Twin Cities Family Fun Spots

First Edition

By
Lisa Sabroski

Co-sponsored by

Solid Advice. Discount Price.

KOOL108
GOOD TIMES • GREAT OLDIES

FAMILY TIMES

BLUE SKY
MARKETING INC.

Twin Cities Family Fun Spots
First Edition

by Lisa Sabroski

Copyright © 1995 by Lisa Sabroski

ISSN: 1081-003X
ISBN: 0-911493-16-6

Cover Design by Amy Beyer
Cover photo by Jacqueline Gilchrist with additional
        permission from Valleyfair Inc.
Edited by Cathlene Taylor

Printed in the United States of America

Published by:

BLUE SKY MARKETING INC.
PO Box 21583-S
St. Paul, MN 55121
(612) 456-5602
SAN 263-9394

8   7   6   5   4   3   2   1

TABLE OF CONTENTS

Preface & Notice 5

Acknowledgments 6

Amusement Places 7

    Amusement Parks & Centers 7

    Batting Cages 17

    Miniature Golf Courses 18

    Play Centers 23

    Pools/Water Slides 32

Art & Craft Centers 39

Campgrounds 49

Excursions 63

Fairs 71

    County 71

    State 76

Horse Riding, Hay & Sleigh Rides 77

    Hay & Sleigh Rides 77

    Horse Riding 81

Museums & Historical Sites 83

Orchards & Berry Picking Farms 115

Parks & Nature Centers 125

    Arboretums/Gardens 125

    Nature Centers/Wildlife Areas 127

    Regional Parks 131

    State Parks 156

Performing Arts 161

Recreational Equipment Rentals 193

    Master List 193

    Bicycles 202

    Boats 202

    Child Carrier Rentals 203

    Cross-Country Skis 203

Downhill Skis .... .203

Ice Skates .... .204

In-line/Roller Skates .... .204

Snow, Ice, & Wind Surfboards .... .204

Snowshoes .... .205

Tent & Camping Accessories .... .205

Seasonal Events .... .207

Winter .... .207

Spring .... .211

Summer .... .216

Fall .... .227

Multi-Season .... .234

Shopping .... .235

Downtown Minneapolis .... .235

Downtown St. Paul .... .240

Suburbs & Neighborhoods .... .245

Skating Arenas .... .255

Ice .... .255

In-line/Roller .... .272

Stadiums, Arenas, Convention Centers, & Sports Teams ... .277

Stadiums, Arenas, & Convention Centers .... .277

Sports Teams .... .292

Stock Car Racing .... .301

Winter Sports .... .303

Downhill Skiing .... .303

Sledding Hills .... .308

Zoos .... .311

Supplementary Listings .... .313

Biking Trails .... .313

Cross-Country Skiing .... .316

Fishing .... .317

Hotlines/Visitors Bureaus/Community Calendars .... .318

Park Departments' Addresses & Numbers .... .319

Index .... .325

PREFACE

Two summers ago, while I was at Crystal Lake beach with my two children, I met a very nice woman who had recently moved from Texas to Apple Valley. During our conversation, she told me wanted to explore the Twin Cities and find fun places to visit with her family, and asked for my recommendations.

I turned out to be a surprisingly poor source of information, despite having been a resident of the Twin Cities area for the past 8 years. I was only able to give key information for a few of the most popular attractions, and only vague information for places I had heard about but never visited.

Though I considered myself an active parent, I realized I usually chose routine activities due to a lack of ideas, or concrete dates, prices, and directions to the places or events I thought about visiting.

The nice woman from Texas said she wished there was a book she could buy that would include all the information she wanted about Twin Cities attractions. I agreed, and thus the seed of an idea for this book was planted.

My hope is that Twin Cities Family Fun Spots will become a valuable guide for anyone who wants to become more active with their families and explore the Twin Cities and surrounding areas. Use this book to generate new ideas and don't forget to take it with you when you rush out the door on your way to new adventures.

NOTICE

Notice: the objective of this guidebook is to provide a greater awareness of the myriad of activities and fun places to visit in and around the greater Twin City area of Minneapolis/St. Paul. Every effort was made to ensure that the information was accurate as of the date this book went to press. Nevertheless, the author and publisher strongly encourage you to call ahead to verify hours, costs, and directions, because of road construction, or changes in hours, costs, etc. made by the management of the individual attractions.

ACKNOWLEDGEMENTS

Dedicated to my husband Bob, and children Caleb and Hope, with whom I look forward to creating many memories with while exploring the Twin Cities fun spots.

In grateful acknowledgment to: Cam Loftness and Debbie Otterblad for surpassing their role as friends and helping me to gather information.

Terri Fogarty for her wonderful care of my children.

Catherine Pringle for her enthusiasm, marketing savvy and great advice.

Jo Nelsen for all her hard work behind the scenes, and in helping to collect information.

Also, many thanks to
> David Undlin
> Catherine Taylor
> Robert Spivey
> Joy McComb

I owe a great debt to my publisher, Vic Spadaccini, of Blue Sky Marketing, for believing in the need for this type of book, and for his unending patience, enthusiasm and encouragement from the beginning of this project through its end.

AMUSEMENT PLACES AMUSEMENT PARKS & CENTERS

▲▲▲▲▲▲▲▲▲▲▲▲▲▲▲▲▲▲▲▲▲▲▲▲▲▲▲▲▲▲▲▲▲▲▲▲▲▲

ALADDIN'S CASTLE

Burnsville Center, Burnsville, MN (612) 435-3887

Maplewood Mall, Maplewood, MN (612) 770-8161

Rosedale Center, 1595 W. Hwy. 36, Roseville, MN (612) 628-9515

The newly remodeled Aladdin's Castle is even more inviting as a family entertainment center, and is filled with popular arcade-style video games for excitement and fun.

COST: Pay as you play. Tokens 25¢.

HOURS: Monday-Friday 10 a.m.-9 p.m.
Saturday 10 a.m.-8 p.m.
Sunday 11 a.m.-6 p.m.

> Burnsville location: Burnsville Center. From I-35W or I-35E southbound, take the Co. Rd. 42 exit and go west to Burnsville Center.
>
> Maplewood location: Maplewood Mall, S.W. corner of I-694 and White Bear Ave.
>
> Roseville location: Rosedale Center, north side of Hwy. 36 between Fairview and Snelling Aves.

AMUSEMENT CITY

1870 Rice St., St. Paul, MN 55113 (612) 487-1025

A place to race your family and friends or enjoy other activities, which include two go-kart tracks; batting cages; bumper boats; an arcade; miniature golf, and a driving range.

COST: Pro-track for young adults 13 and over $3
Small go-kart track for children 7 and over $2.50
Bumper boats $2.50 per ride
Water wars: eight balloons $1, 18 balloons $2
Batting cages: 20 balls $1
Miniature golf: 18-hole game $2.50.

HOURS: April-October: daily 10 a.m.-11 p.m.

> From I-35E northbound, exit on Hwy. 36 west, go to Rice St. Go south to Amusement City on the left.
>
> From I-35W northbound, exit on Hwy. 36, go east to Rice St. Go south to Amusement City on the left.

▲▲▲▲▲▲▲▲▲▲▲▲▲▲▲▲▲▲▲▲▲▲▲▲▲▲▲▲▲▲▲▲▲▲▲▲▲▲▲

Future Indy 500 driver.

GASOLINE ALLEY

10300 Central Ave., Blaine, MN 55434 (612) 784-7223

Gasoline Alley features a very challenging 18-hole miniature golf course, three classes of go-karts, kiddie rides, two game rooms, and concessions.

COST: Pay as you play. Go-karts $2.85-$4, price reflects class of go-kart. Choice of higher-class go-karts requires purchase of license on site. Miniature golf: children 12 and under $2.50, adults $3.50.

HOURS: May through mid-October open 7 days a week, 10:30 a.m.-11 p.m. Open weekends only in April and late October, weather permitting. Call to verify times.

From I-35W northbound, exit on Hwy. 118, go west to Hwy. 65. Go north to 105th St. and make a (legal) U-turn at the light. Come back south on Hwy. 65 to 103rd St. Gasoline Alley is on the west side of Hwy. 65 at 103rd St.

▲▲▲▲▲▲▲▲▲▲▲▲▲▲▲▲▲▲▲▲▲▲▲▲▲▲▲▲▲▲▲▲▲▲▲▲▲▲

GRAND SLAM SPORTS

3984 Sibley Memorial Hwy., Eagan, MN 55122 (612) 452-6485

This indoor family entertainment center is filled with 45,000 square feet of fun, including miniature golf; batting cages; train ride; arcade; play zone; laser tag, and basketball court.

COST: Individual pricing.
Some packages available for $5 and $6.

HOURS: Sunday-Thursday 10 a.m.-10 p.m.
Friday and Saturday 10 a.m.-midnight.

> From Cedar Ave. southbound, exit on Hwy. 13 going north. From Hwy. 13, turn right on Silver Bell Rd. Take another immediate right onto Cedarvale Blvd. Go 1/4 mile to Grand Slam Sports, located on the left in the Cedarvale Shopping Center.

JUMPIN' JAX

Burnsville Center, Burnsville, MN 55337 (612) 898-9798
Maplewood Mall, Maplewood, MN 55109 (612) 770-9860

Jumpin' Jax pushes technology to its limits and puts it within your reach. Have a space-age adventure with an extraordinary brand of Laser Tag, challenge your senses with the Virtual Reality video adventure or have a 'mazing good time in a colossal DynaMaze, which includes a 450-foot obstacle course. Hourly child care is offered with creative play activities for younger children. Jax Diner offers a variety of kid-tested favorites to eat and drink. For children who want a birthday party that's different from the norm, there are seven theme party areas to choose from. Themes include construction site, circus tent, clubhouse, boat, van, Hollywood, and a hot air balloon.

COST: $5.99 admission gets you into one of these areas: DynaMaze, Virtual Reality, or Laser Tag. DynaMaze admission includes unlimited play with free admission for accompanying parents. Virtual Reality and Laser Tag admission includes one game.
Additional games of Virtual Reality and Laser Tag or extra admission into DynaMaze costs $3.99.
Coupons are available for reduced prices on subsequent games.

HOURS: Monday-Thursday 9 a.m.-9 p.m.
Friday and Saturday 9 a.m.-10 p.m.
Sunday 10 a.m.-8 p.m.

AMUSEMENT PLACES

▲▲▲▲▲▲▲▲▲▲▲▲▲▲▲▲▲▲▲▲▲▲▲▲▲▲▲▲▲▲▲▲▲▲▲▲▲▲▲

Burnsville location: Burnsville Center. From I-35W or I-35E southbound, take the Co. Rd. 42 exit west to Burnsville Center. Jumpin' Jax is on the lower level, Dayton's side of the Mall, across from Schmitt Music.

Maplewood location: Maplewood Mall, S.W. corner of I-694 and White Bear Ave. Go to the east Mall entrance. Jumpin' Jax entrance is on the second level of the Mall.

KNOTT'S CAMP SNOOPY

Mall of America, 5000 Center Court, Bloomington, MN 55425-5500 (612) 883-8600

Experience the nation's largest indoor theme park. Located in the Mall of America, Knott's Camp Snoopy features 24 rides and attractions, 11 places to eat, four entertainment stages and seven specialty shops.

COST: Admission is free.
              Guests pay per ride or attraction.

HOURS: Operating hours can vary throughout the year, so please call to
            verify hours.
            Mall hours: Monday-Friday 10 a.m.-9:30 p.m.
                         Saturday 9:30 a.m.-9:30 p.m.
                         Sunday 10 a.m.-7 p.m.

Located in the Mall of America in Bloomington, just 5 minutes from the Minneapolis/St. Paul International Airport. From I-494, take the 24th Ave. exit and follow signs to Mall and parking ramps.

From Cedar Ave. (Hwy. 77),take the Killebrew Drive exit and follow signs to Mall and parking ramps.

From I-35W, take I-494 east to the 24th Ave. exit. Follow 24th Ave. to Mall and parking ramps.

▲▲▲▲▲▲▲▲▲▲▲▲▲▲▲▲▲▲▲▲▲▲▲▲▲▲▲▲▲▲▲▲▲▲

Knott's Camp Snoopy is the largest indoor theme park in the nation.

Photo courtesy of Knott's Camp Snoopy.

AMUSEMENT PLACES

▲▲▲▲▲▲▲▲▲▲▲▲▲▲▲▲▲▲▲▲▲▲▲▲▲▲▲▲▲▲▲▲▲▲▲▲

LILLI-PUTT AMUSEMENT PARK

1349 Coon Rapids Blvd., Coon Rapids MN 55433 (612) 755-1450

Host of the Pepsi and Tom Thumb miniature golf classic for three years, Lilli-putt is one of the largest and most challenging of the mature miniature golf courses in the Twin Cities area. Enjoy 1,600 square yards of miniature golf greens, plus bumper boats and go-karts.

COST: Adults $3.50 per round, seniors and children $2.50.
Bumper boats and go-karts $2.50.

HOURS: Mid-April—mid-October: daily, weather permitting
10 a.m.-midnight.

> From I-694, take the Hwy. 252 exit and go north to the 610 bridge river crossing. On the second exit after the bridge is Coon Rapids Blvd. Turn left on Coon Rapids Blvd. and go 1 mile to the Amusement Park on the right.

SPLATBALL INC.

1955 Johnson St. N.E., Minneapolis, MN 55418 (612) 788-6392

Experience the thrill of playing Capture The Flag, with CO2-powered airguns which fire non-toxic, washable paint pellets. Capturing your opponents' flag and returning it to your own flag station without being "tagged" with a paint pellet is truly a game of strategy, planning and teamwork. There are two outdoor field locations for play: one in Rosemount, MN and the other in Hudson, WI. With advance reservations, they also offer full-service, catered games daily at the location of your choice. When you reserve a field for play, everything you need is supplied, including an airgun, goggles, face mask, paintballs and CO2. Minimum of 16 players (including the organizer) to reserve a field. Players under the age of 18 must have parental permission.

COST: Playing fee $15; C/A gun rental $10; Paint $7 per 100 balls; CO2 refills $2 any size bottle; Season pass $100

HOURS: Reserved game sessions are offered Monday-Friday in four-hour time slots of your choice at either the Rosemount or Hudson field.
Open-game sessions are offered Saturday mornings at either location 8:30 a.m.-12:30 p.m.
Saturday and Sunday playing times are four-hour slots, 8:30 a.m.-12:30 p.m. or 1:30-5:30 p.m.
To choose a date, time, and field location call 788-6392 Monday-Friday noon-6 p.m.

▲▲▲▲▲▲▲▲▲▲▲▲▲▲▲▲▲▲▲▲▲▲▲▲▲▲▲▲▲▲▲▲▲▲▲▲▲▲

Hudson playing field: from Minneapolis/St.Paul, take I-94E across the St. Croix River into Wisconsin. Exit and go north on U.S. Hwy. 12, crossing over the Interstate. Watch for a small sign that says "Road to Willow River State Park (Cty. U)." Turn left and go north on Cty. U, which becomes Cty. A. Continue north on Cty. A through the small town of Burkhardt until you come to a stop sign (Cty. E). Turn right and continue approximately one-half mile to a large blue sign reading SPLATBALL. Turn right into this driveway and continue to follow the SPLATBALL signs until you reach the parking area for the fields.

Rosemount field: from Minneapolis/St. Paul, go south on Hwy. 55 or 56. The two highways merge in Rosemount. Follow Hwy. 55 past Co. Rd. 42 and take the first left onto Fahey Ave. Follow the dirt road down to where the field meets the trees. Turn left at the sign.

Rosemount field: from south suburbs, go east on Co. Rd. 42 past the city of Rosemount. Continue past the Hwy. 52 underpass to where 42 dead-ends at Hwy. 55. Turn right on 55 and take an immediate left on Fahey Ave. Follow the dirt road down to where the field meets the trees. Turn left at the sign.

SPLATBALL INDOOR

3820 Sibley Memorial Hwy., Eagan, MN 55122 (612) 683-1180

Experience the thrill of playing Eliminate The Competition In The Ultimate Indoor Game, with CO_2-powered airguns which fire non-toxic, washable paint pellets. Playing elimination without being "tagged" with a paint pellet is truly a game of strategy, planning and teamwork. There are two indoor arena locations for play under the same roof. With advance reservations, they also offer private games for groups of twelve or more.

COST: 3 hour private session or open play fee $18 per player
$5–$10 gun rental
Paint balls, $6 per 100 balls
Season pass $125
Call for complete details.

HOURS: Regular business hours Monday–Friday 11 a.m.–10 p.m.
Saturdays and Sundays 11 a.m.–7 p.m.
Private reservations available 24 hours a day.

From Hwy. 77 (Cedar Ave.), take Hwy. 13 north to first stop lights. Turn right onto Silver Bell Rd. and go to Beau De Rue Dr. Take another right. Splatball parking lot is approximately 3 buildings down on the right facing Beau De Rue Dr.

13

AMUSEMENT PLACES

▲▲▲▲▲▲▲▲▲▲▲▲▲▲▲▲▲▲▲▲▲▲▲▲▲▲▲▲▲▲▲▲▲▲▲▲

SPORTS SPREE FUN PARK

1001 East Moore Lake Dr., Fridley, MN 55432 (612) 571-3000

Sports Spree Fun Park is a family entertainment center featuring miniature golf, batting cages, basketball and volleyball courts, bumper cars, a creative play area, an arcade room with over 50 electronic games, and a Bridgeman's restaurant with a large party/banquet room.

COST: Free admission. Pay as you play.

HOURS: Sunday-Thursday 10 a.m.-10 p.m.
Friday and Saturday 10 a.m.-midnight.

From I-694, take the Central Ave. (Hwy. 65) exit and go north. Look for Sports Spree Fun Park at the second stoplight.

SPRING LAKE PARK AMUSEMENT

1066 N.E. Hwy. 10, Spring Lake Park, MN 55432 (612) 786-4994

Spring Lake Park Amusement offers a variety of summer fun activities. Attractions include three 18-hole miniature golf courses; a video arcade with concessions; battery cars; water wars (participants fill balloons, get into a cage and launch them at each other); and Hoops USA (a basketball version of miniature golf).

COST: Miniature Golf Championship Course $5 for first round,
$3 for second round
Executive Miniature Golf Courses I & II $4 for first round,
$2 for second round
54-Hole Golf Special, which includes all three courses $8
Water wars: eight balloons $1, 18 balloons $2.

HOURS: April-October: daily, 10 a.m.-midnight, weather permitting.

From I-35W, take the Hwy. 10 exit and go west 3 miles. Follow Hwy. 10 past Hwy. 65 and turn left onto Able St. Turn left again onto the service road and follow to Spring Lake Park Amusement.

▲ ▲

STARBASE OMEGA

318 South Ave., Mall of America, Bloomington, MN 55425 (612) 858-8015

Starbase Omega allows the players to simulate a battle between the Galactic Council of Starbase Omega and a renegade life form of mutant creatures called the Kytef which threaten to capture Starbase Omega and a planet called Previa. Players fight the inter-galactic battle on the planet Previa with Lazer Blasters and Power Vests. Each of these 21st-century combat games lasts about 20 minutes. Starbase Omega was voted Best Birthday Adventure by Minneapolis/St. Paul magazine (December '94 issue).

COST: Single play $7.99; Double play $11.97; All-day pass $21.98; Observation pass $1; Tax not included in prices.

HOURS: Monday-Thursday 10 a.m.-10 p.m.; Friday and Saturday 10 a.m.-11 p.m.; Sunday 11 a.m.-8 p.m. ; Call for mission times.

> Located in the Mall of America in Bloomington, just 5 minutes from the Minneapolis/St. Paul International Airport.
>
> From I-494, take the 24th Ave. exit and follow signs to Mall and parking ramps. From Cedar Ave. (Hwy. 77), take the Killebrew Drive exit and follow signs to Mall and parking ramps.
>
> From I-35W, take I-494 east to the 24th Ave. exit. Follow 24th Ave. to Mall and parking ramps.

THOMPSON'S FAMILY FUN CENTER

3013 27th Ave., S. Minneapolis, MN 55406 (612) 722-7474

This Christian-owned and -operated family fun center promotes safe, friendly fun and features video arcades, pinball machines, and a small snack bar.

COST: Pay as you play.

HOURS: Tuesday-Saturday noon to 11 p.m.
             Sunday 3-11 p.m.

> From Crosstown Hwy. 62 eastbound, take the Hwy. 55 exit (Hiawatha Ave.) going north to E. Lake St. Follow Lake St. east to 27th Ave. S. Turn right onto 27th Ave. S. Thompson's Family Fun Center is on the left side of 27th.
>
> From I-35W northbound, exit at 31st St./ Lake St. and go east (right) on Lake St. 3 miles to 27th Ave. S. Turn right onto 27th Ave. S. Thompson's Family Fun Center is on the left side of 27th.

AMUSEMENT PLACES

▲▲▲▲▲▲▲▲▲▲▲▲▲▲▲▲▲▲▲▲▲▲▲▲▲▲▲▲▲▲▲▲▲

VALLEYFAIR

One Valleyfair Drive, Shakopee, MN 55379 (612) 445-7600

Valleyfair is the largest amusement park in the upper midwest. With over 75 rides and attractions, it is the ideal setting for groups of all ages. Valleyfair's one-price admission gives guests unlimited use of all rides, shows and attractions, plus Whitewater Country Waterpark. The park also has four areas designed especially for children under 48" tall, including Berenstein Bear Country (see front cover photo), Tot Town and Half Pint Park. Whitewater Country Waterpark lets guests experience the thrill of flying down the Hurricane Falls raft ride or enjoy a leisurely turn around Ripple Rapids in an inner tube. There are special areas for young guests too, with Splash Station and Giggle Run.

The park is more than just rides. Guests enjoy over four hours of live entertainment daily. There are more performances in the Amphitheater each evening from June through Labor Day. An entertaining, educational movie is shown in the six-story Pepsi IMAX Theater.

COST: Regular admission $20.95
Children 4 and up to 48" tall and seniors 60 and over $4.95
Children 3 and under free.

HOURS: May-September. Daily Memorial Day-Labor Day and most weekends in May and September.
The park opens at 10 a.m.
Closing times vary.

> From I-35W, take the Hwy. 13 exit west towards Shakopee. Follow Hwy. 13 until it meets Hwy. 101 and continue straight on Hwy. 101. Valleyfair is on Hwy. 101 on the right.

▲▲▲▲▲▲▲▲▲▲▲▲▲▲▲▲▲▲▲▲▲▲▲▲▲▲▲▲▲▲▲▲▲▲▲▲▲▲▲

AMUSEMENT CITY

1870 Rice St., St. Paul, MN 55113 (612) 487-1025

See AMUSEMENT CITY listing under AMUSEMENT PARKS & CENTERS.

GRAND SLAM SPORTS

3984 Sibley Memorial Hwy., Eagan, MN 55122 (612) 452-6485

See GRAND SLAM SPORTS listing under AMUSEMENT PARKS & CENTERS

INSIDE SPORTS TRAINING CENTER & BATTING CAGES

1550 Rice St., St. Paul, MN 55117 (612) 489-5019

Inside Sports offers six baseball and softball batting cages, a video game arcade and party room, 4,800 square feet of astroturf practice space for throwing and fielding, and team clinics along with private lessons.

COST: Varies.

HOURS: Open year round, 7 days a week. Hours change seasonally. Call first.

> From I-35E, take the Larpenteur Ave. exit and go west 1 mile to Rice St. Head south (left) on Rice St. 3 blocks. Inside Sports is on the left.

AMUSEMENT CITY

1870 Rice St., St. Paul, MN 55113 (612) 487-1025
See AMUSEMENT CITY listing under AMUSEMENT PARKS & CENTERS.

CHALLENGE PARK

One Valleyfair Drive, Shakopee, MN 55379 (612) 445-7600

Located next to Valleyfair, Challenge Park provides more opportunities for fun with adventure golf, two 18-hole courses, go-karts, and bumper boats. Take a break and visit the clubhouse with arcade and concessions.

> COST: Round of golf $4.95, session of go-karts $4, session of bumper boats $2.50.

> HOURS: May–September. Open daily Memorial Day through Labor Day and most weekends in May and September. The park opens at 10 a.m. Closing times vary.

> From I-35W, take the Hwy. 13 exit west towards Shakopee. Take Hwy. 13 to Hwy. 101. Challenge Park is on Hwy. 101 on the right.

EKO BAKEN

22570 Manning Trail, Scandia, MN 55073 (612) 433-2422

Located only 25 minutes from the Minneapolis/St. Paul metro area, Eko Baken offers a very challenging and unique nine-hole round of miniature golf in a natural setting. Picnic grounds and a waterslide are available for those who want to make an afternoon of it. The chalet is also open for concessions.

> COST: $2.99 per person or $1.50 with a waterslide ticket. Group rates available.

> HOURS: Memorial Day–Labor Day
> Daily 10 a.m.–7 p.m.

> Eko Baken is 6 miles east of Forest Lake. From I-35E or I-35W northbound, take the Hwy. 97 exit and go east 7 miles to Manning Trail. Follow Manning Trail north 1-1/2 miles to Eko Baken.

FORE SEASONS GOLF

2465 West Industrial Blvd., Long Lake, MN 55356 (612) 473-4813

This challenging 18-hole miniature golf course features a waterfall, pond, and plenty of water hazards.

▲▲▲▲▲▲▲▲▲▲▲▲▲▲▲▲▲▲▲▲▲▲▲▲▲▲▲▲▲▲▲▲▲▲▲▲▲▲

COST: Adult rates weekdays before 6 p.m. $3, after 6 p.m. and on weekends $4. Children 15 and under $2.50.

HOURS: Daily, weather permitting. Hours vary with seasons, weather and holidays; call for information.

> From I-494 take the Hwy. 394 (Hwy. 12) exit. Follow Hwy. 394 west to Long Lake. Turn left at Willow Drive, then right on West Industrial Blvd. Fore Seasons Golf is on the left side of West Industrial Blvd

GOLF MOUNTAIN

N. 376 North Garden, Mall of America, Bloomington, MN 55425 (612) 883-8899

Golf Mountain, the largest indoor 18-hole miniature golf course in the U.S., is on the third floor of the Mall of America, on the north side directly across from the food court. This multi-level course features a waterfall, live plant life and a cave hole.

COST: Adults $5; Children 4 yrs. and under $4

HOURS: Monday–Thursday 10 a.m.–9:30 p.m.
Friday and Saturday 10 a.m.–10 p.m.
Sunday 11 a.m.–7 p.m.
Call for special holiday hours.

> Located in Bloomington, just 5 minutes from the Minneapolis/St. Paul International Airport. From I-494, take the 24th Ave. exit to the Mall of America and parking ramps.
>
> From Cedar Ave. (Hwy.77), take the Killebrew Drive exit to the Mall of America and parking ramps.
>
> From I-35W, take I-494 east to the 24th Ave. exit. Follow 24th Ave. to the Mall of America and parking ramps.

GRAND SLAM SPORTS

3984 Sibley Memorial Hwy., Eagan, MN 55122 (612) 452-6485

This family entertainment center has 45,000 square feet of fun. Activities include an 18-hole miniature golf course with a Boundary Waters theme; batting cages; a train ride; arcade; play zone; laser tag, and a basketball court.

COST: $2.95 per person.

HOURS: Sunday–Thursday 10 a.m.–10p.m.
Friday and Saturday 10 a.m.–midnight.

AMUSEMENT PLACES

▲▲▲▲▲▲▲▲▲▲▲▲▲▲▲▲▲▲▲▲▲▲▲▲▲▲▲▲▲▲▲▲▲▲▲▲▲▲

> From Cedar Ave. southbound, take the Hwy. 13 exit. Follow Hwy. 13 north to Silver Bell Rd. Turn right onto Silver Bell Rd. Take another immediate right onto Cedarvale Blvd. Go 1/2 mile on Cedarvale Blvd. Grand Slam Sports is on the left in the Cedarvale Shopping Center.

GREAT NORTHERN GOLF RANGE

14630 Hwy. 65 N.E., Ham Lake, MN 55304 (612) 434-4109

Great Northern Golf Range provides a bucket of 100 balls to use on their driving range for just $5. Having trouble with your swing? A full-time golf instructor is available to give helpful tips. Daily specials until 6 p.m. include: Senior Day Wednesday, Ladies' Day Thursday, and Kids-under-12 Day Tuesday.

COST: Bucket of 100 balls $5
                Lunch bucket of balls available Monday–Friday (purchase a large bucket and get a half bucket free).

HOURS: April 1–October 1
              Daily 7 a.m.–10 p.m.

> From I-694 take the Hwy. 65 exit north approximately 15 miles to 147th Ave. Great Northern Golf Range is at the intersection of Hwy. 65 and 147th Ave.

LAVA LINKS

1655 W. Co. Rd. B-2, Roseville, MN 55113 (612) 628-9956

When the winter gets long and you could use a touch of the exotic, try visiting Lava Links, a year-round indoor 18-hole putting course. This simulated paradise features tropical surroundings, an active volcano, running waterfalls, real sand traps, and bubbling lava pits. A game area and laser tag in the Magma Chamber are available.

COST: $3–$4.50 depending on age.
                Special rates available for seniors 55 and over, children 10 and under, and juniors 11–15.
                Reduced weekday rates Monday–Thursday.
                Group discounts available with advance reservations.

HOURS: Daily 10 a.m.–10 p.m.

> Located across from Rosedale Mall in the Crossroads Shopping Center, Roseville. From I-35W, take the Hwy. 36 exit east and follow to Snelling Ave. Go north on Snelling to Co. Rd. B-2 W. Lava Links is on the corner of Co. Rd. B-2.

▲▲▲▲▲▲▲▲▲▲▲▲▲▲▲▲▲▲▲▲▲▲▲▲▲▲▲▲▲▲▲▲▲▲

LILLI-PUTT AMUSEMENT PARK

1349 Coon Rapids Blvd., Coon Rapids MN 55433 (612) 755-1450

Host of the Pepsi and Tom Thumb miniature golf classic for three years, Lilli-putt is one of the largest and most challenging of the mature miniature golf courses in the Twin Cities area. Enjoy 1,600 square yards of miniature golf greens, plus bumper boats and go-karts.

COST: Adults $3.50 per round, seniors and children $2.50.
Bumper boats and go-karts $2.50.

HOURS: Mid-April—mid-October: daily, weather permitting
10 a.m.-midnight.

> From I-694, take the Hwy. 252 exit and go north to the 610 bridge river crossing. On the second exit after the bridge is Coon Rapids Blvd. Turn left on Coon Rapids Blvd. and go 1 mile to the Amusement Park on the right.

PUTT PUTT® GOLF

3118 W. Lake St., Minneapolis, MN 55416 (612) 920-2992

Visit "forthefunofit"® and try your hand at miniature golf on an 18-hole course.

COST: Please call for prices and specials.

HOURS: April–October. Daily from Memorial Day to Labor Day
10 a.m.–10 p.m.
Spring and fall: Monday–Thursday 3–10 p.m.; Friday 3 p.m.–midnight; Saturday 10 a.m.–midnight; Sunday 10 a.m.–10 p.m.

> From Hwy. 100, take the Minnetonka Blvd. exit. Follow Minnetonka Blvd. east for approximately 1 mile. Minnetonka Blvd. will become Lake St. Putt Putt® Golf is located on Lake St. behind Nora's Restaurant on the left.

PUTT PUTT® GOLF

2601 Southtown Dr., Bloomington, MN 55431 (612) 881-1110

This international miniature golf franchise was voted the best miniature golf establishment by City Pages in 1993. Visit "forthefunofit"® and try your hand at miniature golf on an 18-hole course.

COST: Please call for prices and specials.

▲▲▲▲▲▲▲▲▲▲▲▲▲▲▲▲▲▲▲▲▲▲▲▲▲▲▲▲▲▲▲▲▲▲▲▲▲▲

HOURS: April–October. Daily from Memorial Day to Labor Day
10 a.m.–10 p.m.
Spring and fall: Monday–Thursday 3–10 p.m.
Friday 3 p.m.–midnight
Saturday 10 a.m.–midnight
Sunday 10 a.m.–10 p.m.

From I-494, take the Penn Ave. exit and go south. Take an immediate right onto Southtown Dr. (frontage road) and go to Putt Putt®.

SECOND SEASON GOLF CENTER INC.

16655 Kenyon Ave., Lakeville, MN 55044 (612) 892-1661

This unique golf center, housed in the Second Season Golf Dome, is considered the largest golf dome in the midwest. The facilities are comfortably heated or air-conditioned according to the time of year. Second Season Golf Center features a 50-stall driving range and an18-hole championship miniature golf course. A running stream cascading from the top of a mountain makes a stunning backdrop for your golfing experience.

COST: Miniature golf: adults $3.50
Children 10 and under $2.50.

HOURS: Open year round, daily 9 a.m.–9 p.m.

From Hwy. I-35W, take the Hwy. 50 (Lakeville) exit. As you come off the exit, turn right onto the frontage road and double back 1/2 mile to Second Season Golf Center on the left.

TROON GOLF CENTER

8400 Co. Rd. 42, Savage, MN 55378 (612) 445-0077

Troon Golf Center features an 18-hole miniature golf course, 60 grass hitting stations, and target greens. The course is lighted for late-night hitting. A PGA professional instructor is available for golf lessons.

COST: Prices are subject to change
Please call for information.

HOURS: March–October: daily 10 a.m.–10p.m.

From I-35W or I-35E southbound, take the Co. Rd. 42 exit west. Follow Co. Rd. 42, 4-1/2 miles west of the Burnsville Shopping Center to the Troon Golf Center.

CIRCUS PIZZA

See below for seven Twin Cities locations. Fun hotline: (612) 593-2770

When it's too cold to ski, skate or sled, families find Circus Pizza to be the perfect spot for indoor adventure. Catering to all ages, Circus Pizza offers: musical, bigger-than-life, animated stage shows; a full-service restaurant; electronic games; carnival rides, and the popular ball crawl. With seven Twin Cities locations, Circus Pizza is easily accessible to almost everyone. You'll want to try out the new Edina Circus Pizza, which houses a two-story ball crawl filled with huge slides, climbing ladders and tubes.

Circus Pizza also plans custom parties for all types of gatherings of eight to 800.

COST: Reasonably priced.

HOURS: Monday–Thursday: restaurant 11 a.m.–9 p.m.; arcade 10 a.m.–10 p.m. Friday: restaurant 11 a.m.–10 p.m.; arcade 10 a.m.–11 p.m. Saturday: restaurant 11 a.m.–10 p.m.; arcade 10 a.m.–11 p.m. Sunday: restaurant noon–8 p.m.; arcade 11 a.m.–9 p.m.

BLAINE location: (612) 780-5334

From I-694 eastbound, take the Hwy. 10 exit. Follow Hwy. 10 north to University Ave. Circus Pizza is located at the intersection of Hwy. 10 and University Ave. (across the street from Northtown Mall next to K-Mart).

BROOKLYN BLVD. location: (612) 560-4422

From I-694, take the Brooklyn Blvd. exit. Follow Brooklyn Blvd. northwest about 1-1/2 miles to Welcome Ave. N. Follow Welcome Ave. N. to the Village North Shopping Center located on the left. Circus Pizza is in North Shopping Center.

From Hwy. 169 (Old Co. Rd. 18), take the 77th Ave. N. (Brooklyn Blvd.) exit. Take 77th Ave. N. east to Welcome Ave. N. Follow Welcome to the Village North Shopping Center on the right. Circus Pizza is located in North Shopping Center.

BURNSVILLE location: (612) 435-3095

From I-35W or I-35E southbound, take the Co. Rd. 42 exit. Turn right onto Co. Rd. 42 and go west to Burnhaven Dr. Take a left onto Burnhaven Drive and proceed one block to the stoplight. Go past the light a few feet and turn right at Frank's Nursery sign. Circus Pizza is straight ahead on the left (across the street from the Burnsville Mall).

EDINA location: (612) 831-4077

From I-494, take the France Ave. exit and go north on France Ave. to 76th St. Take a right onto 76th St., then turn left immediately after McDonald's.

▲ ▲

Circus Pizza is at the far end of Centennial Lakes Plaza. You can enter at both levels of the store.

MAPLEWOOD location: (612) 770-7676

From I-94 eastbound, take the I-35W exit north to Hwy. 36. Follow Hwy. 36 east to White Bear Ave. Go north on White Bear Ave. to Maplewood Mall on the left. Circus Pizza is located on the northeast corner of the mall.

From I-694 eastbound, take the White Bear Ave. exit south to the Maplewood Mall on the right.

NEW HOPE location: (612) 533-2282

From I-394 (Hwy. 12) or Hwy. 55, take the Winnetka Ave. exit. Follow Winnetka Ave. north to Winnetka Center. Turn left into the Winnetka Center. Circus Pizza is straight ahead.

From Hwy. 169 northbound, take the Rockford Rd. (Co. Rd. 9) exit. Follow Rockford Rd. east about 3 blocks to Winnetka Ave. Turn left onto Winnetka. Circus Pizza is about 1/2 block north on Winnetka Ave. in Winnetka Center, located on the left.

WEST ST. PAUL location: (612) 455-4247

From Hwy. 52 (Lafayette Freeway), take the Thompson Ave. exit. Go west on Thompson Ave. to the first light (S. Robert St.). Turn right onto S. Robert and go 1/2 block to Circus Pizza.

DESERT LINKS MIDWAY

175th E. 5th St., Galtier Plaza, St. Paul, MN 55101 (612) 222-1714

Desert Links Midway offers a wide variety of video and skill games. No concessions available.

COST: Games cost 25¢–$1.

HOURS: Monday–Friday 11 a.m.–9 p.m.; Saturday noon–midnight; Sunday noon–8 p.m.

From I-94 in St. Paul, take the 6th St. exit. Go 3 blocks on 6th St. and look for Desert Links Midway on the left.

▲▲

DISCOVERY ZONE

5 Center locations listed below

Discovery Zones are indoor fun centers designed for children 1-12, with health, fitness, safety and fun in mind. Two separate play areas feature an infant/toddler area for children 40" and under and a larger area for children above 40". Both areas feature spiral slides; colorful tunnels; moon walks; giant ball bins; padded mountains, and catwalks. Also featured are skill games which concentrate on hand-eye coordination, and a dining area with pizza, hot dogs, and other favorites. Check into the great birthday party packages and group trip rates.

COST: Children 2–12 $5.99 for unlimited play
Children 24 months and under $2.99 for unlimited play.

HOURS: Monday–Thursday 10 a.m.–8 p.m.
Friday and Saturday 10 a.m.–10 p.m.
Sunday 10 a.m.–7 p.m.

YORKTOWN MALL DISCOVERY ZONE: 3441 Hazelton Rd., Edina, MN 55435, (612) 893-9950

From I-494, take the France Ave. exit. Follow France Ave. north to Hazelton Rd. Proceed east on Hazelton for about 6 blocks. Discovery Zone is on the right in Yorktown Mall.

WOODBURY VILLAGE DISCOVERY ZONE: 1505 Queens Drive #117, Woodbury, MN 55125 (612) 735-4386

From I-494, take the Valley Creek Rd. exit. Follow Valley Creek Rd. east to Queens Drive. Go south on Queens Drive to the Woodbury Village Mall, where Discovery Zone is located.

MARKET PLACE OF WAITE PARK DISCOVERY ZONE: 110 2nd St., South #118, Waite Park, MN 56387 (612) 240-1330

From I-94 northbound, take the Hwy. 15 exit. Follow Hwy. 15 north to Hwy. 23. Go west on Hwy. 23 about 1 block to Market Place on the left.

COON RAPIDS DISCOVERY ZONE: 8601 Springbrook Drive N.E., Coon Rapids, MN 55433 (612) 785-8905

From I-694, take the Hwy. 47 (University Ave.) exit. Go north on Hwy. 47 to 85th Ave. N.W. Proceed east on 85th about 1 block. Turn right at the stop light and Discovery Zone is one block ahead on the right.

BURNSVILLE DISCOVERY ZONE: 14103 Irving Ave. S., Burnsville, MN 55337 (612) 898-2314

From I-35W southbound, take the Co. Rd. 42 exit. Follow Co. Rd. 42 to Irving Ave. S. Turn right onto Irving and go 1 block to Discovery Zone on the right.

▲▲▲▲▲▲▲▲▲▲▲▲▲▲▲▲▲▲▲▲▲▲▲▲▲▲▲▲▲▲▲▲▲

Play centers offer a variety of challenging obstacles.

▲▲▲▲▲▲▲▲▲▲▲▲▲▲▲▲▲▲▲▲▲▲▲▲▲▲▲▲▲▲▲▲▲▲▲▲

GAME TIME

10 E. 7th St., St. Paul, MN 55101 (612) 222-0682

Located in the World Trade Center, Game Time features a wide variety of video and skill games. No concessions available.

COST: Games cost 25¢–$1.

HOURS: Monday–Friday 9 a.m.–8 p.m.; Saturday 10 a.m.–6 p.m.; Sunday noon–5 p.m.

> From I-94, take the 6th St. exit. Follow 6th St. to Wabasha. Turn right onto Wabasha and look for Game Time across from the new Children's Museum.

McDONALD'S PLAYLANDS

Note: With young children needing to expend energy outside the house during the long, cold winter months, I have become a connoisseur of McDonald's Playlands. Visiting the various McDonald's Playlands was an inexpensive way to get out of the house and give my kids fun exercise through multiple levels of tubes, slides and ball pits. McDonald's Restaurants have 14 indoor/outdoor play centers in the Twin Cities area, each different in personality and size. I have listed locations and descriptions of each play center below.

APPLE VALLEY McDONALD'S

7667 150th St., Apple Valley, MN 55124 (612) 432-2185

This McDonald's features a single-level play area with a slide, ball pit and small-fry ball pit.

> Take Cedar Ave. (Hwy. 77) southbound into Apple Valley to Co. Rd. 42. Follow Co. Rd. 42 to Granada Ave. and turn right. From Granada turn right onto 150th St. and follow to McDonald's.

BLAINE McDONALD'S

22401 Ulysses St. N.E., Blaine, MN 55434 (612) 755-2660

This elaborate indoor McDonald's play area features three levels of tubes for climbing in and out; two tube slides; a ball pit, and CD Interactive Educational Programs.

AMUSEMENT PLACES

▲▲▲▲▲▲▲▲▲▲▲▲▲▲▲▲▲▲▲▲▲▲▲▲▲▲▲▲▲▲▲▲▲▲▲▲

> From Hwy. I-694, take the Hwy. 65 exit. Follow Hwy. 65 north about 10 miles to Hwy. 242. Turn left onto Hwy. 242, turn left again onto the frontage road and follow to McDonald's on the corner of Hwys. 242 and 64.

BLOOMINGTON McDONALD'S

8040 Nicollet Ave., Bloomington, MN 55420 (612) 888-6844

Bloomington McDonald's features a two-level play area; slide; cargo net, and single ball pit.

> From I-494 take the Nicollet Ave. exit. Follow Nicollet south 1-1/2 blocks to McDonald's.

BURNSVILLE McDONALD'S

14200 Grand Ave., Burnsville, MN 55337 (612) 435-6688

The Burnsville McDonald's features a two-level Playland with single ball pit and covered slide.

> From I-35W, take the Co. Rd. 42 exit. Follow Co. Rd. 42 east 1 block to Nicollet Ave. From Nicollet Ave, turn left onto Grand Ave. and follow to McDonald's on the left.

CIRCLE PINES McDONALD'S

1 Central St., Circle Pines, MN 55014 (612) 780-3937

The Circle Pines McDonald's features indoor and outdoor Playlands. The indoor Playland consists of one level of climbing tubes; a single ball pit; covered slide, and cargo nets. The outdoor Playland includes a push-button merry-go-round; tornado slide; bouncing rides, and picnic tables.

> From I-35W northbound, take the Lake Drive exit. Follow Lake Drive about 1-1/2 mile to McDonald's at the intersection of Lake Drive and Lexington Ave.

▲▲▲▲▲▲▲▲▲▲▲▲▲▲▲▲▲▲▲▲▲▲▲▲▲▲▲▲▲▲▲▲▲▲

COON RAPIDS McDONALD'S

3080 Coon Rapids Blvd., Coon Rapids, MN 55433 (612) 427-9650

The Coon Rapids McDonald's has a two-level Playland with one slide; a single ball pit, and cargo nets.

> From Hwy. 10, take the Coon Rapids Blvd. exit. Turn left onto Coon Rapids Blvd. and proceed about 5 miles to McDonald's on the left.

COTTAGE GROVE McDONALD'S

7355 Point Douglas Rd., Cottage Grove, MN 55016 (612) 459-9415

The Cottage Grove McDonald's features a unique two-level Playland with a Fun Hut in the center, filled with noise-maker buttons. The Playland also includes two slides; a large and small ball pit; three CD Interactive Educational Programs; a light tree that lights up and plays music; a life-size Ronald McDonald kids love to hug and climb on; and a Lego table.

> From I-494 take the Hwy. 61 exit. Follow Hwy. 61 south to 80th St. Take a left onto 80th St. and proceed to Point Douglas Rd. Take a right onto Point Douglas Rd. McDonalds will be located on the left.

EAGAN McDONALD'S

4565 Erin Lane, Eagan, MN 55121 (612) 452-3179

The Burnsville McDonald's has a two-level Playland; a slide; two ball pits for older and younger children; two video game machines, and a game machine for young children.

> From Hwy. 77 (Cedar Ave.) take the Cliff Rd. exit. Go east on Cliff Rd. to Nichols Rd. Turn left onto Nichols Rd., take another quick left onto Erin Lane and follow to McDonalds.

LAKEVILLE McSTOP

21044 Kenrick Ave., Lakeville, MN 55044 (612) 469-5010

The Lakeville McStop features an indoor and outdoor Playland. The two-level outdoor Playland consists of tubes; a cargo net; a slide; one large ball pit and one small-fry ball pit; character riding toys, and picnic tables. The newer indoor two-level Playland is handicapped-accessible and consists of climbing tubes; a large spiral slide; ball pit; CD Interactive Educational Programs, and three Lego tables.

AMUSEMENT PLACES

▲▲▲▲▲▲▲▲▲▲▲▲▲▲▲▲▲▲▲▲▲▲▲▲▲▲▲▲▲▲▲▲▲▲▲▲

From I-35W southbound, take the Lakeville/Farmington exit to Co. Rd. 70 eastbound and follow to McStop on the right.

MAPLE GROVE McDONALD'S

6255 Sycamore Lane North, Maple Grove, MN 55369 (612) 559-1560

The Maple Grove McDonald's Playland features two levels of climbing tubes; a single ball pit; a slide, and a Lego table.

From I-494, take the Bass Lake Rd (Co. Rd. 10) exit. Go east on Bass Lake Rd. about 1 block to Sycamore Lane. Turn left onto Sycamore Lane and proceed about 1 block to McDonald's.

MINNEAPOLIS McDONALDS

4605 Central Ave., N.E., Columbia Heights, MN 55418 (612) 571-7416

The Minneapolis McDonald's features two levels of tubes; a slide; a single ball pit, and two Lego tables.

From Hwy. 694, take the Central Ave. exit (Hwy. 65) south about 1 mile to McDonald's.

PRIOR LAKE McDONALD'S

16831 Hwy. 13 S.E., Prior Lake, MN 55372 (612) 447-8511

The Prior lake McDonald's features 1 level of tubes; a slide, and ball pit.

Located on Hwy. 13 S.E. at the south end of Prior Lake.

ROSEMOUNT McDONALD'S

15035 Canada Ave, Rosemount, MN 55068 (612) 423-1030

The Rosemount McDonald's has a large seating capacity and features an elaborate three-level Playland decorated with large stuffed animals. The Playland also has a large ball pit; two tunnel slides; two CD Interactive Educational Programs, and a Lego table.

Follow Co. Rd 42 east into Rosemount to Canada Rd. and take a right. From Hwy. 3 take Co. Rd. 42 west to Canada Ave., turn left.

▲▲▲▲▲▲▲▲▲▲▲▲▲▲▲▲▲▲▲▲▲▲▲▲▲▲▲▲▲▲▲▲▲▲▲▲▲

SPRING LAKE PARK McDONALD'S

8124 Hwy. 65, Spring Lake Park, MN 55432 (612) 786-6260

The Spring Lake Park McDonald's features a Lego table and a two-level Playland with a ball pit; a slide, and cargo nets.

> From Hwy. I-694, take the Hwy. 65 (Central Ave.) exit. As you come off the exit you will see McDonald's to the left at the intersection of Hwy. 65 and 81st. St.

PLAY AND LEARN SOFTWARE INC. (PALS)

Minnetonka location: 12949 Ridgedale Drive, 50305 (612) 542-9696

Burnsville location: 13903 Aldrich Ave. S., 55337 (612) 882-4909

PALS is much more than a conventional computer-software store. It houses a room called "The Fun Shop," with about 10 computers just waiting for small hands to experience them. Children and adults are invited to play and learn with the software. To help make learning educational and fun, 400 nonviolent programs are networked into the computers. Store employees control the programming, and are also available to tutor children needing help in developing their math, writing and language skills. PALS also features power hours; an after-school computer program; preschool programs (special keyboards are available for toddlers); teen nights complete with pizza; adult programs ranging from basic computing to multimedia; computer camps held during school vacations, and birthday parties. A "play card" entitles you to 10 hours, printouts and a 30% discount on any software item.

COST: $10 per hour; play card $60.

HOURS: Monday–Friday 10 a.m.–9 p.m.
        Saturday 10 a.m.–6 p.m.
        Sunday noon–5 p.m.
        On weekends, it's a good idea to call for reservations due to limited number of computers.

> Minnetonka Location: From I-394 (Hwy. 12), take the Plymouth Rd. exit. Follow Plymouth Rd. south to Ridgedale Drive. Turn right onto Ridgedale Drive and follow to the Ridge Square South Mall. PALS is located in the middle of Ridge Square South Mall.
>
> Burnsville location: From I-35W or I-35E southbound, take the Co. Rd. 42 exit and go west. Follow Co. Rd. 42 a short distance to Aldrich Ave. S. and turn right. PALS is located across from Burnsville Center at the northern end of Burnsville Market Place.

▲▲▲▲▲▲▲▲▲▲▲▲▲▲▲▲▲▲▲▲▲▲▲▲▲▲▲▲▲▲▲▲▲▲▲▲

BEAVER MOUNTAIN WATER PARK

15100 Buck Hill Road, Burnsville, MN 55306 (612) 435-1700

The entire family can slide out of a hot day and rejuvenate themselves at Beaver Mountain Water Park. Beaver Mountain features five water slides, a new Lazy River and a Kids' Pool/Activity Area.

COST: Children and adults 11 and over $12.95 per day
         Children 5–10, $9.95 per day
         Children 4 and under free.

HOURS: Daily Memorial Day–Labor Day 10 a.m.–9 p.m.

> From I-35W or I-35E southbound, take the Co. Rd. 42 exit west to frontage road (just before Burnsville Center) and turn left. Follow frontage road about 1/2 mile and look for Beaver Mountain on the right.

BROOKLYN CENTER COMMUNITY CENTER

6301 Shingle Creek Parkway, Brooklyn Center, MN 55430 (612) 569-3400

Discover family fun at the Brooklyn Center Community Center's indoor pool and waterslide. Make a splash from the one- or three-meter diving boards, slide 150 feet into the Olympic-size pool, or watch your little ones play in the wading pool. This aquatic facility also offers a small exercise room and sauna for adults. To ensure your family's fun and safety, the Community Center is staffed with professional lifeguards. Bargain days, monthly and family special events are all part of the fun!

COST: Children 2–5, 75¢
         6–14, $2
         15–17, $2.25
         18 and over $2.75.
         Add $1.50 for waterslide.

HOURS: Daily including most holidays. Call for hours or monthly schedule.

> From I-94 or I-694 westbound, take the Shingle Creek Pkwy. exit. At end of exit, take a right. At stoplight, turn right into the Community Center lot.
>
> From I-94 eastbound, take the Shingle Creek Pkwy. exit. At stoplight, go straight across Shingle Creek Pkwy. into Community Center lot.

▲▲▲▲▲▲▲▲▲▲▲▲▲▲▲▲▲▲▲▲▲▲▲▲▲▲▲▲▲▲▲▲▲▲▲▲

BUNKER HILLS WAVE POOL

550 Bunker Lake Blvd. N.W., Anoka, MN 55304 (612) 757-3920

This 25,000-square-foot wave pool uses the latest technology in safe water recreation. Air-generated waves up to four feet in height are made with eight pattern variations. Concessions, locker and tube rental are available. No personal items (food, chairs, flotation toys) are allowed in the facility.

COST: Children 12 and under $3, 18 and over $4. Group rates and reservations for 30 or more.

HOURS: Early June–Labor Day: daily, weather permitting, 10 a.m.–6 p.m. Private party rental 6–9 p.m.

> Take Hwy. I-694 to University Ave. N. (Hwy. 47). Go north to Foley Blvd. Follow Foley Blvd. north to Bunker Hills.

Photo courtesy Anoka Co. Parks

Surfs up at a local wave pool

▲▲▲▲▲▲▲▲▲▲▲▲▲▲▲▲▲▲▲▲▲▲▲▲▲▲▲▲▲▲▲▲▲▲▲

CHASKA COMMUNITY CENTER

1661 Park Ridge Dr., Chaska, MN 55318 (612) 448-5633

The Chaska Community Center features a 110-foot water slide; steam room; sauna; two whirlpools; day care; racquetball courts; large gym; ice arena; craft rooms; video games; community room; strength equipment; exercise equipment, and a dance studio.

COST: Adults $3.75 youth $3.25

HOURS: Monday–Saturday 5:30 a.m.–10 p.m.
Sunday 9 a.m.–10 p.m.
Call for open pool and ice times.

From Hwy. 5, take the Hwy. 41 exit. Follow Hwy. 41 south to Engler Blvd. Go east on Engler Blvd. about 2 blocks to Park Ridge Dr. and Community Center.

EDEN PRAIRIE COMMUNITY CENTER

16770 Valley View Rd., Eden Prairie, MN 55346 (612) 949-8460

For the past 13 years the Eden Prairie Community Center has taken pride in creating a friendly, fun atmosphere for all ages at an affordable price. Yearly memberships are offered for youth, individuals, and families, or activities may be enjoyed for a daily fee. In addition to a swimming pool and wading pool, the Community Center offers ice skating; racquetball; wallyball; special events; weight training and aerobics; group activities, and birthday parties.

COST: Open swimming for adults $2, Children 5–18 $1, Children 4 and
under 50¢, Families $4.

HOURS: Open daily year round. Call for open and family swim times.

From I-494 westbound, take the State Hwy. 5 exit. Follow Hwy. 5 west to Co. Rd. 4. Turn right onto Co. Rd. 4 and follow to Valley View Rd. Turn left onto Valley View. Eden Prairie Community Center is on the right.

From Hwy. 169, take the Hwy. 212 exit going west and stay to the far left as Hwy. 212 turns into State Hwy. 5. Follow State Hwy. 5 west to Co. Rd. 4. Turn right onto Co. Rd. 4 and follow to Valley View Rd. Turn left onto Valley View. Eden Prairie Community Center is on the right.

EDINBOROUGH PARK

7700 York Ave. S., Edina, MN 55435 (612) 893-9890

Edinborough Park is a unique community park under glass, run and operated by the City of Edina's Park and Recreation Department. The park features a waterfall water-way; paths and walkways lined with seasonal flowering plants and trees; a tot lot play area; small ice skating rink; small art gallery with monthly art exhibits; indoor heated pool; exercise area with track, and a delicatessen. Children's special events Tuesday and Thursday at noon include musical concerts, clowns, artists, puppet shows and more. Children's special events move outside in the summer to Centennial Lakes Park. A daily pass in the form of a wristband gives you use of the indoor pool, running/walking track, and ice rink. Adult special events take place throughout the week. Call for details and schedule of events.

COST: Daily pass $3; Skate rental $1.50.
Use of the tot lot, Great Hall and entertainment free.

HOURS: Sunday–Thursday 9 a.m.-9 p.m.; Friday and Saturday 9 a.m.–5 p.m.
Call for program and recreation schedules.

> From I-494 take the France Ave. exit. Proceed north on France to 76th St. Turn right onto 76th St. and go to York Ave. Turn right onto York and follow to Edinborough Park in the middle of the block on the right.

EKO BAKEN

22570 Manning Trail, Scandia, MN 55073 (612) 433-2422

Only 25 minutes away from the Minneapolis/St. Paul metro area, Eko Baken combines waterslide excitement with the breathtaking scenery of the St. Croix River Valley. With two new hydrotube water slides, you will wriggle and giggle down 350 feet of pure fun. The beautiful grounds make it easy to relax. Try the picnic area; driving range; volley-ball courts, and snack bar.

COST: Water tubing for youth and adults 13 and over $8.50 per person
Children 12 and under $7 per person, group rates available.
Waterslide rates for Saturday, Sunday, and holidays $8.5,
Monday–Friday $7.50, group of 25 $7.

HOURS: Memorial Day–Labor Day: waterslides available every day
10 a.m.–7 p.m. Hours extended by reservation.

> From I-35E or I-35W northbound, take the Hwy. 97 exit. Follow Hwy. 97 east about 7 miles to Manning Trail. Follow Manning Trail north about 1-1/2 miles. Eko Baken is 6 miles east of Forest Lake.

AMUSEMENT PLACES

▲▲▲▲▲▲▲▲▲▲▲▲▲▲▲▲▲▲▲▲▲▲▲▲▲▲▲▲▲▲▲▲▲▲▲▲▲▲

MAPLEWOOD COMMUNITY CENTER

2100 White Bear Ave., Maplewood, MN 55109 (612) 779-3555

This Community Center offers a variety of activities the entire family will enjoy. Choose from two pools featuring a 120-foot waterslide with water toys, and a six-lane lap pool. Relax in the whirlpool or seek out fitness activities. Also open to the public is a large gym featuring two full-size basketball courts, a 1/11-mile running track, and a fitness area filled with cardiovascular and weight equipment. Drop-in child care is available.

COST: Resident fees: adults $3, youth and seniors $2.25.
Non-resident fees: adult $4, youth and seniors $3.25.
Fee includes all fitness activities.

HOURS: Open year round. Monday–Friday 6 a.m.–10 p.m., Saturday and Sunday 8:30 a.m.–9 p.m. Call for open swim schedule.

> From I-35E or I-35W northbound, take the Hwy. 36 exit east to White Bear Ave. Follow White Bear Ave. south to Co. Rd. B and turn left. On Co. Rd. B, take the first right into the Maplewood Community Center parking lot on the right.

RICHFIELD POOL AND WATERSLIDE

630 E. 66th St., Richfield, MN 55423 (612) 861-9355

The Richfield Pool and Waterslide features a 50-meter pool with diving well and adult lap swim lane; a double flume; a 29-foot-high waterslide; drop slide; a wading pool with one-foot and two-foot depths, and water volleyball. A large deck and picnic area is attached to the pool.

COST: $5 per person
Children under 42" $3.

HOURS: June–August: open swim Monday–Friday 12:30–8 p.m.
Saturday and Sunday 12:30–7 p.m.

> From I-35W, take the 66th St. exit. Follow 66th St. east 1-1/2 miles. Pool is on 66th St., 2 blocks east of Portland Ave.

▲▲▲▲▲▲▲▲▲▲▲▲▲▲▲▲▲▲▲▲▲▲▲▲▲▲▲▲▲▲▲▲▲▲▲▲

RIVER'S EDGE APPLE RIVER RECREATION AREA

E. Hwy.64, Somerset, WI 54025 (715) 247-3305

Located only 45 minutes from St. Paul, this family-oriented recreation area features two "zoom flume" water slides with 10-degree drops per foot, totaling about 350 feet each. River's Edge Apple River Recreation Area, the largest outfitter on the Apple River, is headquarters of the famous Apple River tube trip. The 2-1/2-hour trip includes tubes and free shuttle service.

The recreation area also includes a campground for families who would like to make a weekend of it. The young'uns will love meeting Yogi Bear, who frequents the campground. Other highlights of the area include a swimming pool, miniature golf and hayrides on weekends. Special summer concerts and outdoor shows are also a favorite of visitors.

COST: Tube rental $5, combination of all-day use of waterslide and tube $10. Save 50% with package deal by paying one price for all activities, including camping; unlimited apple river tubing; watersliding; miniature golf and more.
One-day package $15
Two-day package $25
Three-day package $31.95.

DATES: Memorial Day–Labor Day.

Located two miles east of Somerset, WI. From I-94 eastbound, take the Wisconsin 35 exit. Follow Wisconsin 35 north. Hwy. 35 and Wisconsin 64 run together at Holton, WI. Stay on Hwy. 64, and pass Somerset. River's Edge is on Hwy. 64.

From Hwy. 36 eastbound, get on Wisconsin 35/64 in Stillwater. Hwy. 35 and Wisconsin 64 run together at Holton, WI. Stay on Hwy. 64 and pass Somerset. River's Edge is on Hwy. 64.

VALLEY VIEW POOL

201 E. 90th St., Bloomington, MN 55420 Recording: (612) 881-4937

The Valley View Pool facility features a 50-meter pool with a 2,000-foot-long double flume waterslide. Locker room facilities and concessions available. Another feature for families with children is a large wading pool with a walk-under fountain. Admission to the wading pool is free.

AMUSEMENT PLACES

▲▲

COST: 1994 rates: $4 daily admission
         Optional season passes available
         Waterslide admission $2.50
         Half price rates after 5 p.m.

HOURS: Mid-June–August, daily 11 a.m.–7:45 p.m.

> From I-35W, take the 90th St. exit. Follow 90th east to the Valley View Pool.
>
> From I-494 take the Nicollet Ave. exit. Follow Nicollet Ave. south to 90th St. Proceed east on 90th St. to the Valley View Pool.

WILD MOUNTAIN SUMMER WATERPARK

Co. Rd. 16, Taylors Falls, MN (800) 447-4958

Waterpark attractions include: water slides; go-karts; alpine slides; Black Hole Speed Slide; Lazy River, Wild River Rapids Ride; kiddie karts, and kiddie pool.

COST: Variety tickets $6.95–$20.

HOURS: June–August: early season hours 10 a.m.–6 p.m.
         Late season hours 10 a.m.–8 p.m.

> From I-35E or I-35W northbound, take the Hwy. 8 exit to Taylors Falls and follow to Co. Rd. 16. Follow Co. Rd. 16 north 7 miles to Wild Mountain Waterpark.

ART & CRAFT CENTERS

▲▲▲▲▲▲▲▲▲▲▲▲▲▲▲▲▲▲▲▲▲▲▲▲▲▲▲▲▲▲▲▲▲▲▲▲

AMERICAN SWEDISH INSTITUTE

2600 Park Ave., Minneapolis, MN 55407-1090 (612) 871-4907

Swan J. Turnblad, a Swedish immigrant, newspaper publisher and self-made million-aire, donated his personal possessions, business and 33-room mansion in 1929 to help preserve over 150 years of Swedish heritage in America. More than a just a museum, the institute offers classes in Swedish language, folk arts and crafts; weekly films; special exhibits; lectures; and special cultural events.

> COST: Adults $3, students 6-18 $2. Seniors and children 6 and under free.

> HOURS: Tuesday, Thursday, Friday, and Saturday noon-4 p.m.; Wednesday noon-8 p.m.; Sunday 1-5 p.m. Closed Mondays and holidays.

> From I-35W northbound, take the Lake St./31st St. exit and go east to Park Ave. Take Park Ave. north to the Institute.
>
> From I-35W southbound, take the Hiawatha exit to 26th St. and go west. Follow 26th St. to the Institute on the corner of 26th St. and Park Ave.

BLOOMINGTON ART CENTER

10206 Penn Ave., Bloomington, MN 55431 (612) 948-8746

This community art center features professional exhibits and offers visual art classes for all ages and skill levels.

> COST: Exhibits are free, fees for classes vary.

> HOURS: Monday-Thursday 9 a.m.-5 p.m.; evening classes 7-10 p.m.; Saturday 10 a.m.-1 p.m. Closed Sunday.

> From I-35W, take the 98th St. exit and go west to Penn Ave. Turn left (south) on Penn to 102nd St. Turn right (west) onto 102nd St. Art Center is on the south side of 102nd St.

▲▲▲▲▲▲▲▲▲▲▲▲▲▲▲▲▲▲▲▲▲▲▲▲▲▲▲▲▲▲▲▲

The American Swedish Institute offers classes in Swedish language, folk arts and crafts.

Photo courtesy The American Swedish Institute

▲▲

BURNSVILLE AREA SOCIETY FOR THE ARTS

1200 Alimagnet Parkway, Burnsville, MN 55337 (612) 431-4155

Offers quarterly classes for youth and adults; programs, tours, events, and exhibits several times per year, including a Children's Art Festival in the spring. Member discounts available for classes.

COST: Call for class schedule and fees.

HOURS: Office hours Monday, Tuesday, Thursday 9 a.m.-1 p.m. Quarterly classes offered for youth and adults.

> From I-35W or I-35E southbound, take the Co. Rd. 42 exit and go east to Co. Rd. 11. Follow CO. Rd. 11 north to Alimagnet Pkwy. Turn right onto Alimagnet Pkwy. and follow 2/10 mile to art center on the left.

CERAMIC ARTS & SUPPLIES

4634 Humboldt Ave. N., Minneapolis, MN 55412 (612) 521-2229

Take a ceramic class or purchase ceramic pieces to work on at home. Porcelain, china painting, and doll making classes also available. Must be 15 or older to take class.

COST: Vary according to purchase and class.

HOURS: Monday, Thursday, Friday 9:30 a.m.-4:30 p.m.; Tuesday, Wednesday 9:30 a.m.-7:30 p.m.; Saturday 9:30 a.m.-2 p.m.

> From I-94 westbound, take the 49th/53rd Ave. exit and go west about 10-12 blocks to Humbolt Ave. Turn left (south) onto Humbolt Ave. and go 10-12 blocks. Ceramic store is on the left (east) side, on the corner.

CONTINENTAL CLAY COMPANY

1101 Stinson Blvd. N.E., Minneapolis, MN 55413 (612) 331-9332

Continental Clay is a first-rate supplier of pottery and sculpting tools and paints. Kids are invited to watch how clay is made. Colorful air-drying clay is also available.

COST: Varies. Call for details.

HOURS: Monday-Friday 9 a.m.-5 p.m.; Saturday 9-noon. Closed Sunday.

> From I-35W, take the Stinson exit and go south on Stinson one block to Broadway St. Make a (legal) U-turn and head north on Stinson to the end of the block. Continental Clay Co. is on the right side.

▲▲▲▲▲▲▲▲▲▲▲▲▲▲▲▲▲▲▲▲▲▲▲▲▲▲▲▲▲▲▲▲▲▲▲▲

CREATIVE KIDSTUFF

4313 Upton Ave. So., Minneapolis, MN 55410 (612) 929-2431

Named "Best Twin Cities Toy Store" by Child magazine in 1994, Creative Kidstuff has also won numerous other awards because of the floor-to-ceiling selection of imaginative toys, books, music, and other innovative playthings. Most notable is the KidzArt section in each store, with hundreds of creative art and craft projects for kids up to age 12. This is a "hands-on, do-touch" store that knows kids, likes kids, and knows what kids like.

> HOURS: Monday-Friday 9:30 a.m.-8 p.m.; Saturday 9:30 a.m.-6 p.m.; Sunday noon-5 p.m.

> Minneapolis location: 4313 Upton Ave. S. (S.W. Minneapolis in Linden Hills near Lake Harriet). (612) 927-0653. From I-35W southbound, take the 46th St. exit and go west to Lyndale Ave. Take Lyndale south to 50th St. Go west on 50th to Upton Ave. Follow Upton north about 6-1/2 blocks. From I-35W northbound, exit to Diamond Lake Rd., go west until it becomes 54th St. Follow 54th to Upton Ave. and go north on Upton 10 1/2 blocks.
>
> St. Paul location: 1074 Grand Ave. (at Lexington Parkway, off I-94) (612) 222-2472. From I-94, exit Lexington Pkwy. and go south to Grand Ave. Turn left onto Grand Ave. Creative Kidstuff is located on the right (south) within a block.
>
> Woodbury location: 7150 Valley Creek Rd., Woodbury, MN 55125 (612) 735-4060. From I-494, take the Valley Creek Rd. exit going east (left) and follow 1/4 mile to the Woodbury Village Shopping Mall on the left. Creative Kidstuff is in the middle of the strip mall.
>
> Minnetonka location: 13019 Ridgedale Drive, Minnetonka MN 55305 (612) 540-0022. From I-394, exit at Plymouth Rd. and go south to Cartway Lane. Turn right onto Cartway Lane and follow to Ridgedale Drive. Turn left onto Ridgedale Drive and follow to Creative Kidstuff in Ridge Square.

EAGAN CERAMICS, INC.

1979 1/2 Silver Bell Rd., Eagan, MN 55122 (612) 454-5322

There is over 5,000 square feet of pure ceramic fun at Eagan Ceramics Inc. Classes are available for children on Saturdays, adult classes are in the evenings. A large selection of ceramic supplies, greenware, and porcelain dolls are available as well as firing.

> COST: Class fee is $3.50 plus cost of materials for a three-hour class.

> HOURS: Monday-Thursday 9 a.m.-9:30 p.m.; Saturday 9 a.m.-4 p.m. Closed Friday and Sunday.

▲▲▲▲▲▲▲▲▲▲▲▲▲▲▲▲▲▲▲▲▲▲▲▲▲▲▲▲▲▲▲▲▲▲▲▲▲

> From Hwy. 77 (Cedar Ave.), take Hwy. 13 north to first stop lights. Turn right onto Silver Bell Rd. Located in the Silver Bell Shopping Center (strip mall) on the left. From I-35E, exit at Yankee Doodle Rd. and go west to Hwy. 13. Turn left onto Hwy. 13 and go to first set of stoplights. Turn left onto Silver Bell Rd. Eagan Ceramics is on the left in Silver Bell Shopping Center (strip mall).

EDINA ART CENTER

4701 W. 64th St., Edina, MN 55435 (612)929-4555

The Edina Art Center offers classes and workshops in the visual arts for adults and children. Classes include: drawing; oil, acrylic, and water painting; pottery; jewelry-making and more.

> COST: Class fee is about $15 depending on length of class.

> HOURS: Monday-Thursday 9 a.m.-9:30 p.m.; Friday 9 a.m.-3:30 p.m.; Saturday 9 a.m.-1 p.m. Closed Saturdays in the summer.

> From I-494, exit France Ave. and go north to 66th St. Go west on 66th to West Shore Dr.

K & S CERAMICS

109 S. Fillmore St., Shakopee, MN 55379 (612) 445-4920

K & S is a great place to purchase greenware and ceramic supplies at wholesale prices. It's also great for taking ceramic classes or firing your pieces.

> HOURS: Monday and Friday 9 a.m.-4 p.m. Tuesday-Thursday 9 a.m.-10 p.m.; Saturday 9 a.m.-2 p.m. Closed Sunday.

> Located in downtown Shakopee at the cross sections of Hwy. 101 and Fillmore St. across from the Holiday gas station.

▲▲▲▲▲▲▲▲▲▲▲▲▲▲▲▲▲▲▲▲▲▲▲▲▲▲▲▲▲▲▲▲▲▲▲

KADOODLES

7707 W. 147th St., Apple Valley, MN 55124 (612) 431-3030

Kadoodles is an art activity center where kids and parents can decorate ceramic and plaster statues, figurines and characters. This activity is an interactive experience which enhances children's imaginations, allows them to make their own choices and teaches follow-through while promoting a sense of achievement.

COST: Ceramic pieces start at $4, with a one-time charge of $1.25 for paint, glitter and sealant.

HOURS: Monday-Thursday 2-8 p.m. (winter); 10 a.m.-8 p.m. (summer); Friday 2-9 p.m. (winter); Friday-Saturday 10 a.m.-9 p.m. (summer); Saturday 10 a.m.-9 p.m. (winter); Sunday noon-6 p.m. (winter and summer).

> Located in Apple Valley off 147th St. From I-35W or I-35E heading south, take the Co. Rd. 42 exit. Turn left (east) onto Co. Rd. 42 and go about 3 miles. Turn left onto 147th St. (just before Bachman's) and go to first stop sign. Kadoodles is located on the left side in the Granada Shopping Center.
>
> From Cedar Ave. heading south, turn right onto 147th St. and go about 3 blocks. Kadoodles is located on the right in the Granada Shopping Center.

L & K's CERAMICS, INC.

2383 Hwy. 36, N. St. Paul, MN 55109 (612) 779-6937

Ceramics is a craft that fits all. You can create traditional, country, modern, elegant, or anything else your imagination can put together. Age is no restriction at L & K's. All that's required is to have a great time.

HOURS: Monday-Tuesday 9 a.m.-8 p.m.; Wednesday-Friday 9 a.m.-4 p.m.; Saturday 10 a.m.-4 p.m.

> Located in North St. Paul on Hwy. 36. From I-35E, take the Hwy. 36E exit. L & K's Ceramics is on Hwy. 36.
>
> From I-694, take the Hwy. 36E exit and follow to L & K's Ceramics.

▲ ▲

MINNESOTA CLAY

8001 Grand Ave. S., Bloomington, MN 55420 (612) 884-9101

Minnesota Clay has been Minnesota's original potters' supply source for four decades. You will find glazes, underglazes and over 25 pottery clays manufactured on site. Minnesota Clay is also the manufacturer of Rainbow Air-Dry clay, Underglaze Potter's Pens and Potter's Pad Underglaze Stamping Inks. Distributor of wheels, tools and kilns. Firing service available.

> HOURS: Monday 8:30 a.m.-5 p.m.; Tuesday-Friday 8:30 a.m.-4:30 p.m.; Saturday 9 a.m.-1 p.m.

From I-494, take the Lyndale Ave. exit south. Follow Lyndale to 80th St. Go east on 80th 3 blocks to the corner of 80th and Grand Ave. Minnesota Clay is on Grand.

MINNETONKA CENTER FOR THE ARTS

2240 North Shore Drive, Minnetonka, MN (612) 473-7361

MCA offers art instruction in a broad range of disciplines for both children and adults. Classes include pottery, sculpture, drawing and painting, jewelry, paper making and photography, along with a variety of workshops all year round. View frequently-changing art exhibits in the galleries. Located near Lake Minnetonka, the pastoral setting and close proximity to the Twin Cities metro area provide a vital and creative atmosphere in which to explore the arts.

> COST: Free. Fees for classes and workshops vary for children and adults.

> HOURS: Monday-Saturday 9 a.m.-4 p.m. Summer: Monday-Friday 9 a.m.-4 p.m.; Saturday 9-noon.

From I-394 westbound, take the Co. Rd. 15 exit and go west just past Wayzata. Continue 3 miles around Lake Minnetonka and turn right at County Rd. 51W. MCA is 3 blocks from the turnoff, on the right side.

ART & CRAFT CENTERS

▲ ▲

NORTHEAST CERAMICS INC.

212 13th Ave. N.E. Minneapolis, MN, 55413 (612) 378-9549

If you enjoy working with ceramics or would like to try for the first time, visit Northeast Ceramics, where two certified teachers will guide you through beginning and advanced ceramic projects. Mayco and Duncan products, finishing supplies, and electrical kits are also available.

COST: Class fee $3.50, $3 prepaid. Supplies not included in fee. "Pay as you play."

HOURS: Monday, Tuesday, Thursday 9:30 a.m.-7 p.m.; Wednesday and Friday 9:30 a.m.-5 p.m.; Saturday 8:30 a.m.-2 p.m. Evening classes 7-9:45 p.m. Daytime classes 12:30-3 p.m.

> From I-94, take the Broadway exit and go east to 2nd. St. N.E. (second stop light after bridge). Turn left onto 2nd St., go 2 blocks to 13th Ave. and turn right. Northeast Ceramics is in the middle of the block on the right.

NORTHERN CLAY CENTER

2375 University Ave. W., St. Paul, 55114 (612) 642-1735

Classes in wheel throwing and hand building for all ages and skill levels are available at Northern Clay Center. An exhibition gallery features six special exhibitions a year of functional, sculptural, and installation work by selected regional and national artists. Functional pottery by over 50 artists is available for purchase in the retail store. Special workshops are held throughout the year.

COST: Class fees vary; please call for a brochure.

HOURS: Clay Center, shop and gallery: Monday-Saturday 10 a.m.-5 p.m. Closed Sundays. Classes are held after school, evenings and weekends.

> From I-94, take the Hwy. 280 exit. Take Hwy. 280 to University Ave. exit and go east for 2 blocks. Northern Clay Center is located at the intersection of Raymond Ave. and University Ave.

▲▲▲▲▲▲▲▲▲▲▲▲▲▲▲▲▲▲▲▲▲▲▲▲▲▲▲▲▲▲▲▲▲▲▲▲▲▲▲

PLASTER PARADISE (CRAFTERS PARADISE)

Oak Park Plaza, 10763 University Ave. N.E., Blaine, MN 55434 (612) 755-5450

Plaster Paradise is your ceramic bisque and plaster craft headquarters. Workshops are offered throughout the year. Call for more details.

    COST: Workshops $2 per person.

    HOURS: Monday-Friday 11 a.m.-9 p.m.; Saturday 10 a.m.-5 p.m.
            Sunday 1-5 p.m.

> From I-694 eastbound, take the Central Ave. exit north (Hwy. 65) and go to 109th St. Turn left on 109th and take another left just before the next stoplight at University Ave. Plaster Paradise is located on University Ave in the Oak Park Plaza.

ST. PAUL'S LAND MARK MUSEUM SCHOOL

Landmark Center, 75 W. 5th St., St. Paul, MN 55102 (612) 292-4355

St. Paul's Land Mark Museum School celebrates the diversity of art in the region through a rich and diverse blend of exhibits and educational programs.

    COST: Exhibits free; a $2 donation is suggested. Tuition for classes varies.

    HOURS: Tuesday-Saturday 11 a.m.-4 p.m.; Thursday 11 a.m.-7:30 p.m.

> From I-94 eastbound, take the 5th St. exit. Follow 5th St. to the intersection of 5th and Market Sts. The museum is located at 5th & Market facing Rice Park, next to the Ordway Music Theater in downtown St. Paul.

ART & CRAFT CENTERS

▲ ▲

WALKER ART CENTER PROGRAMS

Vineland Place, Minneapolis, MN 55403 Art Center (612) 375-7600 Group tours of 10 or more, call (612) 375-7609 TDD (612) 375-7586 Family Programs (612) 375-7610 Cowles Conservatory (612) 348-7372

The Walker Art Center is located on Vineland Place, where Lyndale and Hennepin Avenues merge, on the southwestern edge of downtown Minneapolis.

From St. Paul, head west on I-94 and take exit 231B, and follow Lyndale Ave./Hennepin Ave. north to the Walker Art Center.

Approaching Minneapolis from the west on I-394, take exit 8A (Dunwoody Blvd/Hennepin Ave.) and follow Hennepin Ave./Lyndale Ave. south to the Walker Art Center.

SUMMER ARTS PROGRAM AT THE WALKER ART CENTER

Vineland Place, Minneapolis, MN 55403 Family Programs (612) 375-7610

The Walker Art Center offers four-day, hands-on classes in the visual, literary, media, and performing arts for young people 3-14. Guided by artists, children will have the chance to explore and learn about the Minneapolis Sculpture Garden and produce artworks with Garden themes.

COST: Call for prices. Parking is available in the Parade lot adjacent to the Cowles Conservatory and costs $2.50 for cars ($3 event price).

DATES: July and August.

SUNDAY AFTERNOON WORKSHOPS AT THE WALKER ART CENTER

Vineland Place, Minneapolis, MN 55403 Family Programs (612) 375-7610

Families with children are invited to participate in Sunday afternoon art workshops at the Walker Art Center. Led by artists, the workshops include gallery activities and related studio projects. Activities are designed to foster creativity and an understanding of contemporary art. Workshops also encourage parent-child participation.

COST: Participants may purchase tickets for the entire series or for individual sessions. Parking is available in the Parade lot and costs $2.50 for cars ($3 event price).

HOURS: Sunday afternoon.

CAMPGROUNDS

▲▲

AFTON STATE PARK CAMPGROUND

Information: Afton State Park Manager, 6959 Peller Ave. S., Hastings, MN 55033

Information phone (612) 436-5391

Reservation phone (612) 922-9000 or (800) 246-CAMP

TDD/TTY–895-0002 (Mpls./St. Paul area) or (800) 285-2029 (Greater MN and other states)

Experience spectacular views of the St. Croix Valley at Afton State Park, which lies on the bluffs overlooking the St. Croix River. The Afton State Park Campground features 24 backpacking campsites, two rustic group camps and a canoe campsite. The campground is located a strenuous 3/4-mile hike from the parking lots.

Minnesota State Park camping reservations can be made 24 hours a day, seven days a week, by calling The Connection, 922-9000. Camping reservations can be made 90 days in advance, lodging reservations one year in advance. Reservation fee is $5.50.

COST: Backpack or canoe-in sites $7; rustic site $8.

HOURS: Open year round. The park gate is closed 10 p.m.–8 a.m., except to registered campers.

> Afton State Park is located 40 minutes east of the Twin Cities. From I-94 eastbound, take the Co. Rd. 15 exit. Proceed about 7 miles south on Co. Rd. 15 to Co. Rd. 20. Go about 3 miles east on Co. Rd. 20 to the Afton State Park.

BAKER PARK RESERVE CAMPGROUND

3800 County Road 24, Maple Plain, MN 55359

Campground office: (612) 479-2258

Reservations: (612) 559-6700

When you have just a short time to get away, experience the north woods at the Baker Park Reserve Campground on beautiful Lake Independence. Located conveniently 30 miles from downtown Minneapolis, the campground offers 210 campsites suited for tents, trailers, or motor homes; modern bathroom facilities with flush toilets and hot showers; swimming beach; 1/2-acre creative play area; bike rentals; 6.2 miles of paved bike/hike trails; public boat access to Lake Independence and Spurzem Lake; canoe and paddleboat rental; horseshoe pits; volleyball courts; and the Baker Park National Golf Course.

CAMPGROUNDS

▲▲▲▲▲▲▲▲▲▲▲▲▲▲▲▲▲▲▲▲▲▲▲▲▲▲▲▲▲▲▲▲▲▲▲▲▲▲▲

COST: Site per night $11. Site with electricity per night $15. Reservation fee $4.

DATES: Reservations are taken beginning April 1.

> Located west of downtown Minneapolis on Co. Rd. 19 between Highways 12 and 55. From Hwy. 12, take Co. Rd. 29 north to Co. Rd. 19 and follow to the campground.
>
> From Highway 55, take Co. Rd. 24 west or Co. Rd. 19 south to the campground.

BROOKSIDE CAMPGROUND

Rt. 1, Box 60A, Blooming Prairie, MN 55917 (507) 583-2979

At Brookside Campground, 100-plus campsites with full hookups lie within a heavily wooded area bordering the Cedar River. Two swimming pools, a recreational area, playground, and wagon rides make Brookside Campground a place the entire family will enjoy.

COST: Average cost for campsite with full hookups is $16.50.

DATES: May-September.

> From I-35W, go south to Owatonna. From I-35W, take the Hwy. 218 exit and go south to Mower County Number 1. Head east 1-1/2 miles. Campground is on the left.

BUNKER HILLS CAMPGROUND

550 Bunker Lake Blvd. NW, Anoka, MN 55304 (612) 757-3920

Nestled on 1,599 acres of regional park land, Bunker Hill's camp sites will be a real treat for families or groups. The family camping area contains 26 sites with picnic tables and stone fireplaces. There are no electrical, water, or sanitary sewer hookups. There is a central restroom with running water (no showers). Group camping is for tents only and can accommodate 200 people. Restrooms, water, and parking are located in the camping area.

▲▲▲▲▲▲▲▲▲▲▲▲▲▲▲▲▲▲▲▲▲▲▲▲▲▲▲▲▲▲▲▲▲▲▲▲▲▲▲

COST: 50¢ per person per night with a $50 damage deposit, which will be returned within 30 days after camping if there is no damage to facilities. Permit required in advance.

DATES: May 1-October 1: 1 p.m. check-in time; 1 p.m. check-out time.

> From I-694, exit University Ave. (Hwy. 47) north and go to Foley Blvd. Follow Foley Blvd. north to Bunker Hills Regional Park.

CAMP IN THE WOODS

14791 289th Ave., Zimmerman, MN 55398
Metro: (612) 427-5050
Princeton: (612) 389-2516

Enjoy a great escape at Camp In The Woods and relax in one of the large wooded campsites, which include electricity, water, picnic tables, and fire rings. Shower rooms are also available. Recreation opportunities and activities include a swimming pool and wading pool; mini-golf; playground; horseshoe pits; recreation building; tennis courts; walking trails; shuffleboard; hay rides; roller skating area; bocce ball; volleyball; kittenball field; and church services. Reservations recommended.

COST: Weekends per night for two people: site with electricity and water $14; site with electricity, water, and sewer $15. Weekdays per night for two people: site with electricity and water $12; site with electricity, water, and sewer $13. Three-night holiday special, per three nights for two people: site with electricity and water $50; site with electricity, water, and sewer $55. Additional charges per night: children under 18 $1; additional adults $2, A/C or electric heat $2.

HOURS: May 15-Labor Day: 2 p.m. check-in time; 2 p.m. check-out time on weekdays, 6 p.m. check-out time on Sundays and holidays.

> Located 40 miles north of the Twin Cities and only 4 miles north of Zimmerman on U.S. Hwy. 169. From I-94, take U.S. Hwy. 169 north to Camp In The Woods.

CAMPGROUNDS

▲▲▲▲▲▲▲▲▲▲▲▲▲▲▲▲▲▲▲▲▲▲▲▲▲▲▲▲▲▲▲▲▲▲▲▲

CAMP WAUB-O-JEEG

1190 Chisago St., Taylors Falls, MN 55084 (612) 465-5721

For a scenic camping experience, try Camp Waub-O-Jeeg, located only 440 ft. from the St. Croix River. Private tent spots are in very wooded areas close to many wonderful hiking trails. Interstate park rangers present special programs Saturday evenings at the campground. A nondenominational church service is held on Saturday evenings.

COST: Tents/primitive campsites per night $14.50; sites with hookups $17; extra charge per additional adult, A/C, etc.

DATES: Mid-April-October 1.

> From I-35 northbound, take the Hwy. 8 exit east to Taylors Falls. From Hwy. 8 turn onto Hwy. 95 and proceed north to Co. Rd. 16. Continue north on Co. Rd. 16 and follow 2 miles to Camp Waub-O-Jeeg.

COUNTRY CAMPING TENT AND RV PARK INC.

750 273rd Ave. N.W., Isanti, MN 55040 (612) 444-9626

"Go with the flow" on the scenic Rum River just 36 miles north of the Twin Cities. Country Camping has 40 acres of rolling wooded and open land with 50 campsites. This campground also offers canoeing; tubing; shuttle service; recreation room; sand court volleyball; playground; store; hot showers; and fishing on the riverbanks.

COST: Site with water and electrical hookups for two adults and two children $12.75.

DATES: May 1-October 1.

> Take Hwy. 65 to the city of Isanti. At the intersection of Co. Rd. 5 and Hwy. 65, turn west on Co. Rd. 5 and follow to Co. Rd. 10. Go south until Co. Rd. 10 becomes Co. Rd. 68. Follow Co. Rd. 68 to Country Camping on the left.

▲▲▲▲▲▲▲▲▲▲▲▲▲▲▲▲▲▲▲▲▲▲▲▲▲▲▲▲▲▲▲▲▲▲▲▲▲▲

FLETCHER CREEK CAMPGROUND

Route 5, Box 93A, Little Falls, MN 56345 (612) 632-9636

The Fletcher Creek Campground is only minutes away from the boyhood home of Charles Lindbergh, the Weyerhauser Museum, and the Minnesota Military Museum at Camp Ripley. You'll find camping sites for tents and RVs with full hookups, water, and electricity; heated swimming pool; miniature golf; walking access to the Mississippi River for fishing; playground; recreation hall; bathroom facilities with hot showers and flush toilets; and a store.

COST: Site without electrical hookups, per night for two people $12; site with electrical hookups per night for two people $14.

DATES: May 1-October 31. Office hours: 9 a.m.-9 p.m.

Take Hwy. 10 to Little Falls. From Hwy. 10 take Hwy. 371 (which branches off from Hwy. 10 at Little Falls) north 6 miles to campground.

HAM LAKE CAMPGROUND INC.

2400 Constance Blvd., Ham Lake, MN 55304 (612) 434-5337

This is a family campground with the following activities: swimming; play area; boating; canoe and paddle boat rentals; fishing; and camping on wooded and grassy sites. Hot showers are available.

COST: Site without electrical hookups $12 per night. Site with electrical hookups $15 per night.

DATES: May 1-November 1.

Only 20 minutes north of the Twin Cities, Ham Lake Campground is located 1 mile east of Hwy. 65 on Constance Blvd. in Ham Lake.

KIESLER'S CAMPGROUND

PO Box 4, Waseca, MN 56093 (507) 835-3179

Get away and relax at Kiesler's shaded tent and RV campsites. Kiesler's offers heated pool; large playground; mini-golf; shuffleboard; volleyball; recreation hall; 750-acre Clear Lake; fishing docks, boat and canoe rentals; live entertainment; laundry facilities; LP gas; free cable TV; laundry facilities; firewood. A Good Sam Park.

CAMPGROUNDS

▲▲▲▲▲▲▲▲▲▲▲▲▲▲▲▲▲▲▲▲▲▲▲▲▲▲▲▲▲▲▲▲▲▲▲▲▲

COST: $17 base rate for two people.

DATES: April 15-October 15.

> From Minneapolis on I-35W, take the Waseca exit and go to Hwy. 14. Follow Hwy. 14 west for 13 miles to the campground, which is on the left side.
>
> From Minneapolis on Hwy. 13, turn left onto Hwy. 14. Go 1 mile east of intersection to the campground on the right.

KOA TWINS CAMPGROUND

3315 W. 166th St., Jordan, MN 55352 (612) 492-6440

KOA Twins Campground is close enough to your favorite Twin Cities attractions, yet far enough away for you to relax in a quiet setting. The campground features a heated indoor pool, playground, and miniature golf.

COST: Tent site $17; site with electricity and water $20; site with electricity, water, and sewer $22.

DATES: April 15-October 15.

> From I-494 westbound, exit on U.S Hwy. 169 going south. Campground is located on Hwy. 169, 6 miles southwest of Shakopee.
>
> From I-35W southbound, exit Hwy. 13 west. Follow Hwy. 13 until it meets Hwy. 101. Continue on Hwy. 101 to U.S. Hwy. 169. Campground is on Hwy. 169, 6 miles southwest of Shakopee.

KRESTWOOD MOBILE HOME AND RV PARK

10225 Lyndale Ave. S., Bloomington, MN 55420-5276
(612) 881-8218

Located near the Minnesota River Valley and the National Wildlife Refuge, this quiet, peaceful RV park has woodland and prairie wildflower gardens to enjoy.

COST: Partial service, which includes electric and water $15.00 daily, $90 weekly rate, $270 monthly; full service, which includes electric, water, and sewer $16.00 daily, $96 weekly rate, $290 monthly.

HOURS: Open year round; however, no water in the winter months of mid-October-mid-April.

▲▲▲▲▲▲▲▲▲▲▲▲▲▲▲▲▲▲▲▲▲▲▲▲▲▲▲▲▲▲▲▲▲▲▲▲▲▲▲

From I-35W, take the 98th St. exit and proceed east on 98th St. to Lyndale Ave. Turn south on Lyndale Ave. and look for Krestwood on the left after you pass 102nd St. There are two entrances into Krestwood, use the second entrance.

LAKE AUBURN FAMILY CAMPGROUND

Carver Park Reserve, 7025 Victoria Drive, Box 270, Victoria, MN 55386
Reservations: 559-6700
Campground office: 443-2911

To break away from city life to a peaceful rustic setting, try Lake Auburn Family Campground, situated on 3,500 acres of Carver Park Reserve land. The park offers 54 campsites for tents, trailers, or motor homes; pit latrines only (no showers or electricity); creative play area; fishing dock; public boat access to Auburn, Zumbra, Stieger, and Parley Lakes; sandy swimming beach; 8 miles of paved bike trails (bike rentals available). The Lowry Nature Center is also located in the Carver Park Reserve. Enjoy floating boardwalks, 6 miles of wood-chip hiking trails, observation decks, and a plant display area at the Nature Center.

COST: Site per night $8. Reservation service fee $4.

DATES: May 1-October 17.

From Hwy. 7 westbound, turn left onto Co. Rd. 11 and follow to campground.

From Hwy. 5 westbound in the city of Victoria, turn right onto Co. Rd. 11 and follow to campground.

LAKE BYLLESBY REGIONAL PARK CAMPGROUND

7650 Echo Point Rd., Cannon Falls, MN 55009 (507) 263-4447

Lake Byllesby Campground is far enough from the metropolitan area for a real vacation, but close enough for a quick get-away. Relax at one of the many campsites located directly at the edge of Lake Byllesby. All RV sites are equipped with water and electrical hookups. Other recreation opportunities available are: swimming at the beach; boating; fishing; horseshoes; and a ball field.

CAMPGROUNDS

▲▲▲

COST: Tent site per night: weekdays $6.75; weekends $9. RV site per night: weekdays $9.75; weekends $13.

DATES: May-mid-October.

> Located on Lake Byllesby Reservoir near Cannon Falls and east of Randolph. From State Hwy. 56 in Randolph, take Co. Rd. 88, 3.5 miles east to park entrance.
>
> From State Hwy. 52, north of Cannon Falls, take Co. Rd. 86 west to Harry Ave. Follow Harry Ave. 1.5 miles to the park.

LAKE ELMO PARK CAMPGROUND

Information: Washington County Parks Division, Lake Elmo Park Reserve, 1515 Keats Ave. N., Lake Elmo, MN 55042 (612) 731-3851

Lake Elmo Park Campground is located in the Lake Elmo Park Reserve. The campground features 80 modern campsites; three primitive campsites; 20 equestrian campsites, and three group campsites. Developed areas of the Reserve offer opportunities for camping; swimming; fishing; boating; 8 miles of horseback riding trails; picnicking; archery; 20 miles of hiking trails; 12 miles of cross-country ski trails, and 5 miles of bicycle trails.

COST: Parking: daily $3, annual $14.

HOURS: Open year round 7 a.m.–1/2 hour after sunset.

> From I-94, take Hwy. 19 north into the Lake Elmo Park Reserve.

LEBANON HILLS REGIONAL PARK CAMPGROUND

12100 Johnny Cake Ridge Road, Apple Valley, MN 55124
(612) 454-9211

This campground is ideal for families looking for a relaxing, centrally located campground from which to experience Twin Cities fun spots. With easy access to I-35E, I-35W, and I-494, you can visit the Minnesota Zoo, Mall of America, Valley Fair, and more. The campground is in the 2,000-acre Lebanon Hills Regional Park, an excellent vacation setting with hiking, swimming, horseback trails, canoeing, and fishing.

▲▲▲▲▲▲▲▲▲▲▲▲▲▲▲▲▲▲▲▲▲▲▲▲▲▲▲▲▲▲▲▲▲▲▲▲

COST: Tent site per night for up to four people $9.50. RV site with water, electrical, and sewer hookups per night for up to four people $17. Children 4 years and under are free. Each additional person: $1.

DATES: May 27-Labor Day.

From I-35W or I-35E, exit Co. Rd. 42 and go east. From Co. Rd. 42, go north on Johnny Cake Ridge Rd. and look for campground on the right.

NERSTRAND BIG WOODS STATE PARK CAMPGROUND

Information: Nerstrand Big Woods State Park Manager, 9700 170th St. E., Nerstrand, MN 55053

Information phone (507) 334-8848

Reservations (612) 922-9000 or (800) 246-CAMP

TDD/TTY—895-0002 (Mpls./St. Paul area) or (800) 285-2029 (greater MN and other states)

Nerstrand Big Woods, a 1,100-acre State Park, is one of the last remnants of the Big Woods. The Nerstrand Big Woods Campground features 61 semi-modern campsites; 23 sites with electrical hookups; 18 rustic pioneer campsites, and a group camp. Recreational activities within the park include 13 miles of hiking trails; 8 miles of cross-country ski trails, and 5 miles of snowmobile trails.

Minnesota State Park camping reservations can be made 24 hours a day, seven days a week, by calling The Connection, (612) 922-9000. Camping reservations can be made 90 days in advance, lodging reservations one year in advance. Reservation fee is $5.50.

COST: Sites with shower $10 or $12; rustic site (no showers, pit toilets) $8; sites with electricity, add $2.50; backpack or canoe-in sites $7. Half-price camping available Sunday–Thursday for Minnesota residents 65 and older or disabled.

HOURS: Open year round. Park hours 8 a.m.–10 p.m. except for registered campers.

Nerstrand Woods is located about 45 miles directly south of the Twin Cities, about 11 miles southeast of Northfield. Take Hwy. 3 into Northfield to Hwy. 246. Follow Hwy. 246 southeast out of Northfield to Co. Rd. 27. Turn right onto Co. Rd. 27 and follow to Nerstrand Big Woods.

From I-35W southbound, take the Hwy. 59 exit. Follow Hwy. 59 into Northfield to Hwy. 3. Follow Hwy. 3 southeast to Hwy. 246. Follow Hwy. 246 southeast out of Northfield to Co. Rd. 27. Turn right onto Co. Rd. 27 and follow to the Nerstrand Big Woods.

CAMPGROUNDS

▲▲▲▲▲▲▲▲▲▲▲▲▲▲▲▲▲▲▲▲▲▲▲▲▲▲▲▲▲▲▲▲▲▲▲▲▲▲

MINNESOTA VALLEY TRAIL RECREATION AREA

Information: Minnesota Valley Trail Manager, 19825 Park Blvd., Jordan, MN 55352

Information phone (612) 492-6400

Reservation phone (612) 922-9000 or (800) 246-CAMP

TDD/TTY–895-0002 (Mpls./St. Paul area) or (800) 285-2029 (greater MN and other states)

The Minnesota Valley Trail Campground features 25 scenic, well-spaced family campsites; eight secluded walk-in campsites; one canoe campsite, and one walk-in/canoe campsite.

The Minnesota Valley Trail Recreation Area provides picnic grounds; fishing; 22 miles of horseback riding, mountain biking and hiking trails.

Minnesota State Park camping reservations can be made 24 hours a day, seven days a week, by calling The Connection, (612) 922-9000. Camping reservations can be made 90 days in advance, lodging reservations one year in advance. Reservation fee is $5.50.

COST: Sites with shower $10 or $12; rustic site (no showers, pit toilets) $8; sites with electricity add $2.50; backpack or canoe-in sites $7. Half-price camping available Sunday–Thursday for Minnesota residents 65 and older or disabled.

HOURS: Open year round. Park hours 8 a.m.–10 p.m. except for registered campers.

The recreation area and facility headquarters for the Minnesota Valley Trail is located between Jordan and Belle Plaine on Co. Rd. 57.

From Hwy. 169 southbound, follow Hwy. 169 to the first set of stoplights in Jordan. Turn right at the light and proceed 3 blocks to Co. Rd. 57. Turn left onto Co. Rd. 57 and proceed about 5 miles to the Lawrence Unit, where the camping areas are found.

From Hwy. 169 northbound, follow Hwy. 169 north of Belle Plaine about 3 miles to Co. Rd. 57. Turn left onto Co. Rd. 57 and follow a little over a mile to the Lawrence Unit, where the camping areas are found.

PEACEFUL VALLEY CAMPSITES

RR2, Box 100, LeSueur, MN 56058

(612) 665-2297, (612) 338-5605, (800) 554-1668

In the valley of the jolly Green Giant, camp in quiet shaded sites. Enjoy recreational activities like volleyball, horseshoes, and swimming in a heated pool or take a courtesy van to the golf course. Clubs are welcome.

COST: Basic site for two adults and two children $12; $2 extra for electrical and water hookup; $2 per extra person.

DATES: Daily April 15-October 15. Check in till 10 p.m.

> Located 1-1/2 miles south of LeSueur, 7 miles north of St. Peter.
>
> From Hwy. 169, take Peaceful Valley Rd. west for 2/10 of a mile to the campground on the north side of the road.

RICE CREEK CAMPGROUND

550 Bunker Lake Boulevard, Anoka, MN 55304 (612) 757-3920

Located in Lino Lakes on 2,500 acres of Rice Creek Chain-of-Lakes Regional Park Reserve land. Campground facilities include 39 RV sites and 25 tent sites with picnic tables and grills; restrooms with hot water and showers; laundry facilities. Recreational activities include fishing; boating; canoeing; a swimming beach; the Wargo Nature Center; and golfing at Chamonix Golf Course.

COST: RV site per night with electricity and water $12. RV site per night without hookups $10. Tent site per night $8.

DATES: May 1-October 1.

> From I 35W or I-35E, exit at Co. Rd. 14. Campground is between 35W and 35E on Co. Rd. 14.

CAMPGROUNDS

▲▲▲

RIVER'S EDGE CAMPGROUND

E. Hwy. 64, Sommerset, WI 54025 (715) 247-3305

River's Edge Apple River Recreation Area is the largest outfitter on the Apple River, and is the headquarters of the famous tube trip down the Apple River. The 2-1/2-hour trip includes tubes and free shuttle service. River's Edge is not just a campground; it's also a family-oriented recreation area located only 45 minutes from St. Paul. Children will love meeting Yogi Bear, who frequents the campground. Other highlights of the area include a swimming pool; miniature golf; hay rides on weekends; special summer concerts and outdoor shows; and two "zoom flume" water slides.

COST: $5 per person with a $20 minimum site charge. $5 extra with water and electricity. Save 50% on a package deal: pay one price for all activities, including camping, unlimited Apple River tubing, watersliding, miniature golf, and more. One-day package $15, two-day package $25, three-day package $31.95.

DATES: Memorial Day–Labor Day.

> Located 2 miles east of Somerset, WI. From I-94 eastbound, take the Wisconsin 35 exit. Follow Wisconsin 35 north. Hwy. 35 and Wisconsin 64 will run together at Holton, WI. Stay on Hwy. 64 and pass Somerset. River's Edge is on Hwy. 64.
>
> From Hwy. 36 eastbound, get on Wisconsin 35/64 in Stillwater. Hwy. 35 and Wisconsin 64 will run together at Holton, WI. Stay on Hwy. 64 and pass Somerset. River's Edge is on Hwy. 64.

SPRINGVALE CAMPGROUND

36955 Palm St. NW, Stanchfield, MN 55080 (612) 689-3208

This 350-acre campground has an abundance of activities for the family. Highlights include heated pool; play area; game room; horseshoe court; volleyball court; wagon rides; canoe rentals; hiking trails; wildlife lake; and showers.

COST: Site with electricity and water $14. Nonelectric site $13. Primitive area $10.

DATES: April 22-October 2.

> Only 50 miles north of the Twin Cities, Springvale Campground is located 6 miles NW of Cambridge. From Hwy. 65 northbound, take the Isanti Co. Rd. 6 exit. Follow Isanti Co. Rd. 6 west for 6 miles to Co. Rd. 14. Go north on Co. Rd. 14 a mile to campground.

▲▲▲▲▲▲▲▲▲▲▲▲▲▲▲▲▲▲▲▲▲▲▲▲▲▲▲▲▲▲▲▲▲▲▲▲

TIMM'S MARINA AND CAMPGROUND

9080 N. Jewel Lane, Forest Lake, MN 55025 (612) 464-3890 (612) 464-9965

Timm's Marina and Campground offers fun and fishing on beautiful Forest Lake.

COST: Reasonable pricing; call for details.

DATES: May 1-October 1: Monday-Friday 8 a.m.-10 p.m.; Saturday and
Sunday 7 a.m.-10 p.m.

From Hwy. I-35W, exit at Hwy. 97 and go east 6 miles to campground.

WAPITI PARK CAMPGROUND

18746 Troy St., Elk River, MN 55330 (612) 441-1396

This picturesque campground features wooded and open campsites along the scenic
Elk River. Primitive, water and electrical, and full-hookup sites are available. Amenities
include two playgrounds; store; volleyball; fishing; tubing with shuttle service; horse-
drawn hay rides and sleigh rides; hot showers and bath house facilities; recreational
building with equipment; and laundry facilities. Leashed pets allowed.

COST: Primitive site $13 plus tax. Water-and-electric site $16 plus tax.

HOURS: Open year round, with a three-day minimum on holiday weekends.

Located two miles west of Elk River on Hwy. 10. From Hwy. 10, take the
frontage road to Wapiti Park Campground.

WILLIAM O'BRIEN STATE PARK

16821 O'Brien Trail North, Marine on the St. Croix, MN 55047
Group site reservations (612) 433-0500
Family sites only 922-9000

Get back to nature and solitude in Minnesota's number-one cross-country ski park.
The campground, close to the scenic St. Croix River, includes 11 miles of hiking and
cross-country skiing trails. In summer months modern shower and bathroom facilities
are available. Canoe rental is also available through a private contractor.

Minnesota State Park camping reservations can be made 24 hours a day, seven days a
week, by contacting The Connection, 922-9000. Camping reservations can be made
90 days in advance, lodging reservations one year in advance. Reservation fee is $5.50.

CAMPGROUNDS
▲▲▲▲▲▲▲▲▲▲▲▲▲▲▲▲▲▲▲▲▲▲▲▲▲▲▲▲▲▲▲▲▲▲▲▲

COST: Reservations encouraged. Rates vary for group campsites on a reserved
          basis. Entrance fee $14.50 with electric/vehicle permit. A $4 permit is
          good for two consecutive days. An $18 annual permit is good for the
          calendar year.

HOURS: Open year round. Office hours 8 a.m.–10 p.m.; may vary. Self-registra-
          tion available when office is closed.

Located within an hour's drive of the Twin Cities area, on the St. Croix River.
William O'Brien State Park is on Hwy. 95, just 2 miles north of Marine-on-
St. Croix.

From I-35W or I-35E. take the I-694 exit. Go east on I-694 to Hwy. 36.
Continue east on Hwy. 36 to Hwy. 95. Follow Hwy. 95 north, go 2 miles past
Marine-On-St. Croix to the William O'Brien State Park.

YOGI BEAR'S JELLYSTONE PARK

1251 East Bluff, Shakopee, MN 55379 (612) 445-7313

Without leaving the Twin Cities area, your family can enjoy campsites along the
Minnesota River or on beautiful wooded and rolling terrain at Jellystone Park. Kids
can meet Yogi in person and go on a hay ride. Amenities include swimming pool; biking or hiking on 4 miles of paved DNR trail; an outdoor recreation area and playground; fishing in the Minnesota River.

COST: Tent sites $15 per two people. RV site with electricity and water
          $18.95. Site with full hookup per night per two people $21.95. $2 per
          extra person. Children under 4 free.

HOURS: 8 a.m.-10 p.m. in season.

From I-35W take the Hwy. 13 exit and go west to Hwy. 101. Take Hwy. 101
into Shakopee. Turn right at the first stoplight and look for Yogi Bear's
Jellystone Park straight ahead.

EXCURSIONS

▲▲▲▲▲▲▲▲▲▲▲▲▲▲▲▲▲▲▲▲▲▲▲▲▲▲▲▲▲▲▲▲▲▲▲▲▲▲

ANDIAMO SHOWBOAT , ANDIAMO, ANDIAMO TOO, MAJESTIC LADY, THE PARTY GIRL, SCHATZE

112 N. Main St., Stillwater, MN 55082 (612) 430-1234

The entire family will enjoy cruising the scenic, historic St. Croix River on any of six paddle-wheel river boats with Southern-style hospitality and food. Call to make reservations and purchase tickets.

COST: Varies from $9.95 to $18.95. Call for brochure on menus and prices. Children under 5 free.

HOURS: June through September. Call for brochure on departure and arrival times.

> Take Hwy. 36 east to downtown Stillwater and look for large public parking lot on east side of road. The Andiamo Showboat is located behind the parking lot on the St. Croix River.

COMO-HARRIET STREETCAR LINE

Queen Ave. S. and W. 42nd St., Minneapolis, MN 55410 Information: (612) 228-0263; charter information and reservations: (612) 291-7588

Enjoy a two-mile, 15-minute round trip aboard beautifully restored Minnesota trolleys. Ride through a scenic wooded area between Lake Harriet and Lake Calhoun on a rebuilt portion of the old Twin City Rapid Transit Company's historic Como-Harriet line. This is the last operating portion of the 523-mile Twin City Lines system, abandoned in 1954.

COST: Regular rides $1, children under 5 free. Charters $40 per half-hour.

HOURS: Open daily, Memorial Day weekend-Labor Day. Open weekends only in May (before Memorial Day weekend), September (after Labor Day weekend), and October.

> Located at the intersection of Queen Ave. S. and W. 42nd St. on the west side of Lake Harriet near the bandshell.
>
> From Crosstown (Hwy. 62), take the Xerxes Ave. exit and go north to 42nd St. Go east on 42nd St. to Queen Ave. S. Streetcar depot is on the corner of Queen Ave. and 42nd. Park in the free bandshell lot or on street.
>
> From I-35W, take the 46th St. exit and go west to Lake Harriet Parkway. Turn north to 42nd St., then right to Queen Ave. S.

▲▲▲▲▲▲▲▲▲▲▲▲▲▲▲▲▲▲▲▲▲▲▲▲▲▲▲▲▲▲▲▲▲▲▲▲

Photo by Aaron Isaacs, courtesy Minnesota Transportation Museum, Inc.

Ride antique Minnesota streetcars aboard the Minnesota Transportation Museum's Como-Harriet Streetcar Line at Lake Harriet in Minneapolis. Here, Twin City Rapid Transit Company No. 1300, built in 1980 in St. Paul, approaches the north end of the line at Lake Calhoun.

▲▲▲▲▲▲▲▲▲▲▲▲▲▲▲▲▲▲▲▲▲▲▲▲▲▲▲▲▲▲▲▲

CREATIVE RIVER TOURS

P.O. Box 151, Shakopee, MN 55379 (612) 445-7491

Creative River Tours is based in Shakopee on the Minnesota River at historic Murphy's Landing. Narrated excursions describe wildlife, the ever-changing river and historical trivia. The Emma Lee is custom-built as an excursion vessel and specially designed to travel on the Minnesota and Mississippi Rivers. You will be served by a licensed captain and crew.

COST: Adults $7, seniors 62 and over $6, students 6-18 $6, children under 6 free.

HOURS: Weekends and holidays, Memorial Day weekend through mid-October. Departure times: 1, 2, 3 and 4 p.m.

> From I-35W southbound, take the Hwy. 13 exit and go west. From Hwy. 13, take Hwy. 101 north to Shakopee. Creative River Tours is located at Murphy's Landing on Hwy. 101 just east of Shakopee.

MINNESOTA ZEPHYR

601 N. Main St., Stillwater, MN 55082 (612) 430-3000

This leisurely three-hour train excursion boards in the historic city of Stillwater and travels along the beautiful St. Croix River Valley. The Zephyr is powered by two 1951 diesel electric engines, one at each end of the train. Five-course dinner re-creates the elegant atmosphere of railroad dining. You can also visit the Stillwater Logging and Railroad Museum.

COST: $49 per person for excursion and dinner.

HOURS: Open year round, but hours and days vary seasonally. Call for current schedule: (612) 430-3000. For Saturday evening excursions, boarding begins at the Stillwater Depot at 6:30 p.m. with departure at 7:30 p.m. sharp. Estimated return time is 10:45 p.m. at the Stillwater Depot. For Sunday excursions, boarding begins at 11:30 a.m. with departure at noon. For weekday and possible Saturday afternoon trips, call the number above for information.

> From the Twin Cities on I-35W, I-35E, or I-694, exit on Hwy. 36 and go east to downtown Stillwater (about 30 miles from the Twin Cities). Hwy. 36 becomes Main Street. Go north on Main Street to the Minnesota Zephyr Depot, the last business on the right.

▲▲▲

OSCEOLA AND ST. CROIX VALLEY RAILWAY

Depot Rd., Osceola, WI 54020

Information: (612) 228-0263; charters and groups: (800) 643-7412

Experience the beautiful St. Croix River Valley on a 90-minute round trip to Marine-on-St. Croix, or view Wisconsin's countryside on a 45-minute round trip to Dresser. Ride beautifully restored passenger cars dating from the 1920s to the 1950s behind either diesel or steam locomotives.

> COST: To Marine-on-St. Croix: adults $10, seniors $8, children $6, children under 5 free. Family $30, $15 first class.
>
> To Dresser: adults $7, seniors $5, children $3, children under 5 free. Family, charter and group rates available. 5.5% sales tax not included.
>
> HOURS: Weekends and holidays, Memorial Day weekend through October. Departures to Marine-on-St. Croix: 11 a.m. and 2 p.m. To Dresser: 12:45 and 3:45 p.m. Charter and group trips by reservation only on Tuesdays in October and on Thursdays, Memorial Day weekend through October. Call for special schedule of steam train tours and fall color tours in September.

From I-35E or I-35W northbound, exit on Minnesota Hwy. 97, then go east to Minnesota Hwy. 243. Take 243 north about 6 miles to the Osceola turnoff. Go east across the river to Osceola and follow the signs to the railway, one block off Wisconsin Hwy. 35 on Depot St. in Osceola.

PADELFORD PACKET BOAT CO., INC.

Harriet Island, St. Paul, MN 55107 (612) 227-1100

Four large, luxurious Mississippi riverboats (Josiah Snelling, Jonathan Padelford, Anson Northrup, Betsey Northrup) depart from two landings: Boom Island in Minneapolis and Harriet Island in St. Paul. Narrated public excursions are available daily at noon and 2 p.m. from both landings, Memorial Day through Labor Day. Dinner cruises are available evenings with prepaid advance reservations. Group packages available.

> COST: Excursion from Boom Island or Harriet Island: adults $8.50, seniors $7.50, children under 12 $5.50, children 3 and under free. Prime Rib Dinner Cruise: $34.95 per person (sales tax included, no tipping). Chicken and Rib Dinner Cruise: $29.95 per person, $14.95 for children under 12 (sales tax included, no tipping).

▲▲▲▲▲▲▲▲▲▲▲▲▲▲▲▲▲▲▲▲▲▲▲▲▲▲▲▲▲▲▲▲▲▲▲▲▲▲

HOURS: Public excursions run from Memorial Day through Labor Day and depart daily at noon and 2 p.m. from both landings. The Prime Rib Dinner Cruise departs at 6 p.m. Sundays in June, July, and August. The Chicken and Rib Dinner Cruise departs at 6 p.m. Fridays and Tuesdays in June, July, August, and September.

Harriet Island Park is located in downtown St. Paul. From I-94, take the Marion St./Kellogg Blvd. exit toward downtown. Follow Kellogg to the Wabasha Street Bridge, turn right to cross the bridge and go about two more blocks to Plato Blvd. Turn right and follow the Harriet Island signs to the free parking lot.

Boom Island Park is located near downtown Minneapolis, just up the river from Nicollet Island. From I-94 northbound, take the Broadway/Washington Avenue exit and turn right onto Washington. Follow Washington to Plymouth, turn left and follow to the east end of the Plymouth Avenue Bridge (N.E. 8th Ave.). Turn right on Sibley St. N.E. and enter the Boom Island free parking lot.

The Jonathan Paddleford departs Harriet Island in St. Paul. The Padelford Packet Boat Co. offers narrated, public excursions aboard four large riverboats departing from two landings, Boom Island in Minneapolis and Harriet Island in St. Paul.

ST. ANTHONY MAIN "TROLLEY" RIDES

125 S.E. Main St., Minneapolis, MN 55414 (612) 673-5123

Take a nostalgic, narrated trolley tour down the beautiful streets of Minneapolis. Trolleys take off from St. Anthony Main and from the Minneapolis Convention Center. Each round trip lasts about 40 minutes. Round trip routes include the 3rd Ave. Bridge Route and the Stone Arch Bridge Route.

COST: Unavailable

HOURS: Monday–Sunday. From the Minneapolis Convention Center (12th St. S. and 2nd Ave. S.) and St. Anthony Main a trolley leaves on the hour (10 a.m., 11 a.m., etc.); 20 minutes after the hour (10:20, 11:20, etc.) and 40 minutes after the hour (10:40, 11:40, etc.).

St. Anthony Main location: From I-35W, take the 4th St. exit. Turn left onto 4th St. and follow to 3rd Ave. S.E. Turn left onto 3rd. Ave. S.E. and follow about 4 blocks to Main St. St. Anthony Main is on Main St.

Minneapolis Convention Center location: From I-35W northbound (from Bloomington), take the downtown exit to the 11th St. exit. Follow 11th St. south to 2nd Ave. S. Turn left onto 2nd Ave. S. and follow to the Convention Center on your left after you cross 12th St. S.

From I-35W sounthbound, take the Washington Ave. exit. Turn right on Washington Ave. S. and follow to 2nd Ave. S. Turn left onto 2nd Ave. S. and follow to the Convention Center on your left after you cross 12th St. S.

WAYZATA TOWNE TROLLEY

402 East Lake St., Wayzata, MN 55391 (612) 473-9595

A bright red trolley provides a free ride to shops, restaurants, and activities in Wayzata through the courtesy of the Greater Wayzata Area Chamber of Commerce and Wayzata area businesses. The Towne Trolley is also available for rental evenings and Sundays.

COST: Free; free parking.

HOURS: May 21-September 2: Monday-Friday 10 a.m.-4 p.m.; Saturday 10 a.m.-2 p.m. September 6-October 8: Monday-Saturday 10 a.m.-2 p.m.

From Minneapolis, take I-394 west toward Wayzata to the East Wayzata Blvd. exit. Take East Wayzata Blvd. to Central Ave., then go south until Central becomes Lake St. Continue on Lake St. to the Wayzata Towne Trolley Depot on the left.

▲▲▲▲▲▲▲▲▲▲▲▲▲▲▲▲▲▲▲▲▲▲▲▲▲▲▲▲▲▲▲▲▲▲▲▲▲▲

Photo by Zintsmaster, courtesy of The Wayzata Historical Society.

Traveling between shops, restaurants, and businesses in beautiful Wayzata is free aboard the Wayzata Towne Trolley.

EXCURSIONS

▲▲▲▲▲▲▲▲▲▲▲▲▲▲▲▲▲▲▲▲▲▲▲▲▲▲▲▲▲▲▲▲▲▲▲

FAIRS

▲▲▲▲▲▲▲▲▲▲▲▲▲▲▲▲▲▲▲▲▲▲▲▲▲▲▲▲▲▲▲▲▲▲▲▲

ANOKA COUNTY FAIR

P.O. Box 278, Anoka, MN 55303 (612) 427-4070

The Anoka County Fair is one of Minnesota's largest and most entertaining events of the year. Pay only once to enjoy all exhibits, entertainment, and special events. Highlights include grandstand events such as the PRCA national rodeo; grand national truck and tractor pulls, the second largest in the country; demolition derbies; six nights of music by regional big-name bands; a full midway; food; 4-H and open class exhibits; special events for kids; and various contests.

> COST: Adults $5, children $2. All grandstand events, ground events, and parking free.

> DATES: Tuesday-Sunday, first week in August.

> From I-35W northbound, exit on Hwy. 10 exit and go into Anoka. From Hwy. 10, turn right onto Ferry St. and follow to fairgrounds.

CARVER COUNTY FAIR

5325 County Rd. 10 North, Watertown, MN 55388
(612) 955-1772; summer season (612) 442-2333

Highlights include livestock exhibits; horse shows; creative activity exhibits, 150 commercial exhibitors; 16 bands throughout fair days; Goldstar Amusements Midway; grandstand shows featuring motor sports (super pulls out of field tractor and two demo derbies); and a large variety of food. The 1995 fair features a parade Sunday (parade is presented only every five years).

> COST: Adults $2.50, children under 10 free. Seniors 1/2 price Thursdays. Limited parking $2.50.

> DATES: Wednesday-Sunday, second week in August.

> From State Hwy. 5, go west into Waconia. Turn right at Maple St. and proceed north 2 blocks to 4th St. Turn left and follow 4th St. into fairgrounds.

DAKOTA COUNTY FAIR AND DAKOTA CITY HERITAGE VILLAGE

4008 220th St., Farmington, MN 55024 (612) 460-8050

County Fair week includes grandstand shows; 4-H and open class exhibits; commercial exhibits; free entertainment; and carnival. Also during fair week, 20 buildings in Heritage Village (a re-created historic village) are open free.

▲▲▲▲▲▲▲▲▲▲▲▲▲▲▲▲▲▲▲▲▲▲▲▲▲▲▲▲▲▲▲▲▲▲▲▲▲▲

COST: Parking fee only.

DATES: Seven days in early August. Heritage Village tours are available May through October by appointment only.

From Hwy. 3 in Farmington, turn west onto 220th Street, follow to 3rd St. and turn left into fairgrounds.

From Highway 50 in Farmington, turn north onto Denmark, go to 220th St. Turn left, then right at 2nd or 3rd St. into fairgrounds.

HENNEPIN COUNTY OLD TYME FAIR

322 Comanche Trail, Hamel, MN 55340 (612) 478-6189

The fair features grandstand events such as demolition derbies, draft horse pulling competition, and motocross racing; a quality carnival with rides; food; and a children's barnyard and petting area. Games for kids include big wheel races, a tractor pedal pull, and coloring contest. Amateur talent contests are open to all ages. Various 4-H and creative activities competitions are open to all residents of Hennepin County. Categories include fine arts, handicrafts, needlework and quilting, baking, flowers, amateur wine-making, dairy, and more. A premium list, explaining rules and prizes for all classes, is available in June at all Hennepin County libraries.

COST: Adult daily admission $4, children 6-12 $2.

DATES: Thursday-Sunday, July 27-July 30.

From I-494, exit Hwy. 55 and go west to Co. Rd. 101. Follow 101 north to the fairgrounds at the corner of Co. Rd. 10.

LESUEUR COUNTY FAIR

LeCenter, MN 56057 (612) 357-4373

In the friendly farming community of LeCenter, the LeSueur County Fair is host to agricultural equipment and livestock shows; 4-H activities; food; free entertainment; demolition derby; 45 commercial exhibitors; midway carnival; home and family activities.

COST: Free.

DATES: Begins Thursday of the week before the Minnesota State Fair. Dates for 1995: August 17-20. For 1996: August 15-18.

From Hwy. 169 southbound: at St. Peter, take State Hwy. 99 east to the fairgrounds.

▲▲▲▲▲▲▲▲▲▲▲▲▲▲▲▲▲▲▲▲▲▲▲▲▲▲▲▲▲▲▲▲▲▲▲▲

RAMSEY COUNTY FAIR

2020 White Bear Ave., Maplewood, MN 55109 (612) 770-2626 (one month before and two weeks after the fair).

Attractions include 4-H, agriculture, and commercial exhibits; craft entries; midway; ethnic displays and activities; daily stage entertainment; petting zoo; and talent contests (winners go on to State Fair).

COST: Parking fee $1 per car.

DATES: Wednesday-Sunday, third week in July.

From I-35W, exit on Hwy. 36 and go east to White Bear Ave. Go south on White Bear about 1/2 mile to fairgrounds on the left.

SCOTT COUNTY FAIR

P.O. Box 176, Jordan, MN 55352 (612) 492-2436

The four-day fair features 4-H; FFA; open class livestock; horse shows; craft exhibits; entertainment; food; commercial exhibits; and grandstand events daily.

COST: Admission free, $3 parking fee per vehicle. $5 for grandstand events.

DATES: 10 a.m.-12 a.m. daily, last week in July.

From the intersection of Hwy. 282 and Hwy. 169 in Jordan, go north on Scott Co. Rd. 9 for 1/2 mile. Turn left onto Scott Co. Rd. 57 and follow to fairgrounds.

SHERBURNE COUNTY FAIR

Box 002, Elk River, MN 55330 (612) 441-3722 (contact Tom Salzmann, treasurer of fair board)

Highlights of the four-day fair include family fair; four horse shows; tractor pulls; diaper derby; pedal tractor pulls; food; midway; over 1,400 4-H exhibits; free entertainment; teen dance; and talent show.

COST: $1 per person, free parking.

DATES: Thursday-Sunday, fourth weekend in July.

One mile west of Elk River on U.S. Hwy. 10.

▲▲▲▲▲▲▲▲▲▲▲▲▲▲▲▲▲▲▲▲▲▲▲▲▲▲▲▲▲▲▲▲▲▲▲▲▲▲▲

WASHINGTON COUNTY FAIR

P.O. Box 159, Lake Elmo, MN 55042
Eileen Tank, fair manager: (612) 459-3377
Fairgrounds phone: (612) 770-0246

This five-day fair features grandstand shows; rodeos; midway; food; races; horse shows; exhibits; livestock, poultry, and rabbit exhibits; nightly entertainment; and much more. All grandstand shows are free.

COST: Adults 16 and over $2, children 6-15 $1, children 5 and under free. Free parking.

DATES: Wednesday-Sunday, first week in August.

> From I-94 eastbound, take the Manning Ave/County Rd. 15 exit and go north 4 miles to the fairgrounds on the right.

WRIGHT COUNTY FAIR

3741 37th St. S.E., Delano, MN 55328 (612) 972-2880

Fair features midway; car races; demolition derby; 4-H exhibits; food; tractor pulls; horse shows; talent shows; senior citizen day; and much more.

COST: Parking $2 per day.

DATES: Wednesday-Sunday, first week in August.

> Located in Howard Lake. From Hwy. 12 westbound, go into Howard Lake, take Co. Rd. 6 and go north 4 blocks to fairgrounds.

▲▲▲▲▲▲▲▲▲▲▲▲▲▲▲▲▲▲▲▲▲▲▲▲▲▲▲▲▲▲▲▲▲▲▲▲

Photo by Colleen Spadaccini

Looking for a parking spot at the Minnesota State Fair, the nation's largest 12-day agricultural and educational exposition.

▲▲▲▲▲▲▲▲▲▲▲▲▲▲▲▲▲▲▲▲▲▲▲▲▲▲▲▲▲▲▲▲▲▲▲▲▲▲▲

MINNESOTA STATE FAIR

1265 Snelling Ave. N., St. Paul, MN 55108 (612) 642-2200

The Minnesota State Fair, the nation's largest 12-day agricultural and educational exposition, attracts 1.5 million people annually. Agricultural and creative competitions draw
more than 35,000 entries each year, with over $450,000 in prize money. More than
1,300 commercial exhibitors offer food, goods, services, and amusements.

> Other attractions include rides, games area, grandstand shows, and the Midwest's
> largest collection of food vendors, with more than 350 culinary conces-
> sionaires.

COST: Adults 13-64 $5; children 5-12 $4, seniors 65 and over $4.

DATES: The 12 days before and on Labor Day. Gates are open 6 a.m.-10:30
          p.m. Fairgrounds close at midnight, except on Labor Day.

From I-94, exit to Snelling Ave. and go north to Commonwealth Ave., west
on Commonwealth to the fairgrounds.

From I-35W northbound or southbound, exit to Cleveland Ave., go south to
Commonwealth Ave. and follow Commonwealth east to the fairgrounds.

From I-35E, exit to Larpenteur Ave. and go west to Snelling Ave. Follow
Snelling south to Commonwealth Ave., go west on Commonwealth to the
fairgrounds.

HORSE RIDING,
HAY & SLEIGH RIDES

▲▲▲▲▲▲▲▲▲▲▲▲▲▲▲▲▲▲▲▲▲▲▲▲▲▲▲▲▲▲▲▲▲▲▲▲▲

APPLESIDE ORCHARD INC.

18010 Chippendale Ave., Farmington, MN 55024 (612) 463-2505

One of Minnesota's largest pick-your-own fruit farms, with over 100 acres of apples, strawberries, raspberries, and pumpkins. A picnic area, pedal tractors for kids, and hay bales to play in enhance the family experience. Special events include free hay rides, storytellers, live bluegrass music, a kite-flying extravaganza in the second week of September, and a scarecrow-building event in the fall. Call to verify hours and crop availability. Send for flyer on dates and times of events at address above.

> COST: Varies. Free hay and pony rides.

> HOURS: Daily in June 7 a.m.-6 p.m. Closed in July. Daily August-October 9 a.m.-6 p.m. In November: Tuesday-Saturday noon-5 p.m.

> From I-35W or Cedar Ave., go east on Co. Rd. 42 to Hwy. 3, go south about 3-1/2 miles. Orchard is on the left side.

BUNKER HILLS STABLE

190 132nd Ave. N.W., Coon Rapids, MN 55448 (612) 757-7010

Enjoy these activities on acres of beautiful regional park land: trail rides; pony trail or ring; carriage rides; hay or sleigh rides; and riding lessons.

> COST: Basic one-hour trail rides $12 per person, One-hour trail ride for 8 or more riders $9 per person.

> DATES: Open year round.

> From I-694, take the State Hwy. 47 (University Ave.) exit. Follow Hwy. 47 north to Foley Blvd. Turn left (north) onto Foley Blvd. and proceed about 4 miles to Bunker Hills. Follow signs to the Activities Center for maps and brochures.
>
> From State Hwy. 65, take State Hwy. 242 west to Foley Blvd. and turn right into Bunker Hills. Follow signs to the Activities Center.

HORSE RIDING, HAY & SLEIGH RIDES

DIAMOND T RANCH

4889 Pilot Knob Rd., Eagan, MN 55122 (612) 454-1464

In addition to 28 miles of wooded trails open to the public for guided trail rides, Diamond T Ranch features hay and sleigh rides. One- and two-horse open sleigh rides last about 1/2 hour, hay rides about one hour.

COST: Hay rides for 12 people or fewer $60, 13-99 people $5 each, 100 people or more $4.50 each. Sleigh rides for one-horse sleigh, maximum 4 adults $35; two-horse sleigh, maximum 8 adults $60.

HOURS: Open year round; hours fluctuate according to daylight.

> From I-35W southbound, exit Cliff Rd. and go east to Pilot Knob. Turn right and go about 1/2 mile to ranch on the right .
>
> From I-35E southbound, take Pilot Knob Rd. exit, turn right and go about 3 miles. Ranch is on the right.
>
> From I-35E northbound, exit to Cliff Rd. and go east about 1/2 mile. Ranch is on the right.

EAGLE CREEK STABLES, INC.

7301 Eagle Creek Blvd., Shakopee, MN 55379 (612) 445-7222

Eagle Creek Stables, 30 minutes from downtown Minneapolis, offers horse rentals; hay rides; sleigh rides; miles of scenic trails; a heated lounge; horse boarding; and indoor/outdoor arenas. Horse-drawn rides last about one hour. Advance reservations are necessary. The lounge is open to groups until 11 p.m. Bonfires are available on prior request.

COST: Hayride: $5 per person, $60 minimum group rate.

HOURS: Open year round for hay and sleigh rides, anytime of day, or evenings at 6, 7:30, and 9 p.m.

> From I-35W, exit on Hwy. 13 going west and continue until Hwy. 13 meets Hwy. 101. Follow 101 west to Co. Rd. 18. Follow 18 south to Co. Rd. 16 (Eagle Creek Blvd.). Turn right onto Co. Rd. 16 and follow to Eagle Creek Stables on the right.

▲▲

SPONSEL'S MINNESOTA HARVEST APPLE ORCHARD

Old Hwy. 169 Blvd., Jordan, MN 55352 (612) 492-2785, 492-7753 (49-Apple) or (800) 662-7753

September and October are the big apple months in Minnesota. Bring the family and pick 'em yourself or buy already picked. Sponsel's celebrates with hay rides; carnival; wagon and pony rides; hiking trails; petting zoo; and live music. The packing house features a gift shop; food products made at the orchard; lunch area; bakery; and observation deck to watch the packing and sorting operation.

COST: Free.

HOURS: Daily in January-July: 9 a.m.-5 p.m. August-October: 9 a.m.-7 p.m.

Daily in November-December: 9 a.m.-6 p.m. Sleigh rides available November-April. Limited services January-July. Please call.

From I-494 westbound, exit on U.S. Hwy. 169 going south through Shakopee. Go 2 miles past the stoplight in Jordan to Co. Rd. 59. Go south (left) on 59 and follow the Minnesota Harvest signs up the hill and into the woods about 1-1/2 mile. At Old Hwy. 169, turn right and follow to Minnesota Harvest at Apple Lovers' Lane.

From I-35W southbound, exit at Hwy. 13 going west to Hwy. 101. Continue on 101 to U.S. Hwy. 169. Take 169 south through Shakopee. Continue 2 miles past the stoplight in Jordan to Co. Rd. 59 and proceed as above to Minnesota Harvest at Apple Lovers' Lane.

▲▲▲▲▲▲▲▲▲▲▲▲▲▲▲▲▲▲▲▲▲▲▲▲▲▲▲▲▲▲▲▲

A trail ride at a local riding stable.

▲▲▲▲▲▲▲▲▲▲▲▲▲▲▲▲▲▲▲▲▲▲▲▲▲▲▲▲▲▲▲▲▲▲▲▲▲▲

DIAMOND T RANCH

4889 Pilot Knob Rd., Eagan, MN 55122 (612) 454-1464

Diamond T Ranch is a great diversion from city life if you enjoy horses and trail riding. Open to the public for guided trail rides, Diamond T Ranch has 28 miles of wooded trails and horses suited for every skill level. Friendly guides are always available. Other features of the ranch include hay and sleigh rides; riding lessons; horse boarding and sales; a Western shop; snack bar; private party rooms; and cross-country skiing. Diamond T also specializes in children's birthday parties.

COST: Basic one-hour trail ride for 1-9 riders $12 each, 10–19 riders $11.50 each, 20 or more riders $11 each. Riding lessons by appointment only. Semi-private lessons $25 per lesson, private lessons $30.

HOURS: Open year round; hours fluctuate according to daylight.

> From I-35W southbound, take the Cliff Rd. exit east to Pilot Knob. Turn right. Ranch is on the right about 1/2 mile.
>
> From I-35E southbound, take the Pilot Knob Rd. exit. Turn right. Ranch is on the right about 3 miles.
>
> From I-35 E northbound, turn right onto the Cliff Rd. exit.
>
> Ranch is on the right about 1/2 mile.

EAGLE CREEK STABLES, INC.

7301 Eagle Creek Blvd., Shakopee, MN 55379 (612) 445-7222

Eagle Creek Stables, only 30 minutes from downtown Minneapolis, is a nice find for horse lovers. It offers horse rentals; hay rides; sleigh rides; miles of scenic trails; a heated lounge; horse boarding; and indoor/outdoor arenas.

COST: Riding rates for first hour $12, second hour $11, each additional hour, $10, full day $50. Group rates available. Hay ride (with a $60 minimum group rate) $5 per person.

HOURS: Riding May–September: daily 9 a.m.–7 p.m.; October–December: 9 a.m.–dusk; December–February: weekends only, 9 a.m.–dusk.

> From I-35W, take the Hwy. 13 exit going west until it meets Hwy. 101. Continue on Hwy. 101 (west) to Co. Rd. 18. Follow Co. Rd. 18 south to Co. Rd. 16 (Eagle Creek Blvd.). Turn right onto Co. Rd. 16 and follow to Eagle Creek Stables on the right.

HORSE RIDING, HAY & SLEIGH RIDES

▲▲▲▲▲▲▲▲▲▲▲▲▲▲▲▲▲▲▲▲▲▲▲▲▲▲▲▲▲▲▲▲▲▲▲

MUSEUMS & HISTORICAL SITES

▲▲▲▲▲▲▲▲▲▲▲▲▲▲▲▲▲▲▲▲▲▲▲▲▲▲▲▲▲▲▲▲▲▲▲▲▲

AMERICAN SWEDISH INSTITUTE

2600 Park Ave., Minneapolis, MN 55407-1090 (612) 871-4907

Swan J. Turnblad, a Swedish immigrant, newspaper publisher, and self-made million-aire, donated his personal possessions, business, and 33-room mansion in 1929 to help preserve over 150 years of Swedish heritage in America. More than a museum, the Institute offers classes in Swedish language, folk arts, and crafts; weekly films; special exhibits; lectures; and special cultural events.

   COST: Adults $3, students 6-18 and seniors $2, children 6 and under free.

   HOURS: Tuesday, Thursday, Friday, and Saturday noon-4 p.m.; Wednesday
            noon-8 p.m.; Sunday 1-5 p.m. Closed Mondays and holidays.

> From I-35W northbound, take the Lake St./31st St. exit and proceed east to Park Ave. Follow Park Ave. north to the Institute.
>
> From I-35W southbound, take the Hiawatha Ave. exit. Follow Hiawatha to 26th St. Go west on 26th St. to the Institute on the corner of 26th St. and Park Ave.

BAKKEN LIBRARY AND MUSEUM

3537 Zenith Ave. S., Minneapolis, MN 55416 (612) 927-6508

The Bakken is a learning center that promotes understanding of the history and appli-cations of electromagnetism in the life sciences. Founded in 1976 by Earl Bakken, inventor of the first wearable cardiac pacemaker, this private, nonprofit institution maintains a collection of over 10,000 books, manuscripts, archival materials, and more than 2,000 artifacts and scientific instruments. This fascinating collection shows the role of electromagnetism in life, and its uses in biology and medicine.

   COST: Adults $3, students and seniors $2, children under 8 free.

   HOURS: Saturdays 9:30 a.m.-4:30 p.m.; weekdays by appointment for group
            tours and workshops.

> From I-35W, take the 35th/36th St. exit. Follow 35th St. west for two blocks. Cut over 1 block south to 36th St. Follow 36th St. west to Lake Calhoun Pkwy. Turn left onto Lake Calhoun Pkwy. and follow around the southern edge of Lake Calhoun until the parkway meets 36th St. again on the west shore of the lake. Turn left onto 36th St. and follow 1 block to Zenith. Turn right onto Zenith and look for the Bakken on the right.

MUSEUMS & HISTORICAL SITES

▲▲▲▲▲▲▲▲▲▲▲▲▲▲▲▲▲▲▲▲▲▲▲▲▲▲▲▲▲▲▲▲▲▲▲▲▲▲

BASEBALL MUSEUM (Dome Souvenirs Plus)

910 Third St. S., Minneapolis, MN 55415 (612) 375-9707

This quaint baseball museum is filled with autographed baseballs, bats, jerseys, and programs, most from the Minnesota Twins. A snack bar and souvenirs are available during events.

COST: Free.

HOURS: Monday-Friday 9 a.m.-4 p.m.; Saturday 11 a.m.-3 p.m. Open before and after all Metrodome events (Vikings, Twins, and Gopher games, and all concerts).

> From I-35W, exit on Washington Ave. and go north to the Hubert H. Humphrey Metrodome. Dome Souvenirs Plus is located one block north of Dome Gate A.

BELL MUSEUM OF NATURAL HISTORY

University of Minnesota 10 Church St. S.E., Minneapolis, MN 55455
Information and reservations (612) 624-7083 Wildlife information (612) 624-1374

Learn about wildlife while viewing the Bell Museum's wide variety of changing exhibits and beautiful wildlife art. Take a nature walk, or meet wildlife artists and world-renowned researchers. Investigate the University's telescope and planetarium. Programs include special field trips; children's programs and classes; family programs; conferences; lectures; interactive tours; classes for groups; and more.

COST: Adults $3; children 3-16, students, and seniors $2; children under 3, U of M students, and members free.

HOURS: Tuesday-Friday 9 a.m.-5 p.m., Saturday 10 a.m.-5 p.m., Sunday noon-5 p.m. The Touch and See Room is open until 5 p.m. Tuesday-Sunday.

> The Bell Museum is located on the Minneapolis campus of the University of Minnesota, at the southwest corner of 17th Ave. (Church St.) and University Ave. S.E.
>
> From I-35W northbound or southbound, take the University Avenue/4th St. exit. Go east on University to 17th Ave. Turn left (north) onto 17th Ave. to reach the 4th St. ramp. Turn right (south) on 17th Ave. to reach the Nolte and Church Street garages, Northrop Auditorium, or the Washington Ave. ramp.

▲▲▲▲▲▲▲▲▲▲▲▲▲▲▲▲▲▲▲▲▲▲▲▲▲▲▲▲▲▲▲▲▲▲▲

From I-94 westbound, take the U of M exit. The exit will become Huron Blvd. Go north on Huron Blvd., crossing University Ave. and following the curve to the west. Huron Blvd. will become 4th St. Continue on 4th St. three blocks to 17th Ave. To reach the 4th St. ramp, turn right onto 17th Ave. To reach the Nolte and Church St. garages, Northrop Auditorium, or the Washington Ave. ramp, turn left on 17th Ave. and proceed past the stoplight on University Ave. (After crossing University Ave., 17th Ave. becomes Church St.)

Photo courtesy of The Brooklyn Park Historical Farm

"Rolling the hoop" at The Brooklyn Park Historical Farm.

▲▲

BROOKLYN PARK HISTORICAL FARM

4345 101st Ave. N., Brooklyn Park, MN 55443 (612) 493-4604

This 10-acre historical farm was owned by the Eidem family for 82 years. You can experience the sights, smells, and sounds of rural Minnesota farm life as it was in the late 19th century and early 1900s through guided tours, displays, pioneer craft demonstrations, and hands-on activities. Children can enjoy the barn and barnyard, which harbors pigs, cows, sheep, goats, chickens, ducks, geese, and cats. Special events include folk dancing; music; hayrides; contests; childhood games and hoop-rolling; classes relating to turn-of-the-century farm life and homemaking; and an old-fashioned Christmas with Norwegian traditions. Groups of 15 or more may make tour reservations by calling the Brooklyn Park Recreation and Parks Department (612) 493-8333.

COST: Tours:$1.50 per person. Open houses: adults $1.50, children 50¢. Special living history events: adults $2.50, seniors and children $2.

HOURS: May-mid-December: Monday-Friday 9 a.m.-5 p.m. Special events: third Sundays in September, October, and November 1-4 p.m.; first weekend in December 1-5 p.m.

> From I-694, take the Hwy. 252 exit and proceed north on Hwy. 252 to 93rd Ave. N. From 93rd turn left (west) onto Regent Ave. N. and go north (right) to 101st Ave. N. Turn right onto 101st and go east to the farm.

CHILDREN'S MUSEUM

1217 Bandana Blvd., St. Paul, MN 55108 (612) 644-5305

Exciting hands-on experiences are in store for every child who visits the Children's Museum. Exhibits challenge the imagination, encourage exploration, and provide physical activity. Each weekend the museum features special programs free with admission. Enjoy live performances by storytellers, puppeteers, and musicians. Join in hands-on workshops like "Art Tickles," "Joyous Junk," and much more.

After June 11, 1995, the Children's Museum will relocate next to the World Trade Center at Seventh and Wabasha Sts. in downtown St. Paul and reopen to the public September 15, 1995. You can look forward to 47,000 more square feet of fun in this new five-story building. Seven new galleries will be added to the new Museum along with a 150-seat theater.

Themes for five gallery environments include Earth World; One World; World Works; Habitot; and Rooftop Garden. Two of the seven galleries will have changing themes.

The theater will feature drama; dance and music performances; films; programs; two Discovery Classrooms adjacent to the galleries; an activity center; and Museum store.

▲▲▲▲▲▲▲▲▲▲▲▲▲▲▲▲▲▲▲▲▲▲▲▲▲▲▲▲▲▲▲▲▲▲▲

COST: $2 for toddlers (12–36 months) and seniors, $3.50 for children and adults 3–60.

HOURS: Tuesday 9 a.m.–5 p.m.; Wednesday–Saturday 9 am.–8 p.m.; Sunday noon–5 p.m.; Monday 9 am–5 p.m. (Memorial Day–Labor Day only).

CURRENT CHILDREN'S MUSEUM, 1217 Bandana Blvd., St. Paul, until June 11, 1995: Take I-94 to Lexington Avenue. Go north on Lexington 2 miles. Turn left onto Energy Park Drive and go 3 blocks. Turn right at Bandana Square.

NEW CHILDREN'S MUSEUM, 7th and Wabasha Sts., downtown St. Paul, starting September 15, 1995: From I-94 eastbound, take the 5th Street exit. Follow 5th St. to 7th St. (second stoplight). Turn left onto 7th St. Follow 7th St. to Wabasha. The new Children's Museum is at the intersection of 7th and Wabasha.

From I-94 westbound, take the 6th St. exit. Follow 6th St. to Wabasha St. Turn right onto Wabasha and proceed to 7th St. The new Children's Museum is at the intersection of 7th and Wabasha.

From I-35E northbound, take the Kellogg Blvd. exit. Follow Kellogg Blvd. to 7th St. Turn left onto 7th St and proceed to Wabasha. The new Children's Museum is at the intersection of 7th and Wabasha.

From I-35E southbound, take the 10th St. exit. Follow 10th St. to Cedar St. (the Science Museum is directly in front of you). Turn left onto Cedar and proceed about 3 blocks to 7th St. Turn right onto 7th St. and follow to Wabasha. The new Children's Museum is at the intersection of 7th and Wabasha.

▲▲

DAKOTA COUNTY HISTORICAL SOCIETY

130 Third Ave. N., South St. Paul, MN 55075 (612) 451-6260

The Society was founded in 1939 to preserve and promote the history of Dakota County and its people through exhibitions, programs, publications, and research. The Society is housed in a large modern building with a spacious exhibition area decorated with a wall and floor mural. Each year, two exhibitions on facets of Dakota County history are mounted in this room. Three case exhibitions are rotated regularly. A permanent exhibition area titled "Old Town" depicts a variety of stores from the turn of the century. The Society presents programs on Dakota County history to residents of all ages. The research library assists hundreds of people each year with genealogy, house and land research, and many other topics.

COST: Free.

HOURS: Tuesday, Wednesday, Friday 9 a.m.-5 p.m.; Thursday 9 a.m.-8 p.m.; Saturday 10 a.m.-3 p.m.

> From Hwy. 3, I-494, or Hwy. 52/55, take the Concord St. exit, turn west at Grand Ave. and go uphill for 1-1/2 blocks. When the road forms a Y, stay to the left. The museum is on the left side of the road, 1/2 block from the Y intersection. A lighted sign says, "Dakota County Museum."

EDINA HISTORICAL SOCIETY AND MUSEUM

4711 W. 70th St., Edina, MN 55435 (612) 920-8952

The Edina Historical Museum provides a permanent exhibit of Edina's cultural and historical background with rotating exhibits of varied artifacts. The museum is situated in a beautiful year-round park.

COST: Free.

HOURS: Thursday 9 a.m.-noon; Saturday 2 p.m.-4 p.m. or by appointment for groups. Closed in August.

> From Hwy. 100, take the 70th St. exit and follow 70th St. east 1/2 block to the Museum.

▲▲▲▲▲▲▲▲▲▲▲▲▲▲▲▲▲▲▲▲▲▲▲▲▲▲▲▲▲▲▲▲▲▲▲▲

FIRE FIGHTERS MEMORIAL MUSEUM

1100 Van Buren St. N.E., Minneapolis, MN 55413 (612) 623-3817

Children are encouraged to see, touch, and explore fire engine trucks, fire fighting equipment and uniforms, a working alarm call box, a video about fire station life. and antique equipment with story boards. The "learn not to burn room" shows the damage a fire can do in only 4-1/2 minutes. A memorable experience for children is a ride on a real fire engine truck.

COST: Adults $4, children $2.

HOURS: Saturday 9:30 a.m.-3 p.m. Other times by appointment.

From I-35W northbound, take the E. Hennepin Ave. exit and proceed about a mile to Broadway. Follow Broadway west about 6 blocks. The Fire Fighters Memorial Museum is on the northwest corner of Broadway and Central Ave.

FOLSOM HOUSE

Government Rd., Taylors Falls, MN 55084 (612) 465-3125

Tour this lovely frame home, located in Taylors Falls' Argel Hill district, a New England-style village. This lumber baron's home features St. Croix River views.

COST: Adults $3, students 6-16 $1, seniors $2.50, children 5 and under free. Special tour rates available.

HOURS: Daily from the last week in May to the second week in October: 1-4:30 p.m.

Take U.S. Hwy. 8 to Bench St. Turn left onto Bench and left again onto First St., then left onto Government Rd. The Folsom House is on the right side.

FOSHAY TOWER OBSERVATION DECK

821 Marquette Ave., Minneapolis, MN 55402 (612) 341-2522

The Foshay Tower observation deck is located on the 31st floor of the historic Foshay Tower. The public can see 30 miles on a clear day and learn the story behind the first skyscraper built west of the Mississippi, and the only one from 1929 to 1971. Wilbur Foshay, the original owner and builder of the 32-story tower, modeled it after the Washington Monument as a tribute to George Washington.

▲▲▲▲▲▲▲▲▲▲▲▲▲▲▲▲▲▲▲▲▲▲▲▲▲▲▲▲▲▲▲▲▲▲▲▲▲▲▲

COST: Call for prices.

HOURS: Monday-Friday noon-4 p.m.; Saturday 11 a.m.-3 p.m. Closed Sunday.

> From I-35W or I-94 heading into downtown Minneapolis, take the 11th St. exit and proceed to 3rd Ave. Turn right onto 3rd and follow for two blocks to 9th St. Turn left and proceed to the Foshay Tower on the corner of 9th St. and Marquette Ave.

GIBBS FARM MUSEUM OF THE RAMSEY COUNTY HISTORICAL SOCIETY

2097 W. Larpenteur Ave., Falcon Heights, MN 55113 (612) 646-8629

This living history farm portraying life in the early 1900s features costumed guides; an original farm house begun in 1854; authentically bred animals; a barn with farm tools and equipment; and more. A one-room schoolhouse provides a summer schoolhouse program for grades 2-7. The farm is also available for birthday parties.

COST: Adults $2.50, children $1, seniors $2, members free.

HOURS: May-October: Tuesday-Friday 10 a.m.-4 p.m.; Saturday and Sunday
         noon-4 p.m.

> From I-35W southbound, exit to Cleveland Ave. and proceed 1.1 miles south on Cleveland to the Gibbs Farm Museum parking lot on the right.
>
> From I-94 westbound, take the Snelling Avenue exit and proceed north on Snelling 2.7 miles to Larpenteur. Turn left onto Larpenteur and follow 1 mile to Cleveland Ave. Turn right onto Cleveland and proceed 1 block to parking lot on the left.
>
> From I-94 eastbound, take the Hwy. 280 exit and proceed north on 280 about 2 miles to Larpenteur. Turn right onto Larpenteur and proceed 1.2 miles to Cleveland. Turn left onto Cleveland and proceed 1 block to parking lot on the left.

ARD GODFREY HOUSE

Central Ave. at University Ave. S.E. on historic Richard Chute Square between Riverplace and St. Anthony Main, Minneapolis, MN 55403 Information (612) 870-8001 Tours (612) 789-7953

▲▲▲▲▲▲▲▲▲▲▲▲▲▲▲▲▲▲▲▲▲▲▲▲▲▲▲▲▲▲▲▲▲▲▲▲

Situated along the falls of St. Anthony on the Mississippi River, the Ard Godfrey House is the oldest residence in Minneapolis. Built in 1849, the home was restored and refurbished in 1979 by the Women's Club of Minneapolis, and is open for public tours each summer.

COST: Adults $1, seniors 50¢, students 6-18 25¢, children under 6 free.

HOURS: June-September: Friday, Saturday, Sunday, and Monday noon-3:30 p.m. Special tours can be arranged year round.

From I-35W northbound, take the 5th Ave. exit. Follow 5th Ave. north (right) to Washington Ave. Turn onto Washington Ave. and follow to 3rd Ave. Turn right onto 3rd Ave. and follow across the Mississippi River.

From I-394 eastbound, take the Washington Ave. exit. Turn right onto Washington and follow to 3rd Ave. Turn left onto 3rd and follow until it becomes Central Ave. Follow Central to the Ard Godfrey house on the left side of the intersection of Central Ave. and University Ave. in Richard Chute Square.

Photo by Minnesota Historical Society

The James J. Hill House, a Minnesota Historical Society Historic Site, located on St. Paul's magnificent Summit Ave.

MUSEUMS & HISTORICAL SITES

▲▲▲▲▲▲▲▲▲▲▲▲▲▲▲▲▲▲▲▲▲▲▲▲▲▲▲▲▲▲▲▲▲▲▲▲▲▲

JAMES J. HILL HOUSE

240 Summit Ave., St. Paul, MN 55102 (612) 297-2555

Craggy brick and stone, massive scale, fine detail, and ingenious mechanical systems recall the powerful presence of James J. Hill, builder of the Great Northern Railway. Tours help visitors imagine family and servant life in the mansion.

COST: Adults $4, children 6-15 $2, seniors $3.

HOURS: Open year round. Wednesday-Saturday 10 a.m.-3:30 p.m.

> From I-94 take the Marion/Kellogg exit. Turn south down Kellogg Blvd. and follow to Summit Ave. Turn right onto Summit Ave. and go 2 blocks. The Hill House is on the left.

HISTORIC FORT SNELLING

Intersection of Minnesota Hwys. 5 and 55, St. Paul, MN 55111 (612) 725-2413 Tours (612) 726-1171

Life at a military outpost in 1827 is re-enacted by soldiers, cooks, laundresses, store-keepers, and craftsmen. The restored stone fortress overlooks the confluence of the Mississippi and Minnesota Rivers.

COST: Adults $4, children 6-15 $2, seniors $3.

HOURS: May-October: Monday-Saturday 10 a.m.-5 p.m.; Sunday noon-5 p.m.

> From I- 494, take the Hwy. 5 exit. Direction signs to the fort are highly visible on Hwy. 5. Fort Snelling exits are located at the intersection of Hwy. 5 and Hwy. 55.

OLIVER H. KELLEY FARM

15788 Kelley Farm Rd., Elk River, MN 55330 (612) 441-6896

Experience a working 1860s farm, pick typical vegetables from the garden, visit the farmhands and animals at the barn, or see what's cooking in the farmhouse. Costumed guides work the fields with oxen and horses.

Continues on page 94.

▲▲▲▲▲▲▲▲▲▲▲▲▲▲▲▲▲▲▲▲▲▲▲▲▲▲▲▲▲▲▲▲▲▲

Some of the many guides in period costumes re-enacting life at Historic Fort Snelling.

▲▲▲▲▲▲▲▲▲▲▲▲▲▲▲▲▲▲▲▲▲▲▲▲▲▲▲▲▲▲▲▲▲▲▲▲▲▲

COST: Adults $4, students 6-15 $2, seniors $3, children 5 and under free.

HOURS: May 1-October 31: Monday-Saturday 10 a.m.-5 p.m.; Sunday
noon-5 p.m. Visitor Center only: open November 1-April 30: Saturday
10 a.m.-4 p.m.; Sunday noon-4 p.m.

> The Kelley Farm is on U.S. Hwy. 10, 2.5 miles S.E. of Elk River.

LANDMARK CENTER

75 W. 5th St., St. Paul, MN 55102 (612) 292-3225

This nationally known monument was built in 1902 as the Federal Courts Building. It
is now a beautifully restored cultural center with tours and frequent special events, such
as ethnic celebrations and family events.

COST: Free; some special events may require nominal adult admission.

HOURS: Monday-Wednesday and Friday 8 a.m.-5 p.m.; Thursday 8 a.m.-7 p.m.;
Saturday 10 a.m.-5 p.m.; Sunday noon-5 p.m.

> Located on 5th St. in downtown St. Paul, across from Rice Park and the
> Ordway Theatre.
>
> From I-94 eastbound, take the 5th St. exit and proceed to Market St.
> Landmark Center is on the left.
>
> From I-94 westbound, take the 6th St. exit. Follow 6th St. 8 blocks to Market
> St. Landmark Center is on the left.
>
> From I-35E southbound, take the 10th St. exit and follow 10th St. 4 blocks to
> 6th St. Turn right onto 6th St. and go 6 blocks to Landmark Center.
>
> From I-35E northbound, take the Kellogg Blvd. exit. Turn right onto Kellogg
> Blvd. and go one block to 7th St. Take a left and get into the right lane
> immediately. The right lane curves into 5th St. Follow 5th St. 1 block to
> Landmark Center.

▲▲▲▲▲▲▲▲▲▲▲▲▲▲▲▲▲▲▲▲▲▲▲▲▲▲▲▲▲▲▲▲▲▲▲▲▲

CHARLES A. LINDBERGH HOUSE

1200 Lindbergh Drive, Little Falls, MN (612) 632-3154

Explore the boyhood home and surroundings of the famous aviator: enjoy the cozy kitchen, hear the whisper of pines from the porch where Lindbergh slept, or walk by the river where he dreamed of flying. A history center tells more of the family's story.

COST: Adults $3, children 6-15 $1, children 5 and under free.

HOURS: May 1-Labor Day: Monday-Saturday 10 a.m.-5 p.m.; Sunday noon-5 p.m. Labor Day-late October: 10 am-4 p.m.; Saturday and Sunday noon-4 p.m. Other times by group reservation. Schedules and fees subject to change.

> Located 2 miles south of Little Falls. From I-94, take U.S. Hwy. 10 northwest to Minnesota Hwy. 27. Go south (left) on Hwy. 27 to Lindbergh Drive S. and turn left. Charles A. Lindbergh House is on the right.

WILLIAM L. MC KNIGHT-3M OMNITHEATER

30 E. 10th St., St. Paul, MN 55101 (Located in the Science Museum of Minnesota) (612) 221-9488

The Omnitheater is designed to enhance the 70mm film-viewing experience. The steep angle of the seats gives everyone an unobstructed view. Images and sounds literally surround the audience and provide the sensation of being "in the picture." The Omnitheater's main projection room, directly under the audience, houses one of the world's largest projection systems. Film is run horizontally through the projector at 24 frames per second (about six feet). During a 40-minute show, nearly three miles of film passes through the projector and appears on the theater's 7,300-square-foot domed screen.

The Science Museum of Minnesota built this, the second Omnimax theater in the world, in 1978. The Science Museum is one of the largest producers of Imax/Omnimax science and educational films. Titles have included The Great Barrier Reef, Darwin on Galapagos, Ring of Fire, Tropical Rainforest, and The Search for the Great Sharks.

▲▲▲▲▲▲▲▲▲▲▲▲▲▲▲▲▲▲▲▲▲▲▲▲▲▲▲▲▲▲▲▲▲▲

COST: Exhibits and Omnitheater combined ticket: adults $7, children 4-12 and seniors $6. Omnitheater only: adults $6, children 4-12 and seniors $5.

HOURS: Call (612) 221-9444 for information about holiday hours and show times or to make advance Omnitheater reservations.

> The Omnitheater is in the Science Museum, located off I-94 and I-35E in downtown St. Paul, 15 minutes from the Mall of America.
>
> From I-35E northbound, take the 11th St. exit and follow 11th St. to the Science Museum.
>
> From I-94 eastbound or I-35E southbound, take the 10th St. exit and follow 10th St. to the Science Museum.
>
> From I-94 westbound, take the 12th St. exit and follow 12th St. to the Science Museum.

MINNEAPOLIS INSTITUTE OF ARTS

2400 Third Ave. S., Minneapolis, MN 55404
24-hour exhibition information: 870-3200 Program and visitor information: 870-3131

This comprehensive fine arts museum, close to downtown Minneapolis, is recognized internationally as one of the great museums in America. The Institute's collection of more than 80,000 objects is known for its quality and range. The Institute's emphasis has been on the careful gathering of works representative of every age and cultural tradition, spanning 4,000 years of world history. Besides unique monthly exhibitions and tours, the Institute also provides art programs for young people, classes for adults, a library, and special events. Call for seasonal information.

COST: General admission is free. Dayton Hudson Gallery special exhibitions: adults $5; children and seniors $3; Thursdays 5-9 p.m. free.

HOURS: Tuesday, Wednesday, Friday, and Saturday 10 a.m.-5 p.m.; Thursday 10 a.m.-9 p.m.; Sunday noon-5 p.m. Closed Monday.

> From I-94 westbound, take the 11th St. exit and turn left at the second set of lights (3rd Ave. S.). Follow 3rd Ave. S. to W. 24th St., and look for the Institute on the right.
>
> From I-94 eastbound, take the Lyndale/Hennepin Ave. exit. Take the Lyndale (left) fork when the road divides. Proceed on Lyndale to W. 24th St. and turn left. Follow W. 24th St. to 3rd Ave. S. and turn right onto 3rd Ave. S. Follow 3rd Ave. S. and look for the Institute on the right.

▲▲▲▲▲▲▲▲▲▲▲▲▲▲▲▲▲▲▲▲▲▲▲▲▲▲▲▲▲▲▲▲▲▲▲▲▲

From I-35W southbound, take the 11th Ave. exit. Turn left onto 11th Ave. and proceed to Franklin Ave. Turn right onto Franklin Ave. and proceed to 3rd Ave. S. Turn left and go to W. 24th St. and look for the Institute on the right.

From I-35W northbound, take the 31st St./Lake St. exit. Turn left onto 31st St., follow to 1st Ave. S. and turn right. Follow 1st Ave. S. to W. 24th St. and turn right. Follow W. 24th to 3rd Ave. S. and turn right. You will see the entrance to the Institute on the right side of 3rd Ave. S.

From I-394 eastbound, take the Hennepin Ave./Dunwoody exit, follow the signs for Lyndale Ave. (stay to the left). Continue south on Lyndale Ave. to W. 24th St. Turn left onto W. 24th St. and proceed to 3rd Ave. S. Turn right and look for the Theatre on the right.

MINNEAPOLIS PLANETARIUM

300 Nicollet Mall, Minneapolis, MN 55401 (Minneapolis Public Library)
Recording for Star Show updates and times: (612) 372-6644

Family and adult Star Shows await your imagination. The planetarium is a remarkable optical instrument that projects a beautiful reproduction of the night sky on a domed ceiling. Each Star Show lasts one hour; the first half is a lively tour of the current night sky, the second half is an engaging multimedia program on various astronomical topics. Shows change every 2-1/2 months, so please call for updates.

COST: Adults 13 and over $3.75, children 12 and under $2.25, children 2 and under free.

HOURS: Show times: Thursday 7 p.m.; Saturday 11 a.m., 1, 2:15, and 3:30 p.m.; Sunday 1, 2:15, and 3:30 p.m. Monday-Friday show times vary, so please call to verify.

From I-94 westbound, take the 5th St. exit and follow 5th for one mile as it curves around the Metrodome to Hennepin Ave. Turn right onto Hennepin and follow 1 block to 4th St. Turn right onto 4th and look for the Planetarium on the left.

From I-94 eastbound, exit to 4th St. and follow 3-4 blocks. The Planetarium is on the left between Hennepin and Nicollet on 4th St.

From I-394 heading into Minneapolis, take the 4th St. exit. Follow 4th St. 3-4 blocks. After you pass Hennepin Ave., the Planetarium is on the left.

▲▲▲▲▲▲▲▲▲▲▲▲▲▲▲▲▲▲▲▲▲▲▲▲▲▲▲▲▲▲▲▲▲▲▲▲▲▲

> From I-35W southbound, take the Washington Ave. exit to the right and follow Washington Ave. 8 blocks. From Washington turn left onto 3rd Ave. and follow about 3 blocks to 5th St. Turn right onto 5th and go 5 blocks to Hennepin Ave. Turn right onto Hennepin and follow 1 block to 4th St. Turn right onto 4th and follow to the Planetarium on the left side.
>
> From I-35W northbound, take the 5th Ave. exit. Follow 5th Ave. 5 blocks to 5th St. Turn left onto 5th St. and go 5-6 blocks to Hennepin Ave. Turn right onto Hennepin and follow 1 block to 4th St. Turn right again onto 4th St. and follow to the Planetarium on the left.

MINNEHAHA DEPOT

4920 Minnehaha Ave, Minneapolis, MN 55417

(612) 228-0263

Built in 1875, the Minnehaha Depot replaced an even smaller station on the same site. Milwaukee Road agents nicknamed the depot the "Princess" because of its intricate architectural details. Closed in 1963, this preserved railroad station features exhibits on area railroading and telegraphy.

COST: Free.

HOURS: Memorial Day weekend-Labor Day: Sundays and holidays
          12:30-4:30 p.m.

> Located in Minnehaha Park near Minnehaha Falls.
>
> From I-94, take the Hwy. 65 exit going south and follow Hwy. 65 to Minnehaha Pkwy. Turn left onto Minnehaha Pkwy. and follow to Minnehaha Ave. Turn right onto Minnehaha Ave. and go 1 block to the depot.
>
> From Crosstown (Hwy. 62), take the Hwy. 55 exit going north to Minnehaha Pkwy. Proceed east on Minnehaha Pkwy. to Minnehaha Ave. Go south on Minnehaha Ave. to the depot.

MINNESOTA AIR GUARD MUSEUM

5800 40th Ave. S., Minneapolis, MN 55450 (612) 725-5609

Get up close and view the impressive static display including a Blackbird Spy Plane, F-4, F-101, F-89, F-94, P-51, T-6, T-33, C-47, C-45, C-131, and L-4, plus artifacts, photos, and memorabilia depicting Minnesota Air Guard history from 1921 to the present.

▲▲▲▲▲▲▲▲▲▲▲▲▲▲▲▲▲▲▲▲▲▲▲▲▲▲▲▲▲▲▲▲▲▲▲▲▲

COST: $1 donation.

HOURS: Mid-April-mid-September: Saturday and Sunday only, 11 a.m.-4 p.m.

> From the intersection of Hwys. 62 and 55, go south at stoplight. Located on the Minnesota Air Guard Base on the right.

MINNESOTA HISTORY CENTER

345 Kellogg Blvd. W., St. Paul, MN 55102-1906 (612) 296-6126

The Minnesota History Center, headquarters of the Minnesota Historical Society, is an architectural masterpiece. With views of downtown St. Paul and the State Capitol, the History Center also houses a modern research center and interpretive exhibits. Two museum stores and a gourmet cafe are also easy to find and enjoy.

COST: Free.

HOURS: Open year round, Tuesday, Wednesday, Friday, Saturday 10 a.m.-5 p.m.; Thursday 10 a.m.-9 p.m.; Sunday noon-5 p.m.

> From I-94, take the Marion/Kellogg exit. Go south down Kellogg Blvd. The History Center is at the intersection of Kellogg and John Ireland Blvd. 1 block from the Cathedral of St. Paul.

MINNESOTA MUSEUM OF AMERICAN ART

Landmark Center, 75 W. 5th St., St. Paul, MN 55102 (612) 292-4355

St. Paul's landmark museum offers a rich and diverse blend of exhibitions and educational programs celebrating the diversity of art in the region.

COST: Exhibits free, $2 donation suggested. Tuition for classes varies. Expect metered parking or parking ramp cost.

HOURS: Tuesday, Wednesday, Friday, Saturday 11 a.m.-4 p.m.; Thursday 11 a.m.-7:30 p.m.; Sunday 1-5 p.m.

> From I-94 eastbound, take the 5th St. exit and follow 5th to Market St. Landmark Center is at the intersection of 5th and Market Sts. facing Rice Park, next to the Ordway Music Theater in downtown St. Paul.
>
> From I-94 westbound, take the 6th St. exit and follow 6th St. to Market St. Landmark Center is located at the intersection of 5th St. and Market St. facing Rice Park, next to the Ordway Music Theater in downtown St. Paul.

MUSEUMS & HISTORICAL SITES

▲▲▲▲▲▲▲▲▲▲▲▲▲▲▲▲▲▲▲▲▲▲▲▲▲▲▲▲▲▲▲▲▲▲▲▲▲▲▲

MINNESOTA PIONEER PARK

725 Pioneer Park Trail, Annandale, MN 55302 (612) 274-8489

This notable park features a collection of historic buildings and housing artifacts pertaining to pioneer life from the late 19th century to the early 1900s. Don't miss the special summer festivals: Voyageur Camp Week in May, Mendota Days in August, Holiday Traditions in October. Guided tours available on request with two weeks' prior notice.

COST: Adults $4, students 6-16 $2.50, seniors $3, children 5 and under free.

HOURS: Memorial Day-Labor Day: Tuesday-Saturday 10 a.m.-5 p.m.; Sunday noon-5 p.m. Closed Monday except on national holidays.

Located at the east end of Annandale on State Highway 55.

MINNESOTA STATE CAPITOL

Aurora and Constitution Aves., St. Paul, MN 55155 (612) 296-2881

A State Capitol tour is an awe-inspiring experience. Majestic in design, the Capitol harmonizes sculpture, stenciled ceilings, murals, stone, and marble. Guided tours begin on the hour.

COST: Free.

HOURS: Open year round. Weekdays 8:30 a.m.-5 p.m.; Saturday 10 a.m.-4 p.m.; Sunday 1-4 p.m.

Approaching downtown Saint Paul from any main highway such as I-35E or I-94, look for the State Capitol exit signs. Follow signs to the Capitol.

▲▲▲▲▲▲▲▲▲▲▲▲▲▲▲▲▲▲▲▲▲▲▲▲▲▲▲▲▲▲▲▲▲▲▲▲▲

MINNESOTA TRANSPORTATION MUSEUM, INC.

PO Box 17240, Minneapolis, MN 55417
General information: (612) 228-0263

The all-volunteer Minnesota Transportation Museum, Inc., a nonprofit corporation, was formed in 1962 to find, restore, and operate vintage transportation equipment for the education and enjoyment of the public. The Museum currently participates in research, restoration, and operations. The public is welcome to come and observe the restoration of the Minnehaha Steamboat and the Excelsior Streetcar, which are scheduled to be operational in 1996. Restoration projects are going on at different locations around the Twin Cities area. Call for current information.

COST: Call for current information.

HOURS: Call for current information.

MURPHY'S LANDING

2187 E. Highway 101, Shakopee, MN 55379 (612) 445-6900

Murphy's Landing is a living history museum presenting the story of the Minnesota River Valley, 1840–1890. Visitors can stroll on their own or ride on horse-drawn trolleys through the 1-1/2-mile village. Experience the early days of the fur trade era; see the bustling village, enhanced by costumed interpretive guides and by craftsmen plying their trades. You'll especially love the music and entertainment, which often are part of the routine.

COST: Adults $7, students and seniors $6, children 5 and under free.

HOURS: May 27–September 29: Tuesday–Sunday 10 a.m.–5 p.m.; closed Monday. Open weekends in September and during "Folkways of Christmas" festival November 24–December 22.

> From I-35W, take the Hwy. 13 exit. Follow Hwy. 13 until it meets Hwy. 101. Continue north on Hwy. 101 to Shakopee. Murphy's Landing is on Hwy. 101 just east of Shakopee.

A historic guide reads to visiting children at Murphy's Landing.

Photo by MaryAnn Johnson, courtesy Murphy's Landing

▲▲

MUSEUM OF QUESTIONABLE MEDICAL DEVICES

219 S.E. Main St., St. Anthony Main, Minneapolis, MN 55414 (612) 379-4046

The Museum of Questionable Medical Devices displays the world's largest collection of quack medical devices from the AMA-FDA St. Louis Science Center Bakken Library and other sources. Visitors are given the opportunity to experience hands-on treatments and demonstrations, including a mechanical phrenology reading, which is said to define your personality. Reprints of historic posters are for sale, along with free handouts of American Medical Association historical documents relating to health fraud.

COST: Free; free parking.

HOURS: Closed Monday, open Tuesday-Friday 5 p.m.-9 p.m.; Saturday 11 a.m.-
10 p.m.; Sunday noon-5 p.m.

> From I-35W, take the 4th St. exit, turn left and follow 4th St. to 3rd Ave. S.E.
> Turn left again onto 3rd Ave. S.E. and follow 3rd Ave. about 4 blocks to Main
> St. Follow Main St. to St. Anthony Main, a historic commercial block. The
> Museum is in St. Anthony Main.

NORTH WEST COMPANY FUR POST

P.O. Box 51, Pine City, MN 55063 (612) 629-6356

Explore a reconstructed trading post and an authentic wigwam and teepee, while costumed guides portray Indians, voyageurs, and fur traders.

COST: Free.

HOURS: May-Labor Day: Tuesday-Saturday 10 a.m.-5 p.m.; Sunday
noon-5 p.m.

> From I-35W northbound, take the Pine City exit (Hwy. 7). Proceed on Hwy.
> 7, approximately 1.5 miles west to the North West Company Fur Post on the
> right.

▲▲▲▲▲▲▲▲▲▲▲▲▲▲▲▲▲▲▲▲▲▲▲▲▲▲▲▲▲▲▲▲▲▲

Planes of Fame Air Museum is the home to 25 flying WWII aircraft.

PLANES OF FAME AIR MUSEUM

14771 Pioneer Trail, Eden Prairie, MN 55347 (612) 941-2633

Home of 25 flying WWII aircraft, Planes of Fame Air Museum also displays uniforms, engines, artifacts, and memorabilia. You can tour one of the last B-17 Flying Fortresses or experience the thrill of riding in an open-cockpit Stearman Trainer. A full aviation gift shop is also available.

COST: Adults $5, children 7-17 $2, children under 7 free. B-17 tours: adults $3, children $1.

HOURS: Tuesday-Sunday 11 a.m.-5 p.m. Closed Mondays. On Memorial Day weekend an air display is open Saturday-Monday.

> From I-494 take the Hwy. 169 exit and follow 169 south to Co. Rd. 1 (Pioneer Trail). Go west on Co. Rd. 1 to the northwest corner of the airfield (1 mile). Watch for signs.

▲▲▲▲▲▲▲▲▲▲▲▲▲▲▲▲▲▲▲▲▲▲▲▲▲▲▲▲▲▲▲▲▲▲▲▲▲▲

ALEXANDER RAMSEY HOUSE

265 S. Exchange St., St. Paul, MN 55102 (612) 296-8760

Visit one of the loveliest preserved Victorian homes in Minnesota. The former residence of Minnesota's first territorial governor features exquisitely carved walnut woodwork, original furnishings, and a glimpse of family life in the 19th century.

COST: Adults $4, students 6-15 $2, seniors $3, children 5 and under free. Special tour rates available.

HOURS: First week in April through the last week in November: Tuesday-Saturday 10 a.m.-4 p.m. Holiday hours: November 25-December 31. Call for information.

From I-35E northbound, take the Grand Ave. exit. Turn right onto Grand and follow about 3-4 blocks. Cross 7th St. and look for the Ramsey House parking lot on the left.

From I-35E southbound, take the I-94 exit. Go west on I-94 to Marion St. and follow Marion to Kellogg Blvd. Turn right onto Kellogg and proceed to 7th St., turn right and go 3 blocks on 7th to Ramsey St., turn left. The Ramsey House parking lot is on the left.

From I-94 eastbound, take the Kellogg Blvd. exit. Turn right onto Kellogg and follow to 7th St. Turn right onto 7th and go 3 blocks to Ramsey St. Turn left and look for the Ramsey House parking lot on the left.

From I-94 westbound, take the Marion St. exit and turn left immediately at the stoplight. Follow Marion St. to Kellogg Blvd., turn right onto Kellogg and go to 7th St. Turn right onto 7th and go 3 blocks to Ramsey St., turn left onto Ramsey. The Ramsey House parking lot is on the left.

ST. ANTHONY FALLS HISTORIC DISTRICT

St. Anthony Main, 125 S.E. Main St., Minneapolis, MN 55414 (612) 627-5433

Tour what was once the largest milling district in the world. One-hour guided walking tours take you to the only falls on the Mississippi, the Stone Arch Bridge, and other historic landmarks. Tour A starts from the east side program office in St. Anthony Main and crosses the river to finish at the Whitney Hotel Plaza. Tour B starts from the west side of the river at the Whitney Hotel Plaza and finishes at St. Anthony Main on the east side. Visitors may combine tours A and B into a two-hour loop or return to their starting point on the River City Trolley.

▲▲▲▲▲▲▲▲▲▲▲▲▲▲▲▲▲▲▲▲▲▲▲▲▲▲▲▲▲▲▲▲▲▲▲▲▲▲

COST: Adults $2, children 6-15 $1.

HOURS: Tours available April 15-October 31 Wednesday-Sunday. Weekend
tours leave on the hour, noon-4 p.m. from both sides of the river.
Weekday tours Wednesday-Friday leave on the hour, noon-4 p.m. from
the east side only, and return to the starting point at St. Anthony Main.

Directions to the St. Anthony Main location: From I-35W, take the 4th St.
exit. Turn left onto 4th St. and follow 4th St. to 3rd Ave. S.E. Turn left onto
3rd. Ave. S.E and follow about 4 blocks to Main St. St. Anthony Main is on
Main St.

Directions to the Whitney Hotel Plaza location: the Whitney Hotel is located
on South 2nd St. and Portland Ave., 1 block north of the
Portland/Washington intersection.

From I-35W northbound, follow the downtown exits to the 5th Ave. exit.
Continue on 5th Ave. 8 blocks to Washington Ave., turn right onto
Washington and follow 1 block to Portland Ave. Turn left onto Portland and
follow to the Whitney Hotel Plaza.

From I-35W southbound, take the Washington Ave. exit. Turn right onto
Washington Ave. and follow 9 blocks to Portland Ave. Turn right onto
Portland and follow to the Whitney Hotel Plaza.

SCIENCE MUSEUM OF MINNESOTA

30 E. 10th St., St. Paul, MN 55101 (612) 221-9444

At the Science Museum of Minnesota, visitors can get their hands-on science through
fun and exciting exhibits. Special new exhibits open every four months. The Science
Museum is also home to the William L. McKnight-3M Omnitheater (refer to separate
listing in this chapter for more information on the Omnitheater).

COST: Exhibit: adults $5, children 4-12 $4, seniors 65 and over $4.
Omnitheater: adults $6, children 4-12 $5, seniors 65 and over $5.
Combination of exhibits and Omnitheater: adults $7, children 4-12 $6,
seniors 65 and over $6.

EXHIBIT HOURS: Monday-Saturday 9:30 a.m.-9 p.m.; Sunday 10 a.m.-9
p.m. Closed: Mondays after Labor Day-mid-December; Thanksgiving,
and Christmas Day.

Continues page 108

▲▲▲▲▲▲▲▲▲▲▲▲▲▲▲▲▲▲▲▲▲▲▲▲▲▲▲▲▲▲▲▲▲▲▲▲

The Science Museum of Minnesota is home to the William L. McKnight-3M Omnitheater plus changing exhibits ranging from dinosaurs to birds of prey.

▲▲▲▲▲▲▲▲▲▲▲▲▲▲▲▲▲▲▲▲▲▲▲▲▲▲▲▲▲▲▲▲▲▲▲▲

> The Science Museum is located off I-94 and I-35E in downtown St. Paul, 15 minutes from the Mall of America.
>
> From I-35E northbound, take the 11th St. exit and follow 11th St. to the Science Museum.
>
> From I-94 eastbound or I-35E southbound, take the 10th St. exit. Follow 10th St. to the Science Museum.
>
> From I-94 westbound, take the 12th St. exit to the Science Museum.

SIBLEY HISTORIC SITE

55 D St., Mendota, MN 55150 (612) 452-1596

Tour the homes of Minnesota's first governor, Henry Hastings Sibley, and Jean Baptiste Faribault, a farmer and fur trader. View and understand the life and times of the pre-territorial, territorial, and early statehood years of Minnesota. The Sibley Historic Site now houses one of the largest collections of 19th century Dakota and Ojibway artifacts.

COST: Adults $3, students 6-16 $1, seniors $2.50, children 5 and under free. Special tour rates available.

HOURS: Tuesday-Saturday 10 a.m.-5 p.m.; Sunday noon-5 p.m. Tours start on the hour.

> From I-94 westbound, take the Hwy. 55 (Hiawatha Ave.) exit and follow Hwy. 55 south. After crossing over the Mendota Bridge, follow signs for N. Hwy. 13. The Sibley Historic Site is located off Hwy. 13 in Mendota.
>
> From I-35E southbound, take the Hwy. 13 exit. Follow Hwy. 13 southwest into Mendota. The Sibley Historic Site is located off Hwy. 13 in Mendota.
>
> From I-494, take the Hwy. 110 exit. Follow Hwy. 110 north to Hwy. 13. Follow Hwy. 13 southwest into Mendota. The Sibley Historic Site is located off Hwy. 13 in Mendota.

JOHN H. STEVENS INTERPRETIVE HOUSE MUSEUM

4901 Minnehaha Ave., P.O. Box 17241, Minneapolis, MN (612) 722-2220

Built in 1850, the Stevens House is the first permanent settler's home in Minneapolis. Photographic and hands-on exhibits, audiovisual presentations, and historic artifacts tell about the beginnings of the city of Minneapolis and the people who played key roles in its growth and development.

COST: Adults $1, children 25¢.

HOURS: Memorial Day to Labor Day: Tuesday-Friday 1-4 p.m.; Saturday and Sunday 12:30-5 p.m. Closed Monday.

> From the intersection of Highways 62 and 55, go north on 55 past Veterans Hospital to Minnehaha Pkwy. Turn right on parkway and enter Minnehaha Park. Follow signs to Stevens House.

STILLWATER DEPOT, LOGGING AND RAILROAD MUSEUM

601 N. Main St., Stillwater, MN 55082 (612) 430-3000

Step back in time and experience railroad travel as it was in the late 1940s by visiting the Stillwater Logging and Railroad Museum, a national historic site. To re-create the atmosphere and surroundings of railroad dining, take a three-hour dinner excursion on the Minnesota Zephyr, a historic train powered by two 1951 diesel electric engines, one at each end. The three-hour journey boards in the historic city of Stillwater and travels along the river streams and woodland bluffs of the beautiful St. Croix River Valley.

COST: $49 per person for excursion and five-course dinner.

HOURS: Open year round, but hours and days vary seasonally. Call for current schedule: (612) 430-3000. For Saturday evening excursions, boarding begins at the Stillwater Depot at 6:30 p.m. with departure at 7:30 p.m. sharp. Estimated return time is 10:45 p.m. at the Stillwater Depot. For Sunday excursions, boarding begins at 11:30 a.m. with departure at noon. For weekday and possible Saturday afternoon trips, call the number above for information.

> From the Twin Cities on I-35W, I-35E, or I-694, exit on Hwy. 36 and go east to downtown Stillwater (about 30 miles from the Twin Cities). Hwy. 36 becomes Main Street. Go north on Main Street to the Minnesota Zephyr Depot, the last business on the right.

▲▲▲▲▲▲▲▲▲▲▲▲▲▲▲▲▲▲▲▲▲▲▲▲▲▲▲▲▲▲▲▲▲▲▲▲▲▲▲

TRAINS OF BANDANA

1021 Bandana Blvd., St. Paul, MN 55108 (612) 647-9628

The Twin City Model Railroad Club presents an operating model railroad, displays, and art gallery. See various vignettes of Twin Cities scenes carefully reproduced in miniature. Trains are 1/4"-to-the-foot, O-scale models re-creating the romance and history of American railroads in the 1930s, `40s and `50s.

COST: Free parking. Donations welcomed.

HOURS: Friday 10 a.m.-8 p.m.; Saturday 10 a.m.-6 p.m.; Sunday noon-5 p.m.

From I-94, take the Snelling Ave. exit north to Energy Park Dr. Go east on Energy Park Dr. to Bandana Square. The Trains of Bandana exhibit is located in Bandana Square.

UPPER ST. ANTHONY FALLS LOCK AND DAM OBSERVATION DECK

1 Portland Ave., Minneapolis, MN 55401 (612) 333-5336

View the highest lift of river boats and barges on the Mississippi River. The observation deck enables you to view the dam and its 29 locks, which lift various river craft 50 feet above the falls.

COST: Free admission and free parking.

HOURS: April 1-November 1: 9 a.m.-10 p.m. daily.

From I-35W, take the Washington Ave. exit west to Portland Ave. Turn right on Portland Ave. and go 3 blocks to the observation site.

▲▲▲▲▲▲▲▲▲▲▲▲▲▲▲▲▲▲▲▲▲▲▲▲▲▲▲▲▲▲▲▲▲▲▲▲

WALKER ART CENTER

MINNEAPOLIS SCULPTURE GARDEN

Vineland Place, Minneapolis, MN 55403 (612) 375-7600 Group tours of 10 or more, call (612) 375-7609 TDD (612) 375-7586

Located across from the Walker Art Center, the 11-acre Sculpture Garden is one of the largest urban sculpture parks in the U.S. and features more than 40 works of 20th-century sculpture. Designed by Edward Larrabee Barnes, the Sculpture Garden can be likened to Renaissance and 18th-century Italian garden plazas. At the southern end, four plazas (tree-lined, roofless rooms) contain works by leading American and international artists. The northern portion of the Garden is home to permanent and temporary sculptural installations as well as the Alene Grossman Memorial Arbor and Flower Garden.

COST: Free.

HOURS: Open daily 6 a.m.-midnight. Free guided tours of the Garden are given
        on weekends at 1 p.m. May-October. No reservations are needed except
        for group tours (three weeks advance notice required). Meet in the
        Walker lobby.

Photo courtesy Walker Art Center

The Minneapolis Sculpture Garden may best be known for the Claes Oldenburg & Coosje van Bruggen Spoonbridge and Cherry 1987-1988. The stainless steel and painted aluminum sculpture was a gift of Frederick R. Weisman in honor of his parents, William and Mary Weisman, 1988.

▲▲▲▲▲▲▲▲▲▲▲▲▲▲▲▲▲▲▲▲▲▲▲▲▲▲▲▲▲▲▲▲▲▲▲▲▲

WALKER ART CENTER

Vineland Place, Minneapolis, MN 55403 Art Center (612) 375-7600 Group tours of 10 or more, call (612) 375-7609 TDD (612) 375-7586 Family Programs (612) 375-7610 Cowles Conservatory (612) 348-7372

The internationally renowned Walker Art Center is one of the nation's primary resources for modern and contemporary art. The Walker's exhibitions and related programs are intended to foster greater awareness of the integral role art plays in life and culture. The Art Center's permanent collection of paintings, artists' books, prints, videos, sculpture, drawings, photographs, and installation works, consists of some 7,000 pieces.

The Walker Art Center's Educational Programs give the public a chance to interact directly with artists and modern art forms through lectures, tours, workshops, art classes, and audio-visual presentations.

Free admission and a full day of family activities is presented on the first Saturday of every month. Families can take part in hands-on studio activities; enjoy music, dance, or theater performances; view a film series, or take part in special gallery activities.

Adjacent to the Sculpture Garden is the Cowles Conservatory, a greenhouse which showcases botanical installations; Frank Gehry's 22-foot-tall Standing Glass Fish; the *Spoonbridge and Cherry,* a 29 foot high fountain-sculpture; and the Irene Hixon Whitney bridge, a 375 foot long footbridge which connects the Garden to Loring Park. The Alene Grossman Memorial Arbor and Flower Garden is located in the expanded north end of the garden.

COST: Adults $4; students and children 12-18, seniors and groups of 10 or more $3. Free admission on Thursday and the first Saturday of each month. Parking is available in the Parade lot adjacent to the Cowles Conservatory and costs $2.50 for cars ($3 event price).

HOURS: Tuesday-Saturday 10 a.m.-8 p.m.; Sunday 11 a.m. -5 p.m. Closed Monday.

The Walker Art Center is located on Vineland Place, where Lyndale and Hennepin Avenues merge, on the southwestern edge of downtown Minneapolis.

From St. Paul, head west on I-94 and take exit 231B, and follow Lyndale Ave./Hennepin Ave. north to the Walker Art Center.

Approaching Minneapolis from the west on I-394, take exit 8A (Dunwoody Blvd/Hennepin Ave.) and follow Hennepin Ave./Lyndale Ave. south to the Walker Art Center.

▲▲▲▲▲▲▲▲▲▲▲▲▲▲▲▲▲▲▲▲▲▲▲▲▲▲▲▲▲▲▲▲▲▲▲▲

FREDERICK R. WEISMAN ART MUSEUM

University of Minnesota, 333 E. River Road, Minneapolis, MN 55455 (612) 625-9494

This visually striking art museum fills an important role in the thriving arts community of the Twin Cities and greater Minnesota. Designed by internationally acclaimed architect Frank O. Gehry, the Weisman presents and interprets works of art, and mounts exhibitions to place art in cultural, social, and historical contexts. Several major exhibitions are presented each year, as well as organized lectures, symposia, tours, and special events. Both the Weisman Art Museum and Museum garage are handicapped-accessible. Wheelchairs are available at the museum information desk.

COST: Free.

HOURS: Tuesday, Wednesday, Friday 10 a.m.-5 p.m.; Thursday 10 a.m.-8 p.m.; weekends 11 a.m.-5 p.m. Closed Mondays and all major holidays.

The Weisman Art Museum is on the East Bank of the University's Minneapolis campus. The Museum's public parking garage and lower entrance are located at 333 E. River Road. The Museum also may be entered from the parking ramp elevator. The main pedestrian entrance is located off the walkway of the Washington Avenue Bridge.

From St. Paul, take I-94W to the U of M exit and follow to Fulton. Turn left on Fulton and proceed to River Road. Turn right on River Road and follow 1/2 mile to Museum garage entrance.

From I-35W northbound, take the U of M exit and stay to the right, taking the East Bank exit. Follow the exit ramp, crossing the Washington Avenue Bridge. Take the first right to River Road and the Museum garage entrance.

From I-35W southbound, take the Washington Ave. exit left to Seven Corners. At Seven Corners turn right onto Cedar Avenue and then take the first left. Follow signs leading to the University's East Bank. Turn left and follow the ramp crossing the Washington Avenue Bridge. Take the first right to River Road and the Museum garage entrance.

From I-394, go to I-94E and follow to the U of M exit. Take the U of M exit to Fulton and turn left. Follow Fulton to River Road and turn right. Follow River Road for 1/2 mile to Museum garage entrance.

WORLD WAR II AIR POWER DISPLAY SHOW

St. Paul Downtown Airport (Holman Field), St. Paul, MN (612) 455-6942

For three days a year, contemporary aircraft and three dozen World War II, Korean War, and Vietnam-era aircraft are displayed for the public. Get a close look at the B-29 Super Fortress, the airport's only flying World War II aircraft (the same design as the plane that dropped the atomic bomb on Japan), and the

▲▲▲▲▲▲▲▲▲▲▲▲▲▲▲▲▲▲▲▲▲▲▲▲▲▲▲▲▲▲▲▲▲▲▲▲▲

B-24 Liberator, a heavy four-engine bomber from World War II. Many other displays and guest speakers add to the experience. The purpose of the world show is to raise funds for restoration and educational programs for the aircraft restoration group, the Confederate Air Force.

COST: Adults $7, children 12 and under $2.
             Donations welcome.

HOURS: August 4-6, gates open 9 a.m.-6 p.m.

> From I-94, take the Hwy. 52 exit south to Plato Blvd. and follow signs to airport. The display is at the main terminal. Police give directions to parking areas.

The Frederick R. Weisman Art Museum on the University of Minnesota campus.

Photo courtesy The Frederick R. Weisman Art Museum

ORCHARDS & BERRY PICKING FARMS

▲▲▲▲▲▲▲▲▲▲▲▲▲▲▲▲▲▲▲▲▲▲▲▲▲▲▲▲▲▲▲▲▲▲▲▲▲

AAMODT'S APPLE FARM, INC.

6428 Manning Ave. N., Stillwater, MN 55082 (612) 439-3127

Visiting this 44-year-old orchard is fun, relaxing, and educational. A turn-of-the-century farm village and orchard yields apples and more: entertainment; hay rides; apple picking in mid-September; an old-fashioned bakery; catering for groups of 30–300; visits to the pumpkin patch; rides in a hot air balloon; sleigh rides; groomed trails for cross-country skiing. Lanterns are hung along the trail for night-time skiing on Saturday nights. The Old Farm Village is available for weddings, anniversaries, reunions, or business meetings. Call for a schedule of events.

> HOURS: August–December: daily 9 a.m.–9 p.m.

> Located between North St. Paul and Stillwater. From Hwy. 36, exit on Manning Ave. Go north on Manning about 1/2 mile to Aamodt's on the left.

AFTON APPLE ORCHARD

14421 S. 90th St., Afton, MN 55033 (612) 436-8385

You will want to visit this orchard over and over throughout the summer and fall. Pick your own apples, raspberries, strawberries, and pumpkins. Prepicked fruits are also available. Make a day of it and enjoy the picnic areas and playground for the kids. Free hayrides on weekday afternoons and weekends. Call to verify hours and crop availability.

> COST: Varies.

> HOURS: June–July: daily 8 a.m.–6 p.m. Usually closed first part of August. Mid-August–October 31: 10 a.m.–6 p.m.

> From I-94 eastbound, take the Manning Ave. (Co. Rd. 15) exit. Go south on Manning 8 miles to 90th St. Turn left onto 90th, go about 2-1/2 miles and follow signs to orchard.

APPLESIDE ORCHARD INC.

18010 Chippendale Ave., Farmington, MN 55024 (612) 463-2505

One of Minnesota's largest pick-your-own fruit farms, with over 100 acres of apples, strawberries, raspberries, and pumpkins. A picnic area, pedal tractors for kids, and hay bales to play in enhance the family experience. Special events include free hay rides; storytellers; live bluegrass music; a kite-flying extravaganza in the second week of

ORCHARDS & BERRY PICKING FARMS

▲▲▲▲▲▲▲▲▲▲▲▲▲▲▲▲▲▲▲▲▲▲▲▲▲▲▲▲▲▲▲▲▲▲▲▲

September; and a scarecrow-building event in the fall. Call to verify hours and crop availability. Send for flyer on dates and times of events at address above.

COST: Varies. Free hay and pony rides.

HOURS: Daily in June 7 a.m.–6 p.m. Closed in July. Daily August–October: 9 a.m.–6 p.m. November: Tuesday–Saturday noon–5 p.m.

> From I-35W or Cedar Ave., go east on Co. Rd. 42 to Hwy. 3, go south about 3-1/2 miles. Orchard is on the left side.

BAUER BERRY FARM

Co. Rd. 121, Champlin, MN (612) 421-4384

This is a pick-your-own strawberry and blueberry farm. Prepicked sweet corn also available. Call first for crop availability.

COST: Varies.

HOURS: Strawberries, mid-June–mid-July: Monday-Saturday 7 a.m.–1 p.m. Blueberries, July 10–August 1: Monday–Saturday 8 a.m.–noon. Sweet corn, July 20–August 10: daily 9:30 a.m.–4 p.m.

> From Hwy. 694, take the Hwy. 169 exit. Follow Hwy. 169 north toward the Mississippi River. Turn left onto Co. Rd. 12. Follow Co. Rd. 12 about 1/2 mile to Co. Rd. 121. Turn left onto Co. Rd. 121 and proceed about 1 mile to the Bauer Berry Farm on the right.

BROWN'S APPLE ACRES

12727 110th St. S., Hastings, MN 55033 (612) 437-5879

Brown's has an apple salesroom with a large variety of apples, and visitors are encouraged to tour a working dairy farm. Jellies, jams, honey, and maple syrup are also available.

COST: Varies.

HOURS: September 1–December 1: daily 9 a.m.–8 p.m.

> At the junction of Highways 61 and 95, take Hwy. 95 north to 110th St. Turn right onto 110th St. and look for Brown's Apple Acres, the first place on the right.

▲▲▲▲▲▲▲▲▲▲▲▲▲▲▲▲▲▲▲▲▲▲▲▲▲▲▲▲▲▲▲▲▲▲▲▲

EDEN APPLE ORCHARD AND BERRY FARM

Pioneer Trail and Dell Road, Eden Prairie, MN (612) 934-7873

Enjoy a day in the country with your family at Eden Apple Orchard and Berry Farm. Pick from the largest and best varieties of apples, strawberries, and raspberries in this 100-acre orchard. Short trees mean no ladders, so even the smallest child can pluck an apple right off the branch. Hayrides offered on weekends. Call for exact picking dates and prices.

COST: Watch for coupons in local papers and Minneapolis Star Tribune. Cost varies from season to season, so call ahead for exact details.

HOURS: Strawberries, June: daily 8 a.m.–6 p.m. Raspberries, September: daily 10 a.m.–6 p.m. Apples, mid-August–October 31: 10 a.m.–6 p.m.

> Located only 3 miles west of Flying Cloud Airport. From Hwy. 169, exit to Co. Rd.1 (Pioneer Trail). On Pioneer Trail, go west 3 miles and follow signs to orchard.

EMMA KRUMBEE'S APPLE ORCHARD, RESTAURANT, BAKERY, DELI, & COUNTRY STORE

Hwy. 169, Belle Plaine, MN 56011 (612) 873-4334

Emma Krumbee's Apple Orchard features 7,500 apple trees yielding 25 varieties of apples in season. There is something for everyone in the family with pick-your-own apples mid-August–mid-October; pumpkins in October; raspberries in July; a petting zoo; and handicapped-accessible wagons that tour the orchard. Groups are welcome, please call for reservations.

COST: Price based on apple variety per peck bag.

HOURS: Daily in season.

> From I-494 heading toward Eden Prairie, take the Hwy. 169 exit. Follow 169 south through Eden Prairie and Shakopee and continue south 15 miles to Emma Krumbee's on the left.
>
> From I-35W, take the Hwy. 13 exit. Follow Hwy. 13 west until it meets Hwy. 101. Take Hwy. 101 north into Shakopee, to Hwy. 169. Follow Hwy. 169 south about 15 miles to Emma Krumbee's which is located on the left.

▲▲

The Apple Barn, part of Emma Krumbee's Apple Orchard complex.

FISCHER CROIX FARM ORCHARD

Co. Rd. 21, Hastings, MN 55033 (612) 437-7126

This beautiful 20-acre orchard overlooking the St. Croix River offers 25 varieties of pre-picked or pick-your-own apples. Pre-picked fall vegetables and cider are also available. Hayrides offered on weekends noon–4.

COST: Varies.

HOURS: September–December; Monday–Saturday 8 a.m.–5:30 p.m.; Sunday 10 a.m.–6 p.m. Hay rides on weekends noon–4 p.m. Average apple harvest season is mid-September–mid-October.

> From I-494, take Hwy. 10/61 south about 14 miles. When Highways 10 and 61 split, take Hwy. 10 east toward Prescott, Wisconsin. Follow Hwy. 10 about 3 miles to Co. Rd. 21. Follow Co. Rd. 21 north 1 mile. Orchard is on the right.

▲ ▲

HOMESTEAD ORCHARD

Co. Rd. 92, Maple Plain, MN 55359 (612) 479-3186

Your children can experience picking apples and visit a petting zoo. Enjoy a free pony ride (includes a picture), or a free hayride. The entire family will rave over the cider press and delicious caramel apple sundaes. Types of apples you can expect to find and pick include Harelson, Fireside, Prairie Spy, Early Blush, Regent, Honey Crisp, and Keepsake.

COST: Varies. Free hay and pony rides.

HOURS: August 15–November 15: 10 a.m.–6 p.m., hayrides on weekends.

> Located 20 miles west of Minneapolis. From Hwy. 394, take the Co. Rd. 92 exit. Follow Co. Rd. 92 south about 2 miles and look for the orchard on the east side of the road.

LORENCE'S STRAWBERRY AND RASPBERRY FARMS

28625 Foliage Ave., Northfield, MN 55057 (507) 645-9749 or (612) 944-1412

Lorence's Strawberry and Raspberry Farm offers pick-your-own and pre-picked berries. There are many varieties of berries from the U.S., Holland, and Canada. Containers supplied.

COST: Competitive prices.

HOURS: June–October: daily 6 a.m.–8 p.m. Strawberries are in season from June to mid-July, raspberries continue through October. Picking hours may vary due to weather conditions. Please call first to confirm.

> Located on Cedar Ave. (Co. Rd. 23), just 14 miles south of Apple Valley and 7 miles north of Northfield. There are four entrances to the orchard on both sides of the road.

ORCHARDS & BERRY PICKING FARMS

▲▲▲▲▲▲▲▲▲▲▲▲▲▲▲▲▲▲▲▲▲▲▲▲▲▲▲▲▲▲▲▲▲▲▲▲▲ ▲

MC DOUGALL'S APPLE JUNCTION

14325 110th St. S., Hastings, MN 55033 (612) 437-6794

McDougall's Apple Junction features such apple varieties as Haralson, Regent, Honeygold, Honey Crisp, Cortland, McIntosh, Connell Red, and Fireside. Also available are fall vegetables; honey; jam; cider; decorative corn mums; dried flowers; and crafts.

> HOURS: Mid-September–November: weekdays noon–5 p.m., Saturday and
> Sunday 10 a.m.–6 p.m.

Located just north of Hastings. From Hwy. 61 southbound, turn left on Hwy. 95. Go north about 1 mile to Co. Rd. 78 (110th St.). Turn right (east) onto Co. Rd. 78 and follow about 2 miles to the orchard.

MINNETONKA ORCHARDS

6530 Co. Rd. 26, Minnetrista, MN (612) 479-3191

Minnetonka Orchards features apples; cider; jams; honey; mile-hi apple pies; caramel apples; caramel apple sundae; popcorn; pumpkins; winter squash; coffee beans; and craft items. Pick your own pumpkins in October. Free hay rides are offered on weekends, weather permitting.

> COST: Varies.

> HOURS: Mid-August–December: daily 10 a.m.–7 p.m.

From Maple Plain, take Co. Rd. 83 south about 2-1/2 miles to Co. Rd. 26. Follow signs to the orchard.

From Mound, take Co. Rd. 110 about 2-1/2 miles north to Co. Rd. 26 and then follow the signs to the orchard.

MORK'S GROVE ORCHARD

8455 110th St. S., Cottage Grove, MN (612) 459-4752

Enjoy quality time with your family as you walk through this 18-acre orchard featuring pick-your-own apples, plums, grapes, sour cherries, or pears in season. Make a day of it and have a picnic or go on a hayride on the weekend. The Orchard store is filled with apple pies, apple cider, honey, and thrift boxes. Gift boxes available for the holidays.

▲▲▲▲▲▲▲▲▲▲▲▲▲▲▲▲▲▲▲▲▲▲▲▲▲▲▲▲▲▲▲▲▲▲▲▲▲

COST: Varies with fruit. Hayrides are available for groups by appointment, $5 per person.

HOURS: August 15–October 15: daily 9 a.m.–dark. November–December: 9 a.m.–6 p.m. Orchard store is open August 15–December.

> Located only 18 minutes from downtown St. Paul. From St. Paul, take Hwy. 61 south to Jamaica. Turn right onto Jamaica and follow signs to the orchard.

ONEKA BERRIES

13920 Elmcrest Ave. N., White Bear Lake, MN 55110 (612) 429-8761

Oneka Berries features pick-your-own or pre-picked strawberries in season, usually mid-June–early July.

COST: Competitive prices.

HOURS: Vary. Please call before coming to check on berry availability.

> Located 5 miles north of White Bear Lake. Take I-35E to the Hugo Centerville exit (Co. Rd. 14). Follow Co. Rd. 14 east to frontage road. (Otter Lake Rd.) Go 1/4 mile on Otter Lake Rd. to E. Cedar St. Turn left onto E. Cedar St. and proceed 1/4 mile to Oneka Berries.

PETERSEN GLADIOLUS

18040 Hwy. 10, Big Lake, MN 55309 (612) 263-3078

Petersen Gladiolus features pick-your-own strawberries, sweet corn, tomatoes, various kinds of peppers, sugar snap peas, and green beans.

COST: Varies.

HOURS: Daily during daylight hours. Closed Saturday and Sunday evenings. For strawberries, average growing season is mid-June; sweet corn, mid-July–August; tomatoes and peppers, after August 15; sugar snap peas, early to mid-June; green beans, late June.

> From I-94 take the second Monticello exit right to Hwy. 25. Follow Hwy. 25 north about 3 miles to the stoplight in Big Lake. Turn right at stoplight onto Hwy. 10 and proceed about 1 mile to the Petersen Gladiolus farm on the left.

ORCHARDS & BERRY PICKING FARMS

▲▲

PETERSON'S STRAWBERRIES

Co. Rd. 38 & Co. Rd. 71, Rosemount, MN (612) 423-1934

This pick-your-own farm features strawberries and blueberries in season, free containers and recipes.

> COST: Varies.

> HOURS: Daily 8 a.m.–6 p.m. Strawberries available mid-June–early July, blueberries July. Call first about crop availability.

> From I-35W or Cedar Ave., take the Co. Rd. 42 exit. Follow Co. Rd. 42 east past Dakota Technical College to Co. Rd. 71. Turn left (north) onto Co. Rd. 71 and follow about 1/2 mile to Co. Rd. 38. Peterson's Strawberries is at the junction of Co. Rd. 38 and Co. Rd. 71.
>
> From Hwy. 52 turn right onto Co. Rd. 38 and follow about one mile to Co. Rd. 71. Peterson's Strawberries is at the junction of Co. Rd. 38 and Co. Rd. 71.

PINE TREE APPLE ORCHARDS

450 Apple Orchard Rd., White Bear Lake, MN 55110 (612) 429-7202

Pine Tree Apple Orchards feature several varieties of apples, pumpkins, and pick-your-own strawberries. You'll want to visit the Pine Tree Apple Orchard in winter to buy from the bakery filled with apple desserts and mouth-watering breads, or for cross-country skiing throughout 300 acres of winter wonderland.

> COST: Varies.

> HOURS: June–March. Apples available August–February, pumpkins in October, pick-your-own strawberries in June. Call first for hours and crop availability.

> Follow Hwy. 61 north through White Bear Lake to E. Hwy. 96. Turn right onto E. Hwy. 96 and proceed about 2 miles to Apple Orchard Rd. Turn left (north) onto Apple Orchard Rd. and follow to the Pine Tree Apple Orchard.

RAINBOW RIDGE FARM

20175 Rhoda Ave., Welch, MN 55089 (612) 437-7837

This unique berry farm features pick-your-own or picked-to-order strawberries and blueberries. A playground is available for small children, along with picnic tables. Observe flocks of geese as they descend on the farm in November and December.

HOURS: Open June, July, and August when crops are in season: 8 a.m.–noon, 4 p.m.–7 p.m. or until picked out. Call for appointment if hours not convenient or at times other than June, July, and August.

> Located 6 miles south of Hastings on Rhoda Ave. Follow Hwy. 316 south from Hastings about 6 miles to 200th St. Follow 200th to Ravenna Trail. Take a right onto Ravenna Trail and proceed to 205th St. Turn left onto 205th St. and follow to Rhoda. Turn left onto Rhoda and look for Rainbow Ridge, the first farm on the left.

SMITH'S BERRY FARM

98th & Winnetka Ave. N. (Co. Rd. 103), Osseo, MN (612) 425-5715

This pick-your-own farm offers strawberries, peas, beans, cucumbers, tomatoes, squash, corn, pumpkins, watermelons, potatoes, etc. Please call first about crop availability.

COST: Varies.

HOURS: Early June–November: daily 8 a.m.–5 p.m. Call for directions.

SPONSEL'S MINNESOTA HARVEST APPLE ORCHARD

Old Hwy. 169 Blvd., Jordan, MN 55352 (612) 492-2785, 492-7753 (49-Apple) or (800) 662-7753

September and October are the big apple months in Minnesota. Bring the family and pick 'em yourself or buy already picked. Sponsel's celebrates with hay rides; carnival; wagon and pony rides; hiking trails; petting zoo; and live music. The packing house features a gift shop; food products made at the orchard; lunch area; bakery; and observation deck to watch the packing and sorting operation.

COST: Free.

HOURS: Daily in January–July: 9 a.m.–5 p.m. August–October: 9 a.m.–7 p.m. Daily in November–December: 9 a.m.–6 p.m. Sleigh rides available November–April. Limited services January–July. Please call.

▲▲▲▲▲▲▲▲▲▲▲▲▲▲▲▲▲▲▲▲▲▲▲▲▲▲▲▲▲▲▲▲▲▲▲

From I-494 westbound, exit on U.S. Hwy. 169 going south through Shakopee. Go 2 miles past the stoplight in Jordan to Co. Rd. 59. Go south (left) on 59 and follow the Minnesota Harvest signs up the hill and into the woods about 1-1/2 mile. At Old Hwy. 169, turn right and follow to Minnesota Harvest at Apple Lovers' Lane.

From I-35W southbound, exit at Hwy. 13 going west to Hwy. 101. Continue on 101 to U.S. Hwy. 169. Take 169 south through Shakopee. Continue 2 miles past the stoplight in Jordan to Co. Rd. 59 and proceed as above to Minnesota Harvest at Apple Lovers' Lane.

WITHROW BERRY FARM

12515 Keller Ave. N., Hugo, MN 55038 (612) 439-4481

Pick-your-own strawberries.

COST: Varies.

HOURS: Mid-June–July 4: daily 7 a.m. until picked out. Call ahead for daily information.

From St. Paul, go east on Hwy. 36 to Washington Co. Rd. 15 (Manning Ave.). Go north on Washington 15 to Washington Co. Rd. 7 and follow signs to farm.

WYATT STRAWBERRIES

10370 180th St., Hastings, MN 55033 (612) 437-8479

This berry farm features fresh asparagus and strawberries. Asparagus is pre-picked for you by order. Pick your own strawberries, or purchase pre-picked strawberries.

COST: Varies.

HOURS: Daily in season 7 a.m.–8 p.m. Strawberries' average season is mid-June–early July. Asparagus' average season is mid-May–July 1.

Take Hwy. 52 south to the town of Colt. From Hwy. 52 take the Co. Rd 48 exit to the left. Follow Co. Rd. 48 to Co. Rd. 47 and take a right onto Co. Rd. 47. Follow Co. Rd. 47 to Joan Ave. and take a left. Wyatt Strawberries is located on the corner of Joan Ave. and 180th St.

PARKS & NATURE CENTERS

▲▲

ELOISE BUTLER WILDFLOWER GARDEN AND BIRD SANCTUARY

Theodore Wirth Pkwy., Minneapolis, MN 55415-1400 (612) 348-5702

This 14-acre wildflower garden, established in 1907 by Eloise Butler, is a testament to her lofty goal of preserving and planting all the flora of Minnesota within the boundaries of the garden. The sanctuary is bowl-shaped, low in the center with a wooded slope around the outside. The eastern side of the garden is a rolling, less-wooded area. Within the sanctuary lies a trail, a little over 2/3 of a mile long, which explores four kinds of plant and animal habitats. Naturalists offer tours and programs on evenings and weekends.

COST: Free.

HOURS: April 1–October 31: daily 7:30 a.m.–dusk.

> Located in Theodore Wirth Regional Park. From I-94 westbound, take the Hwy. 55 exit. Proceed west on Hwy. 55 to Theodore Wirth Regional Park.

MINNESOTA LANDSCAPE ARBORETUM

3675 Arboretum Dr., Chanhassen, MN 55317 (612) 443-2460

The Minnesota Landscape Arboretum is Minnesota's largest public garden and horticultural resource. This 905-acre park of tulips, hostas, and forests features a seasonal tram; walking tours through woods, prairie, and bogs; and cross-country ski trails. In addition to spectacular gardens and scenery, enjoy a tea room and gift shop. Room and garden rentals are available. Gardening and landscape classes for the entire family are offered throughout the year.

COST: Adults 16 and over $4, children 6-15 $1. Children 5 and under free. No fee after 4:30 p.m. on Thursdays May–August. Tram ride $1.50.

HOURS: Grounds open year round, daily 8 a.m.–sunset. Snyder Building open Monday–Friday 8 a.m.–4:30 p.m.; weekends 11 a.m.–4:30 p.m. Tearoom open daily 11:30 a.m.–1:30 p.m.

> Trumpet Creeper Tram tours available Wednesday–Sunday 11:30 a.m., 1 p.m., and 2:30 p.m. Free walking tours Tuesday, Wednesday, and Thursday at 10 a.m., and the first Saturday of the month at 10 a.m.
>
> Located 2 miles south of Excelsior on Hwy. 41 and 1/2 mile west on Hwy. 5. From I-494, take the Hwy. 5 exit west and follow about 9 miles to the Arboretum.

▲▲▲▲▲▲▲▲▲▲▲▲▲▲▲▲▲▲▲▲▲▲▲▲▲▲▲▲▲▲▲▲▲▲▲▲

Courtesy of Minnesota Landscape Arboretum

The Minnesota Landscape Arboretum has 905 acres of spectacular scenery and gardens.

▲▲

NOERENBERG MEMORIAL GARDENS

2840 North Shore Dr., Wayzata, MN 55391 (612) 476-4666

Enjoy excellent views of Lake Minnetonka from this inspirational formal flower garden. Noerenberg Memorial Gardens is open for tours, informal viewings, and weddings. However, picnics and water-based activities are prohibited.

COST: Parking fee: daily $4. Hennepin Parks annual permit $20.

DATES: Open year round.

> Located on Crystal Bay on Lake Minnetonka. Take Hwy. 12 west to Co. Rd. 15. Proceed south on Co. Rd. 15 and follow to Co. Rd. 51. Turn right onto Co. Rd. 51 and go 1 mile to the junction of 51 and Co. Rd. 84. The entrance will be on the left side of the road.

NATURE CENTERS/WILDLIFE AREAS

CROSBY PARK NATURE CENTER

Information: City of St. Paul, Division of Parks & Recreation, 300 City Hall Annex, 25 W. 4th St., St. Paul, MN 55102 (612) 292-6548

The Crosby Park Nature Center lies within the 729-acre Hidden Falls/Crosby Farm Regional Park. Open year round, the Nature Center offers a variety of nature programming for school classes, groups, special events, and family events. A self-guided trail with numbered posts is located within the park. Trail guides on Crosby's plants and wildlife are available by purchase.

COST: Free.

HOURS: Open year round, Monday–Friday, 8 a.m.–5 p.m.

> From I-35E, take the Shepard Rd. exit southwest. You can reach the park off Shepard Rd. from Crosby Lake Rd. or Crosby Farm Rd. Crosby Farm Rd. brings you to the Nature Center and Watergate Marina. Crosby Lake Rd. brings you to Crosby Lake.

▲▲▲▲▲▲▲▲▲▲▲▲▲▲▲▲▲▲▲▲▲▲▲▲▲▲▲▲▲▲▲▲▲▲▲▲▲▲

EASTMAN NATURE CENTER

13351 Elm Creek Rd., Osseo, MN 55369 (612) 420-4300

Eastman Nature Center, located in Elm Creek Park Reserve, displays exhibits and offers imaginative programming.

    COST: Parking: daily $4, annual permit $20.

    HOURS: Open year round, daily 9 a.m.–5 p.m.

> Located northwest of Osseo, between the communities of Champlin, Dayton, and Maple Grove. From I-94 westbound, take the Co. Rd. 81 exit. Go northwest on 81 to Co. Rd. 121. Proceed north on 121 to Elm Creek Rd. Turn right onto Elm Creek Rd. and follow to the Nature Center.

LOWRY NATURE CENTER

7025 Victoria Dr., Victoria, MN 55386 (612) 472-4911

Established in 1969, the Lowry Nature Center was the first nature center in the metro area. With 450 acres of marsh, forest, and meadows, the nature center has a lot to offer anyone wanting to observe the great diversity of plants and animals. Watch an osprey diving for fish, look at a rare metro-area plant community, or hike the floating boardwalk through the tamarack bog.

Nature programs at Lowry Nature Center focus on Carver Park Reserve's abundant natural resources. They range from watching waterfowl and the fall bird migration to maple syrup-making in the springtime, or stargazing in the summer.

Habitats is a new and popular feature of the Lowry Nature Center. The first of its kind in the Twin Cities, Habitats is an outdoor educational play area featuring larger-than-life flowers to climb, huge dragonfly eyes to peer through, vine-like slides to glide down, and a beaver lodge to sit in. Everything is built on a scale designed for use by preschool- and elementary-school-age children. Self-guided educational kits will be available to families and school groups to enhance their experience.

    COST: Parking: daily $4, annual $20.

    HOURS: Open year round, daily 9 a.m.–5 p.m.

▲▲▲▲▲▲▲▲▲▲▲▲▲▲▲▲▲▲▲▲▲▲▲▲▲▲▲▲▲▲▲▲▲▲▲▲▲▲

> Lowry Nature Center is located in Carver Park Reserve.
>
> From I-494, take the Hwy. 5 exit. Proceed west on Hwy. 5 to Co. Rd. 11. Turn right onto Co. Rd. 11. Carver Park Reserve and the Nature Center are within 1 1/2 miles.
>
> From Hwy. 100, take Hwy. 7 west to Co. Rd. 11. Turn left onto Co. Rd. 11. Carver Park Reserve and the Nature Center are within 1 mile on Co. Rd. 11.

MINNESOTA VALLEY WILDLIFE REFUGE

3815 E. 80th St., Bloomington, MN 55425 (612) 335-2299

Located in the heart of the Twin Cities area is the 8,000-acre Minnesota Valley Wildlife Refuge. The Refuge runs along the Minnesota River for 34 miles from Fort Snelling to Jordan.

Wildlife programs and exhibits operated by the U.S. Fish and Wildlife Service are available. The Visitor Center features many hands-on exhibits and computer games. Visitors can imagine themselves a fire boss on a pre-described burn area or a refuge manager of a deer herd. A spectacular 12-projector slide presentation is shown regularly. Naturalist-led programs are available.

COST: All programs and admissions free.

HOURS: April–December 31: Tuesday–Sunday 9 a.m.–9 p.m. January 1–March 31: Tuesday, Friday, Saturday, and Sunday 9 a.m.–5 p.m.; Wednesday and Thursday 9 a.m.–9 p.m.

> From I-494, take the 34th Ave. exit. Proceed south on 34th Ave. to E. 80th St. Proceed east on 80th St. about 1/2 mile to the Refuge entrance.

RICHARDSON NATURE CENTER

8737 Bush Lake Rd., Bloomington, MN 55438 (612) 941-7993

Located in the Hyland Lake Park Reserve, the Richardson Nature Center is the host of year-round nature programs. Park naturalists are available to explain the habits of the abundant area wildlife. Deer, pheasants, and wild songbirds feed outside the Richardson Nature Center, oblivious to their human observers.

COST: Parking: daily $4, annual $20.

HOURS: Open year round, daily 9 a.m.–5 p.m.

▲▲

> Located in Bloomington. From I-494, go south on Normandale Blvd. (Hwy. 100) to 84th St. Turn right onto 84th St. and follow to E. Bush Lake Rd. Go south on E. Bush Lake Rd. and follow the signs to Richardson Nature Center.

TAMARACK NATURE CENTER

5287 Otter Lake Rd., White Bear Township, MN 55110 (612) 429-7787

The Tamarack Nature Center is located on a 320-acre site at the heart of the Bald Eagle-Otter Lakes area. The Nature Center provides programs to the public throughout the year such as bird banding, wildflower hikes, snowshoeing, and more. Three miles of hiking and cross-country ski trails begin at the Center and go throughout the site.

COST: Free.

HOURS: Open year round, daily 1/2 hour before sunrise–1/2 hour after sunset.

> From I-35E northbound, take the Hwy. 96 exit. Turn right onto Hwy. 96 and go east to Hwy. 61. Turn left onto Hwy. 61 and proceed north to Buffalo St. Turn left onto Buffalo and go west to Hugo Rd. Turn right onto Hugo Rd. and go north to the entrance of the park on the left.

WARGO NATURE CENTER

7701 Main St., Hugo, MN 55038 (612) 429-8007

Rice Creek Chain of Lakes Park Reserve is home to the Wargo Nature Center, which offers environmental programs for children, families, and school groups. Call for a detailed schedule of upcoming programs and events.

COST: Parking: $2.

HOURS: Open 7:30 a.m.–9:30 p.m.

> From I-35W, take exit #36 (Lake Dr.). Follow Lake Dr. north to Co. Rd. 14. Go east on Co. Rd. 14 about 3 miles to the Park Reserve.
>
> From I-35E, take County State Aid Hwy. 14 exit. Proceed west on Hwy. 14 to the Park Reserve entrance.

▲▲▲▲▲▲▲▲▲▲▲▲▲▲▲▲▲▲▲▲▲▲▲▲▲▲▲▲▲▲▲▲▲▲▲▲

ANOKA COUNTY REGIONAL PARKS

ANOKA RIVERFRONT REGIONAL PARK

5100 E. River Rd., Fridley, MN 55432 (612) 757-3920

This beautiful 150-acre park extends along the banks of the Mississippi River. You can enjoy biking, picnicking, 1.5 miles of hiking trails, fishing, and boating throughout the summer months. There is also an exercise area and playground. The Islands of Peace recreation area has special outdoor access facilities for people with physical handicaps. The bike trail connects with Islands of Peace and the Minneapolis parkway system.

COST: Free.

HOURS: 7:30 a.m.–9:30 p.m.

From I-694 (heading toward Fridley), take the E. River Rd. exit south to the park entrance.

BUNKER HILLS REGIONAL PARK

550 Bunker Lake Blvd. N.W., Anoka, MN 55304 (612) 757-3920

This 1,600-acre park is one of Anoka County's most popular regional parks and is home to the Bunker Hills Wave Pool. Notable attractions within the park also include a nine-hole golf course and a 27-hole championship course; the Veterans Memorial; 18 miles of cross-country ski trails; 5.5 miles of hiking trails; biking trails; an archery range; campgrounds; nature study areas; picnic grounds; and horseback riding stables.

COST: No parking fee.

HOURS: 7:30 a.m.–9:30 p.m.

From I-694, take the State Hwy. 47 (University Ave.) exit going north to Foley Blvd. Go north (left) on Foley Blvd. about 4 miles to Bunker Hills. Follow signs to the Activities Center for maps and brochures.

From State Hwy. 65, take State Hwy. 242 west to Foley Blvd. and turn right into Bunker Hills. Follow signs to the Activities Center for maps and brochures.

▲▲▲▲▲▲▲▲▲▲▲▲▲▲▲▲▲▲▲▲▲▲▲▲▲▲▲▲▲▲▲▲▲▲▲▲

Cenaiko Lake in the Coon Rapids Dam Regional Park.

COON RAPIDS DAM REGIONAL PARK

9760 Egret Blvd., Coon Rapids, MN 56433 (612) 757-4700

The 600-acre Coon Rapids Dam Regional Park surrounds Cenaiko Trout Lake, a 29-acre artificial lake stocked with rainbow and brook trout. A variety of appealing recreational activities include hiking; 3 miles of biking trails; boating; fishing; picnicking; nature study; and 2 miles of cross-country skiing.

COST: Parking fee $2.

HOURS: 7:30 a.m.–9:30 p.m.

> Located in Coon Rapids. From State Hwy. 65 take the U.S. Hwy. 10 exit.
> Proceed northwest on Co. Rd. 10 and stay to the right until you reach Coon
> Rapids Blvd. Follow Coon Rapids Blvd. to Egret, turn left onto Egret and fol-
> low to Coon Rapids Dam Regional Park.

▲▲▲▲▲▲▲▲▲▲▲▲▲▲▲▲▲▲▲▲▲▲▲▲▲▲▲▲▲▲▲▲▲▲▲

LAKE GEORGE REGIONAL PARK

Lake George Blvd., 217th Ave., Anoka, MN 55304 (612) 757-3920

This 800-acre park features recreational areas and activities including boating; fishing; picnic grounds; and the largest swimming beach in Anoka County.

COST: Parking fee $2.

HOURS: 7:30 a.m.–9:30 p.m.

> Take State Hwy. 65 north toward Oak Grove. From State Hwy. 65, take the Co. Rd. 74 exit. Follow Co. Rd. 74 west to Lake George Blvd. and follow south to Lake George Regional Park.

RICE CREEK CHAIN OF LAKES PARK RESERVE

7701 Main St., Lino Lakes, MN 55038 (612) 757-3920

Recreational activities on this 2,500-acre reserve include boating; camping; fishing; golfing; hiking; picnicking; swimming beach on Centerville Lake; and cross-country-skiing.

Rice Creek Chain of Lakes Park Reserve is also home to the Wargo Nature Center.

COST: Free.

HOURS: 7:30 a.m.–9:30 p.m.

> From I-35W, take exit #36 (Lake Dr.). Proceed on Lake Dr. north to Co. Rd. 14. Proceed east on Co. Rd. 14 about 3 miles to the Park Reserve.
>
> From I-35E, take County State Aid Hwy. 14 exit. Proceed west on Hwy. 14 to the Park Reserve entrance.

RICE CREEK TRAIL WEST REGIONAL PARK (LOCKE PARK)

550 Bunker Lake Blvd. N.W., Anoka, MN 55304 (612) 757-3920

Rice Creek Trail West Regional Park has 250 acres with 4 miles of hiking and biking trails, which follow Rice Creek to the Mississippi River. Picnic grounds are available, and fishing opportunities abound.

COST: Free.

HOURS: 7:30 a.m.–9:30 p.m.

> Rice Creek Trail West Regional Park is located off State Hwy. 65. Park entrances off 69th St. and 71st Ave. in Fridley.

CARVER COUNTY REGIONAL PARKS

BAYLOR REGIONAL PARK

Carver County Parks, 10775 Co. Rd. 33, Young America, MN 55397
Metro phone (612) 361-1000 Local phone (612) 467-3145

Baylor Regional Park features picnic grounds; trail system; ball field; volleyball courts; tennis courts; horseshoe pits; play lots; and a 50-site tent and RV campground.

Prairie trails, hardwood forests, and floating board walks through marsh are ideal settings for avid wildlife seekers to study a wide variety of animals in their natural habitats. A community room in the park barn is available for group use with advance reservations.

COST: Parking fee: daily $3. Annual parking fee $14.

HOURS: Open year round, 8 a.m.–9 p.m. or sunset.

> Located on Co. Rd. 33, 2-1/2 miles north of State Hwy. 212 or State Hwy. 5, near Norwood-Young America.
>
> From I-494 westbound, take the Hwy. 5 exit. Go west on Hwy. 5 to Co. Rd. 33. Proceed north on Co. Rd. 33 to Baylor Regional Park.

LAKE MINNEWASHTA REGIONAL PARK

Carver County Parks, 10775 Co. Rd. 33, Young America, MN 55397 Metro phone (612) 361-1000, local phone (612) 467-3145

Offering a wide range of activities the whole family will love, this 350-acre Regional Park is one of Carver County's best! A very unique tiered play structure built with kid appeal is a big draw. Lifeguards are on duty daily at Lake Minnewashta's swimming beach for those who enjoy cooling off from the heat in the summer. Four large picnic areas are great gathering points for family get-togethers. Woodlands along the shore of Lake Minnewashta provide an ideal setting for hiking or cross-country skiing on 5.5 miles of trails. If you enjoy boating or fishing, you won't be disappointed in Lake Minnewashta. A field game area and volleyball courts are available for sports-minded visitors.

COST: Parking fee: daily $3. Annual parking fee $14.

HOURS: Open year round, 8 a.m.–9 p.m. or sunset.

> Located off State Hwy. 41 between State Hwys. 5 and 7, west of Chanhassen.
>
> From I-494 westbound, take the Hwy. 5 exit. Go west on Hwy. 5 to Hwy. 41. Proceed north on Hwy. 41 to Lake Minnewashta Regional Park on the left.

▲▲▲▲▲▲▲▲▲▲▲▲▲▲▲▲▲▲▲▲▲▲▲▲▲▲▲▲▲▲▲▲▲▲▲

DAKOTA COUNTY REGIONAL PARKS

LAKE BYLLESBY REGIONAL PARK

7650 Echo Point Rd., Cannon Falls, MN 55009 (507) 437-6608

Twin Cities families have easy access to water recreational activities such as swimming, fishing, sailing, and water skiing at Lake Byllesby Regional Park. Lake Byllesby's 1,490-acre reservoir is the largest body of water in the metropolitan area, south of the Minnesota and Mississippi Rivers. Other recreational opportunities include picnic areas; hiking trails; horseshoes; and camping.

COST: No Parking fee.

HOURS: Open year round.

> Located on Lake Byllesby Reservoir near Cannon Falls and east of Randolph. From State Hwy. 56 in Randolph, take Co. Rd. 88 east about 3.5 miles to park entrance.
>
> From State Hwy. 52, north of Cannon Falls, take Co. Rd. 86 west to Harry Ave. Take Harry Ave. about 1.5 miles to the park.

LEBANON HILLS REGIONAL PARK–EAST SECTION

Contact Dakota County Parks Department, 8500 127th St. E., Hastings, MN 55033 (612) 437-6608 24-hour park info line 438-6313

Lebanon Hills has picnic grounds in several beautiful settings; 10.7 miles of hiking trails, which wind through hilly woodlands and grassy plains and around lakes and ponds; sunbathing or swimming at Schultz Lake Beach; canoeing; mountain biking on 2.5 miles of hilly trail; horseback riding and rental; fishing; and camping at Lebanon Hills Regional Campground. Lebanon Hills also offers cross-country skiing in the winter with .8 miles of trails for the beginning skier and 7 miles of trails for the intermediate skier. It also has 3.4 miles of snowmobile trails and ice fishing.

COST: No parking fee. Swimming beach admission: daily 75¢, family pass $15, last Wednesday of each month free.

HOURS: Open year round 5 a.m.–11 p.m. Swimming beach hours 11 a.m.–8 p.m.

▲▲▲▲▲▲▲▲▲▲▲▲▲▲▲▲▲▲▲▲▲▲▲▲▲▲▲▲▲▲▲▲▲▲

This 2,000-acre park is located in Apple Valley and Eagan.

Directions to Jensen Lake Park entrance: From 35E, take the Cliff Rd. exit and go east to Pilot Knob Rd. Turn right (south) and turn left on Carriage Hill Dr.

From Co. Rd. 42, take the Pilot Knob Rd. exit and go north about 2/3 mile to Carriage Hill Dr. on the right.

Directions to Shultz Lake Park entrance: From 35E, take the Cliff Rd. exit and go east for 1.5 miles. Park entrance is on the right.

From State Hwy. 3, turn left on Cliff Rd. and go west for 1/2 mile. Park entrance is on left.

SPRING LAKE PARK RESERVE (SCHAAR'S BLUFF)

Contact Dakota County Parks Department, 8500 127th St. E., Hastings, MN 55033 (612) 437-6608 24-hour park info line 438-6313

Spring Lake Park features scenic high bluffs overlooking a backwater of the Mississippi River. Spring Lake was formed by the dam at Hastings. Use the picnic grounds for a fun day out, or take in the scenery through 3.6 miles of hiking and cross-country ski trails, plus 1.5 miles of ski skating trails.

COST: No parking fee.

HOURS: Open year round. Summer hours 8 a.m.–11 p.m.; winter hours 8
a.m.–10:30 p.m.

Located 3 miles northwest of Hastings. From the Twin Cities, go east on Hwy. 55 to Co. Rd. 42 (Mississippi Tr.) and turn left (northeast). Follow Co. Rd. 42 to Idell Ave. Turn left (north) on Idell and go about 1 mile to the park.

▲▲▲▲▲▲▲▲▲▲▲▲▲▲▲▲▲▲▲▲▲▲▲▲▲▲▲▲▲▲▲▲▲▲▲▲

HENNEPIN COUNTY REGIONAL PARKS

The following regional parks and park reserves are operated by Hennepin Parks, 12615 County Road 9, Plymouth, MN 55441-1248 General information (612) 559-9000, reservations (612) 559-6700, TDD (612) 559-6719, Ski & Hiking Trail Hot Line (612) 559-6778, Public Safety Dept. (612) 479-1172.

BAKER PARK RESERVE

2301 Co. Rd. 19, Maple Plain, MN 55359 (612) 476-4666

Centrally located in Hennepin County on Lake Independence, Baker Park Reserve is only a 20-minute drive from much of the metro area. This 2,700-acre reserve hosts a stunning maple forest. Enjoy 6.2 miles of paved bicycling trails that wind through meadows and a "big woods" forest. Baker Park Reserve also features picnic grounds; a campground; a large, unique creative play area; fishing and boating in three lakes (Lake Independence, Spurzem Lake, Half Moon Lake); rental of rowboats, paddleboats, canoes, bikes, and skis; golfing at Baker National Golf Course, with 18-hole regulation and nine-hole executive course (473-0800); 7.1 miles of groomed cross-country ski trails; and a chalet and sliding hill for winter activities.

COST: Parking fee: daily $4. Hennepin Parks annual permit $20. Call for other fees.

DATES: Open year round. Swimming beach: Memorial Day weekend–Labor Day.

> Located 20 miles west of downtown Minneapolis on Co. Rd. 19 between Hwy. 12 and Hwy. 55. From Hwy. 12 take Co. Rd. 29. Go north on Co. Rd. 29 to Co. Rd. 19. Follow 19 north to the main park entrance.
>
> From Hwy. 55, take Co. Rd. 24 west to Co. Rd. 19. Proceed south on Co. Rd. 19 to the main park entrance.

▲▲▲▲▲▲▲▲▲▲▲▲▲▲▲▲▲▲▲▲▲▲▲▲▲▲▲▲▲▲▲▲▲▲▲▲▲▲

BRYANT LAKE REGIONAL PARK

6400 Rowland Rd., Eden Prairie, MN 55344 (612) 941-7922

After extensive redevelopment, this 170-acre park reopens in the spring of 1995. Nestled among rolling hills, Bryant Lake Regional Park is a great getaway for the family. Picnic; sun at the Bryant Lake beach; swim; go boating; fish; or bike and hike the trails.

>   COST: Parking fee: daily $4. Hennepin Parks annual permit $20.

>   DATES: Open year round beginning in spring 1995. Swimming beach: Memorial Day weekend–Labor Day.

> Located in Eden Prairie. From I-494, take the Crosstown 62 exit and go east. Follow Hwy. 62 to Shady Oak Rd. (Hwy. 61). Go south on Shady Oak Rd. to Rowland Rd. Turn right onto Rowland Rd. Park entrance is within 1/2 mile on the left side.

CARVER PARK RESERVE

7025 Victoria Dr., Victoria, MN 55386 (612) 472-4911

If you're a wildlife enthusiast, you'll have a memorable experience at Carver Park Reserve. Located west of Chanhassen on 3,500 acres, the reserve is home to deer, fox, owls, hawks, and many other animals. Located here is the Lowry Nature Center, where you can expect to find naturalists and recreation staff providing a variety of fun activities and programs. Exhibits, displays, and maps are made available to familiarize you with the plants and animals you'll discover as you explore the interpretive trails, floating boardwalks, and observation blinds. Wetland animals can be seen from more than 1,700 feet of boardwalk that take you through marsh and tamarack swamps. You won't want to miss a view of the trumpeter swans. Carver Park Reserve is also home to the new outdoor Habitats educational play area, featuring larger-than-life flowers and vines to play on and a beaver lodge to sit in.

Carver Park Reserve also includes picnic grounds; a public campground; swimming beach designated for campers; small play area; 8.5 miles of paved biking and hiking trails; over 9 miles of turf hiking trails; rental of bikes and skis; fishing on four lakes (Lake Auburn, Stieger Lake, Lake Zumbra, Parley Lake); 12.7 miles of cross-country ski trails; and a designated winter sliding hill.

>   COST: Parking fee: daily $4. Hennepin Parks annual permit $20.

>   HOURS: Open year round.

Lowry Nature Center (612) 472-4911

>   HOURS: Monday–Saturday 9 a.m.–5 p.m.; Sunday noon–5 p.m.

▲▲▲▲▲▲▲▲▲▲▲▲▲▲▲▲▲▲▲▲▲▲▲▲▲▲▲▲▲▲▲▲▲▲▲▲▲▲

> From I-494, take the Hwy. 5 exit. Proceed west on Hwy. 5 to Co. Rd. 11.
> Turn right onto Co. Rd. 11 and continue to Carver Park Reserve and the
> Nature Center, within 1-1/2 miles on Co. Rd. 11.
>
> From Hwy. 100, take Hwy. 7 west to Co. Rd. 11. Turn left onto Co. Rd. 11
> and continue to Carver Park Reserve and the Nature Center, within 1 mile on
> Co. Rd. 11.

CLEARY LAKE REGIONAL PARK

18106 Texas Ave. S., Prior Lake, MN 55372 (612) 447-2171

If you are looking for a popular southern metro park, Cleary Lake will be a relaxing surprise. This 1,045-acre Regional Park is located just southwest of Burnsville.

Cleary Lake is best known for its excellent spring fishing, so look for the boat launch and fishing pier. Walkers, bikers, and in-line skaters will enjoy the 3.5-mile paved trail surrounding the lake. The park also includes picnic areas; a three-season pavilion; play area; sandy swimming beach; par-3 length nine-hole course and driving range for golfers; rental of boats, bikes, in-line skates, and cross-country skis; and cross-country skiing on 9.7 miles of groomed trails.

> COST: Parking fee: daily $4. Hennepin Parks annual permit $20.
>
> HOURS: Open year round. Swimming beach: Memorial Day weekend–Labor
>   Day.

> From I-35W, take the Co. Rd. 42 exit. Proceed west on Co. Rd. 42 to Co.
> Rd. 27. Take Co. Rd. 27 south about 3-4 miles to Cleary Lake Regional Park.

COON RAPIDS DAM REGIONAL PARK (West Side)

10360 W. River Rd., Brooklyn Park, MN 55444 (612) 424-8172

If you would like a more intimate view of the Coon Rapids Dam and Mississippi River, visit the west side of the Coon Rapids Dam Regional Park, located in Brooklyn Park on the banks of the Mississippi River. Interpretive programs and displays of artifacts from the years when the dam was in operation are offered at the West Visitor Center. The park also offers fishing from the river shoreline; picnic areas; 1-1/2 miles of hiking trails along the river; and access to the North Hennepin Regional Trail Corridor.

> COST: Parking fee: daily $4. Hennepin Parks annual permit $20.
>
> · DATES: Open year round.

> Located on the Mississippi River between Coon Rapids and Brooklyn Park.
> Take I-94 north until it turns into Hwy. 252. Follow Hwy. 252 north to 93rd
> Ave. and turn left. From 93rd Ave. turn right on Co. Rd. 12. Follow Co. Rd.
> 12 about 2 miles to the Coon Rapids Dam Regional Park which will be locat-
> ed on the right.

CROW-HASSAN PARK RESERVE

11629 Crow-Hassan Park Rd., Rogers, MN 55374 (612) 476-4666

Experience the colorful and ever-changing prairie at Crow-Hassan Park Reserve located
west of Rogers. This park contains the largest and oldest prairie area within the park
system, with 515 acres of restored prairie sweeping over gently rolling terrain. Observe
the habitat of native prairie animals like prairie skink, deer, fox, migrating nighthawks,
and many more. The Park Reserve is also the site of the annual September Prairie Fest,
including re-enactment of the early pioneers' crossing of the wilderness in covered wagons.

This 2,600-acre park also boasts 11.8 miles of hiking and horseback riding trails weav-
ing through prairie and woodlands; group campsites, including a canoe site along the
Crow River; fishing in the Crow River; and 10.9 miles of groomed cross-country ski
trails (ski-in winter camping facilities available).

COST: Parking fee: daily $4. Hennepin Parks annual permit $20.

DATES: Open year round.

> Located west of Rogers on Sylvan Lake Rd. From I-94 take the Rogers exit.
> Proceed south on Co. Rd. 150 to Co. Rd. 116. Turn right onto Co. Rd. 116
> and go to Co. Rd. 203. Turn left on Co. Rd. 203 and follow 203 to the park
> entrance.

ELM CREEK PARK RESERVE

13080 Territorial Rd., Maple Grove, MN 55369 (612) 424-5511

Numerous recreation activities offered at the Elm Creek Park Reserve can keep even
the most active family occupied for a full day. This 5,000-acre Park Reserve is the
largest in the Hennepin Parks system and is home to the Eastman Nature Center.
Interpretive naturalists are on staff to enhance your experience at the Nature Center
and provide a variety of fun activities and programs. The abundant wildlife can be
observed in diverse settings. In the numerous streams and marshes, herons, ducks, and
beavers are popular sights.

▲▲▲▲▲▲▲▲▲▲▲▲▲▲▲▲▲▲▲▲▲▲▲▲▲▲▲▲▲▲▲▲▲▲▲▲▲▲

The Park Reserve also provides 20 miles of turf hiking trails; 9.1 miles of paved biking and hiking trails through gently rolling open land to hilly, wooded sections; 4.9 miles of mountain bike trails; picnic areas; a creative play area; swimming in a sand-bottom pond; archery range; 14 miles of horseback trails; a visitor center with concessions and bike and ski rentals; group campsites (559-9000); 9.2 miles of ski trails; and a designated winter sliding hill.

COST: Parking fee: daily $4. Hennepin Parks annual permit $20.

DATES: Open year round. Swimming beach: Memorial Day weekend–Labor Day.

> Located northwest of Osseo, between the communities of Champlin, Dayton, and Maple Grove. For the recreation area, take Co. Rd. 81 northwest to Territorial Rd. Turn right onto Territorial Rd. and follow to the park entrance.
>
> From I-94/U.S. Hwy. 52 north of Maple Grove, take Co. Rd. 30 (93rd Ave.) east to Glacier Lane. Glacier Lane will become Fernbrook Lane. Follow Fernbrook north to Co. Rd. 81. Take Co. Rd. 81 southeast to Territorial Rd. Turn left onto Territorial Rd. and follow to the park entrance.

FISH LAKE REGIONAL PARK

14500 Bass Lake Rd., Osseo, MN 55311 (612) 420-3423

Looking for a wooded, lakeside setting for a family picnic? This 160-acre Regional Park, located in Maple Grove, won't disappoint the family. You'll enjoy the swimming beach; boating; fishing; biking, hiking, or in-line skating on 1 mile of paved trail; 3.7 miles of turf hiking trails; rental of volleyball horseshoes, in-line skates, and boats; visitor center with concessions; and a designated winter sliding hill.

COST: Parking fee: daily $4. Hennepin Parks annual permit $20.

DATES: Memorial Day weekend–Labor Day weekend. Swimming beach: Memorial Day weekend–Labor Day.

> Located in Maple Grove. From I-494, take the Bass Lake Rd. (Co. Rd. 10) exit and go west for 1-1/2 miles. Park is on the right.

FRENCH REGIONAL PARK

12605 Co. Rd. 9, Plymouth, MN 55441 (612) 559-8891

Amid rolling hills, French Regional Park possesses 310 acres on Medicine Lake, featuring woodland trails and a variety of water-based activities. Enjoy an intimate view of wetland wildlife on a self-guided canoe tour through the backwaters of Medicine Lake. Monthly outdoor education programs feature such topics as maple syrup making, ospreys, and beaver lodges. A shuttle tram runs throughout the summer season between the visitor center and the beach. Winter months are special because of 3.7 miles of lighted cross-country ski trails open until 9 p.m. daily, weather permitting.

French Regional Park also offers a boat launch and fishing pier; swimming beach; picnic areas; creative play area filled with cargo climbing nets; 3 miles of paved biking and hiking trails; 7 miles of turf hiking trails; 5.4 miles of cross-country ski trails; a designated sliding hill; and a visitor center with a concession area and rental equipment for all seasons (boat, ski, volley, etc.).

COST: Parking fee: daily $4. Hennepin Parks annual permit $20.

DATES: Open year round. Swimming beach: Memorial Day weekend–Labor Day.

> Located in Plymouth on Medicine Lake. From I-494, take the Co. Rd. 9 exit. Proceed east 1 mile to French Regional Park. Entrance is on the right.
>
> From Hwy. 169, take Co. Rd. 9 west about 2 miles to the French Regional Park entrance.

HYLAND LAKE PARK RESERVE

10145 Bush Lake Rd., Bloomington, MN 55438 (612) 941-4362
Richardson Nature Center (612) 941-7993

The City of Bloomington surrounds the Hyland Lake Park Reserve, a 1,000-acre oasis of wildlife and woods. Deer, pheasants and wild songbirds are common sights in the Richardson Nature Center, located in the Park Reserve. Learn about maple syrup making or bird watching at one of the many naturalists' programs offered year round. Hike on wood-chip nature trails and experience restored prairie, marsh, and woodlands. Hyland Lake Park Reserve is home to the famous creative play area dubbed "Chutes and Ladders" by Twin City parents. Built on the side of a hill, it has many ladders and slides of different shapes and lengths to thrill and entertain the kids for a whole afternoon.

Hyland Lake Park Reserve also offers picnic areas; 7.4 miles of turf hiking trails; visitor center with concessions; nearly 5 miles of paved biking and hiking trails; fishing pier on Hyland Lake; boat, bike, and ski rental; 6.7 miles of cross-country ski trails; a light-

▲▲▲▲▲▲▲▲▲▲▲▲▲▲▲▲▲▲▲▲▲▲▲▲▲▲▲▲▲▲▲▲▲▲▲

ed sliding hill open until 9 p.m. Friday and Saturday only; downhill skiing at Hyland Hills.

COST: Parking fee: daily $4. Hennepin Parks annual permit $20.

DATES: Open year round.

> Located in Bloomington. From I-494, go south on Normandale Blvd. (Hwy. 100) to 84th St. Turn right and follow 84th St. to E. Bush Lake Rd. Go south on E. Bush Lake Rd. and follow the signs to Richardson Nature Center and Hyland Outdoor Recreation Center. The Hyland Hills Downhill Ski Area is located south of 84th St. on Chalet Road.

LAKE REBECCA PARK RESERVE

9831 Co. Rd. 50, Rockford, MN 55377 (612) 476-4666

Take advantage of this 2,200-acre Park Reserve with its gently rolling landscape and numerous wetland areas. Canoe on the Crow River or fish for everything from bass and muskie to panfish and bullheads on Lake Rebecca. You might recognize Lake Rebecca; it was featured in ice fishing scenes in the movie "Grumpy Old Men." This Park Reserve is one of the sites for trumpeter swan restoration programs.

Lake Rebecca Park Reserve also provides picnic areas; a creative play area; fishing piers; boat launch for nonmotorized boats; boat rentals (canoes, row boats, paddle boats); a swimming beach; 13 miles of turf hiking trails; and 6.5 miles of paved bike and hiking trails.

COST: Parking fee: daily $4. Hennepin Parks annual permit $20.

DATES: April 1–November 15. Swimming beach: Memorial Day weekend–Labor Day.

> Located 30 miles west of Minneapolis on Co. Rd. 50. Take Hwy. 55 west to Co. Rd. 50. Turn left onto Co. Rd. 50 and follow to the park entrance.

MURPHY-HANREHAN PARK RESERVE

15501 Murphy Lake Rd., Savage, MN 55378 (612) 447-2171

Because of its glacial ridges and hilly terrain, this pristine 2,400-acre Park Reserve is popular with horseback riders, mountain bikers, hikers, and cross-country skiers. If challenge is what you are looking for, you won't be disappointed. You'll find 2 miles of turf hiking trails; 6 miles of mountain bike trails; 9.6 miles of horseback riding trails with trailer parking; 12 miles of groomed cross-country ski trails designed for interme-

▲▲▲▲▲▲▲▲▲▲▲▲▲▲▲▲▲▲▲▲▲▲▲▲▲▲▲▲▲▲▲▲▲▲▲

diate to advanced level skiing, and ski skating.

COST: Parking fee: daily $4. Hennepin Parks annual permit $20.

DATES: Open year round.

> Located near Prior Lake on Scott Co. Rd. 75. From I-35W, take the Co. Rd.
> 42 exit. Go west on Co. Rd. 42 to Co. Rd. 27. Proceed south on 27 to Co.
> Rd. 74. Go east on Co. Rd. 74 to Co. Rd. 75 and follow south to the park
> entrance.

NORTH HENNEPIN TRAIL CORRIDOR

Hennepin Parks, 12615 Co. Rd. 9, Plymouth, MN 55441-1248 (612) 424-5511

Connecting the Coon Rapids Dam Regional Park in Brooklyn Park to Elm Creek Park Reserve in Maple Grove are 7.2 miles of paved trails. Also, look for the 7.2 miles of turf horseback riding trails and the 7.2 miles of winter trails for snowshoeing and snowmobiling.

Parking fee: daily $4. Hennepin Parks annual permit $20.

> To the Elm Creek Park Reserve entrance: From I-94, take the Hwy. 169 exit.
> Proceed north on Hwy. 169 to Co. Rd. 81. Follow Co. Rd. 81 north toward
> Osseo. From 81, turn right onto Territorial Rd. Elm Creek Park Reserve is on
> Territorial Rd.
>
> To the Coon Rapids Dam entrance: Take I-94 north until it becomes Hwy.
> 252. Follow Hwy. 252 north to 93rd Ave. Turn left onto 93rd and follow to
> Co. Rd. 12. Turn right onto Co. Rd. 12 and follow about 2 miles to the
> entrance on the right.

▲▲▲▲▲▲▲▲▲▲▲▲▲▲▲▲▲▲▲▲▲▲▲▲▲▲▲▲▲▲▲▲▲▲▲

MINNEAPOLIS PARKS

CENTRAL MISSISSIPPI RIVERFRONT REGIONAL PARK

Information: Minneapolis Park & Recreation Board, 200 Grain Exchange Bldg., 400 S. 4th St., Minneapolis, MN 55415-1400 (612) 661-4800

The Central Mississippi Riverfront is a 150-acre Regional Park which extends along both banks of the Mississippi River from Plymouth Ave. to the I-35W Bridge, and includes interpretive displays and plaques recording the rich heritage of the area.

The East Bank portion of the park includes the following notable areas and sites:

Boom Island is the largest Riverfront park in Minneapolis. This 24-acre artificial land formation originated from deposit buildup on a log boom caught on a shallow point of the river. Facilities on Boom Island include a meadow area; Riverfront promenade; picnic tables; walks; boat launch; and parking lots. Public excursions aboard the sternwheeler Anson Northrup leave from this park daily in the summer. Boom Island is between 8th Ave. N.E. and Nicollet Island.

Nicollet Island offers a dramatic view of St. Anthony Falls and downtown Minneapolis. Other popular features include historic homes restored by the Minneapolis Community Development Agency (MCDA); a wonderful park pavilion; and an amphitheater that offers free concerts five nights a week between Memorial Day and Labor Day. Nicollet Island is at the easterly end of the Hennepin Avenue Bridge.

Main Street runs along the east bank parkway system between 3rd Ave. S.E. and Hennepin Ave. Originally built in 1857 as the central street for the Village of St. Anthony, Historic Main Street has been rebuilt with some of its original cobblestones. Brick walks, unique lighting, restored buildings, and bike paths also help evoke the atmosphere of the 19th century.

Father Hennepin Bluff Park is a wonderful place to experience a dramatic view of the Mississippi River, St. Anthony Falls, and the downtown skyline. Steps, footpaths, and bridges provide direct access to the river and spectacular views of the river gorge and the Stone Arch Bridge. The park area closest to Main St. has designated areas for picnicking. The park is connected to Nicollet Island Park by Historic Main Street and is located at the corner of Main and 5th St. S.E.

The West Bank portion of the park includesThe West River Parkway (Great River Road), which will eventually run the length of the Mississippi River in Minneapolis. The Great River Road features pedestrian paths and bicycle trails along the west bank of the central Riverfront, and the Mills District Interpretive Park, which includes the historic water power canal. The Great River Road is on the west side of the river

▲▲▲▲▲▲▲▲▲▲▲▲▲▲▲▲▲▲▲▲▲▲▲▲▲▲▲▲▲▲▲▲▲▲▲▲▲

between Plymouth Ave. and Portland Ave.

COST: Free.

DATES: Open year round.

> East Bank portion of the park: From I-35W, take the University Ave. exit.
> Proceed west on University to 6th Ave. S.E. Turn left (south) onto Sixth Ave.
> and go to Main St. S.E. You can follow Main St. west along a significant por-
> tion of the East Bank area of the park until you reach the corner of 4th Ave.
> N.E. and Main.
>
> From Main St., you can reach the West Bank portion of the park by proceed-
> ing south across the Mississippi River on 3rd Ave. or Hennepin Ave.

MINNEAPOLIS CHAIN OF LAKES REGIONAL PARK

Information: Minneapolis Park & Recreation Board, 200 Grain Exchange Bldg., 400 S. 4th St., Minneapolis, MN 55415-1400 (612) 661-4800

The Minneapolis Chain of Lakes Regional Park surrounds Lake Harriet, Lake Calhoun, and Lake of the Isles. Popular features of Lake Harriet include the Lake Harriet Bandshell (located on Lake Harriet Pkwy. and William Berry Pkwy.), which presents nightly concerts in the summer, and the Historic Lake Harriet Streetcar, which offers a 2-mile trip aboard a trolley through a scenic wooded area between Lakes Harriet and Calhoun. These lakes also provide sailboat buoys and launches for use by city residents. Sailboat races are a spectacular sight in the warm season.

Lake Calhoun is a popular site for fishing, windsurfing, sailing, canoeing, and in-line skating. Lake of the Isles is noted as a refuge for wildlife: two small islands in the lake provide shelter for water birds. Resident Canada geese, black-crowned night herons, and great egrets can often be seen by observers as they stroll around the Isles.

Recreational opportunities you can expect to find at the Minneapolis Chain of Lakes include biking and hiking trails; picnic grounds; boating; fishing; swimming; in-line or roller skating; nature interpretation; ice fishing; and cross-country skiing.

COST: Free.

DATES: Open year round.

> Lake Calhoun: From I-35W, take the 35th/36th St. exit to 35th St. Follow
> 35th St. west to Nicollet Ave. Turn left onto Nicollet and follow 1 block to
> 36th St. Turn right onto 36th St. and proceed to Calhoun Pkwy., which sur-
> rounds Lake Calhoun.

Lake Harriet: From I-35W, take the 35th/36th St. exit to 35th St. Follow
35th St. west to Nicollet Ave. Turn left onto Nicollet Ave. and follow 1 block
to 36th St. Turn right onto 36th St. and proceed to Calhoun Pkwy. Turn left
onto Calhoun Pkwy. and proceed to William Berry Pkwy. Turn left onto
William Berry Pkwy. and follow to Lake Harriet.

Lake of the Isles: From I-35W, take I-94 west to the Hennepin/Lyndale Ave.
exit. Get onto Hennepin and follow to Franklin Ave. Proceed west on
Franklin to Lake of the Isles.

MINNEHAHA PARKWAY

*Information: Minneapolis Park & Recreation Board, 200 Grain Exchange Bldg., 400 S.
4th St., Minneapolis, MN 55415-1400 (612) 661-4800*

Minnehaha Pkwy., part of the Grand Rounds Parkway System, connects Lake Harriet
(the Minneapolis Chain of Lakes Regional Park) to Nokomis/Hiawatha Regional Park
and Minnehaha Park. Minnehaha and Wirth Memorial Parkways provide 27 miles of
biking, hiking, and cross-country ski trails with connections to various regional and
local parks.

COST: Free.

HOURS: Open year round.

You can get onto Minnehaha Parkway from the southeast end of Lake Harriet,
or the northwest portion of Lake Nokomis.

Lake Harriet: From I-35W, take the 35th/36th St. exit to 35th St. Follow
35th St. west to Nicollet Ave. Turn left onto Nicollet and follow 1 block to
36th St. Turn right onto 36th St. and go to Calhoun Pkwy. Turn left onto
Calhoun Pkwy. and proceed to William Berry Pkwy. Turn left onto William
Berry Pkwy. and follow to Lake Harriet.

Lake Nokomis: From I-35W, take the Diamond Lake Rd. exit. Proceed east
on Diamond Lake Rd. to 3rd Ave. S. Follow 3rd Ave. going north to
Minnehaha Pkwy. Turn right onto Minnehaha Pkwy. and follow as it winds
its way into Hiawatha Park.

MINNEHAHA REGIONAL PARK

*Information: Minneapolis Park & Recreation Board, 200 Grain Exchange Bldg., 400 S.
4th St., Minneapolis, MN 55415-1400 (612) 661-4800*

Minnehaha Park is immortalized in Henry Wadsworth Longfellow's poem, *The Song of
Hiawatha*. Minnehaha Falls, the setting for Longfellow's poem and home to the famed

▲▲▲▲▲▲▲▲▲▲▲▲▲▲▲▲▲▲▲▲▲▲▲▲▲▲▲▲▲▲▲▲▲▲▲▲

statue of Hiawatha, has attracted admirers since the turn of the century. Minnehaha Park is located off Minnehaha Ave. and Godfrey Rd.

COST: Free.

HOURS: Open year round.

> From I-94, take Hwy. 55 (Hiawatha Ave.) southeast to Minnehaha Pkwy. Turn left onto Minnehaha Pkwy. and look for the parking lot on the right.

MISSISSIPPI GORGE REGIONAL PARK

Information: Minneapolis Park & Recreation Board, 200 Grain Exchange Bldg., 400 S. 4th St., Minneapolis, MN 55415-1400 (612) 661-4800

The Mississippi Gorge Regional Park is scenically located along the west and east banks of the Mississippi River. The Grand Rounds Parkway System runs through the park with hiking, biking, and cross-country ski trails.

COST: Free.

DATES: Open year round.

> You can reach the park from anywhere off West River Pkwy., East River Rd., or Mississippi River Blvd.

NOKOMIS-HIAWATHA REGIONAL PARK

Information: Minneapolis Park & Recreation Board, 200 Grain Exchange Bldg., 400 S. 4th St., Minneapolis, MN 55415-1400 (612) 661-4800

Nokomis-Hiawatha Regional Park surrounds Lake Hiawatha and Lake Nokomis. As an unusual feature, Lake Nokomis provides sailboat buoys and launches for use by city residents. During warmer months, sailboat races are a spectacular sight.

The Grand Rounds Parkway System continues around Lake Nokomis (Lake Nokomis Pkwy.) with 2.78 miles of biking/roller-skating trails and 2.70 miles of walking trails. A popular feature of the shore of Lake Hiawatha is the 18-hole Hiawatha Golf Course. In the winter, cross-country skiers can follow marked and lighted trails.

You will find a variety of recreational activities at the Nokomis-Hiawatha Regional Park, including biking; hiking; skating; fishing; boating; picnicking; swimming; ice fishing; and cross-country skiing.

COST: Free.

DATES: Open year round.

▲▲▲▲▲▲▲▲▲▲▲▲▲▲▲▲▲▲▲▲▲▲▲▲▲▲▲▲▲▲▲▲▲▲▲▲▲▲▲

> From I-35W, take the Diamond Lake Rd. exit. Proceed east on Diamond Lake Rd. to Portland Ave. Follow Portland Ave. north to Minnehaha Pkwy. Proceed east on Minnehaha Pkwy. to Nokomis-Hiawatha Regional Park. Lake Nokomis is on the right and Lake Hiawatha is on the left.

THEODORE WIRTH REGIONAL PARK

Information: Minneapolis Park & Recreation Board, 200 Grain Exchange Bldg., 400 S. 4th St., Minneapolis, MN 55415-1400 (612) 661-4800

Natural woodlands surround Theodore Wirth Regional Park, the largest of the Minneapolis regional parks. Popular attractions include the Eloise Butler Wildflower Garden and Bird Sanctuary, the J.D. Rivers 4-H Children's Garden, the Daylily-Perennial Garden, a tamarack bog, and an 18-hole, par 3 golf course. The 14-acre Eloise Butler Wildflower Garden and Bird Sanctuary is the oldest public wildflower garden in the U.S. Naturalists offer tours and programs on evenings and weekends. The Theodore Wirth Golf Course can be enjoyed year round. In the winter the golf course is transformed into the Wirth Winter Sports Complex. Downhill and cross-country skiers, snowshoers, snow tubers, and sledders have opportunities for recreation in the snow.

Theodore Wirth Regional Park surrounds Birch Pond, Wirth Lake, and Bassett Creek, and borders the southern end of Twin Lake and the southwestern end of Sweeney Lake.

The Grand Rounds Parkway system runs through the park and to the north (Victory Memorial Parkway) with 3.54 miles of bike trails and 3.54 miles of walking trails. Victory Memorial Parkway, bordering the northwest edge of Minneapolis, is lined with plaques memorializing the servicemen from Hennepin County who died in World War I. Other memorial features along the Parkway include a War Shrine, a Grand Army Circle, and the Lumberman Statue.

The full list of recreational activities to be enjoyed at Theodore Wirth Regional Park includes biking; hiking; skating; boating; fishing; golfing; nature interpretation; picnicking; swimming; ice fishing; downhill skiing; and cross-country skiing.

COST: Free.

DATE: Open year round.

> The Eloise Butler Wildflower Garden and Bird Sanctuary is open April 1–October 31: daily 7:30 a.m.–dusk.
>
> From I-94 westbound, take the Hwy. 55 exit. Proceed west on Hwy. 55 to Theodore Wirth Regional Park.

149

▲▲▲▲▲▲▲▲▲▲▲▲▲▲▲▲▲▲▲▲▲▲▲▲▲▲▲▲▲▲▲▲▲▲▲▲▲▲

RAMSEY COUNTY PARKS

Information: Ramsey County Parks and Recreation Department, 2015 N. Van Dyke St., Maplewood, MN 55109-3796 (612) 777-1707

BALD EAGLE-OTTER LAKE REGIONAL PARK

Hugo Rd., White Bear Township, MN 55110 (612) 777-1707

Bald Eagle-Otter Lake Regional Park is a thriving habitat for many species of wildlife such as deer, fox, beaver, and a variety of birds, as well as more scarce species such as ospreys and otters. This thriving habitat has extensive woods, wetlands, and grasslands. At the heart of the park is the Tamarack Nature Center. Hiking and cross-country ski trails begin at the center and go throughout the 320-acre site. The east side of Bald Eagle Lake features great fishing, a picnic area, swimming beach, and boat launch.

COST: Free.

HOURS: Open year round, daily 1/2 hour before sunrise–1/2 hour after sunset.

> From I-35E northbound, take the Hwy. 96 exit. Turn right onto Hwy. 96 and go east to Hwy. 61. Turn left onto Hwy. 61 and proceed north to Buffalo St. Turn left onto Buffalo St. and go west to Hugo Rd. Turn right onto Hugo Rd. and proceed north to the entrance of the park on the left.

BATTLE CREEK REGIONAL PARK

Upper Afton Rd., St. Paul, MN 55119 (612) 777-1707

Battle Creek Regional Park is a 1,840-acre natural area filled with extensive areas of woods, wetlands, and grasslands, located within the highly developed urban environment of St. Paul. The 4 miles of paved biking and hiking trails and 5 miles of groomed cross-country ski trails allow visitors to view the pristine landscape and the many species of wildlife, including deer, fox, herons, egrets, and hawks. At the heart of the park is a large group picnic pavilion. The site includes a children's play area, a large informal game field, and walking paths. An evening concert series is provided Tuesdays throughout the summer season. Sledding and tobogganing hills are also available for winter activities. The lower creek area of the park at Hwy. 61 provides some of the most scenic areas in the Twin Cities, with sandstone bluffs and steep wooded slopes bordering each side of the creek.

COST: Free.

HOURS: Open year round, daily 1/2 hour before sunrise–1/2 hour after sunset.

▲▲▲▲▲▲▲▲▲▲▲▲▲▲▲▲▲▲▲▲▲▲▲▲▲▲▲▲▲▲▲▲▲▲▲▲▲

From I-94 eastbound, take the McKnight Rd. exit. Proceed south on McKnight to Upper Afton Rd. Turn left onto Upper Afton Rd. and go east to the entrance of the park on the left.

LONG LAKE REGIONAL PARK

Old Hwy. 8, New Brighton, MN 55112 (612) 777-1707

This 218-acre Regional Park is comprised of cattail marshes, oak woods, and a nine-acre restored prairie. The park also includes 1-1/2 miles of shoreline on Long Lake and a natural area around Rush Lake. The natural area includes 3 miles of paved bike/hike trails and 2 miles of cross-country ski trails. The park has three main activity areas: a beach, picnic area, and boat launch. The large group picnic area includes a large pavilion; game field; volleyball court; hiking/biking trails; and a handicapped-accessible play area. The boat launch area is on the south end of Long Lake and includes a shore fishing area.

COST: Free.

HOURS: Open year round, daily 1/2 hour before sunrise–1/2 hour after sunset. Swimming at the beach area Memorial Day–Labor Day.

From I-35W northbound, take the Hwy. 96 exit. Go west on Hwy. 96 to Old Hwy. 8. Turn left onto Old Hwy. 8 and follow south to the entrance of the park on the right.

From I-35E northbound, take the I-694 exit. Go west on I-694 to I-35W. Take I-35W north to Hwy. 96. Proceed west on Hwy. 96 to Old Hwy. 8. Turn left onto Old Hwy. 8 and follow south to the entrance of the park on the right.

PHALEN-KELLER REGIONAL PARK

Hwy. 61, Maplewood, MN 55109 Information (612) 777-1707
Phalen Lakeside Activities Center (612) 771-7507
Phalen Beach (612) 776-9833
Phalen Recreation Center (612) 298-5721
Cross-country ski trail information (612) 266-6445
Phalen Golf Course (612) 778-0413
For complete concert schedule for the Phalen Amphitheater, call (612) 266-6400

Keller Regional Park, Ramsey County's oldest park, is comprised of 103 acres. The chain of lakes (Kohlman; Gervais; Spoon; Keller; Round; Phalen) runs through the park. The lakes are popular locations for boating and fishing. A boat access ramp is located at Spoon Lake. Other recreational activities available at Keller Regional Park

▲▲▲▲▲▲▲▲▲▲▲▲▲▲▲▲▲▲▲▲▲▲▲▲▲▲▲▲▲▲▲▲▲▲▲▲▲▲

include volleyball court, baseball and softball fields, archery butts, a tot lot, and a bon-fire area.

Phalen Park highlights include Phalen Lake, Phalen Beach, a picnic area and pavilion. The Phalen Lakeside Activities Center provides rentals (paddleboats, canoes, rowboats, electric trolling motors, windsurfers, and sailboats) and lessons (canoeing, windsurfing, and sailing). Phalen Golf Course is a 6,100-yard par 70 course with a driving range. Phalen 18-hole stretches along the west side of Phalen Lake and picnic grounds. In the winter, Phalen Golf Course provides 10K of groomed intermediate-level cross-country ski trails, instruction, equipment rental, and concessions. An ice rink is available at Phalen Recreation Center in the winter. The Phalen Amphitheater is home to many summer musical and theatrical events.

Paved biking and walking paths connect several segments of the park. These paths also connect to the extensive path system in Phalen Regional Park immediately south of Keller. The path system in Keller Regional Park has a direct connection to the 18-mile Willard Munger State Trail, which extends from St. Paul to Pine Point Park.

COST: Free.

HOURS: Open year round, daily 1/2 hour before sunrise– 1/2 hour after sunset. Phalen Beach is open Memorial Day weekend–Labor Day. Cross-country ski trails are open December–mid-February. Phalen Recreation Center summer hours: Monday–Friday, 10 a.m.–9 p.m.

From I-35E northbound, take the Hwy. 36 exit. Proceed east on Hwy. 36 to Hwy. 61. Proceed south on Hwy. 61 to the Phalen-Keller Regional Park. Several park entrances are located along each side of Hwy. 61. The Phalen Lakeside Activities Center is at 1530 Phalen Drive; Phalen Beach at 1400 Phalen Drive; Phalen Golf Course at 1615 Phalen Drive; Phalen Recreation Center at 1000 E. Wheelock Pkwy.

▲▲▲▲▲▲▲▲▲▲▲▲▲▲▲▲▲▲▲▲▲▲▲▲▲▲▲▲▲▲▲▲▲▲▲

ST. PAUL PARKS

COMO REGIONAL PARK

Information: City of Saint Paul, Division of Parks and Recreation, 300 City Hall Annex, 25 W. 4th St., St. Paul, MN 55102
General parks information (612) 266-6400
Conservatory (612) 489-1740
Picnic permits (612) 488-7291
Como Pool (612) 489-2811
O'Neil Amusement Rides (612) 488-4771

This 450-acre Regional Park truly has something for everyone. Como Regional Park has provided recreational activities for visitors over the past 120 years. Como Lake, located within the park, is surrounded by a 1.67-mile path. The Department of Natural Resources reports excellent bass fishing in the lake along with some walleyes. Only car-top-carried boats are allowed on the lake.

Como Park also features the Lakeside Pavilion (1360 N. Lexington Pkwy.); McMurray Field, the site of many municipal athletic events (N. Lexington Pkwy.); Como Zoo (Midway Pkwy. and Kaufman Dr.); Como Conservatory and Ordway Japanese Garden (1325 Aida Pl.); downhill skiing; 7K of groomed trails and 3K of lighted cross-country skiing trails; 1.75-mile biking trail; 1.54-mile walking trail; 2.3-mile biking/pedestrian trail; Como Pool and a state-of-the art wading pool (Horton Ave. and N. Lexington Pkwy.); O'Neil Amusement Rides, pony rides, and miniature golf at the south end of the Zoo.

COST: Varies according to activities.

HOURS: Open year round, sunrise–11 p.m. Como Pool June 10–Labor Day. O'Neil Amusement Rides spring and summer through Labor Day as weather permits, 10 a.m.–9 p.m. Pony rides and miniature golf Memorial Day–Labor Day: weekdays noon–6 p.m.; weekends and holidays 11 a.m.–7 p.m.

> From I-35W, take Hwy. 36 east to Lexington Ave. Go south on Lexington Ave. to Lexington Pkwy. Lexington Pkwy. takes you into the north end of Como Park.
>
> From I-35W, take Hwy. 36 east to Snelling Ave. (Hwy. 51). Proceed south on Snelling to Larpenteur. Turn left onto Larpenteur and follow to Hamline Ave. Turn right onto Hamline Ave. and follow to Midway Pkwy. Turn left on

▲▲▲▲▲▲▲▲▲▲▲▲▲▲▲▲▲▲▲▲▲▲▲▲▲▲▲▲▲▲▲▲▲▲▲

> Midway Pkwy. and follow into Como Park and the Como Zoo.
>
> From I-35E or I-94, take the Rice St. exit. Follow Rice St. north to Como Ave. Follow Como Ave. northeast to Como Park.
>
> From I-94, take the Snelling Ave. exit. Proceed north on Snelling Ave. to Como Ave. Turn right onto Como Ave. and follow into the park, or from Como Ave. turn left onto Hamline and follow to Midway Pkwy. Turn right onto Midway Pkwy. and follow into the Como Zoo parking lot or the park.

HIDDEN FALLS/CROSBY FARM

Information: City of St. Paul, Division of Parks and Recreation, 300 City Hall Annex, 25 W. 4th St., St. Paul, MN 55102 General parks information (612) 266-6400

This 729-acre Regional Park provides 8 miles of paved trails. They run along wooded bottomlands next to the Mississippi River, along the marshes of Crosby Lake and Upper Lake, and past scenic picnic areas to Mississippi River Blvd. The Regional Park is home to the Crosby Park Nature Center, which offers a variety of nature programming. Watergate Marina is also located within the park boundaries on the banks of the Mississippi River.

COST: Free.

HOURS: Open year round. Crosby and Hidden Falls South: sunrise–9 p.m.
Hidden Falls North: sunrise–10 p.m.

> From I-35E, take the Shepard Rd. exit southwest. You can reach the park off Shepard Rd. from Crosby Lake Rd. or Crosby Farm Rd. Crosby Farm Rd. brings you to the Nature Center and Watergate Marina. Crosby Lake Rd. brings you to Crosby Lake.

▲▲▲▲▲▲▲▲▲▲▲▲▲▲▲▲▲▲▲▲▲▲▲▲▲▲▲▲▲▲▲▲▲▲▲▲▲▲

WASHINGTON COUNTY PARKS

COTTAGE GROVE RAVINE REGIONAL PARK

Information: Washington County Parks Div., Lake Elmo Park Reserve, 1515 Keats Ave. N., Lake Elmo, MN 55042 (612) 731-3851

Cottage Grove Ravine Regional Park is 450 scenic acres of hills, and heavily wooded ravines. The park is used often because of its picnic areas, play structure, and 7 miles of hiking and cross-country skiing trails.

COST: Vehicle permits are required, $3 daily, $14 annual. You can purchase permits at Lake Elmo Park Reserve, the Public Works Department, and the license bureaus of the cities of Cottage Grove, Forest Lake, Stillwater, and Woodbury.

HOURS: Open year round, 7 a.m.–1/2 hour after sunset.

> From I-94, take Hwy. 19 south to the Cottage Grove Ravine Regional Park on the left side.

LAKE ELMO PARK RESERVE

Information: Washington County Parks Division, Lake Elmo Park Reserve, 1515 Keats Ave. N., Lake Elmo, MN 55042 (612) 731-3851

Lake Elmo Park Reserve is comprised of forest and prairie; 80% is set aside for preservation and protection, and will be allowed to return to a natural state. Developed areas of the Reserve offer opportunities for camping; swimming; fishing; boating; 8 miles of horseback riding trails; picnicking; archery; 20 miles of hiking trails; 12 miles of cross-country ski trails; and 5 miles of bicycle trails.

COST: Vehicle park permits are required, $3 daily, $14 annual. You can purchase permits at Lake Elmo Park Reserve, the Public Works Department, and the license bureaus of the cities of Cottage Grove, Forest Lake, Stillwater, and Woodbury.

HOURS: Open year round, 7 a.m.–1/2 hour after sunset.

> From I-94, take Hwy. 19 north into the Lake Elmo Park Reserve.

STATE PARKS

AFTON STATE PARK

Information: Afton State Park Manager, 6959 Peller Ave. S., Hastings, MN 55033 (612) 436-5391

Experience spectacular views of the St. Croix Valley at Afton State Park, which lies on the bluffs overlooking the St. Croix River. The park features rolling grasslands and deep forested ravines, which drop 300 feet to the river. Hikers and skiers enjoy the challenge of the steep, rugged terrain. The forested ravines are home to a wide variety of wildlife. You can often see migrating hawks and eagles soar above the bluffs. Other recreational opportunities include a swimming beach; 18 miles of hiking trail; 4 miles of bike trail; 5 miles of horseback riding trail; picnic grounds; a visitor center with interpretive displays; and 24 backpacking campsites. The campground, swimming beach, and interior of the park are accessible only by trail.

COST: Daily or annual permits, required for all vehicles entering a state park, may be purchased at the park. A $4 permit is good for two consecutive days. An $18 annual permit is good for the calendar year.

HOURS: Open year round. The park gate is closed 10 p.m.–8 a.m., except to registered campers.

> Afton State Park is located 40 minutes east of the Twin Cities. From I-94 eastbound, take the Co. Rd. 15 exit. Proceed about 7 miles south on Co. Rd. 15 to Co. Rd. 20. Proceed about 3 miles east on Co. Rd. 20 to Afton State Park.

FORT SNELLING STATE PARK

Fort Snelling State Park, Hwy. 5 and Post Rd., St. Paul, MN 55111
Reservations or general information (612) 725-2390
Pike Island Interpretive Center (612) 726-9247

Fort Snelling State Park, located at the confluence of the Mississippi and Minnesota Rivers, is a wonderful oasis in the midst of a highly developed urban area. There are two spring-fed lakes within the park. Snelling Lake, the main-use lake, features a wonderful beach staffed with lifeguards in summer. The lake also has a small boat access for electric trolling boats only, and a fishing pier. Pike Island, one of two islands within the park, is accessible only by foot. Picnic Island is accessible by vehicle.

Other recreational opportunities include a 5-mile bike trail down the bluffs of the

▲▲▲▲▲▲▲▲▲▲▲▲▲▲▲▲▲▲▲▲▲▲▲▲▲▲▲▲▲▲▲▲▲▲▲

Mississippi River (Minnehaha Trail); many other bike trails connecting to the State Park; 18 miles of hiking and cross-country ski trails; a specially groomed hiking trail for winter use on Pike Island; Pike Island Interpretive Center, featuring nature programs year round; paddleboat and canoe rental in the warmer months and snowshoe rental in the winter; picnic areas with park shelters; and volleyball courts. An added feature children love is the chance to watch planes land because of the park's close proximity to the International Airport.

COST: Daily or annual permits, required for all vehicles entering a state park, may be purchased at the park. A $4 permit is good for two consecutive days. An $18 annual permit is good for the calendar year.

HOURS: Day use only, year round. Park hours 8 a.m.–10 p.m.

From I-494, take the Hwy. 5 exit (this will be the first exit after the International Airport exit). Go east on Hwy. 5 to Post Rd. Turn right onto Post Rd. and follow until it dead-ends in the park.

WILLIAM O'BRIEN STATE PARK

Information: William O'Brien State Park Manager, 16821 O'Brien Trail N., Marine-on-St. Croix, MN 55047 (612) 433-0500

Camping reservations (800) 246-2267

This 1,353-acre State Park located along the St. Croix River features scenic bluffs; floodplain; forests; lakes; marshes; numerous springs; streams flowing through heavily wooded valleys and ravines; and rolling meadows. Diverse wildlife populations are able to thrive in the rich habitat of William O'Brien State Park. Frequent wildlife sightings include white-tail deer; mink; beaver; woodchucks; fox; herons; raptors; and more. The rare trumpeter swan can be seen in the park during spring and fall migrations. Fishing the St. Croix River for northern pike, walleye, bass, and brown trout is another popular activity. The William O'Brien Interpretive Center offers displays and many programs throughout the year relating to the natural and cultural features of the area. Programs include hikes; demonstrations; canoe floats; bike tours; slide shows; movies; ski tours; and special events. Canoes can be rented within the park, with shuttle service provided in the summer.

William O'Brien State Park's comprehensive list of recreational opportunities includes 11 miles of hiking trails; 10 miles of cross-country ski trails; access to a county bike trail system; summer and winter camping; fishing; swimming at Lake Alice Beach; canoeing; picnic areas with shelters; and nature center programs.

COST: Daily or annual permits, required for all vehicles entering a state park, may be purchased at the park. A $4 permit is good for two consecutive days. An $18 annual permit is good for the calendar year.

▲▲▲▲▲▲▲▲▲▲▲▲▲▲▲▲▲▲▲▲▲▲▲▲▲▲▲▲▲▲▲▲▲▲▲

HOURS: Day use only, year round. Park hours 8 a.m.–10 p.m.

Located within an hour's drive of the Twin Cities area, on the St. Croix River. William O'Brien State Park is on Hwy. 95, just 2 miles north of Marine-on-St. Croix. From I-35W or I-35E, take the I-694 exit. Proceed east on I-694 to Hwy. 36. Proceed east on Hwy. 36 to Hwy. 95. Follow Hwy. 95 north, and 2 miles past Marine-On-St. Croix to William O'Brien State Park.

NERSTRAND BIG WOODS STATE PARK

For further information contact the Nerstrand Woods State Park Manager, 9700 170th St. E., Nerstrand, MN 55053 (507) 334-8848

Nerstrand Big Woods, a 1,100-acre State Park, is one of the last remnants of the Big Woods. With rolling hills and valleys, the Big Woods is comprised of sugar maple, basswood, elm, green ash, and ironwood trees. Visitors love to study the 50 varieties of wildflowers and countless varieties of ferns and mushrooms, or to observe the diverse species of birds that make their home in the Big Woods. Many visit the Big Woods in the autumn because of its spectacular display of fall colors. Prairie Creek and a picturesque waterfall are within the park boundaries. Recreational activities include 13 miles of hiking trails; 8 miles of cross-country ski trails; 5 miles of snowmobile trails; 61 semi-modern campsites; and 18 rustic pioneer campsites.

COST: Daily or annual permits, required for all vehicles entering a state park, may be purchased at the park. A $4 permit is good for two consecutive days. An $18 annual permit is good for the calendar year.

HOURS: Day use, year round. Park hours 8 a.m.–10 p.m. except for registered campers.

Nerstrand Woods is located about 45 miles directly south of the Twin Cities, about 11 miles southeast of Northfield. Take Hwy. 3 into Northfield to Hwy. 246. Follow Hwy. 246 southeast out of Northfield to Co. Rd. 27. Turn right onto Co. Rd. 27 and follow to the Nerstrand Big Woods.

From I-35W southbound, take the Hwy. 59 exit. Follow Hwy. 59 into Northfield to Hwy. 3. Follow Hwy. 3 southeast to Hwy. 246. Follow Hwy. 246 southeast out of Northfield to Co. Rd. 27. Turn right onto Co. Rd. 27 and follow to Nerstrand Big Woods.

MINNESOTA VALLEY TRAIL RECREATION AREA

*Information: Minnesota Valley Trail Manager, 19825 Park Blvd., Jordan, MN 55352
(612) 492-6400*

The Minnesota Valley Trail currently runs from Belle Plaine to Chaska and Shakopee. It was established by the State Legislature in 1969 to provide a recreational travel route "through areas which have significant scenic, historic, scientific, or recreational qualities." When completed eventually, the trail will follow the Minnesota River (the lower Minnesota River Valley) for 75 miles through 24,000 acres of floodplain marsh, grassland, and woodland, from Fort Snelling State Park to the City of LeSueur. Nature and wildlife lovers have ample opportunity to study the diverse plant communities and resident birds and wildlife along the trail. Hundreds of thousands of songbirds and waterfowl are attracted to the extensive wetlands during their annual migrations. In the upland areas, you can see white-tail deer; rabbits; fox; hawks; owls; etc.

The headquarters for the Minnesota Valley Trail provides camping; picnic grounds; fishing; 22 miles of horseback riding; mountain biking; and hiking. Be sure to write for a brochure and map of all the trail entrances and highlights at the Minnesota Valley Trail address listed above; write to the Department of Natural Resources, Division of Parks and Recreation Information Center, 500 Lafayette Rd., St. Paul, MN 55155–4040; or call (612) 296-6157 within the metro area, or toll-free (800) 766-6000 from outside the metro area but within Minnesota.

COST: Daily or annual permits, required for all vehicles entering a state park, may be purchased at the park. A $4 permit is good for two consecutive days. An $18 annual permit is good for the calendar year.

HOURS: Day use only, year round. Park hours 8 a.m.–10 p.m. except for registered campers.

The Recreation Area and Facility Headquarters for the Minnesota Valley Trail is located between Jordan and Belle Plaine on Co. Rd. 57.

From Hwy. 169 southbound, follow Hwy. 169 to the first set of stoplights in Jordan. Take a right at the light and go 3 blocks to Co. Rd. 57. Take a left onto Co. Rd. 57 and proceed about 5 miles to the Lawrence Unit, where the camping areas are found.

From Hwy. 169 northbound, follow Hwy. 169 north of Belle Plaine about 3 miles to Co. Rd. 57. Turn left onto Co. Rd. 57 and follow a little over a mile to the Lawrence Unit, where the camping areas are found.

Many Twin Cities lakes have excellent fishing.

Photo by Susan Schreifels

PERFORMING ARTS

▲▲▲▲▲▲▲▲▲▲▲▲▲▲▲▲▲▲▲▲▲▲▲▲▲▲▲▲▲▲▲▲▲▲▲▲▲▲

CHANHASSEN DINNER THEATRES

501 W. 78th St., Chanhassen, MN 55317 (612) 934-1525 (800) 362-3515

The Chanhassen Dinner Theatre, with four theatres under one roof, is the nation's largest professional dinner theatre. Since 1968, Chanhassen has entertained more than 5 million guests with lavish blockbuster musicals and comedies. Guests relax and enjoy tableside service with entrees selected from a delicious menu. AAA magazine says, "any Twin Cities trip should include an evening at Chanhassen."

COST: Varies upon play choice. Dinner and show tickets range from $27 to $49 per person. Ask about discounts for students, seniors, and groups of 15 or more.

HOURS: Open year round with performances Wednesday–Sunday; Tuesday–Sunday in some seasons. Matinees and evening performances available.

From I-494, exit at State Hwy. 5. Go west on State Hwy. 5 about 6 miles to the intersection of 5 and Great Plains Blvd. Turn right (north) on Great Plains Blvd., go over the railroad tracks, and take the first left.

From I-94 westbound from Wisconsin, North St. Paul, or the U of M, take the I-94 exit going west onto I-35W going south. Follow I-35W south to Crosstown 62 west. Stay in the far left lane of the Crosstown as it branches off to the left and the sign indicates Hwy. 212. When the Crosstown passes under I-494 it becomes State Hwy. 5. Continue 6 miles on State Hwy. 5 to the intersection of 5 and Great Plains Blvd. Turn right (north) on Great Plains Blvd., go over the railroad tracks, and take the first left.

From west of Chanhassen, take State Hwy. 5 east to the intersection of 5 and Great Plains Blvd. Turn left (north) on Great Plains Blvd., go over the railroad tracks, and take the first left.

▲▲▲▲▲▲▲▲▲▲▲▲▲▲▲▲▲▲▲▲▲▲▲▲▲▲▲▲▲▲▲▲

Huck Finn and Tom Sawyer hook a big one in The Children's Theatre Company's performance of The Adventures of Tom Sawyer.

▲▲▲▲▲▲▲▲▲▲▲▲▲▲▲▲▲▲▲▲▲▲▲▲▲▲▲▲▲▲▲▲▲▲▲

CHILDREN'S THEATRE COMPANY

2400 Third Ave. S., Minneapolis, MN 55404 (612) 874-0400

The Children's Theatre Company is the largest professional children's theatre in the nation. It produces significant theater experiences, created especially for young people and their families. Plays have included new works based on contemporary children's literature, such as "Animal Fables from Aesop"; Dr. Seuss' "How the Grinch Stole Christmas"; "Amazing Grace"; timely original works such as "The Troubles: Children of Belfast," "Two African Tales," and "On the Wings of the Hummingbird: Tales of Trinidad"; adaptations of children's classics such as "The Jungle Book," "Little Women," and "Pinocchio"; and fine dramatic literature including "A Midsummer Night's Dream," "Our Town," and "The Miser." A theater arts training program teaching drama, dance, and voice is available for children 8–18 through the Children's Theatre Company.

COST: Regular prices $9.50–$24, depending on age and seating. Ticket discounts available to groups, or for preview performances. Rush tickets are available. Parking free.

HOURS: Tuesday–Saturday 7:30 p.m.; Saturday 11 a.m. and 2 p.m.; Sunday 2 p.m.–5 p.m.

> The Children's Theatre Company is next to the Minneapolis Institute of Arts. Parking is free in the ramp located south of the Theatre and in the adjacent lot.
>
> From I-94 westbound, take the 11th St. exit and turn left at the second set of lights (3rd Ave. S.). Follow 3rd Ave. S. to W. 24th St., and look for the theatre on the right.
>
> From I-94 eastbound, take the Lyndale/Hennepin Ave. exit. Take the Lyndale (left) fork when the road divides. Proceed on Lyndale to W. 24th St. and turn left. Follow W. 24th St. to 3rd Ave. S. and turn right onto 3rd Ave. S. Follow 3rd Ave. S. and look for the theatre on the right.
>
> From I-35W southbound, take the 11th Ave. exit. Turn left onto 11th Ave. and proceed to Franklin Ave. Turn right onto Franklin Ave. and proceed to 3rd Ave. S. Turn left and go to W. 24th St. and look for the theatre on the right.
>
> From I-35W northbound, take the 31st St./Lake St. exit. Turn left onto 31st St., follow to 1st Ave. S. and turn right. Follow 1st Ave. S. to W. 24th St. and turn right. Follow W. 24th to 3rd Ave. S. and turn right. You will see the entrance to the theatre on the right side of 3rd Ave. S.

▲▲▲▲▲▲▲▲▲▲▲▲▲▲▲▲▲▲▲▲▲▲▲▲▲▲▲▲▲▲▲▲

From I-394 eastbound, take the Hennepin Ave./Dunwoody exit, follow the signs for Lyndale Ave. (stay to the left). Continue south on Lyndale Ave. to W. 24th St. Turn left onto W. 24th St. and proceed to 3rd Ave. S. Turn right and look for the Theatre on the right.

CHILDREN'S THEATRE COMPANY
Seating Chart

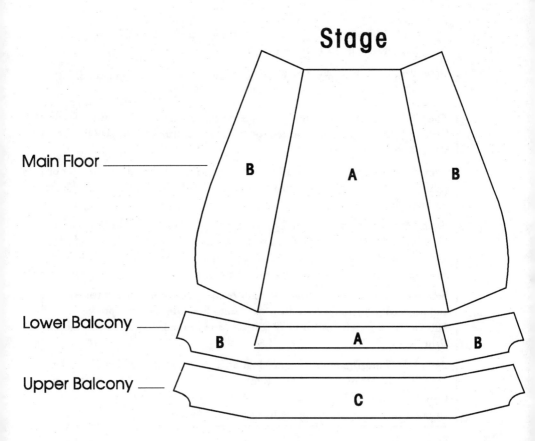

▲▲▲▲▲▲▲▲▲▲▲▲▲▲▲▲▲▲▲▲▲▲▲▲▲▲▲▲▲▲▲▲▲▲▲▲▲▲

CHILD'S PLAY THEATRE COMPANY

1001 Hwy.7, Hopkins, MN 55343 (612) 925-5250

Child's Play Theatre Company has been presenting affordable and innovative productions of classic fairy tales and lesser-known stories since 1984. Child's Play is one of the few professional theatres in the state where young people are cast in almost all the roles. You're invited to experience this theatre's unique world of magic and whimsy.

COST: Adults $8, children and seniors $6, children under 2 free.

HOURS: Show times and locations vary; please call for a complete schedule.

ETHNIC DANCE THEATRE

1940 Hennepin Ave. S., Minneapolis, MN 55403 (612) 872-0024

Through the re-creation and presentation of traditional ethnic dance, music, and arts, the Ethnic Dance Theatre seeks to foster understanding and awareness of world cultures. Performances reflect a strong sensitivity to differences between cultures and their respective dance and musical forms. Since 1974 the Ethnic Dance Theatre has presented performances locally and throughout the Midwest. Audiences can experience everything from a stunning Chinese ribbon dance to an exotic Egyptian woman's dance to a humorous cowboy dance from Mexico's Norteno region. Rehearsals are open to the public beginning the first Sunday after Labor Day and continuing until mid-July.

COST: Attending rehearsals is free.

HOURS: Rehearsal hours Sunday and Thursday 7 p.m.–10 p.m.

> From I-94, take the Hennepin Ave. exit. Follow Hennepin Ave. to Franklin Ave. The Dance Theatre is on the corner of Hennepin and Franklin Ave.

GREAT AMERICAN HISTORY THEATER

30 E. 10th St., St. Paul, MN 55101 (Located in the Science Museum of Minnesota East Building) (612) 292-4323

This professional theatre organization reflects the lives of the people of Minnesota and the Midwest. It dramatizes regional life by commissioning, producing, and touring plays about the history, folklore, and social issues of its own region and other locales.

COST: $9-$15. Additional discounts for groups. Box office telephone 292-4323, group tickets 292-4325.

▲▲

HOURS: Monday-Friday 9 a.m.-5 p.m.; Saturday-Sunday 11 a.m.-5 p.m.

> Located in the Arts and Science Center East Building.
>
> From I-94 eastbound, take the 10th St. exit. Follow 10th St. to the Great American History Theater.
>
> From I-94 westbound, take the 6th St. exit to Wabasha. From Wabasha, follow 10th St. to the Great American History Theater.
>
> From S. 11th St., exit to Cedar St. and follow Cedar to 10th.
>
> From the N. 10th/Wacouta exit, follow 10th to Cedar St.

GUTHRIE THEATER

725 Vineland Place, Minneapolis, MN 55403 Ticket office: (612) 377-2224

The Guthrie Theater is America's leading classical repertory theater. One of its most popular productions, Charles Dickens' "A Christmas Carol," has become a Twin Cities holiday tradition. Access services include interpretation in American sign language, wheelchair accessibility, and audio description. Discounts are available for groups, seniors, schools, students, and corporations. Also available are guided tours, a gift shop, and costume rental.

COST: "A Christmas Carol" $13-$36. Half-price tickets for children available for all performances except Saturday evenings. Student and senior discounts available.

HOURS: Season generally runs May–February. "A Christmas Carol" runs late November–December.

> From I-94 westbound, take the Hennepin/Lyndale exit. Proceed north on Lyndale and get into the left lane. Turn left onto Vineland Place at the second stoplight. Follow Vineland Place to the Theater.
>
> From Hwy. 394, take the Hennepin-Dunwoody Blvd. exit. Turn right onto Lyndale Ave. (first stoplight). Follow Lyndale to Vineland Place. Turn right onto Vineland Place and follow to the Theater.
>
> From I-35W northbound, take the I-94 exit. Go west on I-94 to the Hennepin/Lyndale exit. Follow Lyndale north, and get into the left lane as you come to Vineland Place. Turn left onto Vineland Place at the second stoplight and follow to the Theater.

Continues on page 168

▲▲▲▲▲▲▲▲▲▲▲▲▲▲▲▲▲▲▲▲▲▲▲▲▲▲▲▲▲▲▲▲▲

Photo by Gerald Gustafson, courtesy Great American History Theatre

Great American History Theatre's performance of Days of Rondo re-tells little Evelyn's life in St. Paul's African-American neighborhood from the Post-Depression 30's to the prosperity and promise of the fabulous 40's.

▲▲

From I-94 eastbound, take the Hennepin/Lyndale exit. Go south on Lyndale to Vineland Place. Turn right onto Vineland Place and follow to the Theater.

Parking is available in the lot adjacent to Parade Stadium just north of the Theater, and in the lot next to the Alliance Life Insurance Company of North America building south of the Theater.

HISTORIC ORPHEUM THEATRE *(Seating charts follow State Theater)*

910 Hennepin Ave. S., Minneapolis, MN 55402 Information: (612) 339-7007
Tickets by phone: (612) 989-5151

Built in 1921, this nostalgic Theatre has been completely restored to its original splendor. The Theatre has hosted such diverse attractions as "The Phantom of the Opera," "Miss Saigon," Raffi, Alvin and the Chipmunks, and Shari Lewis and Lambchop. The Theatre is also available for rental.

COST: $15–$67 depending on performance and seating.

HOURS: Box office hours Monday–Friday 9 a.m.–6 p.m.; Saturday and Sunday noon–5 p.m. Performance times vary, so please call for more details.

From I-94 westbound, take the 11th St. exit. Follow 11th St. about 5-6 blocks to Hennepin Ave. Turn right onto Hennepin and follow 1-1/2 blocks to the Orpheum Theatre on the left side of Hennepin between 9th and 10th Sts.

From I-94 eastbound, take the Dunwoody/Hennepin exit. Turn left at the first stoplight (Hennepin Ave.). Follow Hennepin about 6-7 blocks. The Orpheum Theatre is on the left side of Hennepin between 9th and 10th Sts.

From I-35W northbound, take the 11th St./Grant St. exit. Follow 11th about 5-6 blocks to Hennepin Ave. Turn right onto Hennepin and go 1-1/2 blocks north. The Orpheum Theatre is on the left side of Hennepin between 9th and 10th Sts.

From I-35W southbound, take the 11th St. exit. Go about 5-6 blocks to Hennepin Ave. Turn right onto Hennepin and go 1-1/2 blocks. The Orpheum Theatre is on the left side of Hennepin between 9th and 10th Sts.

Ample parking is available on all four sides of the Theatre. Suggested ramps are LaSalle Plaza Parking Ramp at 9th and Hennepin; Dayton's Ramp at 8th St.; the Conservatory Ramp at 9th and LaSalle; and the Target Center at 4th, 5th, and 7th Sts.

▲▲▲▲▲▲▲▲▲▲▲▲▲▲▲▲▲▲▲▲▲▲▲▲▲▲▲▲▲▲▲▲▲▲▲▲

HISTORIC STATE THEATRE *(Seating chart follows Orpheum's chart)*

805 Hennepin Ave. S., Minneapolis, MN 55402

Information (612) 339-7007 Tickets by phone (612) 989-5151

Built in 1921 this nostalgic Theatre has been completely restored to its original splendor. The Theatre has been the host of such diverse productions as "Gypsy," "Joseph and the Amazing Technicolor Dreamcoat," and "Angels in America" (July '95). The Theatre is also available for rental.

COST: Ticket prices range from $15 to $67 depending on the performance and seating.

HOURS: Box office hours are Monday–Friday 9 a.m.–6 p.m. Saturday and Sunday noon–5 p.m.
Performances vary throughout the week so please call for more details.

From I-94 westbound, take the 11th St. exit. Follow 11th St. approximately 5-6 blocks to Hennepin Avenue. Turn right onto Hennepin Ave. The State Theatre is located 3 blocks north on the right side of Hennepin at the corner of 8th and Hennepin.

From I-94 eastbound, take the Dunwoody/Hennepin Ave. exit. Turn left at the first stoplight which is Hennepin Ave. Proceed on Hennepin Ave. approximately 6-7 blocks to The State Theatre on the right side of Hennepin at the corner of 8th and Hennepin.

From I-35W northbound, take the 11th St./Grant St. exit. Follow 11th St. approximately 5-6 blocks to Hennepin Ave. Turn right onto Hennepin Ave. and follow approximately 3 blocks to The State Theatre on the right side of Hennepin at the corner of 8th and Hennepin.

From I-35W southbound, take the 11th St. exit. Follow 11th St. approximately 5-6 blocks to Hennepin Ave. Turn right onto Hennepin Ave. and follow approximately 3 blocks to The State Theatre on the right side of Hennepin at the corner of 8th and Hennepin.

There is ample parking available on all four sides of the Theatre. Suggested ramps are LaSalle Plaza Parking Ramp at 9th and Hennepin; Dayton's Ramp at 8th St.; the Conservatory Ramp at 9th and LaSalle; and the Target Center at 4th, 5th, and 7th Sts.

THE *Orpheum*

BALCONY

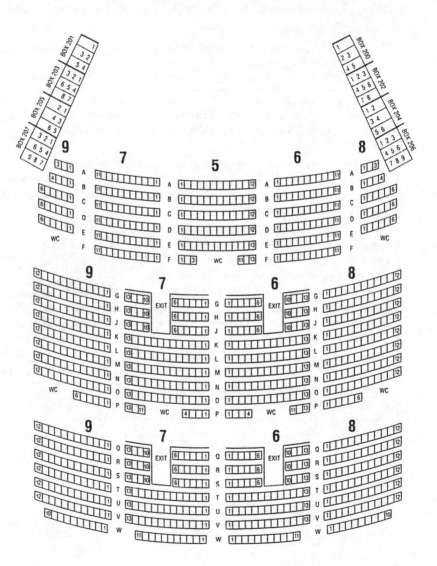

THE *Orpheum*

MAIN FLOOR

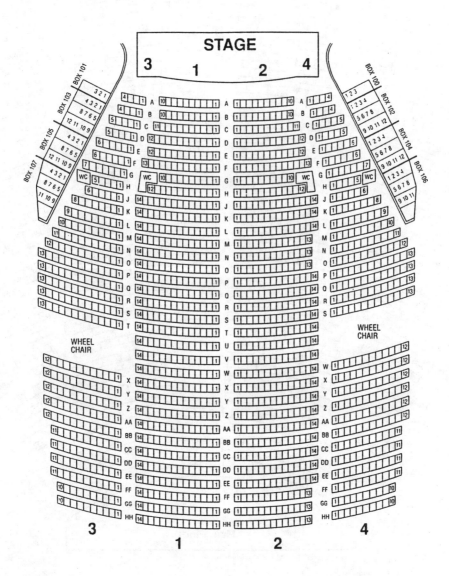

▲▲▲▲▲▲▲▲▲▲▲▲▲▲▲▲▲▲▲▲▲▲▲▲▲▲▲

The State Theatre

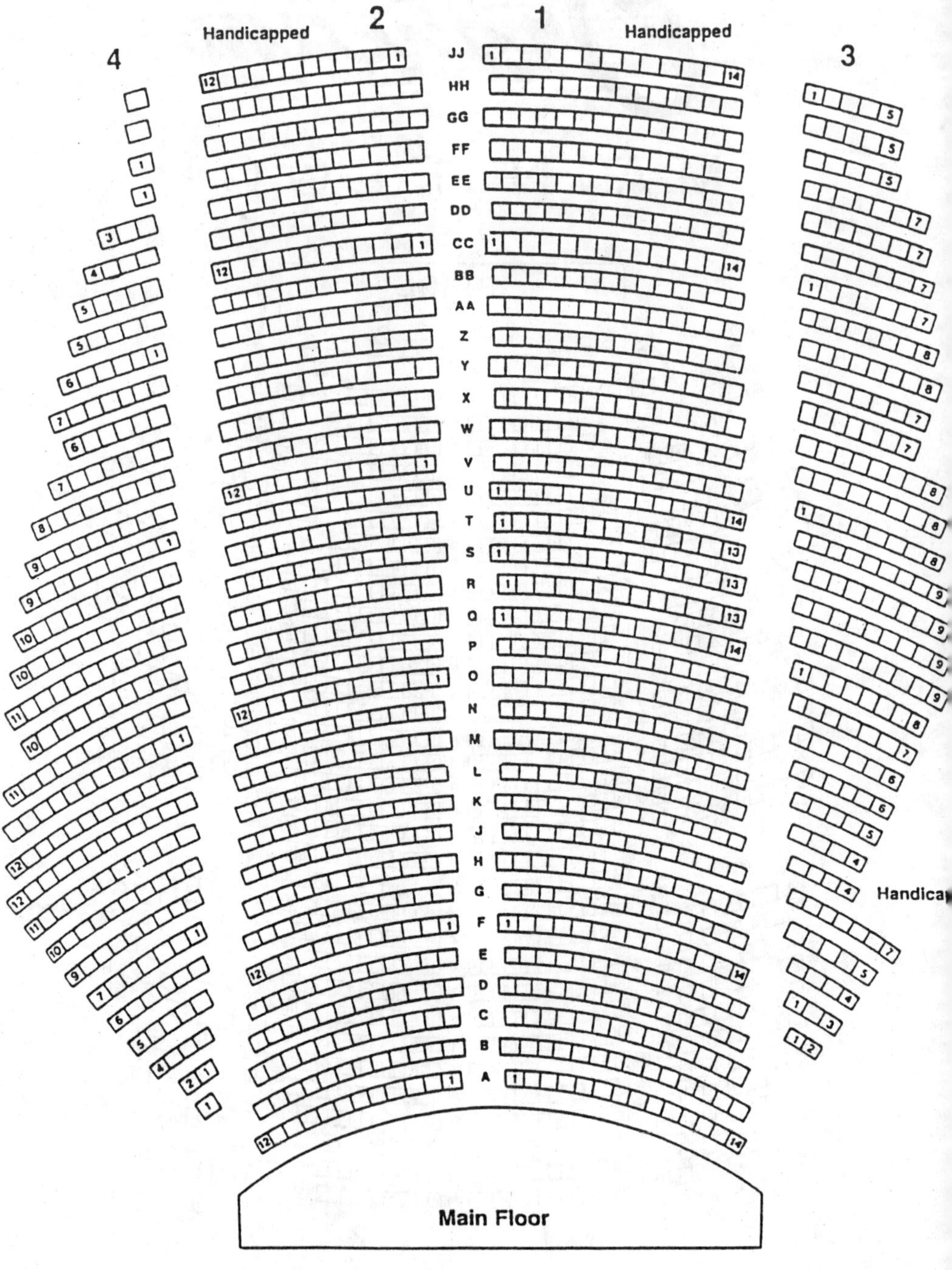

2 **1**

Handicapped   Handicapped

4 **3**

JJ HH GG FF EE DD CC BB AA Z Y X W V U T S R Q P O N M L K J H G F E D C B A

Main Floor

▲▲▲▲▲▲▲▲▲▲▲▲▲▲▲▲▲▲▲▲▲▲▲▲▲▲▲▲

The State Theatre

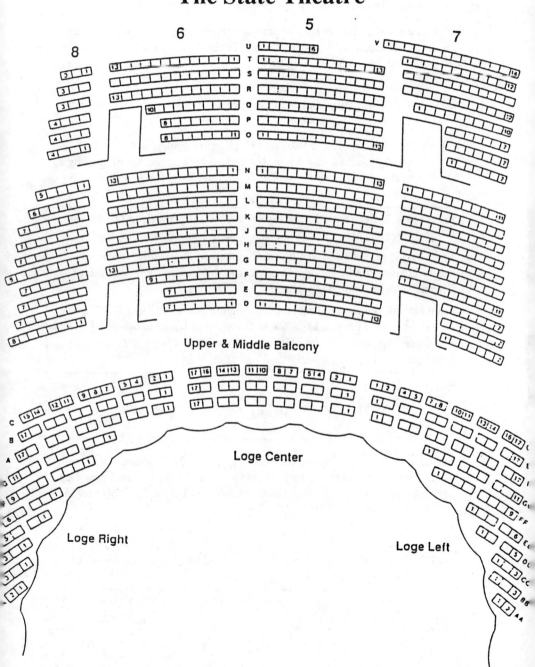

Upper & Middle Balcony

Loge Center

Loge Right

Loge Left

▲▲▲▲▲▲▲▲▲▲▲▲▲▲▲▲▲▲▲▲▲▲▲▲▲▲▲▲▲▲▲▲▲▲▲▲▲▲▲

ILLUSION THEATER

528 Hennepin Ave., Minneapolis, MN 55403 (612) 339-4944 (612) 338-8371

Entering its 21st season, Illusion Theater produces entertaining new works and area premieres about contemporary people and issues. Performances are recommended for middle school-age children and up. Call (612) 339-4944 with questions regarding age appropriateness.

COST: $10–$16; group, student, and senior discounts available. School matinee price $6 per student.

HOURS: Performances in 8th-floor theater Thursday, Friday, and Saturday 8 a.m.–5 p.m.; Sunday 3 p.m. No performance on Sunday of opening weekends. The 7th-floor office is open Monday–Friday 8:30 a.m.–5 p.m.

From Hwy. 394 eastbound, take the 6th St./local streets exit to 6th St. Follow 6th to Hennepin Ave. Theater is at 6th St. and Hennepin.

From I-35W northbound or I-94 westbound, take the 11th St./downtown exit to Hennepin Ave. Follow Hennepin to 6th St. Turn right onto 6th St. Theater is on 6th and Hennepin.

From I-35W southbound, take the Washington Ave. exit. From Washington, turn right onto 1st Ave. and follow to 6th St. Turn left onto 6th and follow to Hennepin Ave. Turn left onto Hennepin Ave. Theater is on 6th and Hennepin.

IN THE HEART OF THE BEAST PUPPET AND MASK THEATRE

1500 E. Lake St., Minneapolis, MN 55407 (612) 721-2535

Now in its 22nd year, In the Heart of the Beast Puppet and Mask Theatre creates full-length original shows for adults and families, and produces the much-loved May Day Parade and Festival every spring. Chosen as Best Children's Theatre by City Pages in 1994.

COST: Tickets for mainstage productions usually $5–$8.

HOURS: Contact the theatre box office for individual show times. Box office (612) 721-2535.

From I-35W, take the 31st St. exit and go 1 block to Lake St. Follow Lake St. east to the theatre.

▲▲▲▲▲▲▲▲▲▲▲▲▲▲▲▲▲▲▲▲▲▲▲▲▲▲▲▲▲▲▲▲▲▲▲

LAKESHORE PLAYERS THEATRE

4820 Stewart Ave., White Bear Lake, MN 55110 (612) 429-5674

Over 42 years of continuous operation has resulted in a highly professional live theater experience in an intimate space. A typical season, September–May, features a blend of musicals, drama, comedy, and children's theater focusing on family entertainment.

COST: Adults $10, students/seniors $9.

HOURS: The box office is open Monday–Friday 2–6 p.m. Performances are on weekends at variable times. Call for schedule.

> Follow Hwy. 96 east or Hwy. 61 north into downtown White Bear Lake. From Hwy. 61 and 96 northbound (Hwy. 96 will temporarily merge with Hwy. 61 before turning east again a few blocks north), turn right onto 4th St. and go 3 blocks to Stewart Ave. Turn left onto Stewart and follow 2 blocks to 6th St. The theater is on the corner of 6th and Stewart.

MINNESOTA ORCHESTRA/ORCHESTRA HALL

1111 Nicollet Mall, Minneapolis, MN 55403 (612) 371-5656

The Minnesota Orchestra presents year-round concerts of classical and popular music. The family classical music series, Adventures in Music, is presented September–May.

COST: Varies by concert.

HOURS: Concert and box office hours vary by program. Ticket office phone hours: Monday–Friday 9 a.m.–7 p.m.; Saturday 10 a.m.–5 p.m.; Sunday noon–5 p.m.

> Orchestra Hall is located in Minneapolis between Marquette Ave. and Nicollet Mall. From Hwy. 394 eastbound, take the 12th St. exit. Go 3 blocks east on 12th St. to Orchestra Hall.
>
> From I-35W northbound, take the 11th St./downtown exit. Follow 11th St. west about 3 blocks to Orchestra Hall.
>
> From I-94 westbound, take the 11th St./downtown exit. Follow 11th St. east about 3 blocks to Orchestra Hall.
>
> From I-35W southbound, take the Washington Ave. exit. Turn right onto Washington and follow to 2nd Ave. Turn left onto 2nd and go to 11th St. Turn right onto 11th and proceed about 1 block to Orchestra Hall.
>
> From I-94 eastbound, take the Hennepin Ave. exit. Turn left (north) onto Hennepin and proceed about 6 blocks to 12th St. Turn right onto 12th St. and follow to Marquette Ave. Turn left onto Marquette and continue 1 block to Orchestra Hall on the left.

Orchestra Hall

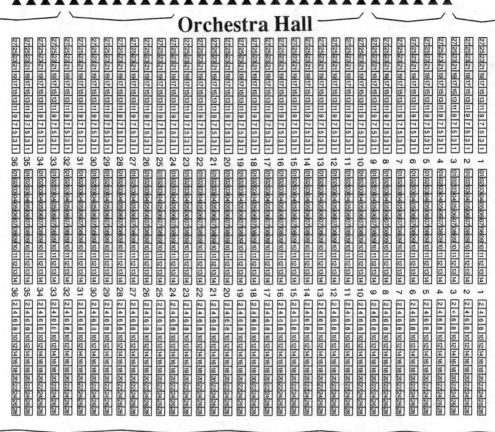

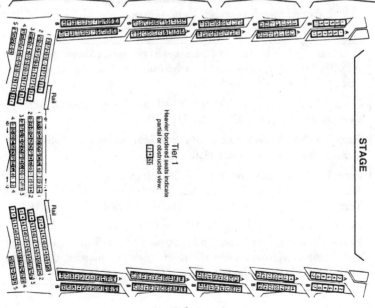

Tier 1
Heavier bordered seats indicate
partial or obstructed view:

STAGE

Orchestra Hall

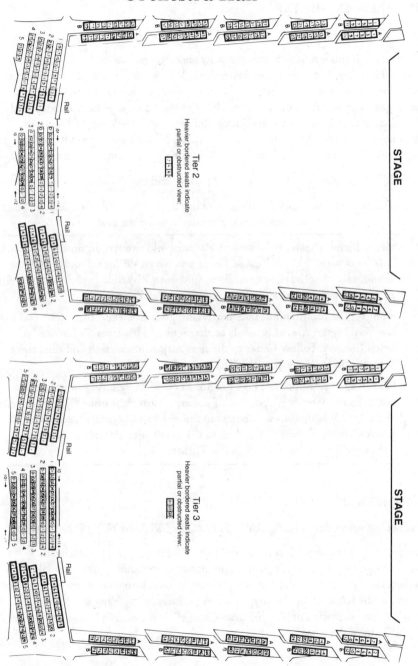

Tier 2

Heavier bordered seats indicate
partial or obstructed view:

STAGE

Tier 3

Heavier bordered seats indicate
partial or obstructed view:

STAGE

▲▲▲▲▲▲▲▲▲▲▲▲▲▲▲▲▲▲▲▲▲▲▲▲▲▲▲▲▲▲▲▲▲▲▲

MIXED BLOOD THEATRE

1501 S. Fourth St., Minneapolis, MN 55454 (612) 338-6131

This multiracial professional theatre company seeks to promote cultural pluralism, individual equality, and artistic excellence through an annual season of novel mainstage productions. The Theatre also offers seven culturally specific shows to schools and other organizations around the country. These productions range from biographical portraits of Martin Luther King and Jackie Robinson to anthologies of American Indian legends and the Asian American experience. Mixed Blood's productions are generally suitable for teenagers and adults and occasionally for younger children.

COST: $7.50–$15, depending on date and seating.

HOURS: Performances generally run Thursday–Sunday and often include Sunday matinees and interpreted performances for the deaf.

Mixed Blood Theatre is located in a century-old fire station on the West Bank in Minneapolis, 1 block west of Cedar and Riverside Aves. From I-94 westbound, take the Riverside exit. Turn right onto Riverside (which becomes 4th St. as it crosses Cedar) and follow 4th St. to the Theatre.

From I-35W southbound, take the Washington Ave. exit. Turn right and follow Washington Ave. as it bends to the right and becomes Cedar Ave. at Seven Corners. Follow Cedar to the next major intersection and turn right onto 4th St. Follow 4th to the Theatre.

From I-35W northbound, take the 3rd St./U of M exit. As you get on the exit, take the West Bank portion of the exit. Turn right onto Washington Ave. and follow Washington as it bends to the right and becomes Cedar Ave. at Seven Corners. Follow Cedar Ave. to the next major intersection and turn right onto 4th St. Follow 4th to the Theatre.

NORTHERN SIGN THEATRE

528 Hennepin Ave., Minneapolis, MN 55403 (612) 338-7876 TTY (612) 338-7549

Northern Sign Theatre is a bicultural and bilingual company that performs in American sign language and English simultaneously. The touring company takes productions throughout the state, produces videotapes, and brings education and residency work to the schools. Popular past productions include "Tickling the Belly of the Earth"; a new adaptation of "A Christmas Carol"; "Deaf Heroes"; "Signs and Stories A-Z"; and "Gift of the Magi."

▲▲▲▲▲▲▲▲▲▲▲▲▲▲▲▲▲▲▲▲▲▲▲▲▲▲▲▲▲▲▲▲▲▲▲▲▲▲

COST: General admission $4–$15, depending on performance, age, and time of day.

HOURS: Performance locations and hours vary; please call.

> The Northern Sign Theatre is located in downtown Minneapolis across from
> City Center. From I-35W, take the I-94 exit west. From I-94 west, take the
> Hennepin Ave. exit north (right) about 8 blocks to the Theatre on the left.

NORTHROP AUDITORIUM

*109 Northrop Auditorium, 84 Church St. S.E., Minneapolis, MN 55455 (612) 624-
2345*

Northrop Auditorium, grand dame of Twin Cities theaters, has been an important center for artistic performances in the Upper Midwest since 1929. The 4,800-seat theater,
located in the heart of the University of Minnesota campus, was named for Cyrus
Northrop, the University's second president. It presents the region's premier series of
dance companies–ballet, contemporary and ethnic–from all over the world. Touring
Broadway shows and other theatrical productions add dynamic elements to the
Northrop season.

Northrop also treats families with its annual holiday presentation of "The Nutcracker"
and with its two months of lively outdoor musical concerts in the summer, most of
which are free and appeal to all ages.

COST: Admission prices for performances and events vary. Expect parking fees.

HOURS: Regular evening shows Wednesday–Saturday 8:30 p.m.; Sunday 7:30
        p.m. Wednesday and Thursday matinees 1:30 p.m. Children's shows,
        four Saturday afternoons before Christmas, 2 p.m.

> From I-35W northbound or southbound, take the University Avenue/4th St.
> exit. Go east on University to 17th Ave. Turn left (north) onto 17th Ave. to
> reach the 4th St. ramp. Turn right (south) on 17th Ave. to reach the Nolte
> and Church Street garages, Northrop Auditorium, or the Washington Ave.
> ramp.
>
> From I-94 westbound, take the U of M exit. The exit becomes Huron Blvd.
> Go north on Huron Blvd., crossing University Ave. and following the curve to
> the west. Huron Blvd. will become 4th St. Continue on 4th St. 3 blocks to
> 17th Ave. To reach the 4th St. ramp, turn right onto 17th Ave. To reach the
> Nolte and Church St. garages, Northrop Auditorium, or the Washington Ave.
> ramp, turn left on 17th Ave. and proceed past the stoplight on University Ave.
> (After crossing University Ave., 17th Ave. becomes Church St.)

Photo by Herbert Migdoll, courtesy Northrop Auditorium

The Nutcracker is a holiday tradition at Northrop Auditorium. Shown is Mother Ginger and Polichinelles from The Joffrey Ballet's Nutcracker.

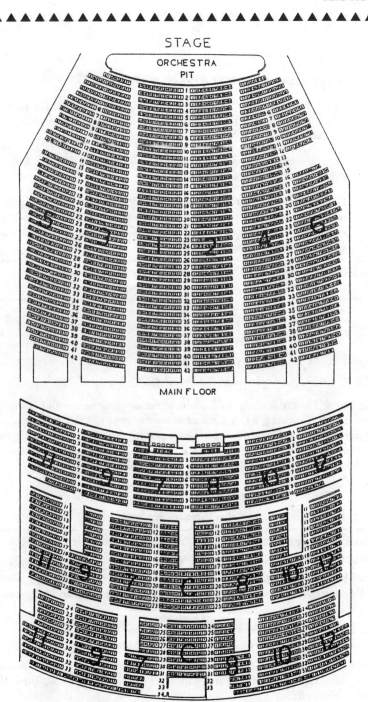

STAGE

ORCHESTRA PIT

MAIN FLOOR

BALCONY
CYRUS NORTHROP MEMORIAL
AUDITORIUM
UNIVERSITY OF MINNESOTA

▲▲▲▲▲▲▲▲▲▲▲▲▲▲▲▲▲▲▲▲▲▲▲▲▲▲▲▲▲▲▲▲▲▲▲▲▲▲

OLD LOG THEATER

5185 Meadville Rd., Excelsior, MN 55331-0250 (612) 474-5951

The Old Log Theater has been running continuously longer than any theater in the country. It presents the best in American comedy and British farce. Special children's shows are featured every year in late November and December.

COST: Regular evening shows $14.50 and $16.50; matinees $11 and $10; children's shows $7 per person.

HOURS: Performances are Wednesday-Saturday 8:30 p.m.; Sunday 7:30 p.m.; matinees on some Wednesdays and Thursdays 1:30 p.m. Meals are served one and one-half to two hours before performance. Performances are about two and one-half hours long.

> From I-494 take the Hwy. 7 exit. Go west on Hwy. 7 to Excelsior. In Excelsior, take the Old Log Way exit and follow signs to the Theater.

ORDWAY MUSIC THEATRE

345 Washington St., St. Paul, MN 55102
Tickets: (612) 224-4222 Administration: (612) 282-3000

The Ordway Music Theatre is recognized as one of the top four nonprofit performing centers in the nation. Providing a performance home for some of the Twin Cities' most vital arts organizations, the Ordway produces outstanding theatrical works and presents the finest performances of theater, ethnic dance, and music. The Ordway presents the First Bank Theater Season and Target's "Planet Ordway" season.

COST: $8–$70.

HOURS: Performances usually run Tuesday–Sunday.

> Located on the corner of Washington and 5th Sts. The Civic Center Ramp on Kellogg Blvd. is recommended for parking.
>
> From I-94 eastbound, take the Kellogg Blvd. exit. Go east on Kellogg Blvd. and follow to Washington St. Turn left onto Washington St. and follow to the Theatre.
>
> From I-94 westbound, take the 6th St. exit. Follow 6th St. 9 blocks to Washington St. Turn left on Washington St.
>
> From I-35E southbound, take the 10th St. exit and follow 10th St. 4 blocks to 6th St. Turn right onto 6th St. and go 7 blocks to Washington St. Turn left on Washington St.
>
> From I-35E northbound, take the Kellogg Blvd. exit. Turn right onto Kellogg Blvd. and follow to Washington St. Turn left to the front of the Ordway.

ORDWAY MUSIC THEATRE

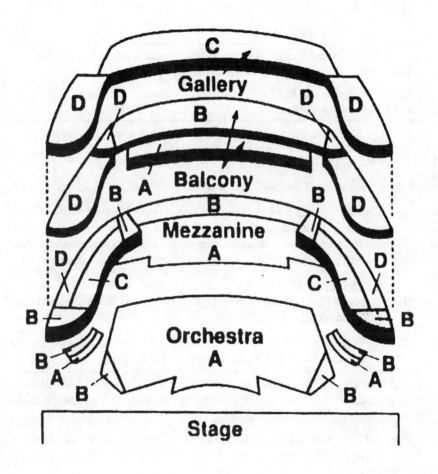

▲▲▲▲▲▲▲▲▲▲▲▲▲▲▲▲▲▲▲▲▲▲▲▲▲▲▲▲▲▲▲▲▲▲▲▲▲▲

O'SHAUGHNESSY AUDITORIUM *(Seating chart follows Penumbra.)*

College of St. Catherine, 2004 Randolph Ave., St. Paul, MN 55105 Ticket office: (612) 690-6700

O'Shaughnessy Auditorium presents the finest in family entertainment at reasonable prices. Call about the O'Shaugnessy Dance series at (612) 690-6700.

COST: Varies.

HOURS: Call for a schedule of events.

> From I-94, take the Cretin Ave. exit. Follow Cretin south to Randolph St. Proceed east on Randolph to O'Shaughnessy Auditorium.
>
> From I-35E, take the Randolph St. exit. Go west on Randolph to O'Shaughnessy Auditorium.

PARK SQUARE THEATRE

Seventh Place Theatre, 20 W. Seventh Place, St. Paul, MN (612) 291-7005

Park Square Theatre mounts six productions per season from the vast literature of Western theatre classics. The season runs January–August. The summer production in July and August is usually a family comedy or mystery. Located in downtown St. Paul, the theatre is within a few blocks of many restaurants, shops, and other family attractions.

COST: Adults $8–$17, students $8, children 10-17 $6. Children under 10 are not admitted.

HOURS: Performances Thursday 7:30 p.m., Friday and Saturday 8 p.m.; Sunday 2 p.m.; Tuesday and Wednesday previews 7:30 p.m.

> The Park Square Theatre is located on Seventh Place, a pedestrian mall running parallel to and between 6th and 7th Sts., between St. Peter and Wabasha across from the World Trade Center.
>
> From I-94 eastbound, take the 10th St. exit. Follow 10th St. 1 block to St. Peter St. Turn right onto St. Peter and proceed about 2-1/2 blocks to Seventh Place on the left.
>
> From I-94 westbound, take the Kellogg Blvd. exit. Follow Kellogg along the river into downtown St. Paul to Wabasha. Turn right onto Wabasha and follow 3-1/2 blocks to Seventh Place on the left.

▲▲▲▲▲▲▲▲▲▲▲▲▲▲▲▲▲▲▲▲▲▲▲▲▲▲▲▲▲▲▲▲▲▲▲▲▲▲

From I-35E southbound, take the Wacouta St. exit. Follow Wacouta to 6th St. Turn right onto 6th and follow about 6 blocks to Wabasha. Turn right onto Wabasha and follow 1/2 block to Seventh Place on the left.

From I-35E northbound, take the Kellogg Blvd. exit. Turn right onto Kellogg and follow to Wabasha. Turn left onto Wabasha and follow about 3-1/2 blocks to Seventh Place on the left.

PENUMBRA THEATRE COMPANY

270 N. Kent St., St. Paul, MN 55102 (612) 224-3180

Penumbra Theatre Company presents critically acclaimed productions that address the African-American experience. In its 18th season, Penumbra achieves its mission by presenting plays, musicals, and performance art pieces that are entertaining, educational, and relevant to issues facing the black community and the community at large. Working here are many influential African-American artists such as Pulitzer Prize-winning playwright August Wilson.

COST: Previews $9, regular run $14 and $17. Student, senior citizen, and group rates available.

HOURS: Season runs August–June with five mainstage shows and two main offerings. Shows typically run Thursday–Sunday with two performances Saturday and Sunday. Box office open Monday–Friday 10 a.m.–6 p.m.

From I-94 eastbound, take the Dale St. exit. Turn right onto Dale St. and follow to Iglehart. Turn left onto Iglehart and follow to the Theatre, which is housed in the Hallie Q. Brown/Martin Luther King Center.

From I-94 westbound, take the Dale St. exit. Turn left onto Dale St. and follow to Iglehart. Turn left onto Iglehart and follow to the Hallie Q. Brown/Martin Luther King Center.

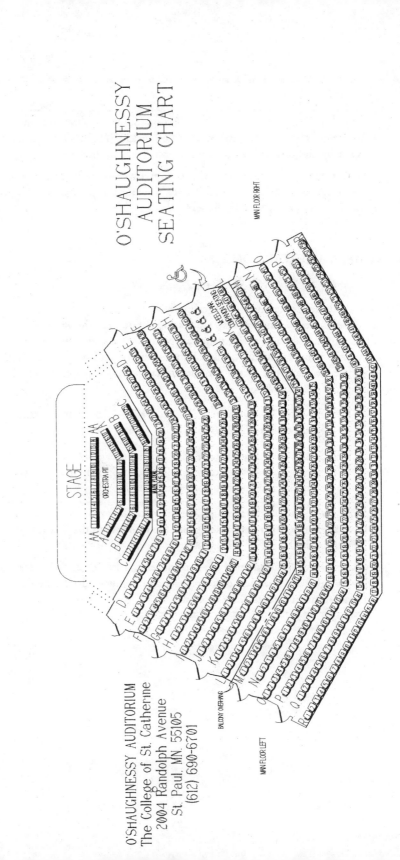

O'SHAUGHNESSY AUDITORIUM
AUDITORIUM
SEATING CHART

O'SHAUGHNESSY AUDITORIUM
The College of St. Catherine
2004 Randolph Avenue
St. Paul, MN 55105
(612) 690-6701

STAGE

ORCHESTRA PIT

MAIN FLOOR RIGHT

MAIN FLOOR LEFT

BALCONY OVERHANG

WHEELCHAIR SEATING

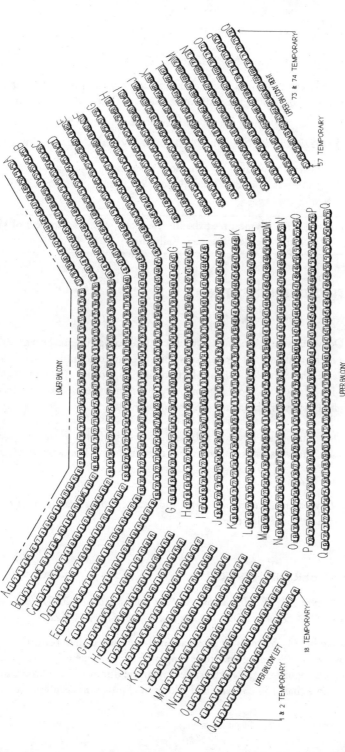

▲▲▲▲▲▲▲▲▲▲▲▲▲▲▲▲▲▲▲▲▲▲▲▲▲▲▲▲▲▲▲▲▲▲▲▲

PLYMOUTH PLAYHOUSE

2705 Annapolis Lane, Plymouth, MN 55441 (612) 553-1600

The Plymouth Playhouse offers fun, lively, and intimate musical comedies suitable for all ages. Dinner is available before the show in the famous Green Mill Restaurant above the Theatre.

COST: $12-$19. Special family nights occasionally with children admitted free.

HOURS: Performances Wednesday, Thursday, and Friday 8 p.m.; Saturday 6 p.m. and 9:30 p.m.; Sunday 2 p.m. Open year round, call for reservations; schedule may vary.

> **Located in suburban Plymouth at the intersection (southeast corner) of Hwy. 55 and I-494 within the Best Western Kelly Inn.**

TEATRO LATINO DE MINNESOTA

3501 Chicago Ave. S., Minneapolis, MN 55407 (612) 432-2314

Teatro Latino De Minnesota is a bilingual, multicultural company established to develop and nurture social and cultural awareness within the Latino community and the community at large. Presentations consist of improvisation, poetry, mime, masks, music, farce, satire, and serious social commentary. All scripts used for tour performances are original pieces or originate from Latino authors.

Teatro Latino De Minnesota is based in Minneapolis, but performs in community centers, parks, prisons, churches, colleges, and other theaters from Minnesota to Mexico.

COST: $8–$12.

HOURS: Vary according to performance and location; please call for performance locations and directions.

ST. PAUL CHAMBER ORCHESTRA

Ordway Music Theatre, 345 Washington St., St. Paul, MN 55102 SPCO Ticket Services Office: (612) 291-1144 Ordway Music Theatre Box Office (612) 224-4222

The St. Paul Chamber Orchestra is an internationally renowned chamber orchestra of 33 virtuosi musicians, performing repertoire ranging from Baroque to contemporary works, featuring distinguished guest artists. Led by music director Hugh Wolff, the SPCO presents more than 150 concerts and educational programs each year, reaching

▲▲▲▲▲▲▲▲▲▲▲▲▲▲▲▲▲▲▲▲▲▲▲▲▲▲▲▲▲▲▲▲▲

audiences through national radio broadcasts, tours, and over 50 recordings.

COST: $7–$34, depending on concert and seating.

HOURS: The SPCO concert season runs September-June. Please call for specific concert dates.

> Located on the corner of Washington and 5th Sts. The Civic Center Ramp on Kellogg Blvd. is recommended for parking.
>
> From I-94 eastbound, take the Kellogg Blvd. exit. Go east on Kellogg Blvd. and follow to Washington St. Turn left onto Washington St. and follow to the Theatre.
>
> From I-94 westbound, take the 6th St. exit. Follow 6th St. 9 blocks to Washington St. Turn left on Washington St.
>
> From I-35E southbound, take the 10th St. exit and follow 10th St. 4 blocks to 6th St. Turn right onto 6th St. and go 7 blocks to Washington St. Turn left on Washington St.
>
> From I-35E northbound, take the Kellogg Blvd. exit. Turn right onto Kellogg Blvd. and follow to Washington St. Turn left to the front of the Ordway.

THEATER MU

1201 Yale Place, #911, Minneapolis, MN 55403 (612) 525-7386

Theater Mu is a professional Asian-American theater company that gives a voice to Asian-Americans, creating and producing works that draw on both Asian and Western performance traditions. Theater Mu presents two or three productions a year, and gives educational and community outreach performances of smaller works.

COST: $8–$12.

HOURS: Hours vary according to performance and location; please call. Performance locations vary; call for directions.

THEATRE DE LA JEUNE LUNE

105 N. 1st St., Minneapolis, MN 55401 (612) 333-6200

This international company is renowned for physically dynamic and visually spectacular productions. Mainstage productions are generally suitable for junior high students and up. Occasional programming is presented for younger children; call for details.

▲▲

COST: Mainstage productions $9–$19. Children's productions $7–$9.
        Discounts available for students and children under 12.

HOURS: Performance times vary; call for schedule.

> From I-94 eastbound, take the 4th St./downtown exit. Turn left on Hennepin
> Ave. and follow to 1st St. Turn left onto 1st St. and follow to the Theatre
> within 1 block on the left.
>
> From I-94 westbound, take the 5th St./downtown exit. Go north on 5th St.
> and follow to Hennepin Ave. Turn right onto Hennepin and follow to 1st St.
> Turn left onto 1st St. and follow to the Theatre within 1 block on the left.
>
> From I-35W northbound, take the Washington Ave. exit. Go north on
> Washington to Hennepin Ave. Turn right onto Hennepin and follow to 1st
> St. Turn left onto 1st St. The Theatre is 1 block ahead on the left.
>
> From I-35W southbound, take the Washington Ave. exit. Proceed north on
> Washington to Hennepin Ave. Turn right onto Hennepin and follow to 1st
> St. Turn left onto 1st St. and follow to the Theatre within 1 block on the left.
>
> From I-394 westbound, take the Washington Ave. exit. Turn right onto
> Washington and follow to 2nd Ave. Turn left onto 2nd and follow to 1st St.
> Turn right onto 1st St. and follow to the Theatre.

THEATRE IN THE ROUND PLAYERS (TRP)

245 Cedar Ave., Minneapolis, MN 55454 (612) 333-3010

The oldest theater company in Minneapolis, Theatre in the Round Players (TRP) has
been producing award-winning drama, comedies, and area premieres for more than 40
years. See your favorite plays and classics in TRP's unique arena stage in the West Bank
theater district. Reservations recommended.

COST: Average price $11; student and senior discounts available.

HOURS: Performances are on weekend evenings; some matinees available. Call
        for times and reservations.

> Located at Seven Corners where Cedar Ave. and Washington Ave. meet. Use
> the 7 Corners Municipal Parking Ramp at 1504 Washington Ave. S. between
> the Holiday Inn Metrodome and Grandma's Restaurant.
>
> From I-94 westbound, take the Cedar Ave. exit. Go north on Cedar to
> Washington Ave. Turn right onto Washington Ave. to get to the parking
> ramp.

▲▲

> From I-94 eastbound or I-35W northbound, go north on I-35W, take the
> Third St./U of M (17C) exit. Follow the west bank lane to Washington Ave.
> and take a right to get to the parking ramp.

UNIVERSITY THEATRE

330 S. 21st Ave., Minneapolis, MN 55455
Tickets: (612) 624-2345 Information: (612) 625-7505

The University Theatre offers high-quality, low-cost live theatre at the University of
Minnesota. University Theatre offers one of the broadest repertoires in the Twin Cities,
from the classics to the newest plays in town.

COST: General admission $9; students, alumni, staff, and faculty of the U of
M $7. Groups of 15 or more $6.

HOURS: October–June season: Wednesday–Saturday 8 p.m.; Sunday 3 p.m.
July–September on the Minnesota Centennial Showboat:
Wednesday–Saturday 8 p.m.; Sunday 3 p.m.

> From I-35W, take the West Bank/3rd Ave. exit. Take West Bank lane to
> Washington. Turn right onto Washington and follow to Cedar Ave. Turn
> right onto Cedar and follow to Riverside. Turn left onto Riverside and follow
> to 21st Ave. S. The University Theatre is on 21st Ave.

PERFORMING ARTS

▲▲▲▲▲▲▲▲▲▲▲▲▲▲▲▲▲▲▲▲▲▲▲▲▲▲▲▲▲▲▲▲▲▲▲▲▲

RECREATIONAL
EQUIPMENT RENTALS

▲▲▲▲▲▲▲▲▲▲▲▲▲▲▲▲▲▲▲▲▲▲▲▲▲▲▲▲▲▲▲▲▲▲▲

MASTER LIST

Why have a "rentals" chapter in a book about family fun spots? It's so you don't miss out on any of the fun things to do, because you don't have the equipment. Renting equipment is a great way to enjoy new experiences at minimal expense. Here's a listing of who rents what. Note that I have presented a master list first, and then listed only the names of rental places under the headings for the equipment they rent. This helped me to avoid repeated duplication of the entire listing.

AARCEE RENTAL

2910 Lyndale Ave. S., Minneapolis, MN 55408 (612) 827-5746

AARCEE Rental has a variety of summer and winter rental equipment available to the public. In summer you can rent camping trailers; tents; camping accessories; canoes; sleeping bags; and roller blades. In the winter, rental equipment includes downhill and cross-country skis, snowboards, and ice skates. If you would rather own your gear and equipment, AARCEE is also a complete camping, clothing, and skiing retail store.

COST: Call for a free rental price sheet.

HOURS: Summer: Monday, Thursday, Friday 9 a.m.–8:30 p.m.; Tuesday and Wednesday 9 a.m.–5:30 p.m.; Saturday 9 a.m.–5 p.m. Winter: Weekdays 9 a.m.-8 p.m.; Saturday 9 a.m.–5 p.m. Closed Sundays year round.

> From I-94, take the Lyndale/Hennepin exit. Travel south on Lyndale Ave. about 1 mile. Store is on the west side of Lyndale Ave.

AREA WIDE CYCLE

229 Water St., Excelsior, MN 55331 (612) 474-3229

Area Wide Cycle is a full-service bicycle store located 1/2 block from the Minnetonka Light Rail (LRT) trail system. You can rent bicycles appropriate for use on the street, or on the limestone surface of the LRT system. There are also child trailers and children's bicycles to rent. The use of bicycle helmets is strongly encouraged. Bicycle helmets are available for a nominal fee, or free with rental of any other equipment. A service department is available to work on all brands of bicycles.

Area Wide Cycle also rents and services cross-country skis and ice skates. With plenty of free parking, renters can get on the LRT trail right at the back door of the store. Ski trail maps are available.

RECREATION EQUIPMENT RENTALS

▲▲▲▲▲▲▲▲▲▲▲▲▲▲▲▲▲▲▲▲▲▲▲▲▲▲▲▲▲▲▲▲▲▲▲▲

COST: Ski rental fees: one day $8, weekend $15, one week $25. Ice skate rental fees: one day $4, weekend $8, one week $15. Bicycle and trailer rental fees: hourly rate $6 with a $10 minimum, 1/2 day $15, one day $20, weekend $35, one week $65.

HOURS: Summer: Monday–Friday 10 a.m.–8 p.m.; Saturday 9 a.m.–5 p.m.; Sunday noon–4 p.m. Call for holiday hours. Winter: Monday, Tuesday, Wednesday, Friday 11 a.m.–7 p.m.; Thursday 11 a.m.–8 p.m.; Saturday 9 a.m.–4 p.m. Closed Sunday.

> From I-494, take the Hwy. 7 exit. Follow Hwy. 7 west 5 miles. There is a lane marked LEFT HAND EXIT for Excelsior. Take the exit and proceed 3 blocks to the municipal parking lot. Area Wide Cycle has a convenient rear entrance facing the parking lot.

BAVARIAN SURF, MINNETONKA

340 Hwy. 7, Excelsior, MN 55331 (612) 474-2885

Bavarian Surf, established in 1984, provides ice and snow surfing; wind surfing; snowboarding; lessons; rentals; sales; service; and accessories year round. Bavarian Surf's head instructor has taught snowboarding and windsurfing at all skill levels for over 14 years. Newly in: 1994 ocean kayaks.

COST: Rentals: $45 first day, $35 second day, $20 third day, $10 fourth day, and so on. Lessons: $45 for three hours.

HOURS: Monday–Friday 10 a.m.–1 p.m.; Saturday 10 a.m.–4 p.m. Lessons are taught after 1 p.m.; call for more details.

> From I-494, take the Hwy. 7 exit. Travel west for 5-1/2 miles. Bavarian Surf, Minnetonka is on the right side of Hwy. 7.

CLEARY REGIONAL PARK 447-2171

FISH LAKE REGIONAL PARK 420-3423

In-line skates may be rented at Cleary and Fish Lake Regional Parks for $4 per hour. Trails are appropriate for beginners. Cleary has 3 miles of paved trails. Fish Lake offers 1.5 miles of paved trails.

HOURS: Fish Lake: daily 9 a.m.–8 p.m.
        Cleary Lake: weekdays 10 a.m.–8 p.m.; weekends 9 a.m.–8 p.m.

> Refer to the Regional Parks chapter to get directions and more information.

COMO SKI CENTER

1431 N. Lexington Pkwy., St. Paul, MN 55108 (612) 488-9673

Como Ski Center offers downhill and cross-country ski rentals for children and adults. One hill with two runs is available for downhill skiing along with 5 kilometers of groomed cross-country ski trails.

COST: Cross-country ski rates per two hours: adults $6, youth 13–17 $4, children 12 and under $2.
Downhill skiing rental package rates for one day: adults $8.50, youth 13–17 $6.50, children $4.50.
Tow ticket rates: adults $5.50, children and youth 17 and under $4.50 weekend; $3.50 weekdays. Lessons in both downhill and cross-country skiing are available.

HOURS: Weekdays 2–9 p.m.; Saturday 9 a.m.–6 p.m.; Sunday 11 a.m.–6 p.m.; holiday hours 10 a.m.–9 p.m.

From I-94, take the Lexington Ave. exit and go north to the Como Ski Center on the left side in the Como Park Golf Course clubhouse building.

EASTERN MOUNTAIN SPORTS

1627 W. Co. Rd. B, Roseville, MN 55113 (612) 631-2900

Eastern Mountain Sports' rental equipment includes tents; sleeping bags; backpacks; skis; snowshoes; and canoes in the summer.

COST: Weekend rates (Friday–Sunday): two-person tents $20, sleeping bags and backpacks $15. Cross-country skis: full pkg. $20. Snowshoes $15. Canoes $40, $10 for each additional day; $5 each additional day for all other rental equipment. One-day rates about $5 less than weekend rates.

HOURS: Weekdays 10 a.m.–9 p.m.; Saturday 9 a.m.–6 p.m.; Sunday noon–5 p.m.

From I-35W, take the Hwy. 36 exit. Follow Hwy. 36 east to the southbound Snelling Ave. exit. From Snelling Ave., turn right at Co. Rd. B and go 1 block. Eastern Mountain Sports is on the north side of the road.

RECREATION EQUIPMENT RENTALS

▲▲▲▲▲▲▲▲▲▲▲▲▲▲▲▲▲▲▲▲▲▲▲▲▲▲▲▲▲▲▲▲▲▲▲▲▲▲

HARRIS WAREHOUSE

501 30th Ave. S. E., Minneapolis, MN 55414 (612) 331-1321

This rental business offers Duluth packs and frame packs at extremely reasonable rates.

COST: $1 per day, $7 per week.

HOURS: Monday & Thursday 8:30 a.m.–8:30 p.m.; Tuesday, Wednesday, Friday, Saturday 8:30 a.m.–5:30 p.m.

> From Hwy. 280, take the University Ave. exit. Follow University Ave. west 1-1/2 miles to 30th Ave. S. E. Go north 2 blocks toward the grain elevators. Parking lot is at the end of the road.

HIGHWAY 55 RENTAL AND SALES

225 Hwy. 55, Plymouth, MN 55340 (612) 478-6448

Highway 55 Rental and Sales, which provides rental equipment for parties, also provides camping equipment such as pop-up tent trailers, tents, campstoves, and lanterns.

COST: Rates based on daily, weekly, or monthly rentals.

HOURS: Monday–Friday 9 a.m.–6 p.m.; Saturday 8 a.m.–5 p.m.; Sunday 10 a.m.–2 p.m.

> From I-494, take the Hwy. 55 exit west for 4-1/2 miles to store on the south side of the highway.

KETTER CANOEING

101 79th Ave. N., Minneapolis, MN (612) 560-3840

Ketter Canoeing was founded in 1970 by a professional racing family to make life easier for the canoeist through equipment, technical advice, and service. Ketter Canoeing sells and rents only the finest designs in canoes, paddles, and accessories such as Kevelar lightweight canoes and Winona canoes. Rental equipment includes solo and two-person canoes, solo yoke, bent paddles, and Seda life vests. Shuttle service is available to the Mississippi, Minnesota, Rum, and Crow Rivers. Ask about canoe delivery anywhere in Minnesota and beyond.

COST: Rental fees: $25 for two-person canoe, 24 hours; $150 for two-person canoe, one week; $15 for solo canoe, 24 hours; $90 for solo canoe, one week.

▲▲▲▲▲▲▲▲▲▲▲▲▲▲▲▲▲▲▲▲▲▲▲▲▲▲▲▲▲▲▲▲▲▲▲▲▲

HOURS: Call anytime Monday–Sunday to make an appointment for rentals.

> From Hwy. 694, take the Hwy. 252 exit. Follow Hwy. 252 north 2 miles to
> Brookdale Dr. Turn right onto Brookdale Dr. and follow to the riverbank,
> turn left. Ketter Canoeing is 1 block on the right (river side of road).

MACALESTER BIKE & SKATE EXCHANGE

370 S. Snelling, St. Paul, MN 55105 (612) 698-3966

Authorized Schwinn, Specialized, Trek, and Rollerblade dealers. Rent new or used
bikes, child trailers, or ice skates. Expert repair service on all bikes.

COST: Rollerblades $12 for 24 hours. Child trailer $10 for 24 hours. Ice skates
$8 for 24 hours.

HOURS: Monday and Thursday 10 a.m.–8 p.m.; Tuesday, Wednesday, Friday 10
a.m.–6 p.m.; Saturday 9 a.m.–5 p.m.; Sunday noon–4 p.m.

> From I-35W, take the 98th St. exit. Turn left onto 98th, then take the first
> left into the Clover Center parking lot. Macalester Bike and Skate Exchange is
> located in the Clover Center.

MARINE LANDING

10 Elm St., P.O. Box 142, Marine-on-St. Croix, MN 55047 (612) 433-2864

Marine Landing is open to the public for aluminum canoe rentals. Shuttle service is
also provided with reservations for a 10-mile trip to Osceola or an 18-mile trip to
Taylors Falls, both on the St. Croix River.

COST: $24 per canoe per day, $12 for each extra day.

HOURS: Monday–Sunday: call anytime for reservations.

> From Hwy. 36, go east to Stillwater. Hwy. 36 ends in Stillwater and becomes
> Hwy. 95. Take Hwy. 95 north. Marine Landing is located 10 miles north of
> Stillwater on Hwy. 95.

RECREATION EQUIPMENT RENTALS

▲▲▲

MIDWEST MOUNTAINEERING

309 Cedar Ave. S. Minneapolis, MN 55454 (612) 339-3433

If you're looking for a place that offers a wide variety and selection of quality rental equipment, you won't be disappointed at Midwest Mountaineering. Winter rentals include cross-country skis; snowshoes; crampons for ice climbing; two- and four-person tents; internal frame back packs; -40°F sleeping bags; foam pads; fuel bottles; one-burner lightweight backpacking stoves; lanterns; four-person cook kits; 9-x-12-foot tarps, and climbing shoes. Additional summer rentals include 20°F sleeping bags; external frame backpacks; canoes; and touring kayaks.

COST: Call for specific rate information. Damage deposit required. Will validate parking in lots

HOURS: Weekdays 10 a.m.–9 p.m.; Saturday 9:30 a.m.–6 p.m.; Sunday noon–5 p.m.

From I- 35W southbound, take the Washington Ave. exit. Turn left onto Washington Ave. Washington becomes Cedar Ave. after 1 block. Continue on Cedar 2 blocks to Midwest Mountaineering on the east side of Cedar Ave.

From I-35W northbound, take the University of Minnesota exit, which will split three ways. Take the middle, which is the West Bank exit, to Washington Ave. and turn right. Washington Ave. becomes Cedar Ave. after 1 block. Continue on Cedar 2 blocks to Midwest Mountaineering on the east side of Cedar Ave.

From I-94 eastbound, use the I-35W northbound exit and the directions above.

From I-94 westbound, take the Cedar Ave. exit. Follow Cedar north about 4 blocks. Midwest Mountaineering is on the east side of Cedar Ave.

P.J. ASCH, OTTERFITTERS

413 E. Nelson, Stillwater, MN 55082 (612) 430-2286

Rock-climbing enthusiasts will be thrilled to discover that P.J. Asch, Otterfitters hosts a 7,000-square-foot, 42-foot-high indoor climbing facility. That's not all; in addition to the retail store, rental equipment for the entire family is available. Rental equipment includes cross-country skis in all sizes, and kayaks in the summer.

COST: Climbing rate: $7 per day on weekends, $5 per day on weekdays. Cross-country ski rental: $10 per day, $15 for weekend. Kayak rental: $35 per day, $50 for weekend.

HOURS: Monday–Saturday 10 a.m.–9 p.m.; Sunday 11 a.m.–7 p.m.

▲▲▲▲▲▲▲▲▲▲▲▲▲▲▲▲▲▲▲▲▲▲▲▲▲▲▲▲▲▲▲▲▲▲▲▲

From Hwy. 36, take the Hwy. 95 exit. Follow Hwy. 95 north to Nelson St. (first stoplight). Follow Nelson to Otterfitters, 1 block on the right in the Old Commander Elevator.

PIERCE SKATE AND SKI

208 W. 98th St., Bloomington, MN 55420 (612) 884-1990

Twin Cities families have known for 58 years that quality skis and skates can be purchased or rented at Pierce Skate and Ski. Recipient of the 1990 Ski Retailer of the Year award, Pierce Skate and Ski still caters to the family, offering ice skating and cross-country ski rental in the winter and in-line skates in the summer.

COST: Ice skate rental $5.50 per day. Cross-country ski rental $9 per day. In-line skate rental $12 per day.

HOURS: Weekdays 10 a.m.–9 p.m.; Saturday 10 a.m.–5:30 p.m.; Sunday noon–5 p.m.

From I-35W, take the 98th St. exit. Follow 98th St. east about 5 blocks. Pierce Skate and Ski is located on 98th St. (Old Shakopee Rd.) and Pleasant St. in the middle of the block. Pierce Skate and Ski is just 5 minutes west of the Mall of America on Old Shakopee Rd.

REI (RECREATIONAL EQUIPMENT INC.)

710 W. 98th St., Bloomington, MN 55420 (612) 884-4315

More than a recreational equipment retail store, REI rents cross-country skis; downhill skis; snowshoes; sleeping bags; thermarest pad; child carrier; rock climbing shoes; tents; Duluth packs; frame packs; internal frame packs; and stoves.

COST: Call for a rate sheet.

HOURS: Monday–Friday 9:30 a.m.–9 p.m.; Saturday 9:30 a.m.–6 p.m.; Sunday 11 a.m.–5 p.m.

REI is located next to the freeway in the Clover Shopping Center. From I-35W, take the 98th St. exit. Head east on 98th St. (left if coming from the north, right if coming from the south).

RECREATION EQUIPMENT RENTALS

▲▲▲▲▲▲▲▲▲▲▲▲▲▲▲▲▲▲▲▲▲▲▲▲▲▲▲▲▲▲▲▲▲▲▲▲▲▲

ROLLING SOLES

1700 W. Lake St., Minneapolis, MN 55408 (612) 823-5711

Established in the spring of 1978, Rolling Soles helped pioneer the sport of outdoor roller skating. In its 18th season of business, Rolling Soles remains entirely owned, managed, and staffed by skaters. Their philosophy is, "If we won't skate it, we won't rent it or sell it."

Rent Rollerblade, Roces, Bauer, and Oxygen in-line skates and ice skates. Safety equipment free with rental fee. A current, valid local picture ID is required. Out-of-state IDs require a credit card or cash deposit as well.

COST: In-line skate rental $5 per hour, $10 per day. Roller skate rental $3 per hour, $7.50 per day. Ice skate rental $3 per hour, $7.50 per day. No overnight rentals.

HOURS: Rental shop open daily. Monday–Friday 10 a.m.–9 p.m.; Saturday and Sunday 9 a.m.–9 p.m. Winter hours vary due to weather, so call first. Retail hours vary with seasons. Closed for rain.

> From I-94 westbound, take the Hennepin Ave. exit. Go south on Hennepin to Lagoon. Proceed west on Lagoon to James Ave. Go south on James to Lake St. Rolling Soles is on the northwest corner of Lake St. and James Ave., 2 blocks east of Lake Calhoun in Uptown.

STUDIO A

1523 W. Lake St., Minneapolis, MN 55408 (612) 825-3077

Studio A offers skate rental.

COST: Ice skate rental $3 per hour, $8 per day. In-line skate rental $5 per hour, $10 per day.

HOURS: Monday–Saturday 10:30 a.m.–9 p.m.; Sunday noon–9 p.m.

> From I-35W, take the W. Lake St. exit. Proceed west on Lake St. about 2 miles. Studio A is on West Lake St. at the intersection of Irving Ave. and Lake St.

▲▲▲▲▲▲▲▲▲▲▲▲▲▲▲▲▲▲▲▲▲▲▲▲▲▲▲▲▲▲▲▲▲▲▲▲▲▲

WAGON BRIDGE MARINA

15862 Eagle Creek Ave. N.E., Prior Lake, MN 55372 (612) 447-4300

The only marina on Prior Lake, Wagon Bridge Marina rents water craft and ski accessories for use on the lake. Rent by the hour or day at reasonable rates. Rental craft include fishing boats; pontoons; and personalized water craft (wave runners, runabouts, and ski boats). Snack bar and live bait also available.

COST: $5–$45 per hour, based on equipment. Call for rates. Free parking.

HOURS: May 1–September 4: rentals daily 6 a.m.–9 p.m.

> From I-35W southbound, take the Co. Rd. 42 exit. Follow Co. Rd. 42 west to Hwy. 13. Turn left onto Hwy. 13 and follow to Co. Rd. 21. Turn right onto Co. Rd. 21 and go about 6 blocks to the Marina on the left after the wagon bridge.

WELCH MILL CANOEING AND TUBING

14818 264th Street Path, Welch, MN 55089 (612) 388-9857 1-800-657-6760

Welch Mill Canoeing and Tubing offers an ideal location for group and family outings in the beautiful Cannon River Valley. Free shuttle service is available with rental equipment. Welch Mill provides canoes; life jackets; paddles; large and small tubes.

HOURS: Daily 10 a.m.; weekends 8 a.m. Closing times determined daily.

> Located less than an hour south of the Twin Cities, between Hastings and Red Wing off Hwy. 61 on Welch Village Road.
>
> From I-35W southbound (from Minneapolis and suburbs), go to Minnesota Hwy. 50 (Lakeville). Follow Hwy. 50 east to U.S. Hwy. 61. Proceed south on Hwy. 61 to Welch Village Rd. (Co. Rd. 7) and turn right.
>
> From St. Paul and suburbs, take U.S. Hwy. 61 south approximately "15 minutes" (per Welch Mill) to Welch Village Rd. (Co. 7).

▲▲▲▲▲▲▲▲▲▲▲▲▲▲▲▲▲▲▲▲▲▲▲▲▲▲▲▲▲▲▲▲▲▲▲

BICYCLES

Bike rentals are available at the following Hennepin County Regional Parks and Reserves: Baker, Elm Creek, and Hyland Lake Park Reserves, and Cleary Lake Regional Park.

COST: Adult bikes $3 per hour, youth bikes $2 per hour, tandems $4 per hour. Toddler seats and helmets are available at no extra charge.

AREA WIDE CYCLE *(see MASTER LIST for full description)*

BOATS

Boat rentals are available at the following Hennepin Regional Parks:

Rowboat rentals $1.50 per 1/2-hour, $15 per day at Baker; Fish Lake; French; Hyland Lake; and Lake Rebecca.

Paddleboat rentals $3–$4 per 1/2-hour at Baker; Cleary Lake; Fish Lake; French; Hyland Lake; and Lake Rebecca.

Canoe rentals $1.50 per 1/2 hour, $15 per day at Baker; Cleary Lake; Fish Lake; French; Hyland Lake; and Lake Rebecca.

AARCEE RENTAL *(see MASTER LIST for full description)*

CANOEING KETTER *(see MASTER LIST for full description)*

EASTERN MOUNTAIN SPORTS *(see MASTER LIST for full description)*

MARINE LANDING *(see MASTER LIST for full description)*

MIDWEST MOUNTAINEERING *(see MASTER LIST for full description)*

P.J. ASCH, OTTERFITTERS *(see MASTER LIST for full description)*

WAGON BRIDGE MARINA *(see MASTER LIST for full description)*

WELCH MILL *(see MASTER LIST for full description)*

▲▲▲▲▲▲▲▲▲▲▲▲▲▲▲▲▲▲▲▲▲▲▲▲▲▲▲▲▲▲▲▲▲▲▲

CHILD CARRIER RENTALS

MACALESTER BIKE & SKATE EXCHANGE *(see MASTER LIST for full description)*

REI *(see MASTER LIST for full description)*

CROSS-COUNTRY SKIS

ELM CREEK PARK RESERVE: *See chapter on parks for rental information.*

CLEARY LAKE REGIONAL PARK: *See chapter on parks for rental information.*

HYLAND LAKE PARK RESERVE: *See chapter on parks for rental information.*

FRENCH REGIONAL PARK: *See chapter on parks for rental information.*

AARCEE RENTAL *(see MASTER LIST for full description)*

AREA WIDE CYCLE *(see MASTER LIST for full description)*

COMO SKI CENTER *(see MASTER LIST for full description)*

EASTERN MOUNTAIN SPORTS *(see MASTER LIST for full description)*

MIDWEST MOUNTAINEERING *(see MASTER LIST for full description)*

P.J. ASCH, OTTERFITTERS *(see MASTER LIST for full description)*

PIERCE SKATE AND SKI *(see MASTER LIST for full description)*

REI *(see MASTER LIST for full description)*

DOWNHILL SKIS

AARCEE RENTAL *(see MASTER LIST for full description)*

COMO SKI CENTER *(see MASTER LIST for full description)*

REI *(see MASTER LIST for full description)*

Also at most downhill Ski Parks

▲▲▲▲▲▲▲▲▲▲▲▲▲▲▲▲▲▲▲▲▲▲▲▲▲▲▲▲▲▲▲▲▲▲▲

ICE SKATES

AARCEE RENTAL *(see MASTER LIST for full description)*

AREA WIDE CYCLE *(see MASTER LIST for full description)*

MACALESTER BIKE AND SKATE EXCHANGE *(see MASTER LIST for full description)*

PIERCE SKATE AND SKI *(see MASTER LIST for full description)*

ROLLING SOLES *(see MASTER LIST for full description)*

STUDIO A *(see MASTER LIST for full description)*

IN-LINE/ROLLER SKATES

AARCEE RENTAL *(see MASTER LIST for full description)*

Cleary and Fish Lake Regional Parks: *See chapter on parks for rental information.*

MACALESTER BIKE AND SKATE EXCHANGE *(see MASTER LIST for full description)*

PIERCE SKATE AND SKI *(see MASTER LIST for full description)*

ROLLING SOLES *(see MASTER LIST for full description)*

STUDIO A *(see MASTER LIST for full description)*

SNOW, ICE, & WIND SURFBOARDS

BAVARIAN SURF, MINNETONKA (see MASTER LIST for full description)

PHALEN-KELLER REGIONAL PARK: Refer to chapter on parks for rental information.

▲▲▲▲▲▲▲▲▲▲▲▲▲▲▲▲▲▲▲▲▲▲▲▲▲▲▲▲▲▲▲▲▲▲

SNOWSHOE RENTAL

FORT SNELLING STATE PARK: *Refer to chapter on parks for rental information.*

MIDWEST MOUNTAINEERING *(see MASTER LIST for full description)*

REI *(see MASTER LIST for full description)*

TENT AND CAMPING ACCESSORIES

AARCEE RENTAL *(see MASTER LIST for full description)*

EASTERN MOUNTAIN SPORTS *(see MASTER LIST for full description)*

HARRIS WAREHOUSE *(see MASTER LIST for full description)*

HIGHWAY 55 RENTAL AND SALES *(see MASTER LIST for full description)*

MIDWEST MOUNTAINEERING *(see MASTER LIST for full description)*

REI *(see MASTER LIST for full description)*

SEASONAL EVENTS

▲▲▲▲▲▲▲▲▲▲▲▲▲▲▲▲▲▲▲▲▲▲▲▲▲▲▲▲▲▲▲▲▲▲▲▲▲

AMERICAN SWEDISH INSTITUTE'S SCANDINAVIAN CHRISTMAS

2600 Park Ave., Minneapolis, MN 55407-1090 (612) 871-4907

If viewing light displays and decorations is your favorite part of the Christmas season, you won't want to miss the elaborate exhibits of Scandinavian decorated trees and table settings at the American Swedish Institute in Minneapolis. Sweden, Norway, Denmark, Iceland, and Finland are represented in this captivating holiday adornment.

COST: Adults $3, seniors and students 6–18 $2, children 6 and under free.

DATES: Late November–early January.

> From I-35W northbound, take the Lake St./31st St. exit and follow 31st St. or Lake St. east to Park Ave. Proceed north on Park Ave. to the Institute.
>
> From I-35W southbound, take the Hiawatha exit. Follow Hiawatha to 26th St. Go west on 26th St. to the Institute on the corner of 26th St. and Park Ave.

DAYTON'S (MINNEAPOLIS)

700 on the Mall (7th St. & Nicollet), Minneapolis, MN 55402-3200 (612) 375-2200

The Upper Midwest's leading department store also hosts extensive events programs throughout the year: personal appearances, exhibits, and fashion shows. Major events include the walk through Auditorium holiday exhibit, and Dayton's/Bachman's Flower Show. Call for schedules and information.

COST: Free. Some selected events are ticketed and may involve charges.

HOURS: Monday–Friday 9:30 a.m.–9:30 p.m.; Saturday 10 a.m.–8 p.m.; Sunday 11 a.m.–6 p.m. Call for holiday hours.

> From I-94 westbound, take the 11th or 5th St. exit. Both intersect with Nicollet Mall.
>
> From I-35W northbound, take the 5th Ave. exit to 9th St., which intersects with Nicollet Mall.
>
> From I-394 eastbound, take the 6th St. exit. 6th St. intersects with the Nicollet Mall.

SEASONAL EVENTS

▲▲▲▲▲▲▲▲▲▲▲▲▲▲▲▲▲▲▲▲▲▲▲▲▲▲▲▲▲▲▲▲▲▲

HOLIDAY IN LIGHTS AT THE MINNESOTA ZOO

13000 Zoo Blvd., Apple Valley, MN 55124 (612) 432-9000 (ZOO-TO-DO)

"Ooh" and "aah" over one of the Twin Cities' most spectacular displays of holiday lights. Over 100,000 lights make hundreds of Christmas trees, holiday characters, and animals come to life at the Minnesota Zoo.

COST: $6 per car..

HOURS: November 23–January 1: Friday–Saturday 5:30 a.m.–11:30 p.m.

> The Minnesota Zoo is located 10 minutes south of the Mall of America. From I-494, take the Hwy. 77 (Cedar Ave.) exit. Follow Hwy. 77 south toward Apple Valley. Follow signs to zoo as you approach the north end of Apple Valley.

HOLIDAZZLE

Nicollet Mall from 12th St. to 4th St., Minneapolis, MN (612) 338-3807

Holidazzle is a series of evening holiday parades celebrating the spirit of the season and the joy and wonder of childhood memories. Each Holidazzle parade features lighted floats with storybook and nursery rhyme characters, marching bands, and choirs. All parades travel down Nicollet Mall from 12th Street to 4th St. For a complete listing of parade dates, call the Minneapolis Downtown Council at (612) 338-3807.

COST: Free.

HOURS: Most evenings, Friday after Thanksgiving–December 30, except Christmas Eve and Christmas Day. All parades start at 6:30 p.m. and last about 30 minutes.

> From I-94 westbound, take the 11th St. or 5th St. exit. Both exits intersect with Nicollet Mall.
>
> From I-35W northbound, take the 5th Ave. exit. Follow 5th Ave. to 9th St., which intersects with Nicollet Mall.
>
> From Hwy. 394 eastbound, take the 6th St. exit. Follow 6th St. until it intersects with Nicollet Mall.

▲▲

Photo by Bob Perzel

Two floats in the annual Holidazzle parade on the Nicollet Mall in downtown

KIDFEST

St. Paul Civic Center, 143 W. 4th St., St. Paul, MN 55401 (612) 224-7361

KIDFEST is a unique opportunity for the entire family to share quality time together at a fun-filled festival and marketplace held in the St. Paul Civic Center. The entire family can enjoy two entertainment stages; a free kiddie midway; several play areas; sports; a petting zoo; games of chance; sing-alongs; and a wide variety of vendors and product sampling.

COST: Varies with each year.

DATES: The last Saturday and Sunday of February.

Refer to ST. PAUL CIVIC CENTER listing under ARENAS for directions.

▲▲▲▲▲▲▲▲▲▲▲▲▲▲▲▲▲▲▲▲▲▲▲▲▲▲▲▲▲▲▲▲▲▲▲▲

ST. PAUL WINTER CARNIVAL

St. Paul Festival and Heritage Foundation, 101 Norwest Center, 55 E. 5th St., St. Paul, MN 55101 (612) 297-6953

The St. Paul Winter Carnival is the largest winter festival in the U.S. This annual 10-day festival, conceived in 1886, relives the legend of Boreas, King of all Winds, who granted each of his four siblings control of one of the four winds. He and the Four Winds traveled to the winter paradise known as Minnesota and made St. Paul and her seven hills the capital and winter playground of the Realm of Boreas. With the Queen of Snows, he created a winter carnival for joyous celebration, music, dancing, feasting, and frolic. The king and queen, along with the Winds and Princesses, reign over the festivities. On the final night of celebration, Boreas must bid farewell to the people of his winter capital because of a fiery confrontation with Vulcanus Rex, king of fire, and his Krewe. Vulcanus Rex restores the warmth of springtime to St. Paul and reigns until the annual return of Boreas and his Winter Carnival.

Over one million people from Minnesota, the U.S., and many foreign countries partic-ipate in and enjoy the Winter Carnival each year. The Carnival has over 100 events, including the Grande Day and Torchlight Parades; the royal coronations; Jazzin' January; snow sculpting competitions; treasure hunt; the Frosty Fingers Kite Fly; sleigh and cutter parades; the Frozen Half Marathon; cross-country ski races; winter camping; dog sled races; and entire days of activities for children, families, and seniors.

COST: Most events are free or require a $3 Winter Carnival button. A few events charge fees.

DATES: Fourth weekend in January–first Sunday in February.

> Most events are held in St. Paul. Many are in Como Park, in downtown's Rice Park, Landmark Center, and the downtown Mississippi River area. Watch the papers and news for details on events and locations, or call 297-6953.

ST. PATRICK'S DAY PARADE

24 E. 4th St., St. Paul, MN 55101 (612) 298-1950

This is a nonmotorized marching parade taking place at noon on St. Patrick's Day. The public is encouraged to participate.

COST: $5 handling charge to participate in parade.

HOURS: St. Patrick's Day (March 17) each year: starts at noon, lasts one hour.

> Parade starts on Wacouta St. and goes up 4th St. to Rice Park in St. Paul. From I-94, take the 10th St. exit to Wacouta St. to reach the general vicinity of the parade.

CINCO DE MAYO CELEBRATION

176 Concord St., St. Paul, MN 55107 (612) 222-6347

Cinco de Mayo (May 5) is a day to celebrate pride and patriotism. The date commemorates the anniversary of a battle in 1862, when the Mexican army defeated the French in their attempt to colonize Mexico. Many celebrate Cinco de Mayo throughout the U.S. The Riverview Economic Development Association Board, staff, and Cinco de Mayo committee invite you to celebrate this gala event in St. Paul's West Side neighborhood.

> COST: Most events free.

> DATE: May 5.

> From I-94, exit on Hwy. 52 (Lafayette Bridge & Freeway) and follow Hwy. 52 south to Concord St. Exit and turn right onto Concord. Festival is on Concord.
>
> From I-494 eastbound or westbound, take the Hwy. 52 exit and follow Hwy. 52 north to Concord St. and exit. Turn left onto Concord. Festival is on Concord.

FESTIVAL OF NATIONS

1694 Como Ave., St. Paul, MN 55108 (612) 647-0191

Over 95 ethnic groups come together at the St. Paul Civic Center for Minnesota's largest multicultural event. This showcase of ethnic diversity provides continuous performances by 75 folk dance ensembles, ethnic foods at 48 cafes, folk art demonstrations by 46 skilled artisans, 65 cultural exhibits, and an international bazaar with 60 shopping booths.

> COST: Adults $7, youth 5–16 $4.

> DATES: For 1995: April 27–30. For 1996: May 2–5.

> Refer to ST. PAUL CIVIC CENTER listing under ARENAS for directions.

▲▲▲▲▲▲▲▲▲▲▲▲▲▲▲▲▲▲▲▲▲▲▲▲▲▲▲▲▲▲▲▲▲▲▲▲▲

One of the many beautiful ethnic costumes at the Festival of Nations.

▲▲

MAYDAY PARADE AND FESTIVAL

Powderhorn Park, 3400 15th Ave. S.. Minneapolis, MN 55407 (612) 721-2535

The much-loved Mayday Parade and Festival is produced every spring by the Heart of the Beast Puppet and Mask Theatre. The festival is held in Powderhorn Park and kicks off with the raising of the Tree of Life. Families can enjoy local bands; a variety of wandering minstrels and entertainers; a children's entertainment and play area; and concessions. The parade starts on the corner of E. 26th St. and Bloomington Ave. in Minneapolis, goes south to 33rd St. and finishes in Powderhorn Park.

COST: Most events free.

DATE: First Sunday in May.

From I-94 westbound, take the Cedar Ave. exit. Follow Cedar south to 35th St. Turn right onto 35th and go about 8 blocks to the park.

From I-35W northbound, take the 36th St. exit. Turn left onto 36th St. and follow to 15th Ave. Turn left onto 15th and follow to park.

From I-35W southbound, take the 36th St. exit. Turn right onto 36th St. and follow to 15th Ave. Turn left onto 15th and follow to park.

MINNESOTA HORSE EXPO

Minnesota State Fairgrounds, St. Paul, MN (612) 922-8666

If you are a horse lover, you won't want to miss this Horse Expo, with horses representing over 30 unique breeds; over 300 exhibitor booths providing horse information and products; and more than 20 daily lectures and demonstrations by horse trainers, judges, and other equine professionals. There's more: free horse rides, the 4-H Used Tack and Clothing Sale, the Saturday evening all-breed Horse and Stallion Service Auction, and the University of Minnesota's Large Animal Hospital tours and lectures. Horse owners and those just interested in learning more about horse care, breeds, and use will enjoy this educational event.

COST: Adults $5, seniors 65 and over $4, children 6–12 $2, children 5 and under free.

HOURS: April 29–30, 1995: Saturday 9 a.m.–8 p.m.; Sunday 9 a.m.–6 p.m.

From I-94, take the Snelling Ave. exit north to Commonwealth Ave. Go west on Commonwealth to the State Fairgrounds.

From I-35W northbound or southbound, take the Cleveland Ave. exit south to Commonwealth Ave. Follow Commonwealth east to the Fairgrounds.

From I-35E, take the Larpenteur Ave. exit and go west to Snelling Ave. Follow Snelling south to Commonwealth Ave. Follow Commonwealth west to the Fairgrounds.

▲▲▲▲▲▲▲▲▲▲▲▲▲▲▲▲▲▲▲▲▲▲▲▲▲▲▲▲▲▲▲▲▲▲▲▲▲▲

OPEN AIR INTERNATIONAL

St. Anthony Main along Historic Main Street, Minneapolis, MN 55401 (612) 378-1226

Enjoy an international blend of imports, ethnic music, steel drummers, and Minneapolis street artists each weekend May–September. For more information call 378-1226.

COST: Most events free.

DATES: Weekends May–September.

> From I-35W, take the 4th St. exit. Turn left onto 4th St. and follow to 3rd Ave. S.E. Take a left onto 3rd Ave. S.E. and follow about 4 blocks to Main St. St. Anthony Main is on Main St.

ROSELAWN STABLES

24069 N. W. Rum River Blvd., St. Francis, MN 55070 Information and reservations (612) 753-5517

Roselawn Stables is a wonderful place to visit with the kids from spring through fall. Children are encouraged to have a hands-on experience with baby animals and their mothers, and gain knowledge of each animal and its usefulness in a 1930s farm setting. Additional activities include sheep shearing; spinning wool; basic horse care; goat milking; pony rides; soap making, leather working, candle dipping, and maple syrup tapping demonstrations; a Horse Day Camp program; and hay and sleigh rides.

COST: Activity fees 50¢–$5. Sleigh and hay rides $35–$50.

HOURS: Please call ahead for reservations and specific dates and times of varying activities.

> From Hwy. 694, take the Hwy. 10 exit. Follow Hwy. 10 north to Co. Rd. 9. Go north on Co. Rd. 9 to Hwy. 24. Follow Hwy. 24 west to #72. Proceed about 1-1/2 miles on #72 to Roselawn Stables.
>
> From Hwy. 65, take the Hwy. 24 exit. Follow Hwy. 24 west to #72. Proceed about 1-1/2 miles on #72 to Roselawn Stables.

TWIN CITIES JUNETEENTH CELEBRATION

1701 Oak Park Ave. N., Minneapolis, MN 55411 (612) 377-7000

Come and enjoy and participate in the largest African-American cultural celebration in Minnesota. It features a festival of African-American films; emerging artists' competitions; a 5K run; re-enactment of the underground railroad; an African village; and a health fair.

COST: Some events have fees.

DATES: May 15–June 30.

> Please call for brochure on events and exact locations throughout the Twin Cities.

APPLESIDE ORCHARD'S SPECIAL EVENTS

18010 Chippendale Ave., Farmington, MN 55024 (612) 463-2505

In addition to 100 acres of apples, strawberries, raspberries, and pumpkins to pick from, Appleside Orchard features special events: free hayrides; storytellers; live bluegrass music; a kite-flying extravaganza in the second week of September; and a scarecrow-building event in the fall. Send for flyer on dates and times of events at address above.

> COST: Varies. Free hay and pony rides.

> HOURS: Daily in June 7 a.m.–6 p.m. Closed in July. Daily August–October: 9 a.m.–6 p.m. November: Tuesday–Saturday noon–5 p.m.

> From I-35W or Cedar Ave., go east on Co. Rd. 42 to Hwy. 3, go south about 3-1/2 miles. Orchard is on the left side.

HASTINGS RIVERTOWN DAYS FESTIVAL

Hastings Area Chamber of Commerce, 119 W. 2nd St., Suite 201, Hastings, MN 55033 (612) 437-6775

Rivertown Days Festival is a community festival for all ages in Hastings, MN. The Festival features a water ski show; fireworks display; carnival; Olde Tyme Ice Cream Social; car show; arts and crafts fair; music; sporting events; parades; and much more.

> COST: Most events free.

> DATES: Third weekend in July: Friday afternoon–Sunday.

> Hastings is approximately 10 miles southeast of the Twin Cities. Take Hwy. 55 or Hwy. 61 into Hastings. Events take place at multiple sites in the community.

HIGHLAND FEST

Highland Business Association, 2004 Ford Pkwy., St. Paul, MN 55116 (612) 699-9042

In mid-August, St. Paul's Highland Village and Hillcrest Park host three fun-filled days of nonstop entertainment and events the whole family will enjoy. You will find the exhibits from 125 of the Midwest's leading artists and crafts people along the sidewalks throughout Highland Village. A children's carnival features clowns; jugglers; games; magicians; puppets; children's music; pony rides; and much more. Write or call for a brochure.

▲▲▲▲▲▲▲▲▲▲▲▲▲▲▲▲▲▲▲▲▲▲▲▲▲▲▲▲▲▲▲▲▲▲▲▲▲

COST: Varies.

HOURS: Call for hours.

Festival is near the intersection of Cleveland Ave. and Ford Pkwy.

From I-35E, take the Randolph St. exit. Follow Randolph west to Fairview. Take Fairview south to Ford Pkwy.

From I-94, take the Fairview exit. Follow Fairview south to Ford Pkwy.

HOPKINS RASPBERRY FESTIVAL

6 Sixth Ave. N., Hopkins, MN 55343 (612) 931-0878

The Hopkins Raspberry Festival is a family-oriented tradition in Hopkins. Special attractions include musical entertainment in the park; fashion show; celebrity golf tournament; kiddie parade; Jaycees tent dance; softball tournaments; ice cream social; variety show; annual fishing contest; sidewalk sales; clowns; magic show; arts and crafts sale; vendors; and more.

COST: Many events are free.

DATES: Third weekend in July. All events are held on Main Street in

Hopkins. From Hwy. 169, take the Excelsior Blvd. exit. Follow Excelsior Blvd. east to 5th Ave. N. and follow to Main St. Turn left onto Main St. and follow to events.

ISANTI RODEO JUBILEE DAYS

Located on Hwy. 65 and Co. Rd. 5 throughout Isanti, MN

Sponsored by the Isanti Fire Department, this pro rodeo has become so prominent that it attracts the top 10 rodeo cowboys/cowgirls in the U.S. Rodeo Jubilee Days also hosts a parade; Heritage Corral, filled with kids' games and pony rides; national clown acts; food; stage shows; softball tournaments; outhouse races; a dance; and "better than most" fireworks.

COST: Adults about $6.50, children about $5. Children free Sunday when accompanied by an adult.

DATES: Third weekend in July.

From Hwy. 694, take the Hwy. 65 exit north about 40 miles. Rodeo grounds are located north of Isanti. Events take place throughout Isanti on Hwy. 65 and Co. Rd. 5.

SEASONAL EVENTS

▲▲▲▲▲▲▲▲▲▲▲▲▲▲▲▲▲▲▲▲▲▲▲▲▲▲▲▲▲▲▲▲▲▲▲▲▲▲

MARKETFEST

Washington Square, White Bear Lake, MN (612) 429-8535

This weekly food and entertainment event is held Thursday nights in Railroad Park in downtown White Bear Lake. Marketfest includes entertainment; crafters; artists; children's activities; a farmer's market, and food.

COST: Many events free or at minimal charges.

HOURS: June 23–August 25: 6–9 p.m.

> Located in downtown White Bear Lake in Railroad Park at the corner of Hwy. 61 and 4th St.
>
> From I-35E, take the Hwy. 96 exit. Follow Hwy. 96 east to Hwy. 61. Follow Hwy. 61 north (left) to the intersection of Hwy. 61 and 4th St. and look for festival site.
>
> From Hwy. 61 northbound, go into White Bear Lake to the intersection of Hwy. 61 and 4th St.

MIDSOMMAR

American Swedish Institute, 2600 Park Ave., Minneapolis, MN 55407-1090 (612) 871-4907

The Midsommar festival re-enacts the well-loved Swedish holiday celebrating the summer solstice, when daylight becomes endless after long winter darkness in the northern reaches of Sweden. Bring the entire family and enjoy this festival of music, folk dancing, arts, crafts, and food.

COST: Most events free.

HOURS: Third Saturday in June 10 a.m.–4 p.m.

> From I-35W northbound, take the Lake St./31st St. exit and go east to Park Ave. Proceed north on Park Ave. to the Institute.
>
> From I-35W southbound, take the Hiawatha exit. Follow Hiawatha to 26th St. Go west on 26th to the Institute on the corner of 26th St. and Park Ave.

▲▲▲▲▲▲▲▲▲▲▲▲▲▲▲▲▲▲▲▲▲▲▲▲▲▲▲▲▲▲▲▲▲▲▲▲

MINNEAPOLIS AQUATENNIAL

Each July, Minneapolis hosts 10 days of traditional and multicultural events, intended to bring people from all of Minneapolis' diverse communities together in celebration of summertime. The Aquatennial is famous for its Grande Day Parade featuring floats, celebrities, and the Midwest's best high school marching bands. The Torchlight Parade, featuring more than 30 elaborately lighted floats, attracts more than a quarter million spectators.

COST: Most events free.

DATES: 10 days beginning the third week in July.

Local newspapers list daily events with times and locations.

MINNEAPOLIS FOURTH OF JULY FIREWORKS

125 S.E. Main St., Minneapolis, MN 55414 (612) 673-5123

Minneapolis fireworks take place along the Mississippi River at historic St. Anthony Main.

HOURS: July 4 at dusk.

From I-35W, take the 4th St. exit. Turn left onto 4th St. and follow to 3rd Ave. S.E. Turn left again onto 3rd Ave. S.E. and follow about 4 blocks to Main St. St. Anthony Main is on Main St.

MINNEAPOLIS-ST. PAUL INTERNATIONAL AIRPORT

Lindbergh Terminal, Minneapolis, MN (612) 726-5574

Visit the Lindbergh Terminal's enclosed observation deck in the Green Concourse for a grand view of the Airport's 3,000-acre airfield, aircraft takeoffs and landings, and airport ground operations. Each August, the Metropolitan Airports Commission also invites you to a behind-the-scenes look at MSP during "Airport Days," with tours, exhibits, and airplanes on display.

COST: Free.

HOURS: The observation deck is open daily 6 a.m.–9 p.m.

Airport Days: third weekend in August 9 a.m.–5 p.m.

To Airport: From I-494 or Hwy. 5, follow the Airport exit signs to Airport.
To Airport Days: From Hwy. 62, take the 28th Ave. exit and follow signs to Airport Days.

▲▲▲▲▲▲▲▲▲▲▲▲▲▲▲▲▲▲▲▲▲▲▲▲▲▲▲▲▲▲▲▲▲▲▲▲▲▲▲

MISSISSIPPI MILE

MCDA Riverfront Team, 105 5th Ave. S., Minneapolis, MN 55401

Mississippi Mile Hotline (612) 673-5123 TDD (612) 673-5154

Minneapolis' Mississippi Mile is a spectacular place to visit in the summer and winter because of its historic sites; one-of-a-kind shops; restaurants; concerts; special events; popular fireworks celebrations; walking tours; and scenic river parks. Call or write for an updated schedule of events, shopping locations, and restaurants.

COST: Varies.

HOURS: Guided walking tours in summer on Saturdays and Sundays. East Bank tours, starting from St. Anthony Main, run hourly noon–4 p.m.

> The Mississippi Mile runs from the I-35 Bridge to Plymouth Ave. with several entry points. The following directions will get you to the St. Anthony Main entry point:
>
> From I-35W, take the 4th St. exit. Turn left onto 4th St. and follow to 3rd Ave. S.E. Take a left onto 3rd Ave. S.E. and follow about 4 blocks to Main St. St. Anthony Main is on Main St.

OPEN AIR INTERNATIONAL

St. Anthony Main along Historic Main Street, Minneapolis, MN 55401 (612) 378-1226

Enjoy an international blend of imports, ethnic music, steel drummers, and Minneapolis street artists each weekend May–September. For more information call 378-1226.

COST: Most events free.

DATES: Weekends May–September.

> From I-35W, take the 4th St. exit. Turn left onto 4th St. and follow to 3rd Ave. S.E. Take a left onto 3rd Ave. S.E. and follow about 4 blocks to Main St. St. Anthony Main is on Main St.

POWDERHORN FESTIVAL

Powderhorn Park, 3400 15th Ave. S., Minneapolis, MN 55407 (612) 721-2535

Powderhorn Festival is a two-day juried art festival featuring 170 top artists from the Midwest. The Festival also features high-class entertainment on two stages; a children's art and craft area; and outstanding ethnic food. An average of 45,000–50,000 visitors attend the Festival, which is set up around beautiful Lake Powderhorn.

▲▲▲▲▲▲▲▲▲▲▲▲▲▲▲▲▲▲▲▲▲▲▲▲▲▲▲▲▲▲▲▲▲▲▲▲

COST: Most events free.

HOURS: First weekend in August: Saturday 10 a.m.–6 p.m.; Sunday 11 a.m.–5
p.m.

> From I-35W, take the 35th/36th St. exit. Go east on 36th St. to any street
> between 10th and 15th Ave., then go north (left) to park.

RICE STREET FESTIVAL

1061 Rice St., St. Paul, MN 55117 (612) 488-1039

The Rice Street Festival is a St. Paul neighborhood tradition that has grown over the
past 80 years. This five-day Festival is kicked off with a large two-hour parade including floats, clowns, and marching bands. A sidewalk extravaganza of arts, crafts, sidewalk sales, and food vendors takes place on Saturday. Throughout the weekend, you
can expect to find several baseball tournaments along with a Kids' Superstar
Competition. The Festival draws over 20,000 visitors.

COST: Most events Most events free.

DATES: Five days beginning with a parade the last Wednesday in July.

> From I-35E, take the Maryland Ave. exit. Follow Maryland west to Rice St.
> Follow Rice south for most activities. Parade starts at Atwater St. and Rice St.
> and ends at Arlington Ave. and Rice St.

RICHFIELD 4TH OF JULY CELEBRATION

66th and Chicago, Richfield, MN 55423. (612) 866-3061

For the past 16 years, Richfield's 4th of July Celebration has attracted over 35,000 people. The festivities start with a parade at 1 p.m. It starts at 70th and Lyndale Ave., goes
north to 66th St. and Lyndale, and east to 12th Ave. The parade breaks up about 2
blocks from Veterans Memorial Park, where most of the celebration takes place. A carnival, concessions, and local performers can be enjoyed by all in the afternoon and
evening hours. Fireworks top off the day at dusk.

COST: Free; you are asked to buy a $2 celebration button to help support the
cost of this celebration.

DATE: July 4.

> From I-494, take the Portland Ave. exit. Follow Portland Ave. north about 10-
> 11 blocks to 66th St. Turn right onto 66th. Veterans Memorial Park is on the
> left.

221

RONDO DAYS PARADE AND FESTIVAL

Martin Luther King Center, 270 N. Kent St., St. Paul, MN 55102 (612) 646-7479
Information hotline: (612) 646-6597

Rondo Days is a one-day festival that celebrates the old Rondo community, a predominantly African-American neighborhood of St. Paul's past. The Festival also seeks to promote good community ties and education. The public is invited to come and learn a little bit of history from people who once lived in the Rondo community.

A parade on Saturday kicks off the Festival, which also features entertainment; food vendors; children's events; promotion of entrepreneurship; and a marching competition held at the Jimmy Griffon Stadium (Central High School Football Stadium). Children's events include games; storytelling; a moon walk; a visit from Ronald McDonald; face painting; entertainment oriented to children; and much more.

COST: Most events free.

HOURS: Third Saturday in July: parade starts 10 a.m. Festival noon–7 p.m.
Marching competition 7 p.m.–10 p.m.

> Festival is located at the Martin Luther King Center. From I-94, take the Dale St. exit. Follow Dale south to Iglehart Ave. Go east (left) on Iglehart to Kent St. Proceed north on Kent. The Martin Luther King Center is on Kent St. Parade starts at St. Peter Claver Church at the corner of Central Ave. and Oxford St. and goes east onto Victoria St. From Victoria the parade heads south to Concordia Ave. (the old Rondo St.), east to St. Albans St., south to Marshall Ave., and east past Martin Luther King Park to Arundel St., where it ends at Marshall and Arundel.

ST. PAUL FOURTH OF JULY FIREWORKS

State Capitol grounds, Saint Paul, MN 55155 (612) 228-0018

St. Paul's fireworks display takes place at "Taste of Minnesota" on the State Capitol grounds.

DATE: July 4.

> Approaching downtown St. Paul from any main highway such as I-35E or I-94, look for the State Capitol exit signs and follow to the Capitol.

▲▲▲▲▲▲▲▲▲▲▲▲▲▲▲▲▲▲▲▲▲▲▲▲▲▲▲▲▲▲▲▲▲▲▲▲▲▲▲

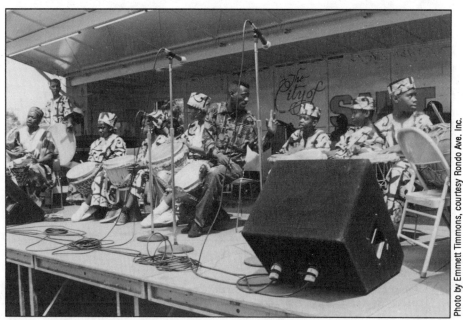

Music is a popular ingredient of the Rondo Days Parade and Festival.

Photo by Emmett Timmons, courtesy Rondo Ave. Inc.

SUMMER MOVIES AND MUSIC IN THE PARK

Loring Park, Minneapolis, MN (612) 348-8226

Summer Movies and Music in the Park is a special event in Loring Park for eight consecutive Monday evenings. The public is invited to come and enjoy evenings filled with diverse musical entertainment and a variety of popular movies.

COST: Free.

HOURS: Monday evenings July–August. Concerts begin at 7 p.m., films follow
         at sunset.

From I-35W, take the I-94 exit. Follow I-94 west to the Lyndale/Hennepin
Ave. exit. As you come off the exit, stay to the right and follow to Lyndale.
Loring Park is on the corner of Lyndale Ave. S. and Harmon Place. Concerts
are in band area in the center of the park.

SEASONAL EVENTS

▲▲▲▲▲▲▲▲▲▲▲▲▲▲▲▲▲▲▲▲▲▲▲▲▲▲▲▲▲▲▲▲▲▲▲

SVENSKARNAS DAG (SWEDES' DAY)

Minnehaha Park, Minneapolis. Sponsored by American Swedish Institute, 2600 Park Ave., Minneapolis, MN 55407-1090 (612) 871-4907

Svenskarnas Dag is the largest midsummer Swedish folk arts and music festival in America. For the past 61 years this festival has taken place each June in Minnehaha Park in Minneapolis. For more information on the day's activities, contact the American Swedish Institute, 871-4907. While in Minnehaha Park, be sure to see Minnehaha Falls, which served as the inspiration for Henry Wadsworth Longfellow's The Song of Hiawatha.

COST: Contributions only.

DATE: Fourth Sunday in June.

> From Hiawatha Ave. or Minnehaha Ave. southbound, turn left (east) on Godfrey Pkwy. Travel east on Godfrey to park entrance.
>
> From Hwy. 62 or Hwy. 55, exit on Minnehaha Ave. and go north to Godfrey Pkwy. Travel east on Godfrey to park entrance.
>
> From Ford Pkwy. westbound, cross the Mississippi River and turn left onto Nawadaha Blvd. Turn left onto Minnehaha Ave. and turn another quick left onto Godfrey Pkwy. to park entrance.

TASTE OF MINNESOTA

State Capitol grounds, St. Paul, MN 55155 (612) 228-0018

This five-day food and music festival is an event you won't want your family to miss. The public enjoys entertainment and samples food specialties from diverse Minnesota restaurants. The last night of the festival is topped off with a spectacular fireworks display.

COST: Food and merchandise have charges.

DATES: June 30–July 4.

> Approaching downtown St. Paul from any main highway such as I-35E or I-94, look for the State Capitol exit signs and follow to the Capitol.

TWIN CITIES JUNETEENTH CELEBRATION

1701 Oak Park Ave. N., Minneapolis, MN 55411 (612) 377-7000

Come and enjoy and participate in the largest African-American cultural celebration in

▲▲▲▲▲▲▲▲▲▲▲▲▲▲▲▲▲▲▲▲▲▲▲▲▲▲▲▲▲▲▲▲▲▲

Minnesota. It features a festival of African-American films; emerging artists' competitions; a 5K run; re-enactment of the underground railroad; an African village; and a health fair.

COST: Some events have fees.

DATES: May 15–June 30.

> Please call for brochure on events and exact locations throughout the Twin Cities.

WHITE BEAR LAKE'S MANITOU DAYS

Contact the White Bear Lake Area Chamber of Commerce, White Bear Lake, MN 55110 (612) 429-8593

White Bear Lake's Manitou Days is an annual five-day June festival to signal the beginning of summer. This family-oriented festival has something for the young and the young at heart. New ideas and events are added every year, but popular events such as the parade, beach dance, and Family Fun Day remain the foundation of this unique community celebration.

COST: Most events free.

DATES: Five days each June. Call for information.

> From I-35E, take the Hwy. 96 exit. Turn right onto Hwy. 96 and follow to Hwy. 61. Go north on Hwy. 61 to downtown White Bear Lake. Event locations vary throughout the town.

WORLD WAR II AIR POWER DISPLAY

St. Paul Downtown Airport (Holman Field), St. Paul, MN (612) 455-6942

For three days each year, contemporary aircraft and three dozen World War II, Korean, and Vietnam-era aircraft are displayed for the public. Have a close-up look at the B-29 Super Fortress, the show's only flying World War II aircraft (the same design as the plane that dropped the atomic bomb on Japan), and the B-24 Liberator, a heavy four-engine bomber from World War II. Many other displays and guest speakers add to the experience. The purpose of the World War II Air Power Display Show is to raise funds for restoration and educational programs for the Confederate Air Force aircraft restoration organization.

COST: Adults $7, children 12 and under $2, donations welcome.

▲▲▲▲▲▲▲▲▲▲▲▲▲▲▲▲▲▲▲▲▲▲▲▲▲▲▲▲▲▲▲▲▲▲

HOURS: August 4–6: gates open 9 a.m.–6 p.m.

From I-94, take the Hwy. 52 exit south to Plato Blvd. and follow signs to the airport. The display is at the main terminal. Police will direct you to appropriate parking.

▲▲▲▲▲▲▲▲▲▲▲▲▲▲▲▲▲▲▲▲▲▲▲▲▲▲▲▲▲▲▲▲▲▲▲▲▲

APPLESIDE ORCHARD'S SPECIAL EVENTS

18010 Chippendale Ave., Farmington, MN 55024 (612) 463-2505

In addition to 100 acres of apples, strawberries, raspberries, and pumpkins to pick from, Appleside Orchard features special events: free hayrides; storytellers; live blue-grass music; a kite flying extravaganza in the second week of September; and a scare-crow-building event in the fall. Send for flyer on dates and times of events at address above.

COST: Varies. Free hay and pony rides.

HOURS: Daily in June 7 a.m.–6 p.m. Closed in July. Daily August–October: 9 a.m.–6 p.m. November: Tuesday–Saturday noon–5 p.m.

> From I-35W or Cedar Ave., go east on Co. Rd. 42 to Hwy. 3, go south about 3-1/2 miles. Orchard is on the left side.

DEFEAT OF JESSE JAMES DAYS

Northfield Convention and Visitors Bureau, 500 Water St. S., P.O. Box 198, Northfield, MN 55057-0198 (507) 645-5604 (800) 658-2548

If you enjoy a good Western, you won't want to miss this four-day festival that com-memorates the James-Younger gang's attempt to rob the First National Bank September 7, 1876, in Northfield, MN. There are re-enactments of the bank raid; an arts festival; arts and crafts shows; a rodeo and rodeo dance; old-time tractor pull; mid-way; carnival; parade; contests; and a variety of musical entertainment, food, and activities. Call for additional information.

COST: Varies according to events.

DATES: Each September the week after Labor Day.

> Travel south on Hwy. 3 or I-35W to Northfield. Events take place in a variety of locations.

EDEN APPLE ORCHARD'S HALLOWEEN HAYRIDES

Pioneer Trail and Dell Road, Eden Prairie, MN (612) 934-7873

Experience thrills and chills as you ride hay wagons through the deep, dark enchanted forest. Encounter witches, ghosts and goblins, and other creepy, crawly creatures of the night. Top off the night with a free fresh apple and cup of cider. Available for sale are fresh-picked apples, pumpkins, and lots of Halloween costumes, make-up and accessories for children and adults in the Witch's Wagon.

COST: Adults $7, children $6. Discount coupons and group discounts available.

HOURS: Wagons leave continuously every night in October 7–9:30 p.m., weather permitting.

> Located 3 miles west of Flying Cloud Airport in Eden Prairie. Take Hwy. 169 to Co. Rd. 1 (Pioneer Trail). On Pioneer Trail, go 3 miles to Dell Road.

EMMA KRUMBEE'S ANNUAL SCARECROW FESTIVAL

Hwy. 169, Belle Plaine, MN 56011 (612) 873-4334

Emma Krumbee's Annual Scarecrow Festival in October is a chance for the entire family to get in the spirit of fall and experience a variety of fun activities. The festival features a unique display of almost 100 scarecrows; wagon rides; festival games; a hay maze; pick-your-own apples and pumpkins; and a friendly petting zoo. The display of scarecrows is actually a contest with entries from all over Minnesota. Scarecrows are judged for originality in the categories of contemporary, traditional, and humorous; children's, teenagers', and adults' scarecrows. Spots fill up fast, so send for your entry form early. Entry forms are available upon request August 30 with a deadline of September 25. Emma Krumbee's awards $4,500 in cash prizes and ribbons. Call for event information and group tour reservations.

COST: Reasonably priced family fun; prices vary depending on activity.

DATES: Open daily during October.

> From I-494 heading toward Eden Prairie, take the Hwy. 169 exit. Follow 169 south through Eden Prairie and Shakopee. Proceed 15 miles south of Shakopee on Hwy. 169 to Emma Krumbee's on the left.
>
> From I-35W, take the Hwy. 13 exit west and follow until it meets Hwy. 101. Take Hwy. 101 north into Shakopee to Hwy. 169. Follow 169 south about 15 miles to Emma Krumbee's on the left.

▲▲▲▲▲▲▲▲▲▲▲▲▲▲▲▲▲▲▲▲▲▲▲▲▲▲▲▲▲▲▲▲▲▲▲▲▲▲

Photo courtesy Emma Krumbee's Apple Orchard.

One of nearly 100 scarecrows at Emma Krumbee's Annual Scarecrow Festival.

EUROPEAN OKTOBERFEST

Kramarczuk's, 225 E. Hennepin Ave., Minneapolis, MN 55414 (612) 379-3018

The increasingly popular European Oktoberfest is a three-day ethnic festival which takes place along E. Hennepin at University Ave. in the Old St. Anthony ethnic district of Minneapolis. Local ethnic restaurants unite to provide the public with a taste of old-world traditions through authentic German, Polish, Ukrainian, Romanian, Italian, and

▲▲▲▲▲▲▲▲▲▲▲▲▲▲▲▲▲▲▲▲▲▲▲▲▲▲▲▲▲▲▲▲▲▲▲▲▲▲

Russian ethnic food specialties; costumed dancers; music; performances; historic and ethnic information booth; genealogy and cultural traditions.

Attractions include the Bavarian Musikmeister; Dolina Polish Folk Dancers; Armenian Dance Ensemble; Cheryvnyky Ukrainian Band; Zuhrah Shrine German Band; Tapestry Folk Dancers; Minneapolis Accordion Club; City Lights Horsedrawn Carriages; Pied Piper Historic Tours of St. Anthony Falls and the ethnic neighborhood; Romanian Dancers; chimney sweeps; Italian puppet shows and clowns; children's "gingerbread" area; perogies; Kramarczuk's Sausage; drawing for European trip; ethnic films; and more.

> COST: Most events free.

> HOURS: September 29, 5 p.m.–10 p.m.; September 30, 11 a.m.–10 p.m.; October 1, noon–6 p.m.

Located along E. Hennepin at University Ave. in the Old St. Anthony ethnic district of Minneapolis.

From I-35W or I-94 eastbound or westbound, take the downtown Minneapolis exit and follow to Hennepin Ave. Proceed on Hennepin north to the Mississippi River. Cross the Hennepin Avenue Suspension Bridge over the river and continue 2 blocks to Oktoberfest at E. Hennepin and University.

EXCELSIOR'S APPLE DAY FESTIVAL

Water St., Excelsior, MN 55331 (612) 474-6461

Excelsior's Apple Day Festival is held on the first Saturday after Labor Day each September. Staged along the main street of this historic town, Apple Day is the premier street festival of the Lake Minnetonka area. The Festival features apples; produce; antiques; crafts; and collectibles. Entertainment includes a calliope; clog dancers; an old-time band; singers; and street musicians. A great variety of food adds to the fun.

> COST: Varies.

> HOURS: First Saturday after Labor Day 8 a.m.–4 p.m.

From I-494 on the west side of Minneapolis, take the Hwy. 7 exit. Follow Hwy. 7 west, and go past Hwy. 101 and Vine Hill Rd. Turn right onto Co. Rd. 19 and right again onto Water St. Water St. is the main street of Excelsior.

MINNESOTA RENAISSANCE FESTIVAL

3525 145th St. W., Shakopee, MN 55379 (612) 445-7361 1-800-966-8215

▲▲▲▲▲▲▲▲▲▲▲▲▲▲▲▲▲▲▲▲▲▲▲▲▲▲▲▲▲▲▲▲▲▲▲▲▲▲

If you enjoy new and unusual experiences, spend a day in this 16th-century village filled with a large array of characters from the Renaissance. Over 600 entertainers create a fun-filled atmosphere you will not soon forget. Children can enjoy a unique variety of rides, animals, and games in the Children's Realm, a challenging play area. Eight stages provide lively entertainment every day.

Choose from over 150 ethnic and American food booths. More than 250 craftspeople display their distinctive wares and perform demonstrations that entertain as well as educate.

COST: Adults $12.95, students and children 5–12 $4.95, seniors $10.95, children under 5 free.

HOURS: Approximately August 13–September 25: gates open 9 a.m.–7 p.m. rain or shine.

> From I-494, take the U.S. Hwy. 169 exit. Go south on 169 to the Renaissance Festival 4 miles south of Shakopee off Hwy. 169.
>
> From I-35W, take the Hwy. 13 exit west until it meets Hwy. 101. Continue on Hwy. 101 to U.S. Hwy. 169. Turn left (south) onto 169 and follow to the Renaissance Festival 4 miles south of Shakopee off Hwy. 169.

RICHFIELD CATTAILS DAYS

6400 Portland Ave., Richfield, MN (612) 866-3061

Over 60 crafters come together for an arts and crafts show during Richfield Cattails Days. On Saturday morning, the Farmer's Market is also open with wonderful harvest buys.

COST: Most events free.

DATES: Third weekend in September.

> From I-494, take the Portland Ave. exit. Follow Portland Ave. north to 64th St. Turn right onto Portland Ave. and proceed to the Farmer's Market lot on the right.

SPONSEL'S MINNESOTA HARVEST APPLE ORCHARD

Old Hwy. 169 Blvd., Jordan, MN 55352 (612) 492-2785, 492-7753 (49-Apple) or (800) 662-7753

September and October are the big apple months in Minnesota. Bring the family and pick 'em yourself or buy already picked. Sponsel's celebrates with hay rides; carnival;

▲▲▲▲▲▲▲▲▲▲▲▲▲▲▲▲▲▲▲▲▲▲▲▲▲▲▲▲▲▲▲▲▲▲

wagon and pony rides; hiking trails; petting zoo; and live music. The packing house features a gift shop; food products made at the orchard; lunch area; bakery; and observation deck to watch the packing and sorting operation.

COST: Most events free.

HOURS: Daily in January–July: 9 a.m.–5 p.m. August–October: 9 a.m.–7 p.m. Daily in November–December: 9 a.m.–6 p.m. Sleigh rides available November–April. Limited services January–July. Please call.

> From I-494 westbound, exit on U.S. Hwy. 169 going south through Shakopee. Go 2 miles past the stoplight in Jordan to Co. Rd. 59. Go south (left) on 59 and follow the Minnesota Harvest signs up the hill and into the woods about 1-1/2 miles. At Old Hwy. 169, turn right and follow to Minnesota Harvest at Apple Lovers' Lane.
>
> From I-35W southbound, exit at Hwy. 13 going west to Hwy. 101. Continue on 101 to U.S. Hwy. 169. Take 169 south through Shakopee. Continue 2 miles past the stoplight in Jordan to Co. Rd. 59 and proceed as above to Minnesota Harvest at Apple Lovers' Lane.

TRICK OR TREAT STREET

St. Paul Civic Center, 143 W. 4th St., St. Paul, MN 55401 (612) 224-7361

Trick or Treat Street brings back the fun and nostalgia of Halloween by providing a safe, happy environment for children to fill up their bags with goodies. Children trick-or-treat in the St. Paul Civic Center down a 300-foot street with 30 stops along the way. After their bags are full of loot, they enter into a festival area providing kid karaoke, a main entertainment stage, miniature golf, computer arcade, a dinosaur dig, and much, much more.

COST: Varies each year.

HOURS: For 1995: Saturday, October 28, 10 a.m.–8 p.m.

> Refer to the ST. PAUL CIVIC CENTER listing under ARENAS for directions.

WELCH VILLAGE AUTUMN FESTIVAL

26685 Co. 7 Blvd., Welch, MN 55089 (612) 258-4567

Autumn colors of the Cannon River Valley dominate the annual Welch Village Autumn Festival. The Festival features musical entertainment (top name Twin Cities bands); food; a ski swap; chair lift rides; arts and crafts; and mountain bike events.

▲▲▲▲▲▲▲▲▲▲▲▲▲▲▲▲▲▲▲▲▲▲▲▲▲▲▲▲▲▲▲▲▲▲▲▲

Children's activities include games; a small carnival area; clowns, face painting, and more.

COST: Around $2.

DATES: First Saturday and Sunday in October.

> Welch Village Ski Area is halfway between the cities of Hastings and Red Wing. From Hwy. 61, take Co. Rd. 7 and follow 3 miles to Welch Village Road.

▲▲▲▲▲▲▲▲▲▲▲▲▲▲▲▲▲▲▲▲▲▲▲▲▲▲▲▲▲▲▲▲▲▲

DAYTON'S (MINNEAPOLIS)

700 on the Mall (7th St. & Nicollet), Minneapolis, MN 55402-3200 (612) 375-2200
  See DAYTON'S (MINNEAPOLIS) listing under WINTER.

EDINBOROUGH PARK CHILDREN'S SPECIAL EVENTS

7700 York Ave. S., Edina, MN 55435 (612) 893-9890

Children's special events are held in Edinborough's unique community park under
glass. They include concerts, clowns, artists, puppet shows, and more. Children's events
move outside in the summer to Centennial Lakes Park. Call for details and schedule.

  COST: Free.

  HOURS: Tuesdays and Thursdays, noon. Call for specific program and recreation
          schedules.

From I-494, take the France Ave. exit north to 76th St. Turn right onto 76th
St. and proceed to York Ave. Turn right onto York and follow to Edinborough
in the middle of the block on the right.

SPONSEL'S MINNESOTA HARVEST APPLE ORCHARD

*Old Hwy. 169 Blvd., Jordan, MN 55352 (612) 492-2785, 492-7753 (49-Apple) or
(800) 662-7753*

  See SPONSEL'S MINNESOTA HARVEST APPLE ORCHARD listing under
  FALL

SHOPPING

▲▲▲▲▲▲▲▲▲▲▲▲▲▲▲▲▲▲▲▲▲▲▲▲▲▲▲▲▲▲▲▲▲▲▲▲

Call the Minneapolis Downtown Council for a map of downtown parking facilities, stores, restaurants, and "Do the Town" (validated parking program) participants.

Minneapolis Downtown Council (612) 338-3807

CITY CENTER

33 S. 6th St., Minneapolis, MN 55402 (612) 372-1200

To experience dynamic downtown shopping, visit the City Center, home to 75 specialty stores and restaurants and Montgomery Ward.

COST: Park in the City Center parking ramp any time after 4 p.m. With a same-day purchase of $20 from City Center merchants, receive free parking. Redeem receipts at the Customer Service Center on the first level of City Center.

HOURS: Monday–Friday 9:30 a.m.–8 p.m.; Saturday 9:30 a.m.–6 p.m.; Sunday noon–5 p.m.

City Center is located 1 block southeast from Target Center. Target Center is on 6th St. and 1st Ave.; City Center is on 6th St. and Hennepin Ave. The following directions will bring you to the City Center.

From I-94 westbound, take the 5th St. exit to 1st Ave. N. Follow 1st Ave. N. to 6th St. Go south on 6th to Hennepin Ave. City Center is at the intersection of 6th and Hennepin.

From I-94 eastbound, take the 4th St. exit. Follow 4th St. to 1st Ave. N. Turn right onto 1st Ave. N. Follow 1st Ave. N. to 6th St. Proceed south on 6th to Hennepin Ave. City Center is located at the intersection of 6th and Hennepin.

From I-35W northbound, take 5th Ave. downtown exit, turn left on 7th St. Go to 1st Ave. N. Follow 1st Ave. N. to 6th St. Proceed south on 6th to Hennepin Ave. City Center is at the intersection of 6th and Hennepin.

From I-35W southbound, take the Washington Ave. exit, turn right, go to 1st Ave. N. and turn left. Follow 1st Ave. N. to 6th St. Go south on 6th to Hennepin Ave. City Center is located at the intersection of 6th and Hennepin.

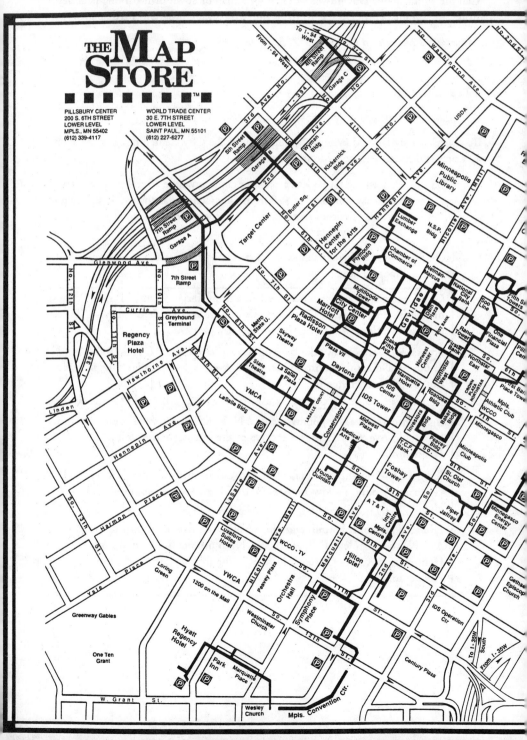

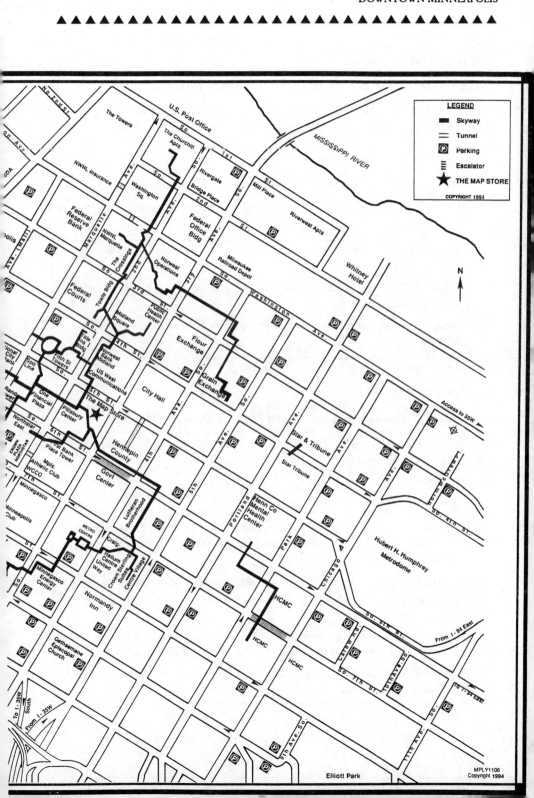

SHOPPING

DAYTON'S (MINNEAPOLIS)

700 on the Mall (7th St. & Nicollet), Minneapolis, MN 55402-3200 (612) 375-220

The Upper Midwest's leading department store also hosts extensive events and programs featuring personal appearances, exhibits, and fashion shows. Major events include the walk through the Auditorium holiday exhibit, and Dayton's/Bachman's Flower Show. Call for schedules and information.

    COST: Free. Some selected events are ticketed and may involve charges.

    HOURS: Monday–Friday 9:30 a.m.–9:30 p.m.; Saturday 10 a.m.–8 p.m.; Sunday 11 a.m.–6 p.m. Call for holiday hours.

> From I-94 westbound, take the 11th St. or 5th St. exit. Both intersect with Nicollet Mall.
>
> From I-35W northbound, take the 5th Ave. exit to 9th St., which intersects with Nicollet Mall.
>
> From I-394 eastbound, take the 6th St. exit. 6th St. intersects with the Nicollet Mall.

GAVIIDAE COMMON

6th and Nicollet, downtown Minneapolis, MN 55402 (612) 372-1222

Gaviidae Common houses Saks Fifth Avenue, Neiman Marcus, and 50 specialty stores, restaurants, and a food court.

    HOURS: Monday–Saturday 10 a.m.–7 p.m.; Sunday noon–5 p.m.

> From I-35W northbound, take the downtown/5th St. exit. Follow 5th St. to 7th St. Turn left onto 7th St. and proceed about 7 blocks to Hennepin Ave. Turn right onto Hennepin and follow 1 block to 6th St. Turn right on 6th St. and proceed 2 blocks to Gaviidae.
>
> From I-94 eastbound, take the 4th St. exit. Proceed east on 4th St. to 1st Ave. Turn right onto 1st Ave. and go 2 blocks to 6th St. Turn left onto 6th St. and proceed 3 blocks to Gaviidae.
>
> From I-94 westbound, go west to 5th St. (Metrodome) exit, 10 blocks to 1st Ave., left on 1st Ave. and immediate left on 6th St., 3 blocks to Gaviidae.
>
> From I-394 eastbound, take the 6th St. exit. Follow 6th St. 4 blocks to Gaviidae.

▲▲▲▲▲▲▲▲▲▲▲▲▲▲▲▲▲▲▲▲▲▲▲▲▲▲▲▲▲▲▲▲▲▲▲▲▲

NICOLLET MALL

For more information on Nicollet Mall, contact: Downtown Council of Minneapolis, 81 S. Ninth St., Suite 260, Minneapolis, MN 55402-3200 (612) 338-3807

> From I-94 westbound, take the 11th St. or 5th St. exit. Both exits intersect with the Nicollet Mall.
>
> From I-35W northbound, take the 5th Avenue exit. Follow 5th Ave. to 9th St., which intersects with Nicollet Mall.
>
> From Hwy. 394 eastbound, take the 6th St. exit. Follow 6th until it intersects with Nicollet Mall.

OPEN AIR INTERNATIONAL

St. Anthony Main along Historic Main St., Minneapolis, MN 55401 (612) 378-1226

Enjoy an international blend of shops. Ethnic music, steel drummers, and Minneapolis street artists each weekend May–September. For more information call (612) 378-1226.

COST: Free.

DATES: May–September weekends.

> From I-35W, take the 4th St. exit. Turn left onto 4th St. and follow to 3rd Ave. S.E. Take a left onto 3rd Ave. S.E. and follow about 4 blocks to Main St.

239

▲ ▲

GALTIER PLAZA

175 E. 5th St., Suite 315, Box 77, St. Paul, MN 55101 (612) 297-6734

Come enjoy St. Paul's exciting dining and entertainment district, including a four-screen movie theater; comedy gallery; night clubs with live entertainment; restaurants for fine dining; billiard parlor; indoor miniature golf course; food court for casual dining; unique gift shops; ethnic food shops; fashions; and more, all under one roof. Galtier Plaza is located in historic lowertown St. Paul overlooking beautiful Mears Park.

HOURS: Monday–Friday 10 a.m.–9 p.m.; Saturday 10 a.m.–6 p.m.; Sunday 11 a.m.–6 p.m.

> From I-35E southbound, take the Waucota exit. Turn right onto 6th St. and follow to Jackson St. Galtier Plaza is at the intersection of 6th St. and Jackson St.
>
> From I-35E northbound, take the Shepard Rd. exit. Follow Shepard Rd. east to Sibley St. Turn left onto Sibley St. and follow to Galtier Plaza, at the intersection of Sibley and 5th St.
>
> From I-94 westbound, take the 6th St. exit. Follow 6th St. west (one-way street) to Sibley St. Galtier Plaza is on the corner of 6th and Sibley.
>
> From I-94 eastbound, take the 5th St. exit and go east on 5th St. past Jackson St. Parking ramp to Galtier Plaza is located on 5th St. between Jackson and Sibley St.

TOWN SQUARE

444 Cedar St., Saint Paul, MN 55101 (612) 298-0900

Located in the heart of downtown St. Paul, Town Square offers more than 40 shops and eateries in addition to an indoor city park.

COST: Free. Receive three hours of free parking with a qualifying purchase at any Town Square store (see store for details).

HOURS: Monday and Thursday 10 a.m.—8 p.m.; Tuesday, Wednesday, Friday, Saturday 10 a.m.—6 p.m.; Sunday 12 p.m.—5 p.m. Longer hours during holiday season.

> From I-94 eastbound or I-35E northbound, take the 5th St. exit. Follow 5th St. to Minnesota St. Take a left onto Minnesota and follow to the Town Square Parking Ramp entrance.
>
> From I-94 westbound or I-35E southbound, take the 10th St. exit. Follow 10th to Cedar St. and turn left. Follow Cedar to the Town Square Parking Ramp on the left between 7th and 6th Sts.

ST. PAUL SKYWAY SYSTEM

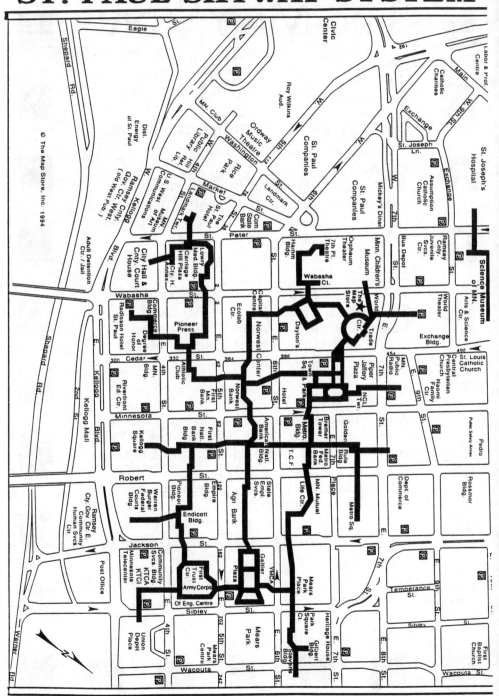

© The Map Store, Inc. 1994

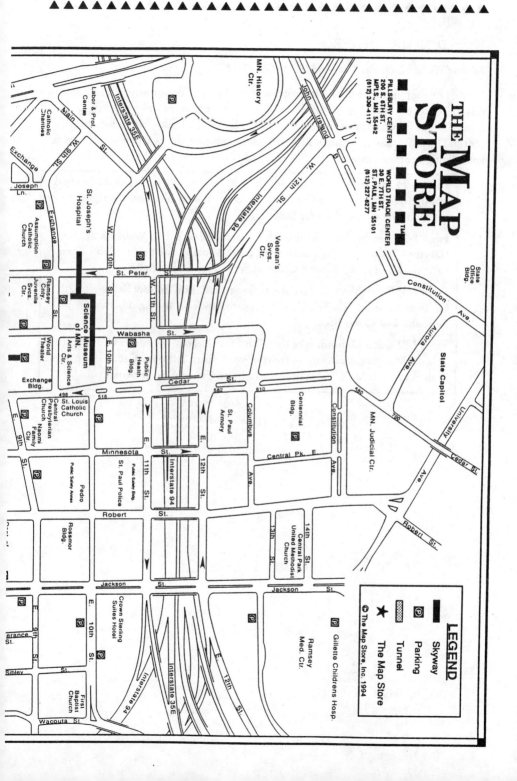

SHOPPING

▲▲▲▲▲▲▲▲▲▲▲▲▲▲▲▲▲▲▲▲▲▲▲▲▲▲▲▲▲▲▲▲▲▲▲▲▲

WORLD TRADE CENTER

7th and Wabasha, St. Paul, MN 55101 (612) 291-1715

A world of shopping and dining is available in the heart of downtown St. Paul. Shop this collection of more than 50 fashion and gift stores and relax while watching a dramatic 52-foot fountain in the spacious atrium. The World Trade Center, located adjacent to Dayton's, also offers three sit-down restaurants and an open food court to meet your dining needs. Complimentary World Trade Center shopping bags are available.

From I-94 eastbound, take the 5th St. exit. Follow 5th St. to 7th St. (second stoplight). Turn left onto 7th St. WTC is the fourth block on the right between Wabasha and Cedar Sts.

From I-94 westbound, take the 6th St. exit. Follow 6th to Wabasha St. (Dayton's is on the right). Turn right onto Wabasha and go to 7th St. Turn right onto 7th and follow to Cedar St. WTC is on your right.

From I-35E northbound, take the Kellogg Blvd. exit. Follow Kellogg to 7th St. Turn left onto 7th. WTC on the fourth block on the right between Wabasha and Cedar Sts.

From I-35E southbound, take the 10th St. exit. Follow 10th to Cedar St. (the Science Museum is directly in front of you). Turn left onto Cedar and proceed 3 blocks to 7th St. WTC is on your right on the southwest corner.

BANDANA SQUARE

1021 Bandana Blvd., St. Paul, MN 55108 (612) 642-1509

Built in 1885, Bandana Square was once a repair and maintenance shop for the iron horses that roared over the tracks of the North Pacific Railroad. Bandana Square is now a redeveloped retail, dining, and entertainment complex featuring turn-of-the-century architecture, 25 local merchants, and plenty of free parking. Included in the complex are the Twin City Terminal Railway; indoor and outdoor courtyards for concerts, dining, and relaxing.

COST: Free.

HOURS: Monday–Friday 10 a.m.–9 p.m.; Saturday 10 a.m.–6 p.m.; Sunday noon–5 p.m.

> From I-94, take the Lexington Pkwy. exit. Proceed north on Lexington to Energy Park Dr. Turn left onto Energy Park Dr. and follow to Bandana Square on the right.
>
> From Larpenteur Ave., take Snelling Ave. south to Energy Park Dr. Go east on Energy Park Dr. and follow to Bandana Square on the left.

BURNSVILLE CENTER

1178 Burnsville Center, Burnsville, MN 55306 (612) 435-8181

Known for its safe, convenient neighborhood shopping experience, Burnsville Center is anchored by four major department stores: Dayton's, Mervyns, J.C. Penney, and Sears. There are also over 155 premier retail stores and 17 dining facilities. Family entertainment is provided each Friday night with local performers like Bob and the Beachcombers. For more information call (612) 435-8182.

HOURS: Monday–Friday 10 a.m.–9 p.m.; Saturday 10 a.m.–8 p.m.; Sunday 11 a.m.–6 p.m.

> Located in Burnsville on Co. Rd. 42 off the intersection of I-35W and I-35E. From I-35W northbound, take the Crystal Lake Rd. exit. As you come off the exit, turn left and cross over I-35W to Buck Hill Road. Turn right onto Buck Hill Road and follow to the Center.
>
> From I-35W or I-35E southbound, take the Co. Rd. 42 exit. Turn right onto Co. Rd. 42 and follow to the Center.

SHOPPING

CALHOUN SQUARE

Refer to Minneapolis' Uptown Shopping District listing.

EDEN PRAIRIE SHOPPING CENTER

1018 Eden Prairie Center, MN 55344 (612) 941-7650

Shop Kohl's; Sears; Target; Mervyns, and over 70 specialty shops, including Kids Quest; UA Theatres; B. Dalton; Radio Shack; The Limited; County Seat; Foot Locker, and Victoria's Secret. For more information, call.

> HOURS: Monday–Friday 10 a.m.–9 p.m.; Saturday 10 a.m.–6 p.m.; Sunday 11 a.m.–6 p.m.

> From I-494 eastbound, take the Valley View Rd. exit. Turn left and follow Prairie Center Dr. to Eden Prairie Center.
>
> From I-494 westbound, take the Hwy. 169 exit going south. Turn left at the traffic light and take another left at Singletree Lane. Follow Singletree Lane to Eden Prairie Center.

HAR-MAR MALL

2100 N. Snelling Ave., Roseville, MN 55113 (612) 631-0340

Har-Mar Mall is home to the 11 Har-Mar Theaters; Marshall's; Michaels Arts and Crafts; Barnes & Noble bookstore; T. J. Maxx; and many more popular stores.

> HOURS: Monday–Friday 10 a.m.–9 p.m.; Saturday 10 a.m.–6 p.m.; Sunday noon–5 p.m.

> From Hwy. 36, go south on Snelling Ave. about 1/4 mile to Har-Mar Mall on the left.
>
> From Larpenteur Ave., go north on Snelling Ave. to Har-Mar Mall on the right.

HORIZON OUTLET CENTER

10150 Hudson Rd., Woodbury, MN 55125 (612) 735-9060

Purchase famous brand-name apparel; shoes; gifts; home furnishings; children's wear; luggage; jewelry; and cosmetics direct from the manufacturer.

▲▲▲▲▲▲▲▲▲▲▲▲▲▲▲▲▲▲▲▲▲▲▲▲▲▲▲▲▲▲▲▲▲▲▲▲▲

HOURS: Monday–Saturday 10 a.m.–9 p.m.; Sunday 11 a.m.–6 p.m. Closed Easter, Thanksgiving, and Christmas.

> Located in Woodbury on I-94 and Co. Rd. 19.
>
> From I-94, take the 251 exit onto Co. Rd. 19. Follow Co. Rd. 19 to Hudson Rd. Turn left onto Hudson Rd. and follow to the Horizon Outlet Center.

KNOLLWOOD MALL

8332 Hwy. 7, St. Louis Park, MN 55426 (612) 933-8041

Main attractions at the Knollwood Mall include Montgomery Ward; Knollwood 4 Theaters; food court; T.J. Maxx; and Kohl's, scheduled to open in August 1995.

HOURS: Monday–Friday 10 a.m.–9 p.m.; Saturday 10 a.m.–6 p.m.; Sunday noon-5 p.m.

> From Hwy. 169, take the Hwy. 7 exit. Proceed east on Hwy. 7 about 1/2 mile to Knollwood Mall on the left.

The Mall of America with the Minneapolis skyline in the distance.

▲▲▲▲▲▲▲▲▲▲▲▲▲▲▲▲▲▲▲▲▲▲▲▲▲▲▲▲▲▲▲▲▲▲▲▲▲

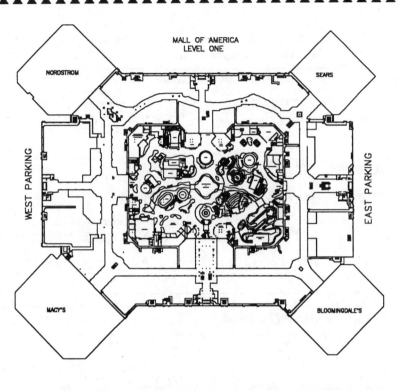

MALL OF AMERICA
LEVEL ONE

NORDSTROM

SEARS

WEST PARKING

EAST PARKING

MACY'S

BLOOMINGDALE'S

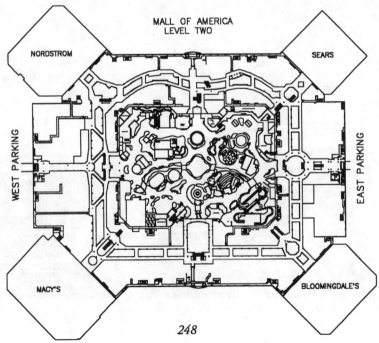

MALL OF AMERICA
LEVEL TWO

NORDSTROM

SEARS

WEST PARKING

EAST PARKING

MACY'S

BLOOMINGDALE'S

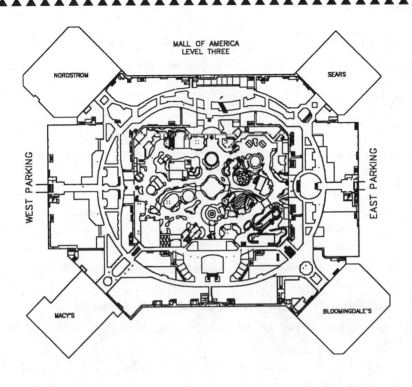

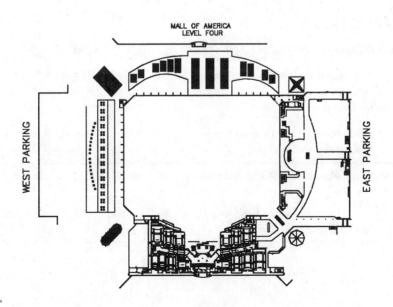

▲▲▲▲▲▲▲▲▲▲▲▲▲▲▲▲▲▲▲▲▲▲▲▲▲▲▲▲▲▲▲▲▲▲▲▲▲

MALL OF AMERICA

Bloomington, MN 55425 at the crossroads of I-494 and Hwy. 77 (Cedar Ave.) (612) 883-8800

Mall of America is the largest fully enclosed retail and entertainment complex in the United States. Over 400 specialty stores join the anchor tenants: Bloomingdale's, Macy's, Nordstrom's, and Sears. Added to the experience is Knott's Camp Snoopy, the Lego Imagination Center, Golf Mountain, and more than 30 sit-down restaurants and nightclubs. For more information call (612) 883-8800.

> HOURS: Retail: Monday–Saturday 10 a.m.–9:30 p.m.; Sunday 11 a.m.–7 p.m.
> Entertainment: Monday-Saturday 10 a.m.–1 a.m.; Sunday 11 a.m.–1 a.m.
> Extended hours during summer and holiday periods.

Located in Bloomington, just 5 minutes from the Minneapolis/St. Paul International Airport.

From I-494, take the 24th Ave. exit to Mall and parking ramps.

From Cedar Ave. (Hwy. 77), take the Killebrew Dr. exit to Mall and parking ramps.

From I-35W, take I-494 east to the 24th Ave. exit. Follow 24th Ave. to Mall and parking ramps.

MAPLEWOOD MALL

3001 White Bear Ave. N. Maplewood, MN 55109-1202 (612) 770-5020

Every week Maplewood Mall is proud to present Friday Family Fun Nights, 5:30–7 p.m., featuring Brian Z. of KMSP-TV in an entertaining activity program for children, plus specials on food court purchases.

> HOURS: Monday–Friday 10 a.m.–9 p.m.; Saturday 9:30 a.m.–6 p.m.; Sunday 11 a.m.–6 p.m.

From Hwy. 694, exit at White Bear Ave. and go south. Mall is on the southwest corner of I-694 and White Bear Ave.

From Hwy. 36, take White Bear Ave. north. Mall is about 1-1/2 miles on the west side of White Bear Ave.

SHOPPING

▲▲▲▲▲▲▲▲▲▲▲▲▲▲▲▲▲▲▲▲▲▲▲▲▲▲▲▲▲▲▲▲▲▲▲▲▲▲

MINNEAPOLIS' UPTOWN SHOPPING DISTRICT

Uptown Association, 1455 W. Lake St., Minneapolis, MN 55402 (612) 823-4581

Uptown offers a wide variety of shopping experiences with over 200 distinct businesses located in the Hennepin-Lake area. Enjoy one of over 20 unique restaurants, view films at Uptown theaters, or relax at Lake Calhoun or Lake of the Isles.

> From I-35W, take the Lake St./31st St. exit. Go west on Lake St. about 2-1/2 miles. Calhoun Square and many other specialty shops are located at the intersection of W. Lake St. and Hennepin Ave.

MIRACLE MILE SHOPPING CENTER

Hwy. 100 and Excelsior Blvd., St. Louis Park, MN 55416 (612) 929-3423

"Park at the front door of your favorite store" at Miracle Mile Shopping Center.

COST: Free.

HOURS: Some stores have different hours, but the shopping center is typically open Monday–Friday 10 a.m.–9 p.m.; Saturday 10 a.m.–6 p.m.; Sunday noon–5 p.m.

> From Hwy. 100, take the Excelsior Blvd. exit. Miracle Mile Shopping Center is located at the intersection of Hwy. 100 and Excelsior Blvd.

RIDGEDALE CENTER

12401 Wayzata Blvd., Minnetonka, MN 55305 (612) 541-4864

Ridgedale Center is a two-level indoor mall comprised of over 140 top retailers, which include the anchor stores: Dayton's, Sears, and JC Penney. A unique feature of Ridgedale Center is the Minnetonka Market, where local merchants and entrepreneurs set up shop in the Commons Area. In the fall of 1995, Ridgedale will become the only center in the Twin Cities area to have two Dayton-Hudson department stores.

COST: Free parking.

HOURS: Monday–Friday 10 a.m.–9 p.m.; Saturday 10 a.m.–8 p.m.; Sunday 11 a.m.–6 p.m.

> From Hwy. 394, take the Ridgedale Dr. exit and follow to the Ridgedale Center parking lot.

▲▲▲▲▲▲▲▲▲▲▲▲▲▲▲▲▲▲▲▲▲▲▲▲▲▲▲▲▲▲▲▲▲▲▲

> From I-494, take the I-394 exit. Follow I-394 east to Ridgedale Dr. Follow to the Ridgedale Center parking lot.
>
> From Hwy. 169, take the Hwy. 394 exit. Follow Hwy. 394 west to Ridgedale Dr. and follow to the Ridgedale Center parking lot.

ROSEDALE CENTER

10 Rosedale Center, Roseville, MN 55113 (612) 638-3553

Rosedale Center is a 1.14 million-square-foot, enclosed regional center with four anchor stores: Dayton's, Mervyns, J.C. Penney, and Montgomery Ward. Included are strong stores such as Warner Brothers Studio Store, Ann Taylor, Talbots, and the Disney Stores. Rosedale draws over nine million customers annually.

HOURS: Monday–Friday 10 a.m.–9 p.m.; Saturday 10 a.m.–6 p.m.; Sunday 11 a.m.–5 p.m. Holiday hours are extended.

> From I-35E or I-35W, take the Hwy. 36 exit. Rosedale Center is located on the north side of Hwy. 36 between Snelling and Fairview Aves.

SOUTHDALE CENTER

10 Southdale Center, Edina, MN 55435 (612) 925-7885

Southdale continues its tradition of delivering original ways to make your shopping better than ever. With over 180 retailers, anchored by Dayton's, J.C. Penney, and Marshalls, Southdale has popular stores such as Talbot's Kids; Eddie Bauer; J. Crew; Gymboree; Gap; and Banana Republic. Southdale has the distinction of being the first indoor shopping mall in the country.

COST: Free parking.

HOURS: Monday–Friday 10 a.m.–9 p.m.; Saturday 10 a.m.–8 p.m.; Sunday 11 a.m.–6 p.m. Department store hours and holiday hours may vary.

> From I-494, take the France Ave. exit and follow 9 blocks to the Center on the right.
>
> From Hwy. 62 (Crosstown), take the France Ave. exit and go south to the Center on the left.

▲▲▲▲▲▲▲▲▲▲▲▲▲▲▲▲▲▲▲▲▲▲▲▲▲▲▲▲▲▲▲▲▲▲▲▲▲

SOUTHTOWN SHOPPING CENTER

I-494 and Penn Ave. S., Bloomington, MN 55431 (612) 375-1077

Southtown includes over 60 stores and amusements, including Montgomery Ward; T.J. Maxx; Southtown Cinema; and Southtown Bowl.

> HOURS: Monday–Friday 10 a.m.–9 p.m.; Saturday 10 a.m.–5:30 p.m.; Sunday noon–5 p.m.

Southtown Shopping Center is located on the southeast corner of Penn Ave. S. and I-494 in Bloomington. From I-494, take the Penn Ave. exit and proceed south to Southtown.

From I-35W, take the 82nd St. exit and proceed west to Southtown.

TANGER FACTORY OUTLET CENTER

38573 Tanger Dr., North Branch, MN 55056 (612) 674-5885

Save 30-70% off retail prices by buying direct from over 32 upscale designer manufacturers such as Reebok; Carter's Childrenwear; Levi; Bugle Boy; Nine West; Capezio; Corning Revere; and many more.

> HOURS: January–March: Monday–Friday 10 a.m.–8 p.m.; Saturday 10 a.m.–6 p.m.; Sunday noon–6 p.m. April–December: Monday–Saturday 10 am–9 p.m.; Sunday 11 a.m.–7 p.m.

Less than 45 minutes north of Minneapolis/St. Paul. Take I-35 to the Hwy. 95 exit. Tanger is on the southwest corner of I-35 and Hwy. 95.

SKATING ARENAS

▲▲▲▲▲▲▲▲▲▲▲▲▲▲▲▲▲▲▲▲▲▲▲▲▲▲▲▲▲▲▲▲▲▲▲▲▲▲

ALDRICH ARENA

1850 White Bear Ave., St. Paul, MN 55109 (612) 777-1707
Recording (612) 777-1361

This indoor spectator arena offers open skating; adult open hockey; long blade sessions; skate rental; and skate sharpening.

COST: Open skating $3, open hockey $5, skate rental $2, skate sharpening $2.50.

HOURS: Open late September–mid-March. Open skating winter schedule: Monday–Friday noon–1:30 p.m.; Tuesday evening 6:30–8 p.m.; Saturday 11 a.m.–12:30 p.m.; Sunday 1 p.m.–2:30 p.m. Adult open hockey winter schedule: Monday and Friday 8–9:30 a.m. Long blade winter session: Sunday 10:30 a.m.–12:30 p.m.; Thursday 9:30 a.m.–11:30 a.m.

> From I-35E, take the Hwy. 36 exit east to White Bear Ave. Follow White Bear Ave. approximately 1-1/2 miles south. Facility is located on White Bear Ave. 1/2 block south of Frost Ave.

ANOKA AREA ICE ARENA

4111 7th Ave. N., Anoka, MN 55303 (612) 427-8163

Anoka Area Ice Arena is a private nonprofit organization that offers open skating only on Sunday afternoons. In the off-season, Anoka Ice Arena offers indoor soccer for children 5-17. Call for more details.

COST: Open skating $2, skate sharpening $2.

HOURS: Open skating Sunday 12:30 p.m.–2:45 p.m.

> From I-35W, take the Co. Rd H (Hwy. 10) exit and go west to 7th Ave. Turn right (north) onto 7th Ave. and go approximately 1-1/4 mile to the Arena on the left.

BIFF ADAMS ARENA

743 N. Western Ave., St. Paul, MN 55103 Recording (612) 488-1336

Open skating mid-October through early March.

SKATING ARENAS

▲▲▲▲▲▲▲▲▲▲▲▲▲▲▲▲▲▲▲▲▲▲▲▲▲▲▲▲▲▲▲▲▲▲▲▲▲▲▲

COST: Adults $2.50, 17 and under $2, skate sharpening $2.

HOURS: Open skating Friday 6:40–8:30 p.m.; Sunday 2–3:50 p.m.

> From I-35E, take the Pennsylvania Ave. exit west to Como Ave. Turn right
> (north) onto Como and follow to Minnehaha Ave. Turn left (west) on
> Minnehaha and go 2 blocks. Biff Adams Arena is at the corner of Western St.
> and Minnehaha.
>
> From I-94 eastbound, take the Dale St. exit north to Minnehaha and go east.
> Follow Minnehaha 4 blocks to Arena on the corner of Minnehaha and
> Western St.

BLOOMINGTON ICE GARDEN

3600 W. 98th St., Bloomington, MN 55431 (612) 948-8842

Bloomington Ice Garden features three ice rinks under one roof. They are open year
round for open skating, open hockey, skating lessons, a figure skating club, and hockey
schools. Skate rental and sharpening are also available. In summer the Ice Garden is the
site of four large baseball card shows, craft shows, dances, and a juke box/game room
show.

COST: Open skating for adults $2.50, children 17 and under $2, adult open
         hockey $4, skate rental $1.50, skate sharpening $2.

HOURS: Open year round. Open skating, winter schedule: Tuesday 12:30
         p.m.–2 p.m.; Wednesday and Friday 10:30 a.m.–noon; Saturday and
         Sunday 2–3:30 p.m. Open hockey Monday, Wednesday, and Friday
         11:30 a.m.–1:30 p.m.

         Summer schedule for open skating: Monday, Wednesday, and Friday
         4–5:30 p.m. Hours are subject to change; call to verify. Open hockey
         offered on Tuesday and Thursday 4:15–5:45 p.m.

> From I-35W, take the 98th St. exit. Follow 98th St. west about a mile to
> Arena on the right.
>
> From I-494, take the France Ave. exit south to 98th St. Turn left (east) onto
> 98th St. and proceed 2 blocks to Arena on the left.

▲▲▲▲▲▲▲▲▲▲▲▲▲▲▲▲▲▲▲▲▲▲▲▲▲▲▲▲▲▲▲▲▲▲▲▲▲▲▲

BRAEMAR ARENA

7501 Hwy. 169, Edina, MN 55439 (612) 941-1322

Open ice skating sessions are available for children and adults. For other arena activities (skating lessons, high school hockey games, etc.), please call.

COST: Open skating $2.50 per person, skate rental $1.25.

HOURS: September–mid-April open skating (subject to change): Tuesday, Thursday, Friday 10:30 a.m.–12:30 p.m.; Tuesday and Friday evenings 8–10 p.m.; Saturday 1:15–3:15 p.m.; Sunday 8:30–10:30 a.m. and 2–4 p.m. Please call for possible cancellations.

From I-494, take Hwy. 169 north to the Valley View Road exit. As you come off the exit, you will see the Arena immediately. From Crosstown 62, take Hwy. 169 south to the Valley View Road exit.

BROOKLYN PARK COMMUNITY ACTIVITY CENTER

5600 85th Ave. N., Brooklyn Park, MN 55443 Recording for updates: (612) 493-8181

The Brooklyn Park Community Activity Center has a standard-size ice rink featuring open skating; open adult hockey and some youth hockey; skating lessons; skate rental and sharpening.

COST: Open skating for adults $2.50, students $2, skate rental $1, skate sharpening $2.50.

HOURS: Winter hours Tuesday and Thursday noon–2 p.m.; Friday 8–9 p.m.; Sunday 2:30–4 p.m. with 1/2 price admission. Extra open skating time on holidays and school days off. Times are subject to change, so call to verify.

From I-94 northbound, take the Hwy. 252 exit. Follow Hwy. 252 north to 85th Ave. Follow 85th west 3 miles to the Community Center on the right.

From I-494, take the Hwy. 694 exit. Follow Hwy. 694 east to Hwy. 169. Follow Hwy. 169 north to 85th Ave. and follow 85th 3 miles to the Community Center on the left.

SKATING ARENAS

▲▲▲▲▲▲▲▲▲▲▲▲▲▲▲▲▲▲▲▲▲▲▲▲▲▲▲▲▲▲▲▲▲▲▲▲▲

BURNSVILLE ICE CENTER

251 Civic Center Pkwy., Burnsville, MN 55337 (612) 895-4650 or 895-4651

Burnsville Ice Center is home to the Burnsville boys' and girls' hockey teams. The Ice Center also offers open skating, open hockey, a variety of skating lessons, and a figure skating club.

COST: Open skating $2, skate rental $1, skate sharpening $2.50.

HOURS: Open skating daily: Monday–Friday 11 a.m.–1 p.m.; Friday and Saturday 7:30–9 a.m.; Sunday 2:30–4 p.m. Open hockey Monday and Friday 8–9:30 a.m.; Sunday 9–10:30 a.m. Times are subject to change, so call to verify.

> From I-35W, take the Burnsville Pkwy. exit east to Nicollet Ave. Follow Nicollet south to Civic Center Pkwy. Go east 1 block to the Arena on the right.

CENTENNIAL SPORTS ARENA

4707 North Rd., Circle Pines, MN 55014 (612) 780-7699

Centennial Sports Arena was the Twin Cities' first Olympic-sized ice surface. Skating opportunities include open skating; three seasonal learn-to-skate programs; adult open hockey on Sunday evenings; fall hockey leagues; and skate sharpening. Summer activities include: indoor soccer; T-ball and golf in April and May, and four hockey schools for all age groups, including girls.

COST: Adults $2.50, students $2. No skate rental available.

HOURS: Wednesday 11:30 a.m.–1 p.m.; Sunday noon–1:30 p.m.

> From I-35W, take the Lexington Ave. exit. Follow Lexington Ave. east to Co. Rd. 10 (North Rd.). Turn left onto Co. Rd. 10 and go 1/2 mile to arena on the left.

CHASKA COMMUNITY CENTER

1661 Park Ridge Dr., Chaska, MN 55318 Recording (612) 448-5633

The Chaska Community Center features open skating; men's open hockey; figure skating lessons; and preschool skating lessons. Skate rental available.

▲ ▲

COST: Open skating: nonresident adults $2.25, nonresident youth $1.75, resident adult $1.50, resident youth $1, skate rental $1, skate sharpening $2.50.

HOURS: Open skating Monday, Wednesday, and Friday 11:30 a.m.–1 p.m.; Wednesday 7:15–8:30 p.m.; Friday 7:15–9:15 p.m.; Saturday 11:30 a.m.—2 p.m. Open skating Sunday 12:30–3 p.m.

> From I-494, take the Hwy. 61 exit. Follow Hwy. 61 south about 5 miles to 80th St. S. Turn left (east) at top of exit ramp onto 80th St. and go about 1 mile. Arena is on the left side of 80th St. next to Park High School.

EAST BETHEL ICE ARENA

20675 Hwy. 65, East Bethel, MN 55011 (612) 434-7579

Come out to the country and visit the East Bethel Ice Arena which offers open skating in the summer and winter months, open hockey, skating lessons, a youth hockey program, and skate sharpening.

COST: $2 per person No skate rental available.

DATES: Open year round. Please call for open skating and open hockey times, which vary.

> From I-35W, take the Hwy. 118 exit which will connect you to Hwy. 65. Proceed 12 miles north on Hwy. 65. The Arena is located on Hwy. 65 about 1-1/4 miles from Co. Rd. 22.

EDEN PRAIRIE COMMUNITY CENTER

16770 Valley View Rd., Eden Prairie, MN 55346 (612) 949-8460

The entire family will enjoy ice skating on this Olympic-size ice rink. In addition to open ice skating, the ice arena offers skating lessons; adult open hockey in the winter; youth and adult open hockey in the summer; skate sharpening; and birthday party rental.

COST: Adults $2.50, students $1.50, family $4, birthday party rental $1.50 per child. Skate rental $1.

DATES: Open daily year round. Call for open skating times.

▲▲▲▲▲▲▲▲▲▲▲▲▲▲▲▲▲▲▲▲▲▲▲▲▲▲▲▲▲▲▲▲▲▲▲▲▲▲

> From I-494 westbound, take the State Hwy. 5 exit. Follow State Hwy. 5 west to Co. Rd. 4. Turn right onto Co. Rd. 4 and follow to Valley View Rd. Turn left onto Valley View and look for the Eden Prairie Community Center on the right.
>
> From Hwy. 169, take the Hwy. 212 exit. Follow 212 west and stay to the far left as 212 becomes State Hwy. 5. Follow State Hwy. 5 west to Co. Rd. 4. Turn right onto Co. Rd. 4 and follow to Valley View Rd. Turn left onto Valley View Rd. and look for the Eden Prairie Community Center on the right.

EDINBOROUGH PARK

7700 York Ave. S., Edina, MN 55435 (612) 893-9890

Edinborough Park is a unique community park under glass, run and operated by the City of Edina's Park and Recreation Department. The park features a waterfall waterway; paths and walkways lined with seasonal flowering plants and trees; a tot lot play area; small ice skating rink; small art gallery with monthly art exhibits; indoor heated pool; exercise area with track; and a delicatessen. A daily pass in the form of a wristband gives you use of the indoor pool, running/walking track, and ice rink. Special events for children are Tuesdays and Thursdays at noon, and include musical concerts; clowns; artists; puppet shows; and more. Children's special events move outside in the summer to Centennial Lakes Park. Adult special events take place throughout the week. Call for details and schedule of events.

COST: Daily pass $3, skate rental $1.50. Entertainment and use of the tot lot and Great Hall are free.

HOURS: Sunday–Thursday 9 a.m.–9 p.m.; Friday and Saturday 9 a.m.–5 p.m. Call for specific program and recreation schedules.

> From I-494, take the France Ave. exit north to 76th St. Turn right onto 76th St. and proceed to York Ave. Turn right again onto York and follow to Edinborough Park in the middle of the block on the right.

FARMINGTON CIVIC ARENA

114 W. Spruce St., Farmington, MN 55024 (612) 463-2510

Arena activities include hockey; broomball; skating lessons; patch/freestyle sessions; ice shows; skating competitions; public skating; and figure skating practice.

▲▲▲▲▲▲▲▲▲▲▲▲▲▲▲▲▲▲▲▲▲▲▲▲▲▲▲▲▲▲▲▲▲

COST:　Open skating price schedule: Tuesday and Thursday $1, Sunday $2, school holidays $1.

HOURS: Open skating Tuesday and Thursday 11:30 a.m.–12:45 p.m.; Sunday 1:30–3 p.m.

> From State Hwy. 50, go into Farmington and turn right onto Denmark Ave. Follow Denmark to Spruce St., turn left onto Spruce. Arena is on the left.
>
> From Hwy. 3, go into Farmington and turn onto State Hwy. 50. Follow Hwy. 50 to Denmark Ave. Turn left onto Denmark Ave. and follow to Spruce St., turn left onto Spruce. Arena is on the left.

FOGARTY ICE ARENA

9250 Lincoln St., Blaine, MN 55434 (612) 780-3323

The Blaine High School and Spring Lake Park High School hockey teams are proud to call the Fogarty Ice Arena home. The Arena also offers open skating, open adult hockey, a learn-to-skate program for preschoolers, and skate sharpening.

COST:　Open skating $2; open hockey $3.

HOURS: Open skating in winter is on Wednesday and Friday 8:30–10 a.m.; Sunday 1:30 p.m.–3 p.m. Please call for summer open skating hours. Adult open hockey is played on Wednesday 11:30 a.m.–1 p.m.

> From I-35W, take the Hwy. 118 exit. Follow 118 until it ends at Central Ave. (Hwy. 65). Cross Central Ave., which will bring you to 91st St. Follow 91st to Lincoln St. and turn right. Fogarty Ice Arena is on Lincoln St. on the left.

GUSTAFSON PHALEN ARENA

1320 Walsh St., St. Paul, MN 55106 (612) 776-2554

Open skating mid-October–early March.

COST:　Open skating for adults $2.50, 17 and under $2, skate sharpening $2.

HOURS: Open skating Saturday 2:10–3:50 p.m.; Sunday 3:10–4:50. Call for special holiday hours.

SKATING ARENAS

▲▲▲▲▲▲▲▲▲▲▲▲▲▲▲▲▲▲▲▲▲▲▲▲▲▲▲▲▲▲▲▲▲▲▲

> From I-35E, take the Maryland Ave. exit. Follow Maryland Ave. east to Walsh St. Follow Walsh St. north about 3 blocks. Walsh will dead-end into the Gustafson Phalen Arena parking lot and the Johnson High School parking lot.
>
> From Hwy. 61, take the Maryland Ave. exit. Follow Maryland Ave. west to Walsh St., follow Walsh north to Arena.

HARDING ARENA

1496 E. 6th St., St. Paul, MN 55106 (612) 774-2127

Open skating mid-October–early March.

    COST: Open skating for adults $2.50, 17 and under $2, skate sharpening $2.

    HOURS: Open skating Wednesday 6:40–8:30 p.m.; Sunday 2:10–3:50 p.m.

> Take I-94 to White Bear Ave. and go north on White Bear to 3rd St. Go west on 3rd to Barclay St. Follow Barclay north to the Arena behind Harding High School.

HASTINGS CIVIC ARENA

2801 Redwing Blvd., Hastings, MN 55033 (612) 437-4940

Hastings Civic Arena offers open skating; skate rental; skating lessons; open hockey; and skate sharpening.

    COST: $2.50 per person, skate rental $1.75.

    HOURS: Open skating October 15–March 15: Friday 8–10:30 a.m.; Saturday and Sunday 1:30–3 p.m. Open hockey Thursday 8–10:30 a.m.

> From Hwy. 61, turn left onto Hwy. 316. Arena is on the left immediately.

HIGHLAND ARENA

800 S. Snelling Ave., St. Paul, MN 55116 (612) 699-7156

Open skating mid-October–early March.

    COST: Open skating for adults $2.50, 17 and under $2, skate sharpening $2.

    HOURS: Open skating Wednesday 6:40–8:30 p.m.; Sunday 2:10–3:50 p.m.

▲▲▲▲▲▲▲▲▲▲▲▲▲▲▲▲▲▲▲▲▲▲▲▲▲▲▲▲▲▲▲▲▲▲▲▲

> From I-94, take the Snelling Ave. exit. Follow Snelling south to Ford Pkwy. Follow Ford Pkwy. to the Arena parking lot on the left.
>
> From I-35E, take the W. 7th St. exit. Follow W. 7th south to Montreal Ave. Follow Montreal west to Snelling Ave. Go north on Snelling 6 blocks to Ford Pkwy. and go east. Arena is at the intersection of Snelling Ave. and Ford Pkwy.

HOPKINS PAVILION

1515 2nd St. S., Hopkins, MN 55343 (612) 939-1410

Hopkins Pavilion offers open skating and skate sharpening. No skate rental available. Skating lessons are offered through the Park and Recreation Department.

COST: Open skating for adults $2, students $1.50, skate sharpening $2.50.

HOURS: Open skating Monday, Wednesday, Thursday, and Friday 11:30–1 p.m.; Wednesday 6:45–8:15 p.m.; Sunday 1:30–3 p.m.

> From Hwy. 394, take the Hwy. 169 exit. Follow Hwy. 169 south to Co. Rd. 3 (Excelsior Blvd.) Follow Co. Rd. 3 west about 1 mile to the Hopkins Pavilion in Central Park on the north side of the road.

INVER GROVE HEIGHTS ARENA

2630 80th St. E., Inver Grove Heights, MN 55076 (612) 451-3938

This is mainly an arena for youth hockey; however, open skating is available Sundays.

COST: $1 per person.

HOURS: Sunday 12:15–1:15 p.m.

> From I-494, take the Hwy. 52 exit. Follow 52 south to 80th St. Go east on 80th 1/4 mile and look for the Arena on the right.

JOSEPH COOK MEMORIAL ARENA

11091 Mississippi Blvd., Coon Rapids, MN 55433 (612) 421-5035

Joseph Cook Memorial Arena offers open skating; open hockey; skating lessons; and skate sharpening. No skate rental available.

SKATING ARENAS

▲▲▲▲▲▲▲▲▲▲▲▲▲▲▲▲▲▲▲▲▲▲▲▲▲▲▲▲▲▲▲▲▲▲▲▲

COST: Call for prices.

HOURS: Open July–April, closed May–June. Open skating Wednesday and Friday 11 a.m.–1 p.m.; Sunday 5:20–7:30 p.m. Adult open hockey Tuesday and Thursday 12:30–2:30 p.m. (winter only).

> From I-94 northbound, take the Hwy. 252 exit. Follow Hwy. 252 north until it becomes Hwy. 610. Follow 610 across the river and take the first exit after the river (Coon Rapids Blvd.). Turn left (west) onto Coon Rapids Blvd. and go to Mississippi Blvd. Turn left onto Mississippi Blvd. and go 1 block to the Arena.

KEN YACKEL WESTSIDE ARENA

44 East Isabel St., St. Paul, MN 55107 (612) 228-1145

Open skating mid-October–early March.

COST: Open skating for adults $2.50, 17 and under $2, skate sharpening $2.

HOURS: Open skating Saturday 2:10–3:50 p.m.; Sunday 3:10–4:50 p.m.

> From I-94, take the Lafayette Bridge exit (Hwy. 52) to Concord St. Follow Concord west to Isabel St. Follow Isabel St. west 6 blocks to the Arena.

LAKEVILLE AMES ARENA

19900 Ipava Ave., Lakeville, MN 55044 (612) 469-1248

Lakeville Ames Arena offers open skating, skating lessons, and private rentals.

COST: $2 per person.

HOURS: Tuesday–Friday 11:30 a.m.–1 p.m.

> From I-35W southbound, take the Co. Rd. 50 exit. Follow Co. Rd. 50 southeast (left) about 3-1/2 miles to the intersection of Ipava and Co. Rd. 50. Turn left onto Ipava and look for the Arena on the right.

LILY LAKE ARENA

1208 S. Greeley St., Stillwater, MN 55082 (612) 439-1337

Open skating and skate sharpening daily.

COST: $2 per person. No skate rental.

▲▲▲▲▲▲▲▲▲▲▲▲▲▲▲▲▲▲▲▲▲▲▲▲▲▲▲▲▲▲▲▲▲▲▲▲

HOURS: October 1–March 31: Monday–Friday noon–1:30 p.m.; Saturday and Sunday 6:30 p.m.–8 p.m.

> Take Hwy. 36 east to Greely St. (the second stoplight as you come into town), turn left (north) onto Greely St. and follow 1/4 mile to Arena.

MARIUCCI ARENA

1901 4th St. S.E., Minneapolis, MN (612) 625-6648

Mariucci Arena offers open skating for U of M students and the public. Skate rental and skate sharpening are also available.

COST: Open skating for adults $2.50, students $1.25, children under 15 $1.50, skate rental $2, skate sharpening $2.50.

HOURS: May vary by month; please call 625-6648 for a recorded message on current hours and rates.

> From I-35W northbound or southbound, take the University Ave. exit. Follow University about 10 blocks to Oak St. Turn left onto Oak St. and follow to 4th St. Mariucci Arena is on the left side of 4th St.
>
> From I-94, take the U of M exit and follow until it becomes 4th St. Follow 4th as it veers left and proceed to Oak St. Follow Oak St. to parking for Mariucci Arena on the left.

NEW HOPE ICE ARENA

4949 Louisiana Ave. N., New Hope, MN 55428 (612) 531-5181

The New Hope Ice Arena features public skating twice a week; open hockey; a youth hockey program; and skating classes in fall, winter, and summer sessions. No skate rental available.

COST: Open skating $2, preschool children free. Open hockey $3, skate sharpening $2.50.

HOURS: Open skating Sundays 4–6 p.m.; Monday 11 a.m.–1 p.m.; Friday 6:30–8 p.m. Open hockey Wednesday, Thursday, and Friday, 11:30 a.m.–1 p.m. Times are subject to change, so call to verify.

> From Hwy. 694, take the Hwy. 169 exit. Follow 169 south to 49th Ave. Follow 49th east about 2 miles to Louisiana Ave. N. New Hope Ice Arena is on Louisiana Ave. N.

SKATING ARENAS

▲▲▲▲▲▲▲▲▲▲▲▲▲▲▲▲▲▲▲▲▲▲▲▲▲▲▲▲▲▲▲▲▲▲

NORTHFIELD ARENA

1280 S. Hwy. 3, Northfield, MN 55057 (507) 645-6556

Northfield Arena is home to St. Olaf and Northfield hockey games. Open skating is offered in winter only. In the spring and summer the Arena is used for special events such as the Joses Cole Traveling Circus, book fair, the Jesse James craft show, and other craft shows. No skate rental available.

    COST: Open skating $2, children 5 and under free, skate sharpening $2.50.

    HOURS: Open skating in winter: Saturday and Sunday 2:30 –3:30 p.m. Hours can vary, so please call ahead to verify.

> From I-35, take the Hwy. 19 exit. Follow 19 east to State Hwy. 3. Travel south about 1 mile on Hwy. 3 and look for the Arena on the right.

OSCAR JOHNSON ARENA

1039 Decourcy Ave., St. Paul, MN 55102 (612) 645-7203

Open skating mid-October–early March.

    COST: Open skating for adults $2.50, 17 and under $2, skate sharpening $2.

    HOURS: Open skating Saturday and Sunday 2:10–3:50 p.m. Open Hockey Sunday 8:50–11 a.m.

> From I-94, take the Snelling Ave. exit. Follow Snelling north to Energy Park Drive. Follow Energy Park Drive east 1/2 block to Decourcy Ave. Go north on Decourcy to the Arena.
>
> From Hwy. 36, take the Snelling Ave. exit. Follow Snelling Ave. south to Energy Park Drive. Follow Energy Park Drive east 1/2 block to Decourcy Ave. Go north on Decourcy to Arena.

PARADE ICE ARENA

600 Kenwood Pkwy., Minneapolis, MN 55403 (612) 348-4853

The movie "Mighty Ducks" was filmed at Parade Ice Arena. The Arena has two standard ice rinks and a studio rink, which are open to the public for skating and men's and women's open hockey. Figure skates are available for rental in limited quantities; skate sharpening is available.

▲▲▲▲▲▲▲▲▲▲▲▲▲▲▲▲▲▲▲▲▲▲▲▲▲▲▲▲▲▲▲▲▲▲▲▲▲

COST: Open skating $2.50, skate rental $1.75, skate sharpening $2.50.

HOURS: Open skating Monday–Friday 11:30 a.m.–1 p.m.; Monday 6:30
       p.m.–8:15 p.m.; Tuesday, Thursday, Saturday, and Sunday 4–5:45 p.m.
       Adult-only skating session Friday 7:45–9:30 p.m.

> From St. Paul, head west on I-94 and take exit 231B, Lyndale Ave./Hennepin
> Ave., going north to Kenwood Pkwy. Follow Kenwood Pkwy. west about 3
> blocks and look for the Arena.
>
> Approaching Minneapolis from the west on I-394, take exit 8A (Dunwoody
> Blvd./Hennepin Ave.) and follow Hennepin Ave./Lyndale Ave. south to
> Kenwood Pkwy. Follow Kenwood Pkwy. west about 3 blocks and look for the
> Arena.

PLEASANT ARENA

848 Pleasant Ave., St. Paul, MN 55102 (612) 228-1143

Open skating mid-October–early March.

COST: Open skating for adults $2.50, 17 and under $2, skate sharpening $2.

HOURS: Open skating Tuesday 6:40–8:30 p.m.; Saturday 2:10–3:50 p.m.

> From I-35E, take the St. Clair exit west, and take an immediate left again
> onto Pleasant Ave. and follow to the Arena.

ROSEMOUNT COMMUNITY CENTER

*13885 S. Robert Trail, Rosemount, MN 55068 (612) 322-6000 Pre-recorded message
(612) 891-9431 press #2*

Many windows surrounding this Olympic-sized ice rink enable the public to skate in a
bright, cheerful environment. Skate sharpening available.

COST: $2 per person, no skate rental available.

HOURS: Open skating January 3–April 6: Tuesday 11:30 a.m.–1 p.m.;
       Wednesday 6:45–8:15 p.m.; Thursday 11:30 a.m.–1 p.m.; Sunday
       1:30–3 p.m. Call for specific school vacation open skating hours.

▲▲▲▲▲▲▲▲▲▲▲▲▲▲▲▲▲▲▲▲▲▲▲▲▲▲▲▲▲▲▲▲▲▲▲▲▲▲▲

From I-35E, take the Pilot Knob Rd. exit. Follow Pilot Knob south to Co. Rd. 38. Turn left onto Co. Rd. 38 and follow to ??????????Hwy. 3. Take Hwy. 3 about 1-1/2 miles south to the Rosemount Community Center.

From Co. Rd. 42, go east to Hwy. 3. Follow Hwy. 3 north about 1 mile. Rosemount Community Center is on the left side.

ROSEVILLE ICE ARENA-JOHN ROSE OVAL

1200 Woodhill Dr., Roseville, MN 55113 (612) 484-0269

Recorded message (612) 484-0268

This popular, busy Arena is home to the Roseville and Mounds View High School hockey teams, the Roseville Youth Hockey Association, the Roseville Figure Skating Club, and the Roseville ISIA Figure Skating School. The public is invited to participate in open skating sessions, men's and women's open hockey, adult long blade sessions, and women's skatercise. Skate rental and skate sharpening are available.

The Roseville Ice Arena is also the location of the outdoor John Rose Oval, a 400-meter speed skating oval. The entire infield area is refrigerated for a total of 110,000 square feet of ice skating surface. Special events include the ISIA District 10 Championships, the Roseville Figure Skating Show, and the Roseville Figure Skating Club Open Competition.

COST: Open skating for adults $2.75, 18 and under $2.25, students $2, skate rental $1, skate sharpening $2.50.

HOURS: Indoor Arena winter hours: Monday 10–11:30 a.m. and 1–2:15 p.m.; Wednesday 10–11:30 a.m. and 7–8:30 p.m.; Thursday 11:30 a.m.–1 p.m.; Friday 10–11:30 a.m.; Sunday 12:30–2 p.m. and 8:30–10 p.m..

Outdoor Oval winter hours: Monday 11 a.m.–1 p.m.; Tuesday 11 a.m.-1 p.m. and 7:30 p.m.–9:30 p.m.; Wednesday 7:30–9:30 p.m.; Thursday 11 a.m.–1 p.m.; Friday 11 a.m.–1 p.m. and 7:30 p.m.–9:30 p.m.; Saturday 7:30–9:30 p.m.; Sunday 1:30–3:30 p.m. and 7:30–9:30 p.m. Times are subject to change because of weather, holidays, and special events, so please call to verify.

From I-35W, take the Co. Rd. C exit. Follow Co. Rd. C east about 3-1/2 miles. The Arena is on Co. Rd. C between Hamline and Lexington Aves. on the north side.

From Hwy. 36, take the Lexington Ave. exit. Follow Lexington Ave. north to Co. Rd. C. Turn left onto Co. Rd. C and go 1 block. Turn right onto Civic Center Drive and facility parking lot.

▲▲▲▲▲▲▲▲▲▲▲▲▲▲▲▲▲▲▲▲▲▲▲▲▲▲▲▲▲▲▲▲▲▲▲▲▲

SHOREVIEW ARENA

877 W. Hwy. 96, Shoreview, MN 55126 (612) 484-2400

Open skating mid-October–early March.

COST: Open skating for adults $2.50, 17 and under $2, skate sharpening $2.

HOURS: Open skating Saturday 3:10–4:50 p.m.; Sunday 2:10–3:50 p.m.

> From I-35W, take the Hwy. 96 exit east to Victoria St. Follow Victoria St. north to the Arena parking lot.
>
> From I-35E, take the Hwy. 96 exit and go west to Victoria St. Follow Victoria St. north to the Arena parking lot.

ST. LOUIS PARK RECREATION CENTER

5005 W. 36th St., St. Louis Park, MN 55416 (612) 924-2545

The St. Louis Park Recreation Center offers open skating, open adult hockey, and an instructional skating program for ages 4 years–adult.

COST: Open skating for adults $2, youth $1.50, special open skating admission for all ages Friday evening $1. Open hockey $3, skate rental $1.50, skate sharpening $2.50.

HOURS: Winter open skating daily, twice on weekends: Sunday 3–4:30 p.m.; Monday noon–1:30 p.m. and 8:45–10 p.m. for adults only; Wednesday noon–1:30 p.m.; Friday noon–1:30 p.m. and 8–9 p.m. Schedule varies, please call.

> From I-494, take the Hwy. 100 exit. Follow Hwy. 100 north about 4 miles to W. 36th St. Follow W. 36th St. east 2 blocks to the St. Louis Park Recreation Center on the right.

VICTORY MEMORIAL ICE ARENA

1900 42nd Ave. N., Minneapolis, MN 55412 (612) 627-2953
Recording 627-2952

Victory Memorial Ice Arena's activities include open ice skating; open hockey; summer hockey schools; private ice rentals; high school and youth hockey games; broomball; skate rentals and sharpening.

SKATING ARENAS

▲▲▲▲▲▲▲▲▲▲▲▲▲▲▲▲▲▲▲▲▲▲▲▲▲▲▲▲▲▲▲▲▲▲▲▲▲

COST: Public hockey $4 per two-hour session, open skating $2 per two-hour session, $2 per person skate rental, skate sharpening $2.

HOURS: Open year round, open skating October–March only on Friday, 7:30–9:45 p.m.

From I-35W northbound, take the 42nd Ave. exit. Turn left onto 42nd Ave. and go about 2 blocks to the Arena.

From I-94, take the downtown Minneapolis exit to the Dowling Ave. exit. Turn left onto Dowling Ave. and follow to Lyndale Ave. Turn right onto Lyndale Ave. N. and proceed to 42nd Ave. Turn left onto 42nd Ave. and go about 12 blocks. Victory Memorial Ice Arena is on the north side of 42nd Ave. N.

WEST ST. PAUL ICE ARENA

60 W. Emerson Ave., West St. Paul, MN 55118 (612) 552-4155

The West St. Paul Ice Arena offers open skating, open hockey, and skate sharpening. No skate rental available.

COST: Open skating $2.50, skate sharpening $2.50, open hockey $3.

HOURS: Open October–March. Open skating Tuesday and Thursday 9–11 a.m.; Saturday and Sunday 2–4 p.m. Open hockey for youth 14 and over Monday, Wednesday, and Friday 9–11 a.m. Early October and March: open hockey Monday–Friday 3:30–5:40 p.m. Call for special open skating hours during holidays and school vacations.

From I-94, take the Hwy. 52 (Old Hwy. 3) exit. Follow Hwy. 52 south to the Butler St. exit. Go west on Butler St. to Robert St., then go south on Robert to Emerson Ave. Follow Emerson west 2 blocks. The Arena is on the left side.

From I-494 or Hwy. 110, take the Hwy. 52 exit. Follow Hwy. 52 north to the Butler St. exit. Go west on Butler St. to Robert St., then go south on Robert to Emerson Ave. Follow Emerson west 2 blocks. The Arena is on the left side.

▲ ▲

WHITE BEAR ARENA

2160 Orchard Lane, White Bear Lake, MN 55110 (612) 777-8255

Open skating mid-October–early March.

COST: Open skating for adults $2.50, 17 and under $2, skate sharpening $2.

HOURS: Open skating Saturday 3:10–4:50 p.m. Call for holiday hours.

> From Hwy. 694, take the White Bear Ave. exit. Follow White Bear Ave. north to Orchard Lane. Go east on Orchard Lane about 3 blocks to the Arena.

WHITE BEAR LAKE SPORTS CENTER

1328 Hwy. 96, White Bear Lake, MN 55110 (612) 429-8571

The White Bear Lake Sports Center offers open skating; skating lessons; adult open hockey; holiday open skating; and dead-ice time (when ice isn't rented).

COST: Open skating for adults $3, children $2, skate rental $1. Dead-ice cost $3 for 45 minutes, $5 for 1-1/2 hours for all ages.

HOURS: Closed only during May for maintenance. Open skating for all ages Tuesday, Thursday, and Sundays 9–11:15 a.m. and 1–3 p.m. Adult-only open skating Monday, Wednesday, and Friday 9–11:15 a.m. Call about dead-ice availability and cost.

> From I-35E northbound, take the Hwy. 96 exit. Follow Hwy. 96 east 1/2 mile to Sports Center Drive, turn right. The Sports Center is behind Birch Lake Square Mall off Sports Center Dr.
>
> From Hwy. 61 northbound, take the Hwy. 96 exit. Follow Hwy. 96 west about 3 miles to Sports Center Dr., turn left. The Sports Center is behind Birch Lake Square Mall off Sports Center Dr.

▲▲▲▲▲▲▲▲▲▲▲▲▲▲▲▲▲▲▲▲▲▲▲▲▲▲▲▲▲▲▲▲▲▲

CHEAP SKATE

3075 Coon Rapids Blvd., Coon Rapids, MN 55433 (612) 427-8980

Cheap Skate features family roller skating and in-line skating; fund-raising for schools, churches, and charities; lessons; birthday parties; group rates; public skating sessions on weekends; full snack shop; pro shop; and party rooms.

COST: Roller skating rates affected by length of session. Standard session lasts three hours and costs $3.50, skate rental $1.

HOURS: Family skating session Tuesday 6–9 p.m. Friday evening session 7–11 p.m. Saturday small-fry/tot skating session for children 8 and under 10 a.m.–noon. Saturday afternoon and evening sessions: noon–4 p.m., 4–6:30 p.m., 7–11 p.m. Sunday afternoon sessions 1–5 p.m., 5–8 p.m. Saturday Adult Night session for adults 18 and over 8–11 p.m.

> From I-694, take the Hwy. 252 exit. Follow Hwy. 252 north to the 610 bridge, and take the second exit after crossing the river (Coon Rapids Blvd.). Turn left onto Coon Rapids Blvd. and proceed about 3-1/2 miles. Cheap Skate is on the left side of the road at the intersection of Coon Rapids Blvd. and Mississippi Blvd.

RHYTHMLAND ROLLER RINK

1835 Central Ave. N.E., Minneapolis, MN 55418 (612) 789-3870

Enjoy smooth skating on Rhythmland's unique hardwood floor. Rhythmland is fun for birthday parties, with a visit from a special birthday panda bear. A full snack bar will satisfy you with munchies while you roll the night away. Skating lessons available.

COST AND HOURS: Bargain nights Tuesday and Wednesday: 6:30–9 p.m. $2.50, Scouts $1. Friday 6:30–10 p.m. $4. Saturday morning session reserved for kids under 12 and parents: 10 a.m.–12:30 p.m. $2. Saturday afternoon session 1–4 p.m. $3. Saturday evening session: 6:30–10 p.m. $4. Sunday sessions: 1–4 p.m. and 4–7 p.m. $3 per session, $5 for both sessions. Summer hours may vary.

> From I-35W northbound, take the Johnson St. exit. Follow Johnson to 8th St. (first light). Turn left (west) onto 8th St. and follow to the next stoplight (Central Ave.) Turn right onto Central Ave. and go 1 block. Rhythmland Roller Rink is on the right.

▲▲▲▲▲▲▲▲▲▲▲▲▲▲▲▲▲▲▲▲▲▲▲▲▲▲▲▲▲▲▲▲▲▲▲▲

ROLLER GARDEN

5622 W. Lake St., St. Louis Park, MN 55416 (612) 929-5518

Family-owned and -operated, this historic roller rink has provided family skating for the past 50 years. Roller Garden offers something for everyone: adult-only skating, Christian Contemporary Music Night, Gospel Music Night, children's skating session for kids 12 and under, and open skating sessions for all ages. The rink is also available for birthday parties.

COST: $3–$4 depending on the session, skate rental $1.

HOURS: Open skating Monday noon–3:30 p.m.; Wednesday noon–3:30 p.m. and 7–10 p.m.; Thursday noon–3:30 p.m.; Friday 7–10 p.m.; Saturday 1–4 p.m.; Sunday 7–10 p.m. Skating to Gospel-contemporary music Monday 7–10 p.m. and Saturday 7–11 p.m. Skating for adults only to '60s–'80s classic hits Tuesday 8:30–11 p.m.; Thursday 8:30–11 p.m., and Sunday 10 a.m.–12:30 p.m. Skating for children 12 and under only: Saturday 10 a.m.–1 p.m., Sunday 1–4 p.m.

> Roller Garden is located on the west side of Hwy. 100 on W. Lake St. in St. Louis Park. From Hwy. 100, take the Minnetonka Blvd. (Hwy. 5) exit. Follow Minnetonka Blvd. to W. Lake St. Follow W. Lake St. to Roller Garden.

ROLLERDOME™

HUBERT H. HUMPHREY METRODOME, 900 S. 5th St., Minneapolis, MN 55415 (612) 825-DOME 825-3663

Literally thousands of Twin Cities residents and visitors have rolled the day away at the world's largest skating facility, the HHH Metrodome. Anyone who enjoys in-line skating is invited to try the spacious Rollerblade® Rollerdome™ for optimum fun. A free beginners lesson is available for anyone interested in learning the basic elements of in-line skating. A concession stand is always open.

COST: Adults $5, students $4, pre-teens and seniors $3, skate rental $5. Free parking at the Metrodome lot at the intersection of 5th St. and 11th Ave.

HOURS: Hours and days vary by month; please call HOT-LINE for seasonal brochure and information.

▲▲▲▲▲▲▲▲▲▲▲▲▲▲▲▲▲▲▲▲▲▲▲▲▲▲▲▲▲▲▲▲▲▲▲▲▲

> From I-94W, take the 4th St. exit to Metrodome.
>
> From I-94E, take the 5th St. exit to Metrodome.
>
> From I-35W southbound, take Washington Ave. exit to Metrodome.
>
> From I-35W northbound, take 5th Ave. exit to Metrodome.
>
> From I-394 eastbound, take 6th St. exit to Metrodome.

SAINTS BLOOMINGTON FAMILY ENTERTAINMENT CENTER

311 W. 84th St., Bloomington, MN 55420 (612) 888-9311

Enjoy good clean fun at this family entertainment center. Full concessions available. Saints Bloomington Family Entertainment Center hosts birthday parties as well.

COST: Morning $3, afternoon $3.50, skate rental 75¢.

HOURS: Saturday morning skate time for children 9 and under 10 a.m.–12:30 p.m. Open skating for all ages Saturday 1–4 p.m. For private party rental time, call 888-9312.

> From I-494 eastbound, take the Nicollet Ave. exit. Follow Nicollet Ave. south (right) to 84th St. Turn right onto 84th St. (west) and follow about 4-5 blocks to Saints Bloomington Family Entertainment Center on the left.
>
> From I-494 westbound, take the Nicollet Ave. exit. Proceed south (left) on Nicollet Ave. to 84th St. Turn right onto 84th St. and follow about 4–5 blocks to Saints Bloomington Family Entertainment Center on the left.

SKATEDIUM ROLLER RINK

1251 Arundel Ave., St. Paul, MN 55117 (612) 489-7633

For over 40 years, Skatedium Roller Rink has provided families with adult and open skating sessions, lessons, and private parties.

COST: Adult sessions Monday, Wednesday, and Friday $4.50, skate rental 50¢. Open skating 7:30-11 p.m. Friday and Saturday $4, skate rental 50¢. Open skating 1:30–4 p.m. Saturday and Sunday $3.50, skate rental free.

HOURS: Adult Nights Monday and Wednesday 7:30–11 p.m. Country Western Dance and lessons Tuesday 7–10 p.m. Thursday reserved for private parties. Adult session Friday 9:30 a.m.–noon; open skating 7:30–11 p.m. Open skating Saturday 1:30 p.m.–4 p.m. and 7:30–11 p.m. Open skating Sunday 1:30–4 p.m.

> Go west 10 blocks on Maryland Ave. from Rice St. to Arundel Ave. and turn
> right. Go east 6 blocks from Dale St. to Arundel Ave. and turn left.

SKATELAND SKATE CENTER

7308 Lakeland Ave. N., Brookland Park, MN 55428 (612) 425-5858

In addition to family roller skating and in-line skating, Skateland Skate Center specializes in fund-raising for schools, churches, and charities; lessons; birthday parties; group
rates; and public skating sessions on weekends. Skateland Skate Center also provides a
full snack shop, pro shop, and party rooms.

COST: Roller skating rates affected by length of session. Standard session lasts
three hours and costs $3.50, skate rental $1.

HOURS: Public skating/family session Tuesday 6–9 p.m. Friday evening session
7–10:30 p.m. Saturday small-fry/tot skate session for children 8 and
under 10 a.m.–noon. Saturday afternoon and evening sessions noon–4
p.m., 4–6:30 p.m., and 7–10:30 p.m.. Sunday afternoon and evening
sessions noon–3 p.m., 3–6 p.m., and 6–8 p.m. Monday Adult Night
session for adults 18 and over 8–11 p.m.

> From I-694, take the Co. Rd. 81 exit. Proceed north on Co. Rd. 81 about 8
> blocks to Skateland Skate Center on the right.

SKATEVILLE

201 S. River Ridge Circle, Burnsville, MN 55337 (612) 890-0988

Have the entire family try out Skateville for a fabulous time. Skateville plays a large
variety of music. Specials include Christian Night, Adult Night Wednesday, After-
School Special Friday, and Family Night Sunday. Having a birthday? Skateville specializes in birthdays for children. Birthday package includes admission; skate rental; hot
dog; potato chips; pop; ice-cream bars, and free passes to come again. Private parties
can be scheduled for all occasions.

COST: Regular admission $3, skate rental $1. Family Night $6 (with one par-
ent skating). Adult Night $3.50. Friday After School Special $2.50.

HOURS: Sunday 1–4 p.m.; Sunday Family Night 6:30–9 p.m. Monday and
Tuesday nights reserved for private parties (call for information and
reservations). Wacky Wednesday sessions (watch for specials) 4–8 p.m.
Adult Night Wednesday 8–11 p.m. Thursday night closed for private
parties. Friday's After-School Special 4–6 p.m. Friday evening session

▲ ▲

7–11 p.m. Saturday morning session 10 a.m.–noon. Saturday afternoon and evening sessions noon–4 p.m. and 7–11 p.m.

From I-35W, take the Hwy. 13 exit. Follow Hwy. 13 north to Nicollet Ave. Take a left onto Nicollet and take an immediate left onto the frontage road. Follow the frontage road to S. River Ridge Circle and turn left. Skateville is on the immediate left side of the road.

WOODDALE RECREATION CENTER

2122 Wooddale Drive, Woodbury, MN 55125 (612) 735-6214

Wooddale Recreation Center offers a variety of skating sessions, including Mighty Mites (children 10 and under with parents); TGIF After-School Special; Friday Night Juke Box; Saturday and Sunday Matinee; and Christian Music Night. Rollerblades are welcome.

COST: $3–$5 depending on the session.

HOURS: Mighty Mites Wednesday and Saturday 10 a.m.–noon. Skating to Gospel-contemporary music Saturday 7–11 p.m. TGIF After-School Special Friday 4–6:30 p.m. Friday Night Juke Box 7–11 p.m. Saturday and Sunday Matinee 1–4 p.m. Saturday 4:30–6:30 p.m. Skate and Eat session Wednesday 4–7 p.m.

From I-494, take the Valley Creek Rd. exit east to Woodlane Dr. Follow Woodlane Dr. south to Wooddale Dr. Follow Wooddale 1/2 mile to Wooddale Recreation Center on the right.

STADIUMS, ARENAS, CONVENTION CENTERS & SPORTS TEAMS

▲▲▲▲▲▲▲▲▲▲▲▲▲▲▲▲▲▲▲▲▲▲▲▲▲▲▲▲▲▲▲▲▲▲▲▲

HUBERT H. HUMPHREY METRODOME

900 S. 5th St., Minneapolis, MN 55415 (612) 332-0386

The Metrodome is the home of the Twins baseball, Vikings football, and Gophers football. Other key events in the HHH Metrodome include trade shows, concerts, golf shows, super cross, truck and tractor pulls, state football playoffs, and much more.

COST: Expect to pay $5-$8 for parking in addition to cost of event.

> From I-94W, take 4th St. exit to Metrodome.
>
> From I-94E, take 5th St. exit to Metrodome.
>
> From I-35W northbound, take Washington Ave. exit to Metrodome.
>
> From I-35W southbound, take 5th Ave. exit to Metrodome.
>
> From I-394 eastbound, take 6th St. exit to Metrodome.

MARIUCCI ARENA (Seating chart on page 279)

*1901 4th St. S.E., Minneapolis, MN 55455 Men's Athletic information (612) 625-4838
Tickets (612) 624-8080*

Mariucci Arena is the home to the University of Minnesota Golden Gopher Hockey Team. It also offers open skating for U of M students and the public.

> From I-35W northbound or southbound, take the University Ave. exit. Follow University about 10 blocks to Oak St. Turn left onto Oak St. and follow to 4th St. Mariucci is located on the left side of 4th St.
>
> From I-94, take the U of M exit and follow until it becomes 4th St. Follow 4th St. as it veers left and proceed to Oak St. Follow Oak St. to the parking lot for Mariucci on the left.

Photo courtesy Minnesota Twins Baseball Club.

The Hubert H. Humphrey Metrodome, home of the Minnesota Twins, Minnesota Vikings, and the University of Minnesota Golden Gophers.

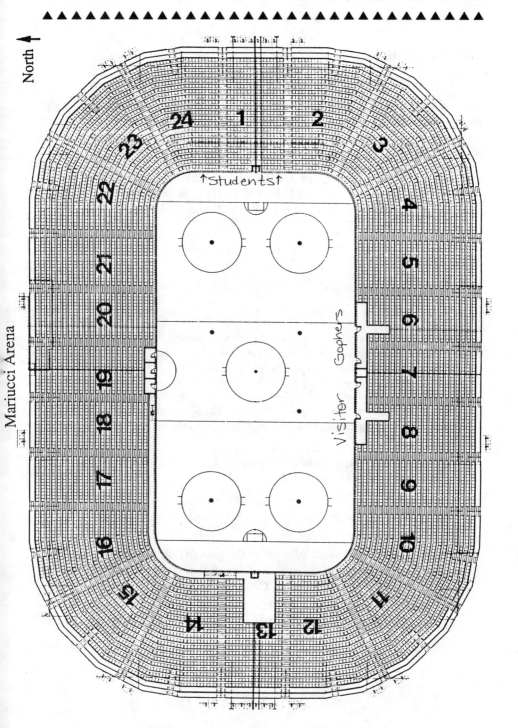

Mariucci Arena

North

↑Students↑

Visitor

Gophers

279

MIDWAY STADIUM

1771 Energy Park Dr., St. Paul, MN 55108 (612) 644-6512

Home to the St. Paul Saints baseball team, Midway Stadium also hosts high school and small college Division III baseball games and tournaments in the spring, plus football games and tournaments in the fall. Midway Stadium is also becoming the site of many popular concerts.

> From I-94, take the Snelling Ave. exit and go north to Energy Park Drive. Turn right onto Energy Park Drive and go 1/4 mile to Midway Stadium on the right. Midway Stadium is 1/4 mile south of the State Fairgrounds.

MINNEAPOLIS CONVENTION CENTER

1301 Second Ave. S., Minneapolis, MN 55403 (612) 335-6000

Hosts many conventions and shows.

HOURS: Vary according to individual events. Municipal Parking Ramps (Leamington, Orchestra Hall, Plaza) open 6 a.m.-11 p.m. or later for events. Hilton Ramp open 24 hours a day.

> From I-94 westbound, take the 11th St. exit and go south to 2nd Ave. S. Turn left onto 2nd Ave. S. and cross 12th St. S. The Convention Center is on the left. The Underground Plaza Parking Ramp is on the right.
>
> From I-94 eastbound and northwest, take the 4th St. exit and follow 4th St. S. to 2nd Ave. S. Turn right onto 2nd Ave. S. and cross 12th St. S. The Convention Center is on the left.
>
> From I-35W northbound, take the downtown exit and follow 11th St. south to 2nd Ave. S. Turn left onto 2nd Ave. S. and cross 12th St. S. The Convention Center is on the left.
>
> From I-35W southbound, take the Washington Ave. exit. Turn right on Washington Ave. S. and follow to 2nd Ave. S. Turn left onto 2nd Ave. S. and cross 12th St. S. The Convention Center is on the left.
>
> I-394 (Hwy. 12) eastbound, take Downtown exit (12th St.) and follow 12th St. to 2nd Ave. S. Turn right. The Convention Center is on the left.

▲▲▲▲▲▲▲▲▲▲▲▲▲▲▲▲▲▲▲▲▲▲▲▲▲▲▲▲▲▲▲▲▲▲▲▲

NATIONAL SPORTS CENTER

1700 105th Ave. N.E., Blaine, MN 55449 (612) 785-5600

The NSC (National Sports Center) is one of the nation's finest sport complexes. This multisport facility features an outdoor stadium, cycling velodrome, indoor and outdoor track and field venues, and 132 acres of playing fields. The NSC is home to the nation's largest international Youth Soccer Tournament-USA CUP. The NSC has also hosted the likes of Carl Lewis, Greg LeMond, the U.S. National Men's and Women's Soccer Teams, the U.S. and Cuba National Wrestling Teams, the National Weight-Lifting Championships, the U.S. Olympic Festival, and the 1991 International Special Olympics.

The NSC is more than sports. It also hosts Blaine's Blazin' 4th, All-Canada Show, craft shows, and other general-interest trade shows. Call for a calendar of upcoming events.

> From I-35W northbound, take the Hwy. 118 exit and go west about 30 miles to Hwy. 65 (Central Ave.). Go north on Hwy. 65 to 105th Ave. Turn right onto 105th Ave. and then take the first right, which is Davenport S. NSC is on the left.

ST. PAUL CIVIC CENTER ARENA
143 W 4TH ST. - ST. PAUL, MN 55102

MAP 20

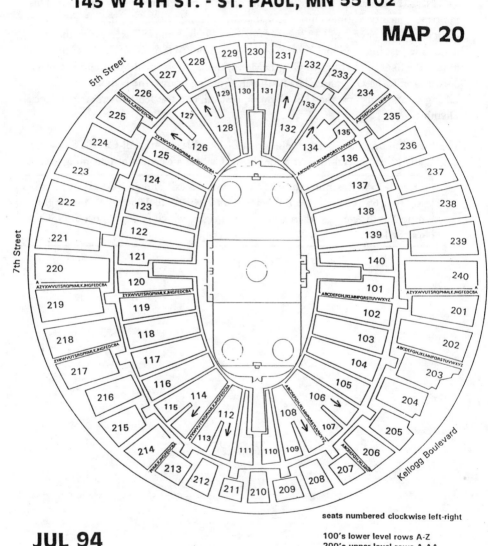

seats numbered clockwise left-right

100's lower level rows A-Z
200's upper level rows A-AA

JUL 94

▲▲▲▲▲▲▲▲▲▲▲▲▲▲▲▲▲▲▲▲▲▲▲▲▲▲▲▲▲▲▲▲▲▲

SAINT PAUL CIVIC CENTER

143 W. Fourth St., St. Paul, MN 55102-1299 (612) 224-7361

The following are examples of annual events at the Saint Paul Civic Center:

JANUARY • Metro Antique Show • Land O'Lakes Kennel Club • Dog Show & Obedience Trials • MN Sportmen's Show	**JULY** • Bridal Show
FEBRUARY • World's Toughest Rodeo • Kidfest • MN State High School Girls Gymnastics Tournament	**AUGUST** • MN Weapons Collectors Show
MARCH • MN State High School Wrestling, • Boys Hockey, & Basketball Tournaments • Twin Cities Indoor Garage Sale • Star of the North Antique Shows	**SEPTEMBER** • Creative Sewing & Needle • Arts Expo
APRIL • Shrine Circus • Festival of Nations • IHL Hockey Games	**OCTOBER** • Great American Train Show • Trick or Treat Street
MAY • Midwest Pet Fair	**NOVEMBER** • Ice Fishing, Snowmobile & • Winter Sports Show • Holiday Art, Gift & Craft Show
JUNE • Bridal Show	**DECEMBER** • MN Weapons Collectors Show • Hmong New Year Celebration

PARKING: Ramp $5, lot $6 for event days. Free bus parking lot behind ramp between Eagle and Shepherd Rds.

From I-94 westbound, exit at 5th St. Turn right at the second stoplight onto 7th St. Take another right at the next stoplight and then a left onto Kellogg Blvd. The Civic Center is on the left and the parking ramp on the right.

From I-94 eastbound, exit at Kellogg Blvd./Mounds and go left on Kellogg Blvd. about 1 mile. The Civic Center is on the right and the parking ramp on the left.

From I-35E southbound, take the Wacouta St. exit (left exit off freeway). Follow Wacouta until it ends at Kellogg Blvd. Turn right onto Kellogg Blvd. and go about 9 blocks to the Civic Center on the right, parking ramp on the left.

From I-35E north the Kellogg Blvd. exit. Go right 1 block. The Civic Center will be on your left and the parking ramp on the right.

From Rochester, take Hwy. 52 to Plato Blvd. and turn left onto Plato. Go about 5 blocks and turn right onto Wabasha. Follow Wabasha to Kellogg Blvd. and turn left. Drive about 3 blocks to the Civic Center on your right and the parking ramp on the left.

From I-494 (Bloomington, International Airport), take I-494E to Hwy. 5, which changes to W. 7th St. Drive east on 7th St. about 3 miles to Kellogg Blvd. Take a right onto Kellogg. The Civic Center is on the left and the parking ramp on the right.

SIEBERT FIELD

Corner of 15th Ave. S.E. and 8th St. S.E., Minneapolis, MN Men's Athletic information (612) 625-4838 Tickets (612) 624-8080

Siebert Field is home to the University of Minnesota Golden Gopher Baseball Team and the Minneapolis Loons, an independent Class A professional baseball team.

From I-35W northbound, take the University Ave. exit. Follow University about 5 blocks to 15th Ave. Turn left onto 15th Ave. and proceed to 8th St. Follow 8th St. to Siebert Field on the corner of 8th and 15th Sts. on the right.

From I-94, take the U of M exit and follow until it becomes 4th St. Follow 4th St. to 15th Ave. Turn right onto 15th Ave. and follow to Siebert Field on the corner of 8th and 15th.

The Target Center, home of the Minnesota Timberwolves NBA team.

Photo by Bruce Kluckhohn, courtesy Minnesota Timberwolves.

THE SPORTS PAVILION

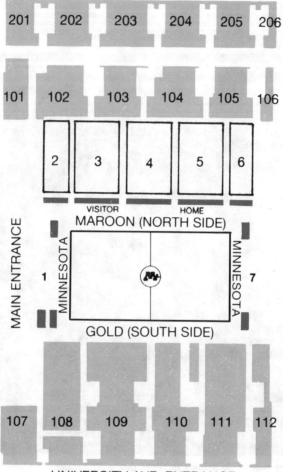

201 202 203 204 205 206

101 102 103 104 105 106

2 3 4 5 6

VISITOR   HOME

MAROON (NORTH SIDE)

MAIN ENTRANCE

MINNESOTA   1   MINNESOTA   7

GOLD (SOUTH SIDE)

107 108 109 110 111 112

UNIVERSITY AVE. ENTRANCE

Courtside - Theatre Style Seating
$6.00 single game
Season ticket holders

General Admission - Bleacher Seating
$5.00 & $3.00

Wheelchair Seating

Women's Athletics
UNIVERSITY OF MINNESOTA

The Sports Pavilion - formerly the old
Mariucci Arena, adjacent to Williams Arena

Gopher Tickets: 624-8080

▲▲▲▲▲▲▲▲▲▲▲▲▲▲▲▲▲▲▲▲▲▲▲▲▲▲▲▲▲▲▲▲▲▲▲▲▲▲

SPORTS PAVILION

1923 University Ave. S.E., Minneapolis, MN 55455 (attached to Williams Arena)
Women's Athletic Information (612) 626-7828 Men's Athletic information (612) 625-4838 Tickets (612) 624-8080

The Sports Pavilion is home to the following Minnesota Gopher Varsity Sports: women's volleyball, basketball, and gymnastics; men's wrestling and gymnastics.

> From I-35W northbound or southbound, take either the Washington Ave. or University Ave. exit and go east about 1 mile to reach Sports Pavilion on the corner of University Ave. S.E. and Oak St. S.E.
>
> From I-94, take the U of M exit and follow until it becomes 4th St. Follow 4th St. as it veers left and proceed to Oak St. Turn left onto Oak St., and follow to the Williams Arena parking lot, which you'll see after you pass over University Ave.

TARGET CENTER

600 First Ave. N., Minneapolis, MN (612) 673-0900

Target Center is a state-of-the-art entertainment facility that hosts a wide range of events from NBA basketball to rock concerts and family shows. Target Center is the home of the Minnesota Timberwolves.

COST: Varies for each event. Weekend and evening parking $4.

DATES: Open only for events.

> Located in downtown Minneapolis on the corner of 1st Ave. N. and 6th St. Call to verify directions at (612) 673-8333.
>
> From I-94 westbound, take 5th St. exit to 1st Ave. N.
>
> From I-94 eastbound, take 4th St. exit, turn right on 1st Ave. N.
>
> From I-35W northbound, take the 5th Ave. downtown exit, turn left on 7th St. and go to 1st Ave. N.
>
> From I-35W southbound, take the Washington Ave. exit, turn right, go to 1st Ave. and turn left.
>
> From I-394 eastbound, take downtown exit, go to parking garage A or B on either side of the arena.

Target Center

MAIN FLOOR ARENA DIAGRAM

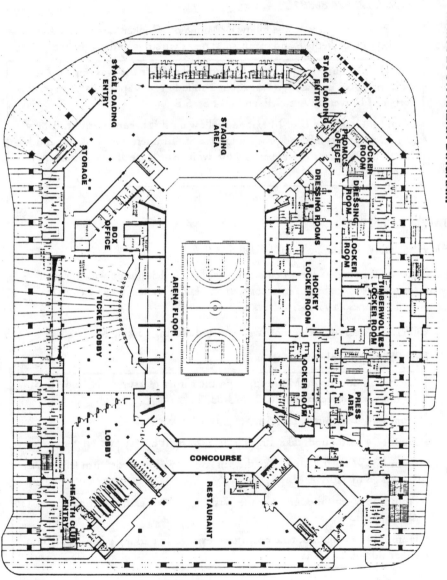

Target Center

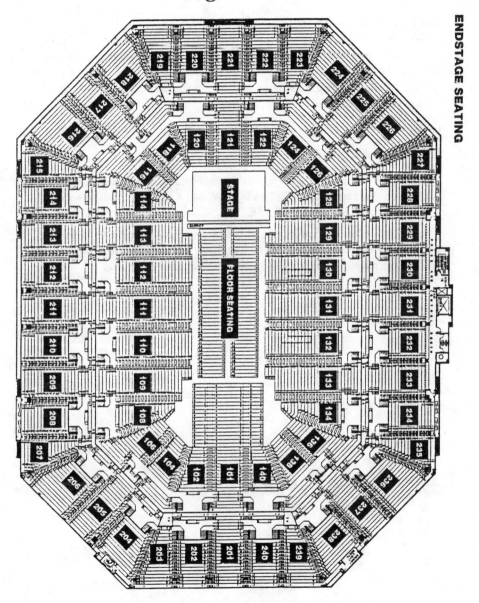

▲▲▲▲▲▲▲▲▲▲▲▲▲▲▲▲▲▲▲▲▲▲▲▲▲▲▲▲▲▲▲▲▲▲▲▲▲▲

WILLIAMS ARENA

4 Oak St. S.E., Minneapolis, MN 55455-2005 Men's Athletic information (612) 625-4838 Tickets (612) 624-8080

Williams Arena is the home of the University of Minnesota Golden Gopher men's basketball team. With a seating capacity for 14,300 fans, "The Barn" turns into a mad frenzy for visiting teams of the Big Ten Conference and other nonconference opponents. Called the "toughest ticket in town," Williams Arena is known as a truly special place to watch college basketball. It was voted among the five best college basketball arenas by Inside Sports in 1990.

COST: Event parking for a $4 fee is just one block northeast of the arena.

DATES: Early November—early March.

From north or south on I-35W, exit either Washington Ave. or University Ave. and travel east approximately 1 mile to Williams Arena, on the corner of University Ave. SE and Oak St. SE.

From I-94, take the U of M exit and follow until it becomes 4th St. Follow 4th St. as it veers left and go to Oak St. Turn left onto Oak St. and follow to the Williams parking lot, visible after you cross University Ave.

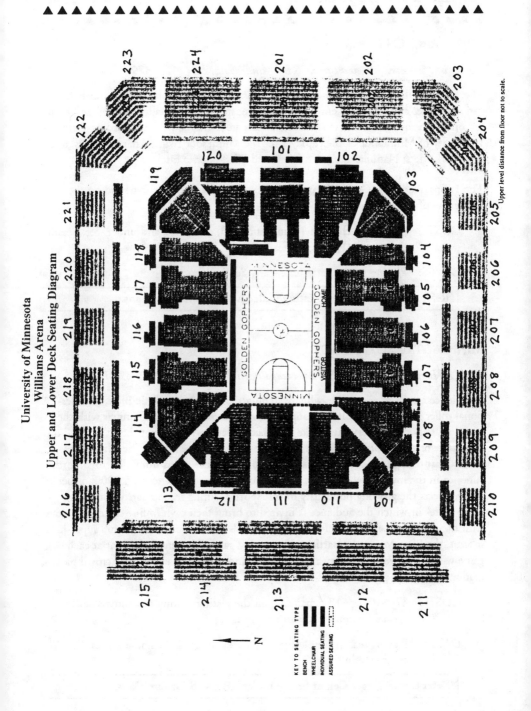

University of Minnesota
Williams Arena
Upper and Lower Deck Seating Diagram

KEY TO SEATING TYPE
BENCH
WHEELCHAIR
INDIVIDUAL SEATING
ASSURED SEATING

Upper level distance from floor not to scale.

291

▲▲▲▲▲▲▲▲▲▲▲▲▲▲▲▲▲▲▲▲▲▲▲▲▲▲▲▲▲▲▲▲▲▲

MINNEAPOLIS LOONS

Corner of 15th Ave. S.E. and 8th St. S.E., Minneapolis, MN (612) 379-7404

The Minneapolis Loons is an independent Class A professional baseball team. Each game provides a great family entertainment atmosphere with quality baseball and exciting on-field promotions and events. The Loons are managed by Greg Olson—former University of Minnesota Gopher; player for the Minnesota Twins, Atlanta Braves, and New York Mets; National League All-Star and World Series catcher.

The Loons' pledge is "Good, cheap fun." Games are played at Siebert Field on the University of Minnesota campus.

COST:　　Adults $6, children 12 and under $3, children 2 and under free. Season tickets for 41 home games $199.

DATES:　　Playing season early June–early September.

> Refer to the Siebert Field listing under ARENAS for directions.

MINNESOTA ARCTIC BLAST

3800 1st Bank Pl., P.O. Box 357, Minneapolis, MN 55440-357 (612) 376-PUCK

Experience a rush of adrenaline while watching the Minnesota Arctic Blast, a professional roller hockey team, blast its opponents. For those who are unfamiliar with the sport, roller hockey is very much like professional ice hockey, except that it's played on a concrete or plastic playing surface and players wear in-line skates. The Minnesota Arctic Blast team is in its second season and plays against teams from all across North America in the lower level of Target Center. An average attendance of 5,000 fans per game reflects the growing popularity of this sport. Gaining in popularity is the "pre-game skate" in which the audience is invited to bring their own in-line skates and skate with the players for an hour before the game. Kids will also enjoy the team's super-hero mascot, the Blast Man, who participates in every game. Live entertainment at each game will double your pleasure, and includes dancers, music, and a lot of crowd participation during the game and half-time.

COST:　　$7, $10, or $13 depending on the seating. Group discounts available; special discount with concessions.

DATES:　　Playing season June–August. Of 24 games, 12 are home games. Call for exact schedule.

> Refer to the Target Center listing under ARENAS for directions.

▲▲▲▲▲▲▲▲▲▲▲▲▲▲▲▲▲▲▲▲▲▲▲▲▲▲▲▲▲▲▲▲▲▲▲▲

The Minnesota Moose Professional Hockey Team plays its home games at the St. Paul Civic Center.

Photo courtesy Minnesota Moose Professional Hockey Team.

▲▲▲▲▲▲▲▲▲▲▲▲▲▲▲▲▲▲▲▲▲▲▲▲▲▲▲▲▲▲▲▲▲▲▲▲▲

MINNESOTA MOOSE

28 W. 6th St., St. Paul, MN 55102 (612) 26-MOOSE (Ticket hotline)

Minnesota Moose, the only professional hockey team in Minnesota, belongs to the International Hockey League, the second best league in the world. Six out of the 22 players are from Minnesota, 15 are from Canada, and one is from Russia. In an 81-game schedule, 41 games are played at home in the St. Paul Civic Center. Call for a schedule.

COST: $4.50–$22.50. Children under 15 and seniors receive a $2 discount. Discounts available for groups of 20 or more.

HOURS: Playing season October–April 1: weekdays 7 p.m., Saturday and Sunday 3 p.m.

Refer to the St. Paul Civic Center listing under ARENAS for directions.

MINNESOTA THUNDER PRO SOCCER

P.O. Box 19378, Minneapolis, MN 55419 THUNDER LINE (612) 893-1442

Minnesota Thunder, the 1994 USISL Midwest Division Champions, is a professional soccer team organized after the loss of the Minnesota Strikers in 1988. The goal of the team is to provide a high level of competition for Minnesota players, and to be an affordable entertainment, educational, and charitable resource for Minnesota fans and the soccer community. Home games are played in the National Sports Center.

COST: Adults $8, youth $5, group rates available.

HOURS: Season home opener is played May 13. The last game before playoffs will fall on August 5, 1995. Games are generally played Saturday nights at 7 or 7:30 p.m.

Refer to the National Sports Center listing under ARENAS for directions.

MINNESOTA TIMBERWOLVES

600 1st Ave. N., Minneapolis, MN 55403 (612) 673-1600

The Minnesota Timberwolves of the National Basketball Association (NBA), started as an expansion franchise in the 1989–1990 playing season. Target Center is home court for the Timberwolves' 41 regular season home games. Fans will also enjoy special half-time entertainment, contests, and Crunch, the team's wolf mascot.

▲▲▲▲▲▲▲▲▲▲▲▲▲▲▲▲▲▲▲▲▲▲▲▲▲▲▲▲▲▲▲▲▲▲▲▲

COST: $9.50–$42.50. Call Ticket Master at (612) 989-5151 or come to the box office of the Target Center lobby. Box office hours are Monday–Saturday 9:30 a.m.–6 p.m.; also open two hours prior to game time Sunday: 12:30 p.m.

HOURS: November–April Monday–Saturday 7 p.m., Sunday 2:30 p.m.

> Refer to the Target Center listing under ARENAS for directions.

MINNESOTA TWINS

The Metrodome, 501 Chicago Ave. S., Minneapolis, MN 55415 (612) 33-TWINS or (800) 33-TWINS

Since moving to the Twin Cities from Washington D.C., in 1961, the Minnesota Twins Baseball Club has had a special place in the hearts of sports fans throughout the Upper Midwest. The Twins organization has produced winning teams that have drawn record crowds and promoted unmatched community pride and spirit. For 35 years, the Twins have treated their loyal fans to four division titles, three American League pennants, and three World Series appearances — including World Series Championships in 1987 and 1991.

COST: Home game tickets start as low as $4. They may be purchased at the Twins ticket office at the Metrodome, or at the Twins Pro Shops in Richfield, Roseville, and Apple Valley. To charge tickets by phone, please call (612) 33-TWINS or (800) 33-TWINS.

DATES: Playing season April–September.

> Refer to the HHH Metrodome listing under ARENAS for directions.

1995 Minnesota Twins Seating

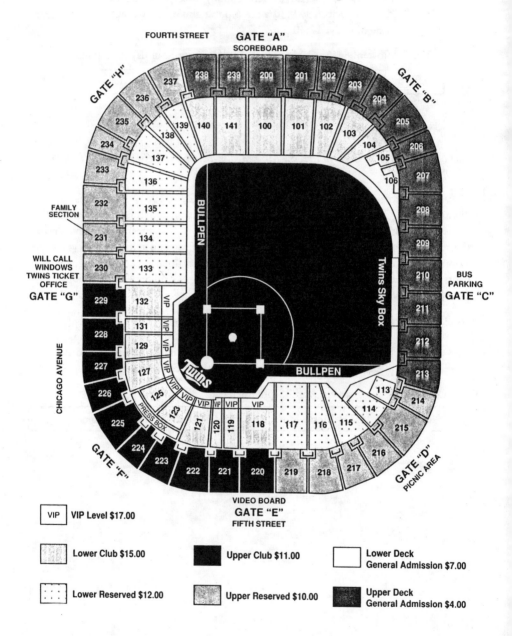

▲▲▲▲▲▲▲▲▲▲▲▲▲▲▲▲▲▲▲▲▲▲▲▲▲▲▲▲▲▲

Minnesota Vikings

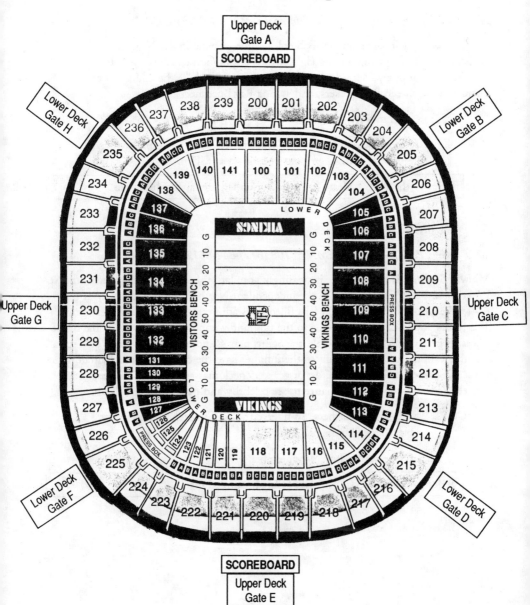

297

MINNESOTA VIKINGS (Seating chart on previous page.)

Hubert H. Humphrey Metrodome, Minneapolis, MN (612) 333-8828

Minnesota's entry in the National Football League, playing in the NFC Central Division, plays two preseason and eight regular season home games a year in the Hubert H. Humphrey Metrodome. Home opponents include the Chicago Bears, Detroit Lions, Green Bay Packers, and Tampa Bay Buccaneers.

COST: $15 to $40.

DATES: Playing season September–December. Games are typically played on Sundays, with some games Mondays and Thursdays.

> Refer to the HHH Metrodome listing under Arenas for directions.

ST. PAUL SAINTS

1771 Energy Park Dr., St. Paul, MN 55108 (612) 644-6512

Midway Stadium is home to the increasingly popular professional baseball team, the St. Paul Saints. The Saints belongs to the independent Northern League and play at the AA levels. Last year over 241,000 fans filled the stadium to 98% capacity every game. The team's popularity is largely due to the fun family atmosphere and affordable ticket prices. Averaging 3–4 games a week, the Saints play 42 home games a year. You'll see a pig, the team mascot, deliver balls to the umpire; have the chance to get a haircut in an authentic barber chair in the stands; or get a $5 neck massage from Sister Rosalind Gefred. You might even get a chance to see celebrity and partial owner Bill Murray.

COST: Adults $4 bleachers, $6 reserved seats. Children 14 and under $3 bleachers, $5 reserved seats.

DATES: Game season June 9–September 4.

> Refer to ST. PAUL CIVIC CENTER for directions.

▲▲▲▲▲▲▲▲▲▲▲▲▲▲▲▲▲▲▲▲▲▲▲▲▲▲▲▲▲▲▲▲▲▲▲

UNIVERSITY OF MINNESOTA'S GOLDEN GOPHERS

226 Bierman Field Athletic Bldg., 516 15th Ave. S. E., Minneapolis, MN 55455 Women's Athletic Information (612) 626-7828 Men's Athletic information (612) 625-4838 Tickets (612) 624-8080 or (800) U-GOPHER. Call for ticket information or to receive a game schedule for any of your favorite Golden Gopher sports teams.

COST: Varies by event.

HOURS: Varies by event.

Refer to the Mariucci Arena, Metrodome, Sports Pavilion, Seibert Field, and Williams Arena listings under STADIUMS & ARENAS for directions.

STOCK CAR RACING

▲▲▲▲▲▲▲▲▲▲▲▲▲▲▲▲▲▲▲▲▲▲▲▲▲▲▲▲▲▲▲▲▲▲▲▲▲▲

RACEWAY PARK

One Checkered Flag Blvd., Shakopee, MN 55379

Recorded information (612) 445-5500 (612) 445-2257

See NASCAR stock car racing at its best. Sunday night's program includes modifieds; short trackers; hobbies; and the famous Figure 8s on the 1/4 asphalt facility.

COST: Adults $8, students and children 5-12 $3, children 4 and under free. Parking free. Specials may be slightly higher.

HOURS: Mid-April–September: Sunday 7 p.m. Call for holiday and special events schedule.

> From I-35W, take the Hwy. 13 exit and go west toward Shakopee. Follow Hwy. 13 until it meets Hwy. 101 and continue on Hwy. 101. Raceway Park is just 5 miles east of Shakopee on Hwy. 101, across from Valleyfair.

WINTER SPORTS

▲▲▲▲▲▲▲▲▲▲▲▲▲▲▲▲▲▲▲▲▲▲▲▲▲▲▲▲▲▲▲▲▲▲▲▲

AFTON ALPS SKI AND GOLF

6600 Peller Ave. S., Hastings, MN 55033 (612) 436-5245

> If you enjoy downhill skiing through spectacular scenery, visit the Afton Alps Ski Area, nestled in the rolling hills of the scenic St. Croix River Valley overlooking Afton State Park. With 37 lighted runs from beginning to advanced level, Afton Alps' downhill area will be enjoyable for the entire family.
>
> COST: Please call for lift ticket prices.
>
> HOURS: November–April: daily 9 a.m.–10 p.m.

From I-94, take exit 253 south about 7 miles to 70th St. Turn left onto 70th St. and go 3 miles to the Afton Alps Ski Area.

COMO SKI CENTER

1431 N. Lexington Pkwy., St. Paul, MN 55108 (612) 488-9673

Without having to leave town, enjoy two lighted downhill ski runs with rope tows; 7 kilometers of groomed cross-country ski trails; and a short sliding hill at the Como Downhill Ski Area. The chalet offers downhill and cross-country ski rental, lessons, an accessory shop, and a snack bar.

> COST: Cross-country ski rates per two hours: adults $6, young adults 13–17 $4, children 12 and under $2.
> Downhill skiing rental package rates for one day: adults $8.50, young adults 13-17 $6.50, children 12 and under $4.50.
> Tow ticket rates: adults $5.50, young adults 17 and under $4.50 weekends, $3.50 weekdays. Lessons offered for both downhill and cross-country skiing.
>
> HOURS: Weekdays 2–9 p.m.; Saturday 9 a.m.–6 p.m.; Sunday 11 a.m.–6 p.m.; holiday hours 10 a.m.–9 p.m.

From I-94, take the Lexington Ave. exit and go north to the Como Ski Center on the left side in the Como Park Golf Course clubhouse building.

▲▲▲▲▲▲▲▲▲▲▲▲▲▲▲▲▲▲▲▲▲▲▲▲▲▲▲▲

Mother Nature deposits fresh powder on Afton Alps.

▲ ▲

BUCK HILL SKI AREA

15400 Buck Hill Rd., Burnsville, MN 65308 (612) 435-7187

Established in 1954 with only one cleared slope and one tow rope, Buck Hill has grown to 11 different runs for skiers and snowboarders of all abilities. Equipped with the latest snowmaking technology, 100% snow coverage is guaranteed.

Buck Hill also has a Sports Learning Center, which was chosen the "Best Place to Learn to Ski" by Mpls./St. Paul magazine. The Sports Learning Center offers training by skilled staff in skiing and snowboarding for all ages and abilities.

From entry-level racing to one of the top-ranked junior teams in the U.S., Buck Hill is an excellent place to race. Ski magazine declared Buck Hill "a legendary capital of American ski racing" in its March 1992 issue. Racing programs offered at Buck Hill include NASTAR; Development Team; Buck Hill Ski Racing Club; Adult Race Clinics; and The Ski Challenge.

Buck Hill is also open during the summer for mountain biking. The 4 miles of trails are specifically designed to accommodate the beginning, intermediate, and advanced rider.

COST: Snow ticket rates $10–$23, depending on age and time of day or week. Call (612) 435-7187 for the most up-to-date prices. Children 5 and under free with a paying adult. Seniors 62 and over ski 1/2 price. Ski rental rates, including skis, boots, and poles, $14. Snowboard rental rates, day and evening, $20.

HOURS: Weekdays 10 a.m.–10 p.m.; weekends 9 a.m.–10 p.m.

From I-35W southbound, take the Co. Rd. 42 exit. Go straight through the light at the top of the intersection, which puts you on Buck Hill Rd. Follow Buck Hill Rd. through two stop signs. After the second stoplight, look for Buck Hill on the right.

From I-35E southbound, take the Co. Rd. 42 exit. Turn right onto Co. Rd. 42 and follow to Buck Hill Rd. Turn left onto Buck Hill Rd. Follow Buck Hill Rd. through two stop signs. After the second stoplight, look for Buck Hill on the right.

▲▲▲▲▲▲▲▲▲▲▲▲▲▲▲▲▲▲▲▲▲▲▲▲▲▲▲▲▲▲▲▲▲▲▲

HYLAND HILLS SKI AREA

8800 Chalet Rd., Bloomington, MN 55438 (612) 835-4604

Come and enjoy one of the best ski and snowboard areas around with 14 downhill runs, 3 triple chair lifts and a full-size half pipe.

COST: Weekend lift ticket $18, weekday lift ticket $13, night skiing $10, complete rental package $12, snowboards $20.

HOURS: Monday–Sunday 9 a.m.–9 p.m.

> From I-494, take the Bush Lake Rd. exit south. Bush Lake Rd. will turn into Chalet Rd. Follow Chalet Rd. into Hyland Hills.

MOUNT FRONTENAC

Box 119, Frontenac, MN 55026 (612) 388-5826

Located 9 miles south of Red Wing in the scenic Hiawatha River Valley, Mount Frontenac features 10 runs, three chair lifts, two tow ropes, and night skiing. A cafeteria and adult lounge help make your stay more comfortable. Ski rental and ski instruction available.

COST: Lift tickets: adults $20, juniors 13–17 $18, children 6–12 $16, children 5 and under free. Ski rental $13.

HOURS: December–March: Wednesday–Friday 4:30–10 p.m.; Saturday 9 a.m.–10 p.m.; Sunday 10 a.m.–8 p.m.

> Follow Hwy. 61 to Red Wing and go 9 miles south. Mount Frontenac is on Hwy. 61 on the right.

WELCH VILLAGE SKI AREA

26685 Co. 7 Blvd., Welch, MN 55089 (612) 258-4567

"Make a run for it" on the slopes of the scenic Cannon River Valley at Welch Village Ski Area. Welch Village began as a family idea in 1965, and 30 years later is still a popular place to bring the entire family to ski or learn to ski. With 36 trails and nine lifts, the area offers an ideal skiing mix for all levels of skiers and snowboarders. The skiing terrain is serviced by two quad chairs, five doubles, one triple, and a Mitey-Mite surface lift that keeps you skiing and not standing in line.

The main chalet has three food service areas, two levels of seating, a ski accessory store,

▲ ▲

video games, and lockers for your convenience. Also available is the east side adult chalet.

Snowboarders have their own niche at the Snowboards Parks area, designed for beginners through advanced riders.

For all skiers at first-time through advanced levels, Welch Village's exclusive SKILINK™ offers the latest in ski learning techniques and technology to make your experience easy, fun, and affordable. SKILINK staff are members of the Professional Ski Instructors of America.

COST: Please call (612) 258-4567 for recorded information on current lift ticket and rental prices.

HOURS: Mid-November–mid- or late March, weather permitting. Skiing daily 9 a.m.–10 p.m.; Friday and Saturday 9 a.m.–midnight.

> Welch Village Ski Area is located 45 minutes southeast of St. Paul. Take U.S. Hwy. 61 southeast through Hastings, then take Co. Rd. 7 or Welch Village Rd. south and follow 3 miles to the Welch Village Ski Area.

WILD MOUNTAIN SKI AREA

Co. Rd. 16, Taylors Falls, MN (800) 447-4958

Experience winter skiing at its best on 22 completely lighted ski runs at Wild Mountain Ski Area. Ski seven days and nights a week, and all night until 3 a.m. Fridays. Complete rentals, ski school, and guaranteed learn-to-ski programs available for adults, teens, and children.

COST: Please call toll-free for rates.

HOURS: November–April: weekdays 10 a.m.–10 p.m.; Friday all night till 3 a.m.; Saturday 9:30 a.m.–10:30 p.m.; Sunday 9:30 a.m.–9 p.m.

> From I-35E or I-35W northbound, take the Hwy. 8 exit to Taylors Falls and follow to Co. Rd. 16. Follow Co. Rd. 16 north 7 miles to Wild Mountain.

▲▲▲▲▲▲▲▲▲▲▲▲▲▲▲▲▲▲▲▲▲▲▲▲▲▲▲▲▲▲▲▲▲▲▲

EKO BAKEN

22570 Manning Trail, Scandia, MN 55073 (612) 433-2422

Located only 25 minutes away from the Minneapolis/St. Paul metro area. Snow tubing at Eko Baken is fast and fun, and makes everyone feel like a kid again. Safe, well-lighted expert and bunny hills available for people of all sizes and abilities. Rope claws make getting up the hill as effortless as getting down the hill. Warm up in a spacious new chalet with a snack bar.

COST: Adults 13 and older $8.50, children 12 and under $7, group rates available.

HOURS: Weekends, holidays, Christmas vacation 11 a.m.–10 p.m.; Friday 6:30–10 p.m.; Monday–Thursday evenings by reservation. Hours extended by reservation.

> Eko Baken is 6 miles east of Forest Lake. From I-35E or I-35W northbound, take the Hwy. 97 exit. Follow Hwy. 97 east 7 miles to Manning Trail. Follow Manning Trail north 1-1/2 miles to Eko Baken.

GREEN ACRES RECREATION

8989 55th St. N. (Co. Rd. 13) at Demontreville Trail, Lake Elmo, MN 55042 (612) 770-1969

Green Acres is a family-oriented recreation area that offers winter tube sliding in sessions lasting two hours. Facilities consist of two hills; three rope tows; lighting; a newly expanded warming chalet; and a friendly staff.

COST: Adults 13 and over $8.50, children 12 and under $7.50, group rates available.

HOURS: Sessions for Saturdays, Sundays, and holidays are 10-noon, 12:30-2:30 p.m., 3-5 p.m., 5:30-7:30 p.m., 8-10 p.m., First and last shift closed on Sunday. Thursday 6-9 p.m. (3 hour) Friday 5:30-7:30 p.m., 8-10 p.m. Sledding available Monday–Wednesday by reservation only for three-hour sessions.
Open daily during Christmas holidays, December 26-January 2.

> From Hwy. I-694/I-494, take the Hwy. 36 exit east to Co. Rd. 13 (55th St. N.) Travel south 1/4 mile on Co. Rd. 13 to Green Acres on the left (at Demontreville Trail).

▲▲▲▲▲▲▲▲▲▲▲▲▲▲▲▲▲▲▲▲▲▲▲▲▲▲▲▲▲▲▲▲▲▲▲▲

HILL BILLY HILLS SNOW TUBING

13414 Co. Rd. 160, St. Joseph, MN 56374 (612) 363-7797

Winter can still be exhilarating at Hill Billy Hills. Experience great family time snow tubing down hills ranging from mild to wild. An automated tow rope takes the effort out of getting back up the hill. Hills are lighted at night. A large warming chalet with full-service snack bar awaits you when you need a break.

COST: Tube and tow ticket: Adults and youth 13 and over $6, children 12 and under $5, $1 off prices for groups of 20 or more.

HOURS: Monday–Friday 6–10 p.m., Saturday and Sunday noon–10 p.m. Dist. 742 school holidays noon–10 p.m.

> From I-94 northbound heading toward St. Joseph, take exit 160 and turn southwest (left) onto Co. Rd. 2. Go 3 miles on Co. Rd. 2 to Jct. 160. Turn right onto Co. Rd. 160 and follow about 1 mile. Hill Billy Hills is on the right side of the road.

SOUTH VALLEY PARK

70th St. and Cahill Ave., Inver Grove Heights, MN 55077 (612) 450-2585

South Valley Park offers a fully lighted sledding hill for wintertime fun.

COST: Free.

HOURS: Regular hours   School vacation hours
           Week Days 4–8 p.m.   10 a.m.–8 p.m.
           Saturday   10 a.m.–8 p.m.   10 a.m.–8 p.m.
           Sunday   1–5 p.m. 1–5 p.m.
           Holiday hours: Christmas Eve 10 a.m.–1 p.m.; closed Christmas Day; New Year's Eve 10 a.m.–8 p.m.; New Year's Day 1–5 p.m.

> Located in Inver Grove Heights. From I-494 (Hwy. 10) going east, take the Lafayette Freeway exit. Proceed south on Lafayette to 70th St. E. Proceed east on 70th St. E. The park is on 70th St. and Cahill Ave.

ZOOS

▲▲▲▲▲▲▲▲▲▲▲▲▲▲▲▲▲▲▲▲▲▲▲▲▲▲▲▲▲▲▲▲▲▲▲▲▲

COMO ZOO/COMO ZOOLOGICAL SOCIETY

Midway Pkwy. and Kaufman Dr., St. Paul, MN 55113 (612) 488-5571

Historic Como Zoo is home to over 350 animals, many of which are threatened or endangered species. The zoo features primates, African hoofed stock, large cats, and aquatic animals. Zoodale, the gift shop, is open daily.

COST: Free.

HOURS: Open year round, including holidays.
Summer hours, April–September: grounds 8 a.m.–8 p.m., buildings 10 a.m.–6 p.m.
Winter hours, October–March: grounds 8 a.m.–5 p.m., buildings 10 a.m.–4 p.m.

> Located in the middle of Como Park just a few blocks east of Snelling Ave. on Midway Pkwy. at Kaufman Drive.
>
> From I-94, take the Lexington Ave. exit. Go north on Lexington Ave. and follow the signs.
>
> From Hwy. 36, take the Lexington Ave. exit. Go south on Lexington Ave. and follow the signs.

MINNESOTA ZOO

13000 Zoo Blvd., Apple Valley, MN 55124 (612) 432-9000 (ZOO-TO-DO).

The Minnesota Zoo exists to strengthen the bond between people and the living earth. The zoo provides award-winning recreational, educational, and conservation programs to the public. Children are always wide-eyed over their encounters with a large variety of native and exotic animals.

COST: Adults $8, children 3–12 $4, seniors 65 and over $5.

HOURS: October–April: 9 a.m.–4 p.m. May–September 9 a.m.–4 p.m.; weekends 9 a.m.–6 p.m.

> The Minnesota Zoo is located 10 minutes south of the Mall of America.
>
> From Hwy. 77 (Cedar Ave.) southbound toward Apple Valley, follow the well-marked signs to zoo as you approach the north end of Apple Valley.
>
> From I-35E, take the Cliff Rd. exit and go east to Johnny Cake Ridge Rd. Turn right (south) and follow to zoo.

▲▲▲▲▲▲▲▲▲▲▲▲▲▲▲▲▲▲▲▲▲▲▲▲▲▲▲▲▲▲▲▲▲▲▲▲▲▲

Dolphins perform for an enthusiastic audience at the Minnesota Zoo.

Photo courtesy Minnesota Zoo.

SUPPLEMENTARY LISTINGS

▲▲▲▲▲▲▲▲▲▲▲▲▲▲▲▲▲▲▲▲▲▲▲▲▲▲▲▲▲▲▲▲▲▲▲▲▲

BIKING TRAILS

Because several fine books already are dedicated entirely to the subject of biking trails in Minnesota and the Twin Cities area, this one chapter could not cover the subject adequately. Instead, the following books, pamphlets, and maps are highly recommended.

"BIKE WAYS" BROCHURES

"Bike Ways" brochures are filled with information and detailed maps of local biking trails. The brochures are distributed through county offices or local park and recreation departments. Phone numbers for these are listed later in this chapter under PARKS DEPARTMENTS' ADDRESSES & NUMBERS. For additional biking information and "Bike Ways" brochures and maps, contact:

Dakota County .... (612) 891-7030

Hennepin Parks .... (612) 559-9000

State Wide Trails-DNR .... (612) 296-6699

MN Dept. of Transportation .... (612) 296-2216

MN Office of Tourism .... (800) 657-3700

BIKING IN VIKINGLAND by Marlys Mickelson

This is one of the best guides for anyone who enjoys biking or hiking a variety of trails. It tells the locations of 27 biking and hiking trails, 62 mountain biking locations, how to get there, and what to expect. The book includes 22 biking/hiking maps of significant trails in the Twin Cities area, the state of Minnesota, and western Wisconsin. The 106-page guide sells for $7.95 and can usually be found in local bookshops or biking stores.

SUPPLEMENTARY LISTINGS

▲▲▲▲▲▲▲▲▲▲▲▲▲▲▲▲▲▲▲▲▲▲▲▲▲▲▲▲▲▲▲▲▲▲▲

BIKING WITH THE WIND by Dixen-Seed-Wilson

This book chronicles bicycling day trips in Minnesota and Wisconsin within reach of the Twin Cities. Whether you enjoy biking for leisure or sport, this book is highly recommended. For each trail, it includes maps and detailed descriptions of terrain; point-to-point mileage; toilet facilities; points of interest; picnic spots; places to eat along the way, and camping and lodging facilities. Routes vary from 10 to 60 miles in length. This 319-page book sells for $16.95 and can be found in almost any Twin City bookstore.

GRAND ROUNDS PARKWAY SYSTEM

Write to the Minneapolis Park & Recreation Board for a brochure with a detailed map of the Grand Rounds Parkway System. The system consists of 53 miles of connecting scenic parks, parkways, bike paths, and pedestrian paths encircling the entire city of Minneapolis. The system includes the chain of lakes; Lake Nokomis; Lake Hiawatha; Minnehaha; Shingle and Bassett Creeks; and the Mississippi River.

Minneapolis Park & Recreation Board 310 4th Ave. S., Minneapolis, MN 55415

THE NORTH COUNTRY GUIDE TO MOUNTAIN BIKING by Cindy Storm, Cindy Bijold, Kelly Owen, and Anne Breckenridge

This guide highlights 55 fat-tire routes and state trails. It includes descriptions, detailed maps, technical hints, and trail tips. The 158-page guide sells for $12.95 and can be found in most bookstores.

TWIN CITIES BIKE MAP by Little Transport Maps

This large, impressive fold-out map boasts that it provides the Twin Cities' most complete bike route information. The map also includes mountain bike trails, road and commuter routes, and park and rail trails. The map can be found in most bookstores and sells for $7.95.

▲▲▲▲▲▲▲▲▲▲▲▲▲▲▲▲▲▲▲▲▲▲▲▲▲▲▲▲▲▲▲▲▲▲▲▲

Biking in Vikingland

Minnesota's Most Popular Biking Trail Guide

Discover the beautiful biking trails Minnesota and Wisconsin have to offer. Choose from short day or longer weekend trips. Biking in Vikingland is convenient, inexpensive and easy-to-use.

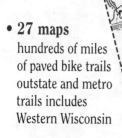

BIKING IN VIKINGLAND

Revised

Bicycle Trails: Where to go • What to expect • How to get there

by Marlys Mickelson

- **27 maps**
  hundreds of miles of paved bike trails outstate and metro trails includes Western Wisconsin

- **Trail Access**
  how to find it where to park points of interest bath rooms

- **Trail Specifics**
  length difficulty grade pavem

- **Lists 62 mountain biking locations**

- **Tips on safety and equipment**

Biking in Vikingland
Softcover $7.95
ISBN 0-934860-00-9

ADVENTURE
PUBLICATIONS, INC.

Get your copy at your local bookstore or bike shop or call (612) 689-9800

▲ ▲

Cross-country skiing opportunities are so numerous that the subject is best left to many of the excellent cross-country ski guides already published. They are available from your local bookstore, local Parks & Recreation Departments, and at State Parks.

Twin Cities Fishing Guide does an excellent job of covering fishing opportunities throughout the Twin Cities. It is available in local bookstores and bait shops.

▲ ▲

- The Connection 922-9000

- DNR Trail and Water Ways (612) 772-7935

- DNR Fish Survey (612) 296-3325

- Greater Minneapolis Convention and Visitors Association 661-4700

Minneapolis Calendar of Events Mail requests to: 4000 Multifoods Tower, 33 S. 6th St., Minneapolis, MN 55402

- Minneapolis Downtown Council (612) 338-3807 offers maps of downtown parking facilities, stores, restaurants, and "Do the Town" (validated parking program) participants.

- Minneapolis Tourism Hotline (612) 370-9103

- Minnesota Office of Tourism (612) 296-5029

- Mississippi Mile Hotline gives updates on year-round events on the Minneapolis river front at (612) 627-5433

- Mississippi National River & Recreation Area (MNRRA) & Park Service activities information is available from the National Park Service at (612) 290-4160

St. Paul Calendar of Events Mail requests to 55 E. 5th St., Suite 101, St. Paul, MN 55101 or call (612) 297-6985

- St. Paul Convention and Visitors Bureau (612) 297-6985 or 800-627-6101

- St. Paul Tourism Hotline (612) 222-1000

- Ticket Master (612) 989-5151

- Twin Cities Tourism Attractions Association of Minnesota (612) 858-8493

Parks & Recreation departments are great resources when you want to know more about your local beaches, parks, walking, biking, and cross-country ski trails. You can often rent recreational equipment and reserve pavilions through Parks & Recreation. Getting a long list of summer activities for kids is also a sure bet.

Afton (No Parks & Recreation)
Stillwater School District
Community Education
1875 S. Greeley St.
Stillwater, MN 55082
(612) 351-8300

Andover (Public Works)
1685 Cross Town Blvd. N.W.
Andover, MN 55304
(612) 755-8118

Anoka
641 Jacob Lane
Anoka, MN 55303
(612) 421-6630

Apple Valley
14200 Cedar Ave.
Apple Valley, MN 55124
(612) 953-2300

Arden Hills
1450 W. Hwy. 96
Arden Hills, MN 55112
(612) 633-5676

Bayport
294 N. 3rd St.
Bayport, MN 55003
(612) 439-2530

Belle Plain
220 South Market St.
Belle Plain, MN 56011
(612) 873-4377

Birchwood
See White Bear Lake
City Hall (612) 426-3403

Blaine
9150 Central Ave. N.E.
Blaine, MN 55434
(612) 784-6700

Bloomington
2215 W. Old Shakopee Rd.
Bloomington, MN 55431
(612) 948-8877

Brooklyn Center
6301 Shingle Creek Pkwy.
Brooklyn Center, MN 55430
(612) 569-3400

Brooklyn Park
5200 85th Ave. N.
Brooklyn Park, MN 55443
(612) 493-8335

Burnsville
100 Civic Center Pkwy.
Burnsville, MN 55337
(612) 895-4500

Champlin
11955 Champlin Dr.
Champlin, MN 55316
(612) 421-2820

Chanhassen
690 Coulter Dr.
Chanhassen, MN 55317
(612) 937-1900

Chaska
1661 Park Ridge Dr.
Chaska, MN 55318
(612) 448-3176

Circle Pines (covers Blaine,
Circle Pines and Lexington)
4707 North Rd.
Circle Pines, MN 55014
(612) 780-7686 or 780-7687

Cologne
110 Louis St. W.
Cologne, MN 55322
(612) 466-2064

Columbia Heights
530 Mill St.
Columbia Heights, MN 55421
(612) 782-2860

Corcoran
9525 Cain Rd.
Corcoran, MN 55340
(612) 520-2288

Cottage Grove
7516 80th St. S.
Cottage Grove, MN 55016
(612) 458-2834

Crystal
4800 Douglas Dr.
Crystal, MN 55429
(612) 531-0052

Deephaven
20225 Cottagewood Rd.
Excelsior, MN 55331
(612) 474-4755

Dellwood
(see Dellwood City Hall
612-429-1356)

Eagan
3830 Pilot Knob Rd.
Eagan, MN 55122
(612) 681-4660

East Bethel
2241 221st Ave. N.E.
East Bethel, MN 55011
(612) 434-9569

Eden Prairie
8080 Mitchell Rd.
Eden Prairie, MN 55344-2230
(612) 949-8442

Edina
4801 W. 50th St.
Edina, MN 55424
(612) 927-8861

Elk River
P.O. Box 490
Elk River, MN 55330
(612) 441-7420

Excelsior
339 3rd St.
Excelsior, MN 55331
(612) 474-5233

Falcon Heights
2077 W. Larpenteur Ave.
Falcon Heights, MN 55113
(612) 644-5050

Farmington
325 Oak St.
Farmington, MN 55024
(612) 463-7111

Forest Lake
Community Services
6100 N. 210th St.
Forest Lake, MN 55025
(612) 464-9110

Fridley
6431 University Ave. N.E.
Fridley, MN 55432
(612) 572-3570

Golden Valley
200 Brookview Pkwy.
Golden Valley, MN 55426
(612) 544-5218

Greenwood
20225 Cottagewood Rd.
Deephaven, MN 55331
(612) 544-5218

▲▲▲▲▲▲▲▲▲▲▲▲▲▲▲▲▲▲▲▲▲▲▲▲▲▲▲▲▲▲▲▲▲▲

Ham Lake
15544 Central Ave. N.E.
Ham Lake, MN 55304
(612) 434-9555

Hamel
2052 County Rd. 24
Medina, MN 55340
(612) 473-4643

Hastings
101 E. 4th St.
Hastings, MN 55033
(612) 437-4127

Hennepin County Parks
12615 Co. Rd. 9
Plymouth, MN 55441
(612) 559-9000

Hopkins
14600 Minnetonka Blvd.
Minnetonka, MN 55345
(612) 939-8203

Inver Grove Heights
8450 Barbara Ave.
Inver Grove Heights, MN 55077
(612) 450-2587

Isanti
P.O. Box 126
Isanti, MN 55040
(612) 492-6211

Jordan
500 Sunset Dr.
Jordan, MN 55352
(612) 492-6211

Lakeville
20195 Holyoke Ave.
Lakeville, MN 55044
(612) 469-4431

Lauderdale
1891 Walnut
Lauderdale, MN 55113
(612) 631-0300

Lexington
Suite 140, 4175 Lovell Rd.
Lexington, MN 55014
(612) 784-2792

Lino Lakes
7204 Lake Dr.
Lino Lakes, MN 55014
(612) 464-5562, Ext. 176

Little Canada
515 Little Canada Rd.
Little Canada, MN 55117
(612) 484-2177

Long Lake
1964 Park Ave, P.O. Box 606
Long Lake, MN 55356

Mahtomedi
Community Services
1520 Mahtomedi Ave.
Mahtomedi, MN 55115
(612) 426-1116

Maple Grove
Box 1180
Maple Grove, MN 55311
(612) 420-4000

Maple Plain
1620 Maple Ave.
Maple Plain, MN 55359
(612) 479-0515

Maplewood
1830 E. County Rd. B
Maplewood, MN 55109
(612) 770-4570

Medina
2052 County Rd. 24
Medina, MN 55340
(612) 473-4643

Mendota Heights
1101 Victoria Curve
Mendota Heights, MN 55118
(612) 452-1850

▲▲▲▲▲▲▲▲▲▲▲▲▲▲▲▲▲▲▲▲▲▲▲▲▲▲▲▲▲▲▲▲▲

Minnesota Office of Tourism
100 Metro Square
121 E. 7th Place
St. Paul, MN 55101
(612) 296-5029

Minnetonka
14600 Minnetonka Blvd.
Minnetonka, MN 55345
(612) 939-8203

Minnetonka Beach
2945 Westwood Rd.
Minnetonka Beach, MN 55361
(612) 471-8878

Minnetrista
7001 County Rd. 110 W.
Minnetrista, MN 55364
(612) 446-1660

Monticello
P.O. Box 1147
Monticello, MN 55362
(612) 295-2711

Moundsview
2401 Highway 10
Moundsview, MN 55112-1499
(612) 784-0618

New Brighton
400 10th St. N.W.
New Brighton, MN 55112
(612) 638-2120

New Hope
4401 Xylon Ave. N.
New Hope, MN 55428
(612) 531-5151

New Prague
118 Central Ave. N.
New Prague, MN 56071
(612) 758-4401

Newport
596 7th Ave.
Newport, MN 55055
(612) 459-5677

North Metro Visitors Center
6205 Earle Brown Dr., Suite 100
Brooklyn Center, MN 55430
(612) 566-7722

North Oaks
North Oaks Homeowners Assoc.
52 Wildflower Way
St. Paul, MN 55127
(612) 484-6005

North St. Paul
Community Center & Recreation
2290 1st St. N.
North St. Paul, MN 55109
(612) 770-4471

Northern Dakota County
Chamber of Commerce
1380 Corporate Center Curve
Suite 116
Eagan, MN 55121-1200
(612) 452-9872

Northfield
Community Services
801 Washington St.
Northfield, MN 55057
(507) 645-1240
(507) 645-8833 City Hall

Oak Grove
19900 Nightingale St. N.W.
Cedar, MN 55011
(612) 753-1920

Oak Park Heights
14168 57th St. N.
Oak Park Heights, MN 55082
(612) 439-4439

Oakdale
1584 Hadley Ave. N.
Oakdale, MN 55128
(612) 739-5086

Orono
705 Old Crystal Bay Rd.
Long Lake, MN 55356
(612) 449-8350

▲▲▲▲▲▲▲▲▲▲▲▲▲▲▲▲▲▲▲▲▲▲▲▲▲▲▲▲▲▲▲▲

Osseo
415 Central Ave.
Osseo, MN 55369
(612) 425-2624 (City Hall)

Plymouth
3400 Plymouth Blvd.
Plymouth, MN 55447
(612) 550-5130

Princeton
706 1st St.
Princeton, MN 55371
(612) 389-4789
(612) 427-9524 (City Hall)

Prior Lake
16200 Eagle Creek Ave. S.E.
Prior Lake, MN 55372
(612) 447-4230

Ramsey
15153 Nowthen Blvd. N.W.
Ramsey, MN 55303
(612) 427-1410 or 427-1741

Richfield
7000 Nicollet Ave. S.
Richfield, MN 55423
(612) 861-9385

Robbinsdale
4139 Regent Ave. N.
Robbinsdale, MN 55422
(612) 537-4534

Rockford (Community Education)
P.O. Box 9
Rockford, MN 55373
(612) 477-5831
(612) 477-6565 (City Hall)

Rogers
1230 School St.
Elk River, MN 55330
(612) 241-3523
(612) 428-2253 (City Hall)

Roseville
2800 Arona St.
Roseville, MN 55113
(612) 628-0088

Savage
6000 McColl Dr.
Savage, MN 55378
(612) 882-2685

Shakopee
129 Holmes St. S.
Shakopee, MN 55379
(612) 445-3650

Shoreview
4580 N. Victoria St.
Shoreview, MN 55126
(612) 490-4750

Shorewood
5755 Country Club Rd.
Shorewood, MN 55331
(612) 474-3236

South St. Paul
125 3rd Ave. N.
South St. Paul, MN 55075
(612) 450-8744

Spring Lake Park
1301 81st Ave. N.E.
Spring Lake Park, MN 55432
(612) 784-6491
(612) 471-9051

St. Anthony
3301 Silver Lake Rd.
St. Anthony, MN 55418
(612) 781-5021
(612) 789-8881

St. Bonifacius
(See Waconia)

SUPPLEMENTARY LISTINGS

▲▲▲▲▲▲▲▲▲▲▲▲▲▲▲▲▲▲▲▲▲▲▲▲▲▲▲▲▲▲▲▲▲▲

St. Francis (for activities information
contact St. Francis School District
Community Education Office)
3325 Bridge St.
St. Francis, MN 55070
(612) 753-2296

St. Louis Park
5005 Minnetonka Blvd.
St. Louis Park, MN 55416
(612) 924-2540

St. Michael (Community Education)
11343 50th St.
Albertville, MN 55301
(612) 497-4948

St. Paul Parks & Rec.
25 W. 4th St.
St. Paul, MN 55102
(612) 266-6400

Stillwater Community Education
1875 S. Greeley St.
Stillwater, MN 55082
(612) 351-8346

Tonka Bay
4901 Manitou Rd.
Tonka Bay, MN 55331
(612) 474-7994

Vadnais Heights
687 E. County Rd. F.
Vadnais Heights, MN 55127
(612) 429-5343

Victoria
P.O. Box 36
Victoria, MN 55386
(612) 443-2363

Waconia (Community Education)
24 S. Walnut
Waconia, MN 55387
(612) 442-6610

Watertown (Community Education)
P.O. Box 938
Watertown, MN 55388
(612) 446-1913

Wayzata (Community Education)
P.O. Box 660
Wayzata, MN 55391
(612) 476-3200

West St. Paul Parks
60 W. Emerson Ave.
West St. Paul, MN 55118
(612) 552-4150

White Bear Lake
3554 White Bear Ave.
White Bear Lake, MN 55110
(612) 773-6077

Woodbury
8301 Valley Creed Rd.
Woodbury, MN 55125
(612) 731-7588

Wyoming
(See Forest Lake)

INDEX

▲▲▲▲▲▲▲▲▲▲▲▲▲▲▲▲▲▲▲▲▲▲▲▲▲▲▲▲▲▲▲▲

3M Omnitheater 106
Aamodt's Apple Farm Inc. 115
Aarcee Rental 193
Adventures in Music 175
Afton Alps Ski & Golf 303
Afton Apple Orchard 115
Afton State Park 15
Afton State Park Campground 49
Airport Days 219
Aladdin's Castle 7
Aldrich Arena 255
Alene Grossman Memorial Arbor & Flower Garden 111, 112
Alexander Ramsey House 105
American Swedish Institute 83
American Swedish Institute's Scandinavian Christmas 207
Amusement City 7, 18
AMUSEMENT PARKS & CENTERS 7–16
    Aladdin's Castle 7
    Amusement City 7
    Berenstain Bear Country 16
    Gasoline Alley 8
    Grand Slam Sports 9
    IMAX Theater 16
    Jumpin' Jax 9
    Knott's Camp Snoopy 10
    Lilli-Putt Amusement Park 12
    Pepsi IMAX Theater 16
    Splatball Inc. 12
    Splatball Indoor 13
    Sports Spree Fun Park 14
    Spring Lake Park Amusement 14
    Starbase Omega 15
    Thompson's Family Fun Center 15
    Valleyfair 16
    Whitewater Country Waterpark 16
Andiamo 63
Andiamo Showboat 63
Andiamo Too 63
Anoka Area Ice Arena 255
Anoka County Fair 71
Anoka County Regional Parks 131

Anoka Riverfront Regional Park 131
Anson Northrup 66
Antique Show 283
Apples 117
Appleside Orchard Inc. 77, 115
Appleside Orchard's Special Events 216, 227
Arboretums/Gardens 125
Ard Godfrey House 90
Area Wide Cycle 193
ART & CRAFT CENTERS 39–48
    Alene Grossman Memorial Arbor & Flower Garden 111, 112
    American Swedish Institute 39
    Bloomington Art Center 39
    Burnsville Area Society for the Arts 41
    Ceramic Arts & Supplies 41
    Continental Clay Company 41
    Creative Kidstuff 42
    Grossman, Alene, Memorial Arbor & Flower Garden 111, 112
    Eagan Ceramics Inc. 42
    Edina Art Center 43
    K & S Ceramics 43
    Kadoodles 44
    L & K's Ceramics Inc. 44
    Minnesota Clay 45
    Minnetonka Center for the Arts 45
    Northeast Ceramics Inc. 46
    Northern Clay Center 46
    Plaster Paradise (Crafters Paradise) 47
    St. Paul's Land Mark Museum School 47
    Summer Arts Program at the Walker Art Center 48
    Sunday Afternoon Workshops at the Walker Art Center 48
    Walker Art Center Programs 48
Arts Expo 283
Asparagus 124
Baker Park National Golf Course 49
Baker Park Reserve 137

▲▲▲▲▲▲▲▲▲▲▲▲▲▲▲▲▲▲▲▲▲▲▲▲▲▲▲▲▲▲▲▲▲

Baker Park Reserve Campground 49
Bakken Library & Museum 83
Bald Eagle–Otter Lake Regional Park 150
Bandana Square 245
Baseball Museum 84
BATTING CAGES 17
    Amusement City 7
    Grand Slam Sports 7
    Inside Sports Training Center &
        Batting Cages 17
Battle Creek Regional Park 150
Bauer Berry Farm 116
Bavarian Surf Minnetonka 194
Baylor Regional Park 134
Beaver Mountain Water Park 32
Bell Museum of Natural History 84
Berenstain Bear Country 16
Betsey Northrup 66
Bicycle Rental 202
Biff Adams Arena 255
BIKE TRAILS 313
    "Bike Ways" Brochures 313
    Grand Rounds Parkway System 313
Bike Ways Brochures 313
Bloomington Art Center 39
Bloomington Ice Garden 256
Blueberries 116, 122, 123
Boat Rental 202
Boom Island 66
Braemar Arena 257
Bridal Show 283
Brooklyn Center Community Center 32
Brooklyn Park Community Activity
    Center 257
Brooklyn Park Historical Farm 86
Brookside Campground 50
Brown's Apple Acres 116
Bryant Lake Regional Park 138
Buck Hill Ski Area 305
Bunker Hills Campground 50
Bunker Hills Regional Park 131
Bunker Hills Stable 77
Bunker Hills Wave Pool 33
Burnsville Area Society for the Arts 41

Burnsville Center 245
Burnsville Ice Center 258
Calhoun Square 246
Camp in the Woods 51
Camp Waub-O-Jeeg 52
CAMPGROUNDS 49–62
    Afton State Park Campground 49
    Baker Park National Golf Course 49
    Baker Park Reserve Campground 49
    Brookside Campground 50
    Bunker Hills Campground 50
    Camp in the Woods 51
    Camp Waub-O-Jeeg 52
    Country Camping Tent & RV
        Park Inc. 52
    Fletcher Creek Campground 53
        Minnesota Military Museum 53
        Weyerhauser Museum 53
    Ham Lake Campground Inc. 53
    Kiesler's Campground 53
    KOA Twins Campground 54
    Krestwood Mobile Home & RV
        Park 54
    Lake Auburn Family
        Campground 55
        Carver Park Reserve 55
        Lowry Nature Center 55
    Lake Byllesby Regional Park
        Campground 55
    Lake Elmo Park Campground 56
    Lebanon Hills Regional Park
        Campground 56
    Minnesota State Park camping
        reservations 57
    Minnesota Valley Trail Recreation
        Area 58
    Nerstrand Big Woods State Park
        Campground 57
    Peaceful Valley Campsites 59
    Rice Creek Campground 59
    River's Edge Campground 60
    Springvale Campground 60
    Timm's Marina & Campground 61
    Wapiti Park Campground 61

▲▲▲▲▲▲▲▲▲▲▲▲▲▲▲▲▲▲▲▲▲▲▲▲▲▲▲▲▲▲▲▲▲▲▲

William O'Brien State Park 61
Yogi Bear's Jellystone Park 62
Carver County Fair 71
Carver County Regional Parks 134
Carver Park Reserve 55, 138
Centennial Sports Arena 258
Central Mississippi Riverfront Regional Park 145
Ceramic Arts & Supplies 41
Challenge Park 18
Chanhassen Dinner Theatres 161
Charles A. Lindbergh House 95
Chaska Community Center 34, 258
Cheap Skate 272
Child Carrier Rentals 203
Child's Play Theatre Company 165
Children's Museum 86
Children's Theatre Company 163, 164
Cinco De Mayo Celebration 211
Circus Pizza 23
City Center 235
Cleary Lake Regional Park 139
Como–Harriet Streetcar Line 63
Como Regional Park 153
Como Ski Center 195, 303
Como Zoo 311
Como Zoological Society 311
Continental Clay Company 41
Coon Rapids Dam Regional Park 132
Coon Rapids Dam Regional Park (West Side) 139
Cottage Grove Ravine Regional Park 155
Country Camping Tent & RV Park Inc. 52
Cowles Conservatory 112
Craft Show 283
Creative Kidstuff 42
Creative River Tours 65
Creative Sewing & Needle Show 283
Crosby Park Nature Center 127
Cross-Country Ski Rental 203
Cross-Country Skiing 115, 122
Crow-Hassen Park Reserve 140
Cycling Velodrome 281

Dairy Farm 116
Dakota County Fair 71
Dakota County Historical Society 88
Dakota County Regional Parks 135
Dayton's (Minneapolis) 207, 238
Dayton's/Bachman's Flower Show 238
Defeat of Jesse James Days 227
Desert Links Midway 24
Diamond T Ranch 78, 81
Discovery Zone 25
DNR Fish Survey 318
DNR Trail & Water Ways 318
Dog Show & Obedience Trials 283
Downhill Ski Rental 203
DOWNHILL SKIING 303–307
Afton Alps Ski & Golf 303
Buck Hill Ski Area 305
Como Ski Center 303
Hyland Hills Ski Area 306
Mount Frontenac 306
Welch Village Ski Area 306
Wild Mountain Ski Area 307
Eagan Ceramics Inc. 42
Eagle Creek Stables Inc. 78, 81
East Bethel Ice Arena 259
Eastern Mountain Sports 195
Eastman Nature Center 128
Eden Apple Orchard's Halloween Hayrides 227
Eden Apple Orchard & Berry Farm 117
Eden Prairie Community Center 34, 259
Eden Prairie Shopping Center 246
Edina Art Center 43
Edina Historical Society & Museum 88
Edinborough Park 35, 260
Edinborough Park Children's Special Events 234
Eko Baken 18, 35, 308
Elm Creek Park Reserve 140
Eloise Butler Wildflower Garden & Bird Sanctuary 125
Emma Krumbee's Annual Scarecrow Festival 228

▲▲▲▲▲▲▲▲▲▲▲▲▲▲▲▲▲▲▲▲▲▲▲▲▲▲▲▲▲▲▲▲▲

Emma Krumbee's Apple Orchard Restaurant Bakery Deli & Country Store 117
Emma Lee 65
Ethnic Dance Theatre 165
European Oktoberfest 229
Excelsior's Apple Day Festival 230
EXCURSIONS 63–70
    Andiamo 63
    Andiamo Showboat 63
    Andiamo Too 63
    Como–Harriet Streetcar Line 63
    Creative River Tours 65
    Emma Lee 65
    Majestic Lady 63
    Minnesota Zephyr 65
        Stillwater Logging & Railroad Museum 65
    Osceola & St. Croix Valley Railway 66
    Padelford Packet Boat Co. Inc. 66
        Anson Northrup 66
        Betsey Northrup 66
        Boom Island 66
        Harriet Island 66
        Jonathan Padelford 66
        Josiah Snelling 66
        Party Girl 63
    St. Anthony Main "Trolley" Rides 68
        Minneapolis Convention Center 68
        St. Anthony Main 68
        Stone Arch Bridge Route 68
    Shatze 63
    Wayzata Towne Trolley 68
FAIRS, COUNTY 71–75
    Anoka County Fair 71
        PRCA National Rodeo 71
    Carver County Fair 71
    Dakota County Fair 71
        Heritage Village 71
    Hennepin County Old Tyme Fair 72
    LeSueur County Fair 72
    Ramsey County Fair 73

    Scott County Fair 73
    Sherburne County Fair 73
    Washington County Fair 74
    Wright County Fair 74
FAIRS, STATE 76
    Minnesota State Fair 76
Farmington Civic Arena 260
Festival of Nations 211, 212
Fire Fighters Memorial Museum 89
Fischers Croix Farm Orchard 118
Fish Lake Regional Park 141
Fletcher Creek Campground 53
Fogarty Ice Arena 261
Folsom House 89
Fore Seasons Golf 18
Fort Snelling 92
Fort Snelling State Park 156
Foshay Tower Observation Deck 89
Frank Gehry's 22-foot-tall Standing Glass Fish 112
Frederick R. Weisman Art Museum 113
French Regional Park 141
Friday Family Fun Nights 250
Galtier Plaza 240
Game Time 27
Gardens 125
Gasoline Alley 8
Gaviidae Common 238
Gibbs Farm Museum of the Ramsey County Historical Society 90
Golf Mountain 19
Grand Rounds Parkway System 313
Grand Slam Sports 7, 9, 19
Grande Day Parade 210, 219
Grapes 120
Great American History Theater 165
Great American Train Show 283
Great Northern Golf Range 20
Greater Minneapolis Convention & Visitor Association 318
Green Acres Recreation 308
Grossman, Alene, Memorial Arbor & Flower Garden 111, 112
Gustafson Phalen Arena 261

▲▲▲▲▲▲▲▲▲▲▲▲▲▲▲▲▲▲▲▲▲▲▲▲▲▲▲▲▲▲▲▲▲▲

Guthrie Theater 166
Ham Lake Campground Inc. 53
Har-Mar Mall 246
Harding Arena 262
Harriet Island 66
Harris Warehouse 196
Hastings Civic Arena 262
Hastings Rivertown Days Festival 216
Hay Rides 115, 117, 118, 119, 120, 123
HAY & SLEIGH RIDES 77–80
     Appleside Orchard, Inc. 77
     Bunker Hills Stable 77
     Diamond T Ranch 78
     Eagle Creek Stables, Inc. 78
     Sponsel's Minnesota Harvest Apple
        Orchard 79
Hennepin County Old Tyme Fair 72
Hennepin County Regional Parks 137
Henry Hastings Sibley 108
Heritage Village 71
Hidden Falls/Crosby Farm 154
Highland Arena 262
Highland Fest 216
Highway 55 Rental & Sales 196
Hiking Trails 123
Hill Billy Hills Snow Tubing 309
Historic Fort Snelling 92
Historic Orpheum Theatre 168,
    170–171
Historic State Theatre 169, 172–173
Hmong New Year Celebration 283
Holiday Art, Gift, & Craft Show 283
Holiday in Lights at the Minnesota
    Zoo 208
Holiday Traditions in October 100
Holidazzle 208
Homestead Orchards 119
Hopkins Pavilion 263
Hopkins Raspberry Festival 217
Horizon Outlet Center 246
HORSE RIDING 81–82
     Diamond T Ranch 81
     Eagle Creek Stables Inc. 81
Hot Air Balloon 115

Hubert H. Humphrey Metrodome 277
Hyland Hills Ski Area 306
Hyland Lake Park Reserve 142
Ice Skates Rental 204
Illusion Theater 174
IMAX Theater 16
In The Heart of the Beast Puppet &
    Mask Theatre 174
In-Line/Roller Skate Rental 204
IN-LINE/ROLLER SKATING
    ARENAS 272–276
     Cheap Skate 272
     Rhythmland Roller Rink 272
     Roller Garden 273
     Rollerdome™ 273
     Saints Bloomington Family
        Entertainment Center 274
     Skatedium Roller Rink 274
     Skateland Skate Center 275
     Skateville 275
     Wooddale Recreation 276
Inside Sports Training Center & Batting
    Cages 17
Inver Grove Heights Arena 263
Irene Hixon Whitney Bridge 112
Isanti Rodeo Jubilee Days 217
James J. Hill House 92
Jazzin' January 210
Jean Baptiste Faribault 108
John H. Stevens House Museum 109
Jonathan Padelford 66
Joseph Cook Memorial Arena 263
Josiah Snelling 66
Jumpin' Jax 9
K & S Ceramics 43
Kadoodles 44
Ken Yackel Westside Arena 264
Ketter Canoeing 196
Kidfest 209, 283
Kiesler's Campground 53
Kite Flying 115, 210
Knollwood Mall 247
Knott's Camp Snoopy 10
KOA Twins Campground 54

Krestwood Mobile Home & RV Park 54
L & K's Ceramics Inc. 44
Lake Auburn Family Campground 55
Lake Byllesby Regional Park 135
Lake Byllesby Regional Park
    Campground 55
Lake Elmo Park Campground 56
Lake Elmo Park Reserve 155
Lake George Regional Park 133
Lake Minnewashta Regional Park 134
Lake Rebecca Park Reserve 143
Lakeshore Players Inc. 175
Lakeville Ames Arena 264
Land O'Lakes Kennel Club 283
Landmark Center 94
Lava Links 20
Lebanon Hills Regional Park–East
    Section 135
Lebanon Hills Regional Park
    Campground 56
LeSueur County Fair 72
Lilli-Putt Amusement Park 12, 21
Lily Lake Arena 264
Live Music 115, 123
Locke Park 133
Long Lake Regional Park 151
Lorence's Strawberry & Raspberry
    Farms 119
Lowry Nature Center 55, 128
Macalester Bike & Skate Exchange 197
Majestic Lady 63
Mall of America 247–249, 250
Map of downtown Minneapolis 236–237
Map of downtown St. Paul 242–243
Map of Mall of America 248–249
Maplewood Community Center 36
Maplewood Mall 250
MAPS
    Mall of America 248–249
    Minneapolis Skyway System
        236–237
    St Paul Skyway System 242–243
    Twin Cities Greater Metro inside
        front cover

Marine Landing 197
Mariucci Arena 265, 277, 279
Marketfest 218
May Day Parade & Festival 174, 213
Mc Dougall's Apple Junction 120
McDonald's Playlands 27
Mendota Days 100
Metro Antique Show 283
Midsommar 218
Midway Stadium 280
Midwest Mountaineering 198
Midwest Pet Fair 283
MINIATURE GOLF 18–22
    Amusement City 18
    Challenge Park 18
    Eko Baken 18
    Fore Seasons Golf 18
    Golf Mountain 19
    Grand Slam Sports 19
    Great Northern Golf Range 20
    Lava Links 20
    Lilli-Putt Amusement Park 12, 21
    Putt Putt® Golf Bloomington 21
    Putt Putt® Golf Minneapolis 21
    Second Season Golf Center Inc. 22
    Troon Golf Center 22
Minneapolis' Fourth of July
    Fireworks 219
Minneapolis' Uptown Shopping
    District 252
Minneapolis Aquatennial 219
Minneapolis Calendar of Events 318
Minneapolis Chain of Lakes Regional
    Park 146
Minneapolis Convention Center 68, 280
Minneapolis downtown parking
    facilities 235
Minneapolis Institute of Arts 96
Minneapolis Loons 292
Minneapolis Parks 145
Minneapolis Planetarium 97
Minneapolis Sculpture Garden 111
Minneapolis Skyway System 236–237
Minneapolis Tourism Hotline 318

▲▲▲▲▲▲▲▲▲▲▲▲▲▲▲▲▲▲▲▲▲▲▲▲▲▲▲▲▲▲

Minneapolis, downtown 235–239
Minneapolis-St. Paul International
    Airport 219
Minnehaha Depot 98
Minnehaha Parkway 147
Minnehaha Regional Park 147
Minnesota Air Guard Museum 98
Minnesota Arctic Blast 292
Minnesota Clay 45
Minnesota History Center 99
Minnesota Horse Expo 213
Minnesota Landscape Arboretum 125
Minnesota Military Museum 53
Minnesota Moose 294
Minnesota Moose Hockey 283
Minnesota Museum of American Art 99
Minnesota Office of Tourism 318
Minnesota Orchestra 175
Minnesota Pioneer Park 100
Minnesota Renaissance Festival 230
Minnesota State Capitol 100
Minnesota State Fair 76
Minnesota State Park camping
    reservations 57
Minnesota Thunder Pro Soccer 294
Minnesota Timberwolves 294
Minnesota Transportation Museum
    Inc. 100
Minnesota Twins 295, 296
Minnesota Valley Trail Recreation Area
    58, 159
Minnesota Valley Wildlife Refuge 129
Minnesota Vikings 297, 298
Minnesota Zephyr 65, 109
Minnesota Zoo 311
Minnetonka Center for the Arts 45
Minnetonka Orchards 120
Miracle Mile Shopping Center 252
Mississippi Gorge Regional Park 148
Mississippi Mile 220
Mississippi Mile Hotline 318
Mixed Blood Theatre Company 178
MN Orchestra/Orchestra Hall 176–177
Mork's Grove Orchard 120

Mount Frontenac 306
Murphy's Landing 100
Murphy-Hanrehan Park Reserve 143
Museum of Questionable Medical
    Devices 103
MUSEUMS & HISTORICAL SITES
    83–114
    American Swedish Institute 83
    Bakken Library & Museum 83
    Baseball Museum 84
    Bell Museum of Natural History 84
    Brooklyn Park Historical Farm 86
    Children's Museum 86
    Dakota County Historical Society 88
    Edina Historical Society &
        Museum 88
    Fire Fighters Memorial Museum 89
    Folsom House 89
    Fort Snelling 92
    Foshay Tower Observation Deck 89
    Gibbs Farm Museum of the Ramsey
        County Historical Society 90
    Ard Godfrey House 90
    James J. Hill House 92
    Historic Fort Snelling 92
    Oliver H. Kelley Farm 92
    Landmark Center 94
    Charles A. Lindbergh House 95
    William L. McKnight–3M
        Omnitheater 95
    Minneapolis Institute of Arts 96
    Minneapolis Planetarium 97
    Minnehaha Depot 98
    Minnesota Air Guard Museum 98
    Minnesota History Center 99
    Minnesota Museum of American
        Art 99
    Minnesota Pioneer Park 100
        Holiday Traditions in
            October 100
        Mendota Days 100
        Voyageur Camp Week 100
    Minnesota State Capitol 100

Minnesota Transportation
    Museum Inc. 100
Murphy's Landing 100
Museum of Questionable Medical
    Devices 103
North West Company Fur Post 103
Planes of Fame Air Museum 104
Alexander Ramsey House 105
Science Museum of Minnesota 106
    William L. McKnight–3M
        Omnitheater 106
Sibley Historic Site 108
    Henry Hastings Sibley 108
    Jean Baptiste Faribault 108
John H. Stevens House Museum 109
Stillwater Logging & Railroad
    Museum 109
    Minnesota Zephyr 109
Trains of Bandana 110
Upper St. Anthony Falls Lock &
    Dam Observation Deck 110
Walker Art Center 112
    Cowles Conservatory 112
    Frank Gehry's 22-foot-tall
        Standing Glass Fish 112
    Irene Hixon Whitney
        Bridge 112
    Minneapolis Sculpture
        Garden 111
    Spoonbridge and Cherry 112
Frederick R. Weisman Art
    Museum 113
World War II Air Power Display
    Show 113
National Park Service 318
National Sports Center 281
Nature Centers/Wildlife Areas 127
Nerstrand Big Woods State Park 158
Nerstrand Big Woods State Park
    Campground 57
New Hope Ice Arena 265
Nicollet Mall 239
Night-Time Skiing 115
Noerenberg Memorial Gardens 127

Nokomis-Hiawatha Regional Park 148
North Hennepin Trail Corridor 144
North West Company Fur Post 103
Northeast Ceramics Inc. 46
Northern Clay Center 46
Northern Sign Theater 178
Northfield Arena 266
Northrop Auditorium 179–181
Nutcracker 179–180
O'Shaughnessy Auditorium 184,
    186–187
Old Log Theater 182
Oliver H. Kelley Farm 92
Oneka Berries 121
Open Air International 214, 220, 239
ORCHARDS & BERRY PICKING
    FARMS 115–124
    Aamodt's Apple Farm Inc. 115
        Cross-Country Skiing 115
        Hay Rides 115
        Hot Air Balloon 115
        Night-Time Skiing 115
        Sleigh Rides 115
    Afton Apple Orchard 115
        Hay Rides 115
    Appleside Orchard Inc. 115
        Hay Rides 115
        Kite-Flying 115
        Live Music 115
        Scarecrow-Building Event 116
        Story Tellers 115
    Bauer Berry Farm 116
        Blueberries 116
        Strawberries 116
    Brown's Apple Acres 116
        Dairy Farm 116
    Eden Apple Orchard & Berry
        Farm 117
        Apples 117
        Hay Rides 117
        Raspberries 117
        Strawberries 117
    Emma Krumbee's Apple Orchard
        Restaurant Bakery Deli &

▲▲▲▲▲▲▲▲▲▲▲▲▲▲▲▲▲▲▲▲▲▲▲▲▲▲▲▲▲▲▲▲▲

Country Store 117
Petting Zoo 117
Fischers Croix Farm Orchard 118
Hay Rides 118
Homestead Orchards 119
Hay Rides 119
Pony Rides 119
Lorence's Strawberry & Raspberry
Farms 119
Raspberries 119
Strawberries 119
Mc Dougall's Apple Junction 120
Minnetonka Orchards 120
Hay Rides 120
Pumpkins 120
Mork's Grove Orchard 120
Grapes 120
Hay Rides 120
Pears 120
Plums 120
Sour Cherries 120
Oneka Berries 121
Strawberries 121
Petersen Gladiolus 121
Strawberries 121
Vegetables 121
Peterson's Strawberries 122
Blueberries 122
Strawberries 122
Pine Tree Apple Orchard 122
Cross-Country Skiing 122
Pumpkins 122
Strawberries 122
Rainbow Ridge Farm 123
Blueberries 123
Strawberries 123
Smith's Berry Farm 123
Strawberries 123
Vegetables 123
Sponsel's Minnesota Harvest Apple
Orchard 123
Hay Rides 123
Hiking Trails 123
Live Music 123

Petting Zoo 123
Pony Rides 123
Withrow Berry Farm 124
Strawberries 124
Wyatt Strawberries 124
Asparagus 124
Strawberries 124
Orchestra Hall 175, 176–177
Ordway Music Theatre 182–183
Oscar Johnson Arena 266
Osceola & St. Croix Valley Railway 66
P.J. Asch Otterfitters 198
Padelford Packet Boat Co. Inc. 66
Parade Ice Arena 266
Park Square Theatre 184
PARKS & NATURE CENTERS
125–161
Arboretums/Gardens 125
Afton State Park 15
Anoka County Regional Parks 131
Anoka Riverfront Regional Park 131
Baker Park Reserve 137
Bald Eagle–Otter Lake Regional
Park 150
Battle Creek Regional Park 150
Baylor Regional Park 134
Bryant Lake Regional Park 138
Bunker Hills Regional Park 131
Carver County Regional Parks 134
Carver Park Reserve 138
Central Mississippi Riverfront
Regional Park 145
Cleary Lake Regional Park 139
Como Regional Park 153
Coon Rapids Dam Regional
Park 132
Coon Rpids Dam Regional Park
(West Side) 139
Cottage Grove Ravine Regional
Park 155
Crosby Park Nature Center 127
Crow-Hassen Park Reserve 140
Dakota County Regional Parks 135
Eastman Nature Center 128

▲▲▲▲▲▲▲▲▲▲▲▲▲▲▲▲▲▲▲▲▲▲▲▲▲▲▲▲▲▲▲▲▲

Elm Creek Park Reserve 140
Eloise Butler Wildflower Garden &
    Bird Sanctuary 125
Fish Lake Regional Park 141
Fort Snelling State Park 156
French Regional Park 141
Gardens 125
Hennepin County Regional
    Parks 137
Hidden Falls/Crosby Farm 154
Hyland Lake Park Reserve 142
Lake Byllesby Regional Park 135
Lake Elmo Park Reserve 155
Lake George Regional Park 133
Lake Minnewashta Regional
    Park 134
Lake Rebecca Park Reserve 143
Lebanon Hills Regional Park–East
    Section 135
Locke Park 133
Long Lake Regional Park 151
Lowry Nature Center 128
Minneapolis Chain of Lakes
    Regional Park 146
Minneapolis Parks 145
Minnehaha Parkway 147
Minnehaha Regional Park 147
Minnesota Landscape
    Arboretum 125
Minnesota Valley Trail Recreation
    Area 159
Minnesota Valley Wildlife
    Refuge 129
Mississippi Gorge Regional Park 148
Murphy-Hanrehan Park Reserve 143
Nature Centers/Wildlife Areas 127
Nerstrand Big Woods State Park 158
Noerenberg Memorial Gardens 127
Nokomis-Hiawatha Regional
    Park 148
North Hennepin Trail Corridor 144
Phalen-Keller Regional Park 151
Ramsey County Parks 150
Rice Creek Chain of Lakes Park

Reserve 133
Rice Creek Trail West Regional Park
    (Locke Park) 133
Richardson Nature Center 129
St. Paul Parks 153
Schaar's Bluff 136
Spring Lake Park Reserve (Schaar's
    Bluff) 136
State Parks 156
Tamarack Nature Center 130
Theodore Wirth Regional Park 149
Wargo Nature Center 130
Washington County Parks 155
Wildlife Areas 127
William O'Brien State Park 157
Party Girl 63
Peaceful Valley Campsites 59
Pears 120
Penumbra Theatre Company 185
Pepsi IMAX Theater 16
PERFORMING ARTS 161–192
    Chanhassen Dinner Theatres 161
    Child's Play Theatre Company 165
    Children's Theatre Company
        163, 164
    Ethnic Dance Theatre 165
    Great American History Theater 165
    Guthrie Theater 166
    Historic Orpheum Theatre 168,
        170–171
    Historic State Theatre 169, 172–173
    Illusion Theater 174
    In The Heart of the Beast Puppet &
        Mask Theatre 174
        May Day Parade & Festival 174
    Lakeshore Players Inc. 175
    Minnesota Orchestra 175
        Adventures in Music 175
    Mixed Blood Theatre Company 178
    Northern Sign Theater 178
    Northrop Auditorium 179–181
        The Nutcracker 179–180
    Old Log Theater 182
    Orchestra Hall 175, 176–177

▲▲▲▲▲▲▲▲▲▲▲▲▲▲▲▲▲▲▲▲▲▲▲▲▲▲▲▲▲▲▲▲▲▲

Ordway Music Theatre 182–183
O'Shaughnessy Auditorium 184,
    186–187
Park Square Theatre 184
Penumbra Theatre Company 185
Plymouth Playhouse 188
St. Paul Chamber Orchestra
    183, 188
Teatro Latino De Minnesota 188
Theater MU 189
Theatre De La Jeune Lune 189
Theatre in the Round Players
    (TRP) 190
University Theatre 191
Petersen Gladiolus 121
Peterson's Strawberries 122
Petting Zoo 117, 123
Phalen-Keller Regional Park 151
Pierce Skate & Ski 199
Pine Tree Apple Orchard 122
Planes of Fame Air Museum 104
Plaster Paradise (Crafters Paradise) 47
PLAY CENTERS 23–31
    Circus Pizza 23
    Desert Links Midway 24
    Discovery Zone 25
    Game Time 27
    McDonald's Playlands 27
    Play & Learn Software Inc.
        (PALS) 31
Play & Learn Software Inc. (PALS) 31
Pleasant Arena 267
Plums 120
Plymouth Playhouse 188
Pony Rides 119, 123
POOLS/WATER SLIDES 32–38
    Beaver Mountain Water Park 32
    Brooklyn Center Community
        Center 32
    Bunker Hills Wave Pool 33
    Chaska Community Center 34
    Eden Prairie Community Center 34
    Edinborough Park 35
    Eko Baken 35

    Maplewood Community Center 36
    Richfield Pool & Waterslide 36
    River's Edge Apple River Recreation
        Area 37
    Valley View Pool 37
    Wild Mountain Summer
        Waterpark 38
Powderhorn Festival 220
PRCA National Rodeo 71
Pumpkins 120, 122
Putt Putt® Golf Bloomington 21
Putt Putt® Golf Minneapolis 21
Raceway Park 301
Rainbow Ridge Farm 123
Ramsey County Fair 73
Ramsey County Parks 150
Raspberries 117, 119
    Hopkins Raspberry Festival 217
REI (Recreational Equipment Inc.) 199
RENTALS 193–205
    Aarcee Rental 193
    Area Wide Cycle 193
    Bavarian Surf Minnetonka 194
    Bicycle Rental 202
    Boat Rental 202
    Child Carrier Rentals 203
    Como Ski Center 195
    Cross-Country Ski Rental 203
    Downhill Ski Rental 203
    Eastern Mountain Sports 195
    Harris Warehouse 196
    Highway 55 Rental & Sales 196
    Ice Skates Rental 204
    In-Line/Roller Skate Rental 204
    Ketter Canoeing 196
    Macalester Bike & Skate
        Exchange 197
    Marine Landing 197
    Midwest Mountaineering 198
    P.J. Asch Otterfitters 198
    Pierce Skate & Ski 199
    REI (Recreational Equipment
        Inc.) 199
    Rolling Soles 200

▲▲▲▲▲▲▲▲▲▲▲▲▲▲▲▲▲▲▲▲▲▲▲▲▲▲▲▲▲▲▲▲▲▲▲▲

Snow Ice & Wind Surfboards 204
Snowshoe Rental 205
Studio A 200
Tent & Camping Accessories 205
Wagon Bridge Marina 201
Welch Mill Canoeing & Tubing 201
Rhythmland Roller Rink 272
Rice Creek Campground 59
Rice Creek Chain of Lakes Park
    Reserve 133
Rice Creek Trail West Regional Park
    (Locke Park) 133
Rice Street Festival 221
Richardson Nature Center 129
Richfield 4th of July Celebration 221
Richfield Cattails Days 231
Richfield Pool & Waterslide 36
Ridgedale Center 252
River's Edge Apple River Recreation
    Area 37
River's Edge Campground 60
Rodeo 217, 283
Roller Garden 273
Rollerdome™ 273
Rolling Soles 200
Rondo Days Parade & Festival 222
Rosedale Center 253
Roselawn Stables 214
Rosemount Community Center 267
Roseville Ice Arena–John Rose Oval 268
Saints Bloomington Family
    Entertainment Center 274
Scarecrow-Building Event 116
Schaar's Bluff 136
Science Museum of Minnesota 106
Scott County Fair 73
SEASONAL EVENTS 207–234
    American Swedish Institute's
        Scandinavian Christmas 207
    Appleside Orchard's Special Events
        216, 227
    Cinco De Mayo Celebration 211
    Dayton's (Minneapolis) 207
    Defeat of Jesse James Days 227

Eden Apple Orchard's Halloween
    Hayrides 227
Edinborough Park Children's Special
    Events 234
Emma Krumbee's Annual Scarecrow
    Festival 228
European Oktoberfest 229
Excelsior's Apple Day Festival 230
Festival of Nations 211, 212
Hastings Rivertown Days
    Festival 216
Highland Fest 216
Holiday in Lights at the Minnesota
    Zoo 208
Holidazzle 208
Hopkins Raspberry Festival 217
Isanti Rodeo Jubilee Days 217
Kidfest 209
Marketfest 218
Mayday Parade & Festival 213
Midsommar 218
Minneapolis Aquatennial 219
    Grande Day Parade 219
    Torchlight Parade 219
Minneapolis' Fourth of July
    Fireworks 219
Minneapolis-St. Paul International
    Airport 219
    Airport Days 219
Minnesota Horse Expo 213
Minnesota Renaissance Festival 230
Mississippi Mile 220
Open Air International 214, 220
Powderhorn Festival 220
Rice Street Festival 221
Richfield 4th of July Celebration 221
Richfield Cattails Days 231
Rodeo 217
Rondo Days Parade & Festival 222
Roselawn Stables 214
St. Patrick's Day Parade 210
St. Paul Fourth of July Fireworks 222
St. Paul Winter Carnival 210
    Grande Day Parade 210

▲▲▲▲▲▲▲▲▲▲▲▲▲▲▲▲▲▲▲▲▲▲▲▲▲▲▲▲▲▲▲▲

Jazzin' January 210
Kite Flying 210
Torchlight Parade 210
Sponsel's Minnesota Harvest Apple
Orchard 231, 234
Summer Movies & Music in the
Park 223
Svenskarnas Dag (Swedes' Day) 224
Taste of Minnesota 224
Trick or Treat Street 232
Twin Cities Juneteenth Celebration
215, 224
Welch Village Autumn Festival 232
White Bear Lake's Manitou
Days 225
World War II Air Power Display 225
SEATING CHARTS
Childrens Theater 164
Historic Orpheum Theatre 170–171
Historic State Theatre, Minneapolis
172–173
Mariucci Arena 279
MN Orchestra/Orchestra Hall
176–177
Northrup Auditorium 181
O'Shaughnessy Auditorium 186–187
Ordway Music Theatre 183
Sports Pavilion 286
St Paul Civic Center 282
Target Center 288–289
Twins 296
Vikings 297
Williams Arena 291
Second Season Golf Center Inc. 22
Shatze 63
Sherburne County Fair 73
SHOPPING 235–254
Bandana Square 245
Twin City Terminal Railway 245
Burnsville Center 245
Calhoun Square 246
City Center 235
Dayton's Minneapolis 238
Dayton's/Bachman's Flower

Show 238
Eden Prairie Shopping Center 246
Galtier Plaza 240
Gaviidae Common 238
Har-Mar Mall 246
Horizon Outlet Center 246
Knollwood Mall 247
Mall of America 247–249, 250
Map of Mall of America
248–249
Maplewood Mall 250
Friday Family Fun Nights 250
Minneapolis, downtown 235–239
Map of downtown Minneapolis
236–237
Minneapolis downtown parking
facilities 235
Minneapolis' Uptown Shopping
District 252
Miracle Mile Shopping Center 252
Nicollet Mall 239
Open Air International 239
Ridgedale Center 252
Rosedale Center 253
St. Paul, downtown 240–244
Map of downtown St. Paul
242–243
Southdale Center 253
Southtown Shopping Center 254
Tanger Factory Outlet Center 254
Town Square 240
World Trade Center 244
Shoreview Arena 269
Shrine Circus 283
Sibley Historic Site 108
Siebert Field 284
Skatedium Roller Rink 274
SKATING ARENAS 255–271
Aldrich Arena 255
Anoka Area Ice Arena 255
Biff Adams Arena 255
Bloomington Ice Garden 256
Braemar Arena 257
Brooklyn Park Community Activity

Center 257
Burnsville Ice Center 258
Centennial Sports Arena 258
Chaska Community Center 258
East Bethel Ice Arena 259
Eden Prairie Community Center 259
Edinborough Park 260
Farmington Civic Arena 260
Fogarty Ice Arena 261
Gustafson Phalen Arena 261
Harding Arena 262
Hastings Civic Arena 262
Highland Arena 262
Hopkins Pavilion 263
Inver Grove Heights Arena 263
Joseph Cook Memorial Arena 263
Ken Yackel Westside Arena 264
Lakeville Ames Arena 264
Lily Lake Arena 264
Mariucci Arena 265
New Hope Ice Arena 265
Northfield Arena 266
Oscar Johnson Arena 266
Parade Ice Arena 266
Pleasant Arena 267
Rosemount Community Center 267
Roseville Ice Arena–John Rose
    Oval 268
St. Louis Park Recreation Center 269
Shoreview Arena 269
Victory Memorial Ice Arena 269
West St. Paul Ice Arena 270
White Bear Arena 271
White Bear Lake Sports Center 271
Skateland Skate Center 275
Skateville 275
Sleigh Rides 115
Smith's Berry Farm 123
Snow Ice & Wind Surfboards 204
Snowshoe Rental 205
Sour Cherries 120
South Valley Park 309
Southdale Center 253
Southtown Shopping Center 254

Splatball Inc. 12
Splatball Indoor 13
Sponsel's Minnesota Harvest Apple
    Orchard 79, 123, 231, 234
Spoonbridge and Cherry 112
Sport Pavilion 286, 287
SPORTS 292–299
    Minneapolis Loons 292
    Minnesota Arctic Blast 292
    Minnesota Moose 294
    Minnesota Thunder Pro Soccer 294
    Minnesota Timberwolves 294
    Minnesota Twins 295, 296
    Minnesota Vikings 297, 298
    St. Paul Saints 298
    University of Minnesota's Golden
        Gophers 299
Sports Spree Fun Park 14
Sportsmen's Show 283
Spring Lake Park Amusement 14
Spring Lake Park Reserve (Schaar's
    Bluff) 136
Springvale Campground 60
St. Anthony Main 68
St. Anthony Main "Trolley" Rides 68
St. Louis Park Recreation Center 269
St. Patrick's Day Parade 210
St. Paul Calendar of Events 318
St. Paul Chamber Orchestra 183, 188
St. Paul Civic Center 282, 283
St. Paul Convention & Visitors
    Bureau 318
St. Paul Fourth of July Fireworks 222
St. Paul Parks 153
St. Paul Saints 298
St. Paul Skyway System 242–243
St. Paul Tourism Hotline 318
St. Paul Winter Carnival 210
St. Paul, downtown 240–244
St. Paul's Land Mark Museum School 47
STADIUMS ARENAS 277–290
    Hubert H. Humphrey
        Metrodome 277
    Mariucci Arena 277

▲▲▲▲▲▲▲▲▲▲▲▲▲▲▲▲▲▲▲▲▲▲▲▲▲▲▲▲▲▲▲▲

Midway Stadium 280
Minneapolis Convention Center 280
National Sports Center 281
    Cycling Velodrome 281
    Youth Soccer Tournament–
        USA Cup 281
St. Paul Civic Center 283
    Antique Show 283
    Arts Expo 283
    Bridal Show 283
    Craft Show 283
    Creative Sewing & Needle
        Show 283
    Dog Show & Obedience
        Trials 283
    Great American Train Show 283
    Hmong New Year
        Celebration 283
    Holiday Art, Gift, & Craft
        Show 283
    Kidfest 283
    Land O'Lakes Kennel Club 283
    Metro Antique Show 283
    Midwest Pet Fair 283
    Minnesota Moose Hockey 283
    Shrine Circus 283
    Sportsmen's Show 283
    Star of the North Antique
        Shows 283
    State High School Boys
        Wrestling, Hockey,
        Basketball Tourna-
        ments 283
    State High School Girls
        Gymnastics Tourna-
        ment 283
    Trick or Treat Street 283
    Twin Cities Indoor Garage
        Sale 283
    Winter Sports Show 283
    World's Toughest Rodeo 283
Siebert Field 284
Sport Pavilion 286, 287
Target Center 287, 288–289

    Williams Arena 290, 291
Star of the North Antique Shows 283
Starbase Omega 15
State High School Boys Wrestling,
    Hockey, Basketball Tournaments 283
State High School Girls Gymnastics
    Tournament 283
State Parks 156
Stillwater Logging & Railroad Museum
    65, 109
STOCK CAR RACING 301
    Raceway Park 301
Stone Arch Bridge Route 68
Story Tellers 115
Strawberries 116, 117, 119, 121, 122,
    123, 124
Studio A 200
Summer Arts Program at the Walker Art
    Center 48
Summer Movies & Music in the
    Park 223
Sunday Afternoon Workshops at the
    Walker Art Center 48
SUPPLEMENTARY LISTINGS 318
    DNR Fish Survey 318
    DNR Trail & Water Ways 318
    Greater Minneapolis Convention &
        Visitor Association 318
    Minneapolis Calendar of Events 318
    Minneapolis Tourism Hotline 318
    Minnesota Office of Tourism 318
    Mississippi Mile Hotline 318
    National Park Service 318
    St. Paul Tourism Hotline 318
    St. Paul Calendar of Events 318
    St. Paul Convention & Visitors
        Bureau 318
    Ticket Master 318
    Twin Cities Tourism Attractions
        Association of Minnesota 318
Svenskarnas Dag (Swedes' Day) 224
Tamarack Nature Center 130
Tanger Factory Outlet Center 254
Target Center 287, 288–289

Taste of Minnesota 224
Teatro Latino De Minnesota 188
Tent & Camping Accessories 205
Theater MU 189
Theatre De La Jeune Lune 189
Theatre in the Round Players (TRP) 190
Theodore Wirth Regional Park 149
Thompson's Family Fun Center 15
Ticket Master 318
Timm's Marina & Campground 61
Torchlight Parade 210, 219
Town Square 240
Trains of Bandana 110
Trick or Treat Street 232, 283
Troon Golf Center 22
Twin Cities Greater Metro inside
    front cover
Twin Cities Indoor Garage Sale 283
Twin Cities Juneteenth Celebration
    215, 224
Twin Cities Tourism Attractions
    Association of Minnesota 318
Twin City Terminal Railway 245
Twins, Minnesota 296
University of Minnesota's Golden
    Gophers 299
University Theatre 191
Upper St. Anthony Falls Lock & Dam
    Observation Deck 110
Valley View Pool 37
Valleyfair 16
Vegetables 121, 123
Victory Memorial Ice Arena 269
Vikings 297
Voyageur Camp Week 100
Wagon Bridge Marina 201
Walker Art Center 112
Walker Art Center Programs 48
Wapiti Park Campground 61
Wargo Nature Center 130
Washington County Fair 74
Washington County Parks 155
Wayzata Towne Trolley 68
Welch Mill Canoeing & Tubing 201

Welch Village Autumn Festival 232
Welch Village Ski Area 306
West St. Paul Ice Arena 270
Weyerhauser Museum 53
White Bear Arena 271
White Bear Lake Sports Center 271
White Bear Lake's Manitou Days 225
Whitewater Country Waterpark 16
Wild Mountain Ski Area 307
Wild Mountain Summer Waterpark 38
Wildlife Areas 127
William L. McKnight–3M Omnitheater
    95, 106
William O'Brien State Park 61, 157
Williams Arena 290, 291
WINTER SLEDDING 308–310
    Eko Baken 308
    Green Acres Recreation 308
    Hill Billy Hills Snow Tubing 309
    South Valley Park 309
WINTER SPORTS 303–310
Winter Sports Show 283
Withrow Berry Farm 124
Wooddale Recreation 276
World's Toughest Rodeo 283
World Trade Center 244
World War II Air Power Display
    113, 225
Wright County Fair 74
Wyatt Strawberries 124
Yogi Bear's Jellystone Park 62
Youth Soccer Tournament–USA Cup 281
ZOOS 311
    Como Zoo 311
    Como Zoological Society 311
    Minnesota Zoo 311